NATO ASI Series

Advanced Science Institutes Series

A series presenting the results of activities sponsored by the NATO Science Committee, which aims at the dissemination of advanced scientific and technological knowledge, with a view to strengthening links between scientific communities.

The Series is published by an international board of publishers in conjunction with the NATO Scientific Affairs Division

A Life Sciences B Physics	Plenum Publishing Corporation London and New York
C Mathematical and Physical Sciences D Behavioural and Social Sciences E Applied Sciences	Kluwer Academic Publishers Dordrecht, Boston and London
F Computer and Systems Sciences G Ecological Sciences H Cell Biology I Global Environmental Change	Springer-Verlag Berlin Heidelberg New York London Paris Tokyo Hong Kong Barcelona Budapest

NATO-PCO DATABASE

The electronic index to the NATO ASI Series provides full bibliographical references (with keywords and/or abstracts) to more than 30000 contributions from international scientists published in all sections of the NATO ASI Series. Access to the NATO-PCO DATABASE compiled by the NATO Publication Coordination Office is possible in two ways:

- via online FILE 128 (NATO-PCO DATABASE) hosted by ESRIN, Via Galileo Galilei, I-00044 Frascati, Italy.
- via **CD-ROM** "NATO-PCO DATABASE" with user-friendly retrieval software in English, French and German (© WTV GmbH and DATAWARE Technologies Inc. 1989).

The CD-ROM can be ordered through any member of the Board of Publishers or through NATO-PCO, Overijse, Belgium.

Series F: Computer and Systems Sciences Vol. 80

The ASI Series Books Published as a Result of Activities of the Special Programme on ADVANCED EDUCATIONAL TECHNOLOGY

This book contains the proceedings of a NATO Advanced Research Workshop held within the activities of the NATO Special Programme on Advanced Educational Technology, running from 1988 to 1993 under the auspices of the NATO Science Committee.

The books published so far as a result of the activities of the Special Programme are:

Vol. F67: Designing Hypermedia for Learning. Edited by D. H. Jonassen and H. Mandl. 1990.

Vol. F78: Integrating Advanced Technology into Technology Education. Edited by M. Hacker, A. Gordon, and M. de Vries. 1991.

Vol. F80: Intelligent Tutoring Systems for Foreign Language Learning. The Bridge to International Communication. Edited by M. L. Swartz and M. Yazdani. 1992.

Intelligent Tutoring Systems for Foreign Language Learning

The Bridge to International Communication

Edited by

Merryanna L. Swartz

Vitro Corporation
Advanced Technology
Building 4, Room 1417H
14000 Georgia Avenue
Silver Spring, MD 20906-2972, USA

Masoud Yazdani

Department of Computer Science
University of Exeter
Prince of Wales Road
Exeter EX4 4PT, UK

Springer-Verlag
Berlin Heidelberg New York London Paris Tokyo
Hong Kong Barcelona Budapest
Published in cooperation with NATO Scientific Affairs Division

Proceedings of the NATO Advanced Research Workshop "The Bridge to International Communication: Intelligent Tutoring Systems for Foreign Language Learning", held in Washington, DC, September 19–21, 1990.

CR Subject Classification (1991): I.2.7., K.3.1.

ISBN-13: 978-3-642-77204-7 e-ISBN-13: 978-3-642-77202-3
DOI: 10.1007/978-3-642-77202-3

Library of Congress Cataloging-in-Publication Data
NATO Advanced Study Institute on the Bridge to International Communication: Intelligent Tutoring Systems for Second Language Learning (1990: Washington, D.C.) Intelligent tutoring systems for foreign language learning: the bridge to international communication/edited by Merryanna L. Swartz, M. Yazdani. p. cm.— (NATO ASI series. Series F, Computer and systems sciences; vol. 80) "Proceedings of the NATO Advanced Study Institute on the Bridge to International Communication: Intelligent Tutoring Systems for Second Language Learning, 19–21 September 1990, Washington, D.C. Includes bibliographical references and index.

1. Language and languages—Computer—assisted instruction—Congresses. 2. Intelligent tutoring systems—Congresses. I. Swartz, Merryanna L. II. Yazdani, Masoud, 1955– . III. North Atlantic Treaty Organization. IV. Title. V. Series. P53.28.N28 1990 418'.0285—dc20 91-39497.

Softcover reprint of the hardcover 1st edition 1992

45/3140-543210 – Printed on acid-free-paper

Preface

Multilingual communication within the world community is important for economic, political, and cultural interactions. In a global environment where other languages are increasing in importance in addition to recognized international standards (i. e., English and French), language learning is becoming more important for improved international relations. At the same time, recent advances in instructional technology make the promise of building intelligent tutoring systems in advanced technology laboratories to teach these language skills a reality in the near future. These tutoring systems, therefore, may help us foster improved methods for acquiring languages.

As active language learners and instructional technology researchers, we felt an international meeting with similar individuals was needed to discuss how such advanced tutoring systems are to be designed and implemented. We held such a meeting, the results of which are presented in this volume. The purpose of this Advanced Workshop, sponsored by the NATO Scientific Affairs Division, was to bring together a multidisciplinary group of researchers who were active in the development of intelligent tutoring systems for foreign language learning. Participants came from computer science, computational linguistics, psychology, and foreign language learning. Washington, D.C. was selected for the Workshop site since it is Merryanna's home city, the capitol of the United States, and an international, multilingual community in its own right. Masoud agreed to the location (with a promise to be shown the White House!) and graciously volunteered to coordinate activities from the European side.

The theme of our Workshop, "The Bridge to International Communication," served as a focal point for our discussions and paper presentations. The metaphor of 'bridge' was used in several ways at the Workshop. To begin with, as our society becomes increasingly multilingual, languages will surely be useful for bridging communication between different peoples in business, education, and cultural activities. The Workshop itself served to bridge current research progress from efforts under way in 10 different countries. Finally, from a technology viewpoint, the Workshop helped us to discuss the possibility of bridging two artificial intelligence technologies into one hybrid instructional system for language learning: intelligent tutoring systems (ITS) and natural language processing (NLP).

Of course, there still remains a substantial amount of work to be done before the effective, efficient integration of ITS and NLP into one system can be accomplished. Nevertheless, we began to lay the groundwork for such an enterprise at this meeting and established a beginning for an international collaboration in order to accomplish the goal of developing a working, intelligent tutoring system that supports foreign language acquisition and that can be used in the language classroom.

Since our meeting, other researchers in this field have contacted us to see how they could participate in this venture. There is active research in this field (that we know of) in Japan and China, Czechoslovakia and Hungary, as well as other work in Europe, the

U. S., and Canada not represented at this Workshop. We hope that the future growth in this field will include the collaboration and sharing of research results that we established at this meeting. Readers are encouraged to become part of the 'bridge' we started to build on September 18-21, 1990 in Washington, D.C., U. S. A.

We dedicate this book to all those who love teaching and learning new languages and cultures. For us, language is the 'bridge' to worldwide communication.

Merryanna L. Swartz, Workshop Director
Masoud Yazdani, Workshop Co-Director

Table of Contents

Section 3. Modeling the Language Learner: Computational Methods

Section 4. Tutoring Knowledge and Learner Control: Knowledge Representation, Computational Strategies, and Environments

Section 5. Computer Systems and Environments for Foreign Language Learning

Acknowledgements

We would like to thank several individuals who contributed to the success of this Workshop and the book. They are: Luis V. da Cunha, NATO Scientific Affairs Division, for his support and guidance; Stefano Cerri and Joseph Psotka as members of our organizing committee; and especially Henry Hamburger, as a member of the organizing committee and for his helpful comments and reviews of some of the papers in this book. Thanks are also given to Scott Blanksteen for his help with checking the manuscripts.

Workshop Participants

Anne Abeillé, Paris, France

Odile Blanvillain, Paris, France

Charles Button, Glasgow, Scotland

Stefano A. Cerri, Milan, Italy

Thierry Chanier, Paris, France

Eleanor Criswell, McLean, VA, USA

Françoise Demaizière, Paris, France

Carl Frederiksen, Montréal, Canada

Danilo Fum, Trieste, Italy

Alec Gogos, Thessaloniki, Greece

H. Altay Güvenir, Ankara, Turkey

Henry Hamburger, Fairfax, VA, USA

Jürgen Handke, Wuppertal, Germany

Gerard Kempen, Nijmegen, Netherlands

Robert Lawler, Indianapolis, IN, USA

Brian MacWhinney, Pittsburgh, PA, USA

George Miller, Princeton, NJ, USA

Joseph Psotka, Alexandria, VA, USA

Daniel Russell, Palo Alto, CA, USA

Roland Sussex, Queensland, Australia

Merryanna L. Swartz, Washington, DC, USA

Carlo Tasso, Udine, Italy

Yorick Wilks, LaPlata, NM, USA

Dieter Wolff, Wuppertal, Germany

Masoud Yazdani, Exeter, UK

Michael Zock, Paris, France

Introduction

Merryanna L. Swartz

Advanced Technology Department, Vitro Corporation, Silver Spring, MD

Advances in artificial intelligence (AI) in education applications have improved the potential of developing intelligent instructional systems that can actually be used in the classroom. Progress in natural language processing (NLP) has also improved the way in which computers handle natural language input. It seems propitious, therefore, that we look at these two technological advances in the application of foreign language (FL[1]) intelligent tutoring systems (ITS). Despite these advances, the challenge of integrating ITS and NLP into one hybrid system is a formidable task. The papers in this book, and others presented at the Workshop, address that challenge and present current research in the field representing laboratories from 10 different countries (Australia, Canada, England, France, Germany, Greece, Italy, Scotland, Turkey, U.S.A.).

Intelligent Tutoring Systems for Foreign Languages

Language instruction delivered on computers is not new, but the enhancement of such instruction with AI technology in computer systems is. Computer-assisted language learning (CALL) has been used in foreign language instruction for some time with varying degrees of success [11]. This CALL approach to computer-delivered instruction generally uses predefined branching routines and static error feedback messages to guide learners. More adaptive, individualized instruction is feasible with AI techniques that model learner performance and deliver goal-based and remedial instruction to move the learner through the material [5, 13, 8]. This kind of computer-based instruction is the basis for ITS. The domains that have been most used in recent ITS development are for the most part tractable and formally defined (mathematics, physics, electronics). Of course, not all of the problems in ITS research have been solved in these domains. Nevertheless, some very promising ITS exist that are used in training settings (e. g., the Geometry ITS [2]).

In less well-defined domains such as language learning, many important issues are emerging that were not encountered in the traditional ITS domains. Some of these issues involve (1) the representation of linguistic knowledge in the expert and learner[2] models, (2)

---

[1] I would like to comment on the use of both foreign and second language learning (FLL and SLL in this book). Both terms refer to the acquisition of a non-native language. In some communities, the language is a second language (e.g., Canada with English and French); in large monolingual societies the second language is often referred to as a foreign language. We argued about appropriate terminology at the Workshop, but no obvious resolution was found. One can argue that for some learners, it is third or fourth language learning- but 'Fourth Language Learning' seems strange to consider! On the other hand, all non-native languages can be viewed as foreign until learned adequately; this seems to be the best general term to use. This definition is not accepted universally in the field. The reader will therefore see both references (FLL and SLL) used in the book which reflect either the sociocultural definition for non-native language learning in a country or personal preference.

[2] In ITS, the term 'student' model is generally used when referring to the person acquiring some skill. We discussed the terms 'student' and 'learner' and their relation to language skill acquisition during our working sessions. Borrowing from Self [12] we use term 'learner' in the editors' introductory comments since it reflects more active participation and collaboration in the learning process on the part of the learner.

NATO ASI Series, Vol. F 80
Intelligent Tutoring Systems for Foreign Language Learning
Edited by M. L. Swartz and M. Yazdani

implementing parsers that must process ungrammatical input and reason about it in view of learners' predictable interlingual productions during learning, (3) representing tutoring knowledge that is appropriate for language learning (teaching strategies and principles for language learning are different from other types of skill learning), and very importantly, (4) understanding the foreign language acquisition process.

Many of these issues will involve a considerable research effort before effective FL ITS becomes a reality in the classroom; and we do not wish to claim that all these problems have to be solved before such a system is developed. Indeed, we shall no doubt be wrestling with some of these issues for some time. Nevertheless, we examined selected issues from those listed above at our Workshop and discussed their role in the development of an ITS architecture for foreign language learning. This book, as a compilation of some of the papers presented at the Workshop, presents an overview of the current state of the art and recent contributions made to the field.

In order to understand the issues that face FL ITS research, the reader should be familiar with the basic architecture for an intelligent tutoring system. An ITS is made up of four basic modules: the expert model, the learner model, the tutor model, and the interface or environment for communicating with the learner. The reader is referred to many excellent books that give more detailed information about ITS in other domains and ITS architectures [8, 12, 14, 16, 17, 19]. These modules are briefly reviewed below with a description of the unique requirements for developing FL ITS.

The Expert Module for a Language ITS

The expert module of an ITS provides the domain intelligence for the system [1], a model of the expert. For any given domain, not only must we decide what knowledge to include in the expert model, but also, how we should represent or encode it. Anderson [1] provides an overview of the three primary approaches to codifying expert knowledge: black box models, expert systems, and cognitive models; and discusses the trade offs for each approach in terms of implementation effort and pedagogical effectiveness. In language domains, we will find that certain approaches are more appropriate than others, given the nature of linguistic knowledge, even though the implementation costs are high.

This ITS module represents the domain-specific expert knowledge and the inferencing or reasoning processes involved in solving problems in the instructional domain. In language domains, this means we need some type of grammar and a lexicon for the target language (the expert knowledge), and a parser (the expert inference engine) to process language inputs.

The grammar is used to define the legal rules for that portion of the language to be taught. This component of the expert knowledge base usually follows some syntactic theory (e. g., Definite Clause Grammar, Functional Unification Grammar, Lexical Functional Grammar, General Phrase Structure Grammar, and Tree Adjoining Grammar (TAG) [3]) used to formally represent a particular grammar. However, a linguist's formal grammar is not the intention in the construction of this portion of the expert knowledge. Foreign language teachers don't teach formal grammars, but rather some subset of the grammatical system for a language that is to be acquired by the learner for productive, communicative purposes. Similarly, the coverage in the language ITS must be mindful of this requirement. The expert model's grammar knowledge need not be exhaustive

---

However, the reader will find both 'student' and 'learner' used in the papers presented herein. These terms can be thought of as synonyms (Ask George what relations WordNet would have for these nouns.)

3 Readers are referred to [9] more more information on these formalisms. Tag is described in Chapter 5 in this book.

therefore, but adequate for the skill level (beginning, intermediate, advanced) to be addressed by the system.

A lexicon is another component in the knowledge base to provide coverage for the words to be acquired by the learner, and that will permit the parser to understand language input during various activities and learning experiences. Some type of formalism is required to represent the semantics for the lexicon so that meaningful parsing can be accomplished for words used in context. Language learning is not simple vocabulary learning where an item in Ll is mapped directly to its correspondent in L2[4]. The context surrounding a word has much to do with specifying what word or idiom is used to appropriately communicate some meaning. But representing semantics and limited pragmatics in an ITS is a very hard research problem. Nevertheless, the system should ideally have some form of world knowledge and context to illustrate how language is used in natural settings.

The parser provides the means for the computer system to reason about and process the language, and it is the last major component in the expert module. In FL ITS, the challenge is not only to provide natural language understanding capabilities, but to allow for processing imperfect input since learners never have complete control of the L2 used. Parsing natural language in a FL ITS involves not only a means of interaction for the learner with the system, but also understanding the domain skill itself that is being taught. This is a unique characteristic for NLP in language ITS implementations. The parser must be capable of accepting divergent input strings from learners and be able to identify a plausible divergence from nonsensical language so as to be capable of reasoning properly about learners' attempts to use the L2.

The Learner Module for a Language ITS

The learner module in an ITS includes the information that describes a learner's knowledge about what is being learned and allows the tutor module to adapt instruction [18] and provide appropriate feedback. Self [11] refers to this model as a set of programs designed to represent a learner's knowledge state. VanLehn [18] specifies two components that make up the learner model: the structure or representation of the knowledge in the model and the process that manipulates that knowledge structure. This process is termed 'diagnosis' and the outcome is termed 'knowledge state assessment'.

In order to properly model the learner and perform diagnosis, the system must have knowledge about learner errors. In traditional ITS, these errors are stored in bug catalogs or lists of mal-rules that get accessed when the system is engaging in learner diagnosis. While similar methods can be employed in FL ITS, the nature of the error and the way the system should understand it are different for foreign language learning (See Chapter 8).

In a foreign language domain, the representation of the knowledge in the learner model must use the same computational formalisms as in the expert model. This is so that during the process of diagnosis, the system can compare the two knowledge states using some acceptable modeling technique. Thus we can expect some type of formal grammar and lexicon in the learner model similar in form to those used in the expert module. The process of diagnosis has traditionally used techniques such as overlay or differential models [14] or model tracing [1, 18]. In language learning where communicative skills are stressed and situation dependent, other modeling techniques may be needed. Several papers in this book describe implementations of these and other techniques more suited to language learning.

Building and maintaining such a learner model is generally considered a difficult and costly task. Constructing a 'deep' model may not be a priority in certain cases (e. g., learning language for communicative purposes where the idea expressed counts more than

4 L2 refers to a foreign or second language; L1 refers to one's native language.

the actual grammatical construction used), but in other circumstances, a deeper learner model is unavoidable (e. g., when diagnosing grammar errors is important). A set of design principles for bypassing some of the problems encountered in constructing a deep model [12] should help FL ITS researchers with this problem.

The Tutor Module for a Language ITS

This module represents the tutoring strategies and instructional goals used to deliver instruction in the system. The tutor module in an ITS is responsible for enabling the student to solve problems in the domain. Teaching students how to acquire a skill is difficult because the computer tutor must be able to adapt the instruction to individual needs. This means that the tutoring system needs to know about the learners' performance, be able to advise them during a learning segment, suggest or present new activities based on inferences made about current performance, and be able to provide meaningful feedback when errors are made. These capabilities indicate how important the communication between the tutor and learner modules is. Tutoring approaches in ITS can vary depending on the skill to be learned and the instructional purpose of the ITS (e. g., discovery learning, grammar drills, review exercises). Traditionally, ITS has used tutorial dialogues, simulations, and plan-based instruction to represent tutoring knowledge in the tutor module. Learning environments are another alternative.

Tutorial dialogues as a means to convey instruction arose from the Socratic method of tutoring [14] and can be used to guide performance and provide hints or coaching to help the learner solve problems. Simulations in ITS are another tutorial technique. They are more easily implemented when the domain knowledge can be represented by formal rules such as electronic troubleshooting or steam plant mechanics [14]. In these domains, the instruction can be presented by having the computer simulate state changes in the device that learners must interact with as they solve problems. Plan-based instruction is another method that uses a set of instructional goals and curricular activities as part of the knowledge base in the tutor module. Plan rules embody pedagogical principles for a domain and are attached to the instructional goals for a particular lesson. Therefore, actual teaching strategies must be codified in the system. This is a particularly difficult approach since we understand so little about good human teaching strategies.

Learning environments, as an alternative to a formal tutor module, present instruction in an open, discovery-based system that students explore. No formal tutoring rules are used to move students from one knowledge state to another. Students are left to their own intellectual devices to experience and learn about what is made available to them. Good tutoring in these environments depends on the organization and presentation of the domain knowledge (See Section Four for some examples). If the student is to discover appropriate knowledge structures in the domain, then the representation of the knowledge must follow organizational principles that support the cognitive processes of the learner as s/he moves through the environment.

In a foreign language ITS, the type of approach selected for representing the tutoring knowledge should be based on an understanding of the unique nature of foreign language acquisition. Current theories of foreign language learning and teaching support the communicative approach [7, 9]. This means that the tutoring should use authentic, realistic language contexts for presenting new material to the learner. The papers we present in this book illustrate some promising methods, as well as challenges, for representing tutoring knowledge in a foreign language ITS.

The Graphical Interface Environment for a Language ITS

The learning environment is characterized by the graphical interface of the tutoring system. The features for this environment include the tools and noninstructional help that will guide the learner as problems get solved [3]. It is through the graphical interface in an ITS that all the instruction is communicated [19]; thus its design becomes very important for a language tutoring system. Burton [3] discusses several important issues for designing instructional interfaces, for example, the level of abstraction required by different domains, and the fidelity of graphical simulations for tutoring aspects of physical systems (steam plant fault diagnosis). In a foreign language ITS, the interface or learning environment should provide a means for entering language input to be parsed by the system as well as the use of different media (graphics, animation, text, sound, video) to present language in meaningful, communicative situations. This suggests the use of some type of mutiwindowing, multimedia design. Different media are especially important for language learning so that acoustic, semantic, and orthographic mappings to the L2 can be made. Current advances in graphical interface and multimedia technology provide us with new, exciting tools for creating the graphical interface. Many of the papers in this book illustrate the different multimedia approaches available for foreign language ITS interface implementations.

The Structure of the Book

The papers in the book represent a selection of those presented at the Workshop, and are organized into five different sections to reflect a conceptual focus for each group of papers. We used the Workshop topics to organize our presentations and focus our discussions (computational and theoretical foundations, learner modeling and error diagnosis, and tutoring strategies and learner control). We found that some of the papers addressed other areas not explicitly covered by these topics. The foreign language experts we invited to the Workshop were most concerned about identifying language learner characteristics and discussing practical issues related to using computers in the classroom. Since understanding these issues is a fundamental prerequisite to foreign language ITS research, we grouped these papers in Section One. The next three sections of the book present papers that explore some of the research problems we face in the development of the three principal ITS modules. These sections propose methods for solving some of the knowledge representation, computational, theoretical, and modeling problems we face. The papers presented in Section Two deal with the first topic. Here we grouped those papers that described theories of foreign language acquisition and processing, and computational formalisms for representing linguistic knowledge, as a theoretical basis for understanding foreign language ITS requirements. Section Three includes papers that describe modeling techniques for understanding what the learner knows about the L2 and methods for constructing learner models. These papers deal with the computational aspects of the second topic, but also depend on an understanding of learner characteristics and errors presented in Section One. Section Four presents papers that describe approaches to tutoring language in an ITS. These papers focus on using principled techniques and environments for presenting communicative foreign language tutoring with innovative use of multimedia. Section Five presents descriptions of working Intelligent CALL prototypes. These papers present current accomplishments and the technology promise in FL ITS research.

All of the Workshop participants are gratefully acknowledged for the lively discussion and critiques of the work presented during the Workshop, and their consideration of the research problems that remain to be solved. Their many fruitful ideas and contributions that arose in the working group sessions are reflected in the introductory comments for each section of the book.

The papers cover many different technical domains and therefore can be read in a modular fashion. We assume that our readers will come from foreign language teaching, computational linguistics, psychology and psycholinguistics, and computer science. You may may feel more familiar with certain sections or papers in the book depending on your background and interest. But we hope that you will read those other sections whose work is less familiar to you in order to understand the interaction between different fields in a multidisciplinary effort such as FL ITS development. We also hope that the reader will be able to gain from the work presented in this book and use it as a guide for continued research in the field.

References[5]

1. Anderson, J. R.: The expert module. In Foundations of intelligent tutoring systems (M. C. Polson and J. J. Richardson, eds.). Hillsdale, NJ: Lawrence Erlbaum Association 1988
2. Anderson, J. R., Boyle, C. F., & Yost, G.: The geometry tutor. Proceedings of the Ninth Joint Conference on Artificial Intelligence, pp. 1-7. Los Altos, CA: Morgan Kaufmann 1985
3. Burton, R. R.: The environment module of ITSs. In Foundations of intelligent tutoring systems (M. C. Polson and J. J. Richardson, eds.). Hillsdale, NJ: Lawrence Erlbaum Association 1988
4. deSaussure, F. Cours de linguistique générale. Payot: Paris, France, 1972.
5. Halliday, M.A.K.: An introduction to functional grammar. London: Edward Arnold 1985
6. Kintsch, W. & van Dijk, T. A.: Toward a model of text comprehension and production. Psychological Review, 85, 363-394 (1978)
7. Littlewood, W.: Communicative language teaching. London, UK: Cambridge University Press 1981
8. Mandl, H. & Lesgold, A.: Learning issues for intelligent tutoring systems. New York, NY: Springer-Verlag 1988
9. Richards, J. C.: The context of language teaching. New York, NY: Cambridge University Press 1985
10. Schwind, C.: An intelligent language tutoring system. International Journal of Man-Machine Studies, 33, 557-579 (1990)
11. Self, J.: Student models in CAI. *International Journal of Man-Machine Studies* 6:261-276, (1974)
12. Self, J.A.: Bypassing the intractable problem of student modelling. Proceedings ITS-88, Montreal, pp. 18-24, 1988
13. Shieber, S. An introduction to unification-based approaches to grammar. Center for the Study of Language and Information: Stanford, CA (1986)
14. Sleeman, D. & Brown, J. S.: Intelligent tutoring systems. New York, NY: Academic Press, Inc 1982
15. Smith, W. F.: Modern issues in foreign language education: Theory and implementation. Lincolnwood, IL: National Textbook Company 1987
16. Polson, M. C. & Richardson, J. J.: Foundations of intelligent tutoring systems. Hillsdale, NJ: Lawrence Erlbaum Association 1988
17. Psotka, J., Massey, L.D., & Mutter, S. A.: Intelligent tutoring systems: Lessons learned. Hillsdale, NJ: Lawrence Erlbaum Association 1988
18. VanLehn, K.: Student modeling. In Foundations of intelligent tutoring systems (M. C. Polson and J. J. Richardson, eds.). Hillsdale, NJ: Lawrence Erlbaum Association 1988
19. Wenger, E.: Artificial intelligence and tutoring systems. Los Altos, CA: Morgan Kaufmann Publishers, Inc 1987

---

[5] These references are also referred to in the five introductory section comments in this book.

Section One

Teaching Practice: Understanding Technology and Language Learners

One of the first steps in the development of a foreign language ITS is to understand the characteristics of language learners and language teaching practice. In this section we present a group of papers that were prepared by foreign language teaching experts invited to our Workshop. In this introduction, we borrow from an essay presented at the Workshop by Alec Gogos, English professor, Aristotle University, on the practical perspective of computer-assisted language learning (CALL) in the classroom.

As a foreign language teaching expert, Dr. Gogos elaborated on two interesting views for CALL. One view embraces all the positive aspects of CALL, new technology, automated instruction, and instructional support for the teacher. Where previously the language teacher has relied on record and audiotape players, videos and filmstrips, and the language laboratory, we are now seeing the language laboratory concept encapsulated in one system: CALL. These systems provide multimedia presentations of language material with sound, animation, and online exercises. This is exciting, but we must not be seduced by mere technology; high tech toys will not in and of themselves perform miracles in the classroom.

The other view for CALL begins with an admission that foreign language learning is very different from learning other subjects. Everyone agrees that to become a graduate in nearly any subject (math, economics, or computer programming), one follows a four year program of study and then gets a diploma. This degree assures us that the graduate is knowledgeable in the subject, indeed a specialist or expert in the field. However, with language learning, the situation is somewhat different. After four years of study, the graduate may be considered a specialist in the field, but there is no guarantee that this individual will be comparable with a native speaker (an 'expert' in the field). This is especially true if the individual started the program with no prior knowledge in the language or if the program of study is in their native language environment.

Nevertheless, CALL has entered the classroom and there it shall stay. To use it effectively in the classroom, and to develop it into a more sophisticated intelligent tutoring system, we must first come to understand the language learner, the acquisition process itself, and how to best utilize this new technology for instructional purposes.

Chapter 1 expands on this practical perspective with a description of an evaluation of a CALL system presently in use at a German university. We are shown how CALL can be used to promote communicative interactions between learner and system. The authors also present a good description of learner characteristics from a psycholinguistic view of language acquisition. Their view of the learner as an 'experimenter' provides a good introduction to more detailed theoretical frameworks on foreign language acquisition presented in Section two of the book.

Chapter 2 in this section discusses language learners' errors and misconceptions that arise during learning. The authors have developed an analytic approach to extract diagnostic information about an individual's errors during a lesson. This approach uses an interactive dialogue where questions are used to probe learners' 'intuitions' regarding novel linguistic phenomena. Such empirical data plays an important role in error diagnosis in ITS research. We will revisit similar issues in error knowledge acquisition and the computational formalisms derived from this analysis in the section on Modeling the Language Learner presented later.

NATO ASI Series, Vol. F 80
Intelligent Tutoring Systems for Foreign Language Learning
Edited by M. L. Swartz and M. Yazdani

STORYBOARD and Communicative Language Learning: Results of the Düsseldorf CALL Project

Lienhard Legenhausen[1] and Dieter Wolff[2]

[1] Anglistisches Institut, Heinrich-Heine-Universität, Universitätsstr. 1, D-4000 Düsseldorf

[2] Fachbereich 4, Bergische Universität Gesamthochschule, Gaußstr. 20, D-5600 Wuppertal

Abstract: The paper is concerned with the evaluation of Computer Assisted Language Learn-ing software. A specific CALL program, STORYBOARD, was assessed in a foreign lan-guage learning context. The results of our experiments which are described in detail show that this program is of interest both as a traditional text reconstruction exercise and as a tool in second language writing activities. When applied conventionally, the program seems to promote language awareness, when used as a word processor it seems to motivate the students to produce highly structured and grammatically well-formed texts.

1. Introduction

The Düsseldorf CALL project is concerned with the evaluation of commercially available language teaching/learning software. CALL programs are tested in everyday classroom situations and assessed on the basis of various evaluative principles. The selection of the programs is largely determined by the varying roles the computer can play in the language classroom. So far we have distinguished between four roles:

- The computer can assist language tutoring. Cf. structural drill-and-practice programs (QUESTIONMASTER, TESTMASTER).
- The computer can simulate reality. Cf. computer simulations which aim at free or communicative practice (GRANVILLE, LONDON ADVENTURE).
- The computer can process language for the learners and thus provide authentic material for the active exploration of language structure. Cf. text manipulation programs of the STORYBOARD type, concordancers.
- The computer enables learners to process language. Cf. utility programs (word processors, data bases) which can be used in the classroom in their real-life function as tools for data storage and data processing.

It is obvious that computer software, serving several diverse functions in the foreign language classroom, cannot be evaluated according to one single methodological principle. What we are trying to do, therefore, is to systematically vary the evaluative principles and techniques according to different software types. Software from each category will be evaluated on the basis of either cognitive psychological, discourse analytical or observational principles.

So far we have used discourse analytical means to analyse the communicative interactions in front of the screen when students work with a computer simulation. We have chosen GRANVILLE as probably the most sophisticated simulation in CALL. Secondly, we have applied techniques borrowed from cognitive psychology in the evaluation of text reconstruction programs of the STORYBOARD type. In the third stage,

NATO ASI Series, Vol. F 80
Intelligent Tutoring Systems for Foreign Language Learning
Edited by M. L. Swartz and M. Yazdani

observational principles were used to assess the applicability and usefulness of utility programs in the foreign language classroom. For various reasons we shall exclude research into the language tutoring function of the computer (cf. Figure 1).

Computer Function	Software Type	Evaluative Principle
Computer assists language tutoring	Drill and Practice: Question master	
Computer simulates reality	Simulations: GRANVILLE	discourse-analytical
Computer processes language (for the learner)	Text reconstructions: STORYBOARD	cognitive-psychological
Computer enables learner to process language	Utility programs: Word processors, etc.	observational-analytical

Figure 1. Software Evaluation

In our paper we will report on our STORYBOARD experiments. STORYBOARD is a popular CALL program in which learners have to (re)construct a text which is presented on the screen as a skeleton of squares (one square for each letter) and punctuation marks. Every time the informant guesses the correct word the computer puts it in its place on the screen.

We will focus on data from various learner groups at different learning stages who were engaged in different classroom activities. We have used STORYBOARD first in its conventional function as a text reconstruction program (cf. category 3), and secondly, we had learners work with the word-processing facility for writing their own texts (cf. category 4). To begin, we briefly discuss some language learning principles and the relationship between language use and language learning, which will form the theoretical background for the evaluation of our experiments.

2. Language Learning Principles

There can be no doubt that the evaluation of what has been called "language teaching" necessitates a theoretical framework, a theory of foreign language learning, which has to supply the criteria for the evaluative process. As we all know, such a theory does not exist yet and probably never will. In research on second language acquisition and foreign language learning, however, a number of general principles have emerged which seem to be accepted by most L2 researchers (cf. [9, 13, 2] this volume). It seems legitimate to adduce these principles for assessing language teaching materials and the role of the microcomputer as a focal point in classroom activities. We would like to distinguish between the importance of language use on the one hand, and of language awareness on the other.

As to language use, it has been emphasized time and again in foreign language teaching and in L2 research that the frequent use of the language to be learnt is of the utmost importance in the learning process. To put it in Rod Ellis' [3] words: "Language learning *is* language use". Many researchers and practitioners agree that *authentic* and *purposeful* language use is one of the utmost important prerequisites for language learning. Learners should produce language pur-posefully, and they should be exposed to language purposefully produced by other 'communicators' in the classroom.

In our research, the principle that language learning is language use has become an important general criterion for the evaluation of the computer's contribution to the language classroom. CALL programs which provide opportunities for authentic and purposeful language use should be ranked high in the hierarchy of language learning software. In working with these programs, the learner takes up his role as a *communicator* in the classroom.

Secondly, we believe that the language learner's role as an *experimenter* and *researcher* in the classroom should not be underestimated. Active experimental exploration of L2 structures (morphological and syntactic) by the learners in the classroom on the basis of authentic materials and research in the communicative functions and processes and strategies of language use are activities which lead to language awareness and thus develop his L2 competence (cf. [13], [14] this volume as examples). This principle supplements the language learning principle discussed above: actively and consciously exploring language and communication should constitute an important activity in the language classroom (cf. Figure 2).

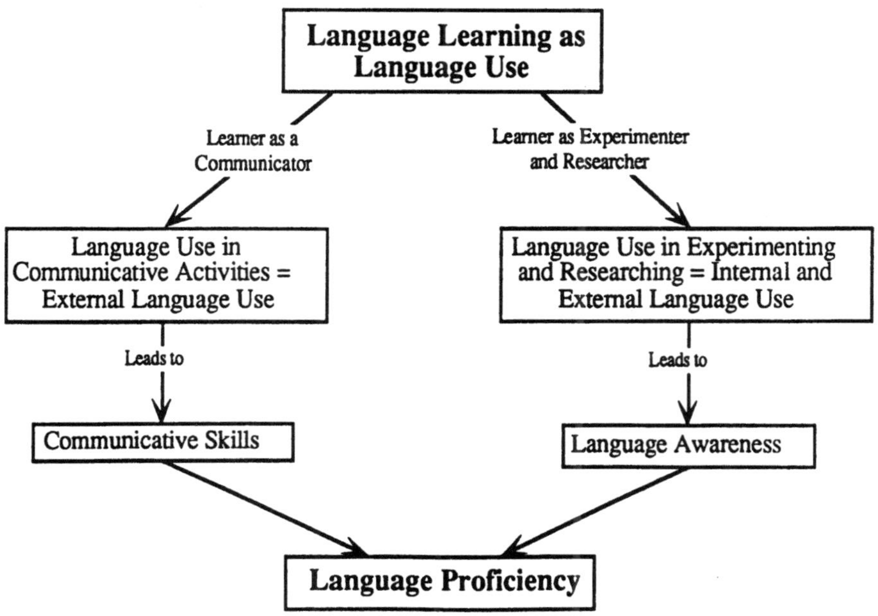

Figure 2. Language Learning as Language Use

3. Language Use and Language Learning: A Psycholinguistic Perspective

Both cognitive psychologists and psycholinguists (cf. [9] this volume) view language use and language learning as complex psychological activities which are, to a large extent, dependent on each other. In order to learn a language, cognitive psychologists claim, language users have to process language (cf. [7] this volume). Language processing involves a host of very complex mental operations which cannot be dealt with here in detail. Let us give a short description of what we know of the processes taking place in receptive processing or language comprehension, however, because these processes are of special interest in the evaluation of the conventional use of STORYBOARD (cf. Figure 3).

In cognitive comprehension research processing is viewed as a psychological activity in which concept-driven and data-driven processes interact with each other. During processing, language users do not passively decode the incoming linguistic stimuli or data: reading or listening are interactive processes which incorporate the linguistic as well as the world knowledge of the language user. Knowledge concepts are activated either by the incoming data (linguistic stimuli, contextual stimuli) or by the reader's or listener's expectancies. Knowledge concepts tentatively activated can be transformed or discarded by the incoming data; the concepts themselves, however, are equally powerful. They can either transform incoming data or even make the reader or listener neglect or discard them. Concept-driven processing is often called top-down processing, and data-driven processing bottom-up processing.

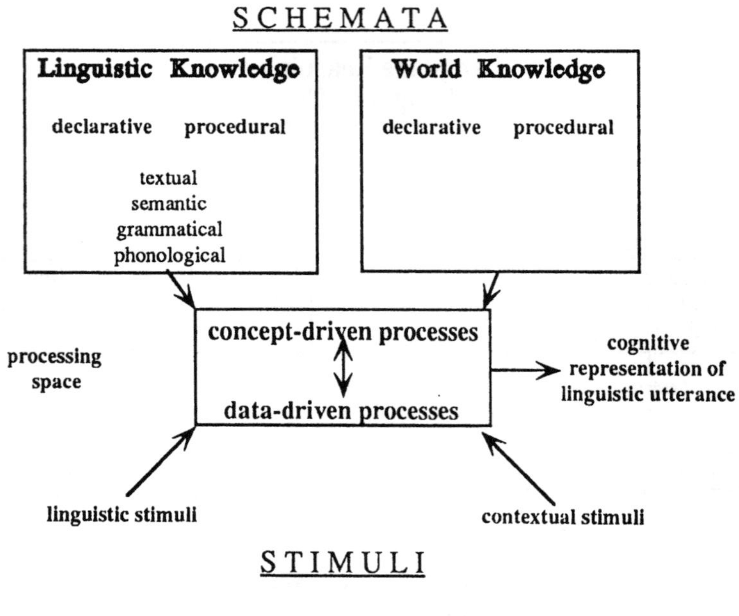

Figure 3. Simplified Linguistic Information Processing Model

Cognitive psychologists believe that linguistic and world knowledge is stored in the language user's memory in the form of schemata [11, 12]. Schemata are either declarative or procedural in nature: declarative schemata comprise the factual knowledge we have about the world (in a restaurant there are waiters and waitresses serving food) or about a language (specific words have specific meanings, texts are constructed in a certain way, etc.). Procedural world knowledge schemata contain our knowledge about what we do in specific situations (what do I do in a restaurant, in a supermarket?) and, similarly, procedural language schemata tell us what to do while processing language.

It must be assumed that language production processes can also be described within the same theoretical framework.

Two points should be retained from this discussion of language use:

(1) Using a language involves a series of complex mental operations which do not depend solely on the incoming linguistic stimuli but also on the language user's linguistic and world knowledge.

(2) From a psycholinguistic perspective, using a language is a prerequisite for learning a language. Language users must process language in order to take up new linguistic knowledge, but also in order to restructure existing knowledge and to automatize it. They do this unconsciously while communicating, but also consciously when exploring language and language use. Language use thus serves three functions in language learning: acquiring new declarative and procedural language knowledge, restructuring this knowledge and preparing it for re-use.

It is against this theoretical background that we will describe our STORYBOARD experiments. The first part is concerned with the conventional use of STORYBOARD as a text reconstruction activity. We focus on different types of strategies employed by learners when reconstructing a text from scratch. In the second part, we report on an integrated writing activity in which learners used the authoring module of STORYBOARD to write a text for a reconstruction exercise.

4. STORYBOARD as a Classroom Activity

4.1 The Conventional or Default Use of the Program

We believe that STORYBOARD as a text reconstruction activity is not so much directed towards promoting communicative skills but rather towards promoting language awareness. At first sight, working with STORYBOARD seems to be just a guessing game. On closer examination, and within the framework of cognitive psychology, however, it is a language processing task, i.e. a special type of text comprehension. Normal text comprehension is hampered by the fact that data-driven processing is only possible within a very limited scope: the learner is provided with a small amount of data. So he is forced to rely more heavily on his declarative and procedural linguistic and world knowledge than in normal text processing. Top-down concept-driven activities will take precedence over bottom-up data-driven activities. His processing difficulties will lead him to focus much more than in normal text processing on what he does while comprehending a text. In experimenting with his procedural and declarative knowledge he will become conscious of the strategies he normally uses in order to process language. To us, STORYBOARD is a problem-solving task which provides a host of opportunities for exploring language structure. It is the learner in his role as an experimenter and researcher who is in the centre of this activity.

4.1.1 Experimental Design

In the context of our STORYBOARD reconstruction experiments we were interested in the following questions:
(1) What are the mental activities which take place while learners work with a STORYBOARD program?
(2) To what extent does the learner use general and linguistic problem solving strategies while he tries to solve this text reconstruction task?

In our experiments we used verbal reporting as our data elicitation technique. The informant reports on his mental activities while solving the task. This psychological data elicitation procedure was (re)discovered by Ericsson/Simon [4,5] (cf. also [6] , [1]).

The reconstruction data we would like to discuss today were elicited from two different groups of informants - 20 students of English language and literature at Düsseldorf University and 20 grammar school students aged between 15 and 16, who on average had had about 5 years of English. Neither grammar school nor university students had worked with STORYBOARD before.

We believe that the informants' comments give valuable clues as to the mental processes going on while searching for a word. We also believe that the words actually chosen, i.e. the products of the informants' mental processes, are an important source of information.

4.1.2 Results and Discussion

A discussion of all our findings is not possible in the context of this paper, we will concentrate on just a few aspects. We discuss briefly some of the words in the sequence they were typed in by the students below. There are some remarkable differences between the grammar school group and the university students:

(1) University students, in general, tend to stick to the global problem-solving strategy which they had decided upon in the first place. On the other hand, grammar school students quite often switch their general problem-solving strategy during the course of the reconstruction process.
(2) University students seem to prefer a general problem-solving strategy which we will call the *paradigmatic strategy*, i.e. they choose a specific word, usually a function word, type it in, and then (quite often independent of the success or failure of their attempt) try out a number of words which stand in a paradigmatic relationship to the word first chosen. (e. g.: *on, in, out*). When a content word is chosen, the same strategy can be observed (e. g.: *woman, girl, lady*).
(3) Grammar school students seem to employ much more frequently a *syntagmatic* general problem-solving strategy. They choose a specific syntagma and type it into the computer word by word. Quite often they continue doing this even if the first or second word is not accepted by the machine (e. g.: *a, fly is, flying*). The paradigmatic problem-solving strategy can also be observed; grammar school students, however, lack detailed knowledge about the paradigmatic structure of the L2, so the strategy is less successful.

From these observations it can be concluded that highly structured paradigmatic declarative language knowledge seems to be a characteristic feature of more competent language learners.

The grammar school students seem to have at their disposal language knowledge which largely consists of lists of automatized syntagmatic structures, although, as we said, some paradigmatic structuring can also be observed. The university students, on the other hand, have restructured their declarative language knowledge to a much larger extent and are able to use this paradigmatic knowledge in this particular problem-solving task.

In the analysis of the process data we have tried to categorize the comments informants give on their choice of a specific word or word form. We assume that these comments are verbalizations of the specific cognitive strategies employed by the informant in order to tap his linguistic and world knowledge in a particular phase of the problem-solving process. Like Faerch and Kasper [6] we regard a strategy as "a potentially conscious plan for solving what, to the individual, presents itself as a problem in reaching a particular goal". These specific cognitive strategies should not be confounded with the more global general problem-solving strategies (syntagmatic vs. paradigmatic strategies) which were discussed in the last section. The former are rather like superordinate plans which are realized through the activation of the latter.

On the whole, we were able to discern six strategy types:

Frequency strategies: The choice of a specific word is influenced by the frequency of the word in English texts.

(1) Und *the* kommt auch ziemlich oft drin vor im Text. (K09)
(*the* also appears quite often in a text)
(2) *to:* Ja, ich such jetzt erst mal nach eigentlich so gängigen Präpositionen, Konjunktionen und so'n Zeug. (S23)
(*to:* to start with, I am looking for some of these more common prepositions, conjunctions and stuff like that)

Form-orientated strategies: The choice of a specific word is influenced by screen display cues, i.e., word-length, apostrophies, quotation marks etc.

(3) *don't:* Ja, ich überlege, was hier vielleicht hinkommt, mit dem anderen Apostroph da. (K05)
(*don't:* Yes, I wonder what I should put here, with the other apostrophy)
(4) *superstition:* Jetzt fang ich an zu zählen, die Lücken bringen mich nicht weiter. (S02)
(*superstition:* Now I shall start counting. The gaps don't get me any further)

Strategies related to *grammatical knowledge:* The choice of a specific word is influenced by the informant's grammatical knowledge:

(5) *that/which:* Ja, weil das halt Nebensätze einleitet. (K12)
(*that/which:* Yes, because this introduces subordinate clauses)
(6) Nach *avoid* muß doch dann die -ing Form kommen. (S16)
(After *avoid* an -ing form can be expected)

Strategies related to *semantic knowledge:* The choice of a word is influenced by the informant´s semantic knowledge:

(7) *beautiful:* Ja, vielleicht 'ne Abwandlung von *pretty* oder so was. (K11)
(*beautiful:* Probably a variant of *pretty* or something like that)
(8) *bad: good* habe ich jetzt, vielleicht *bad.* (S02)
(*bad:* I've tried *good,* maybe *bad*)

Strategies related to *textual* knowledge: The choice of a word is influenced by the informant's knowledge of text structure and of specific story-telling conventions:

(9) *I:* Also, ich denk mir also so, wenn das von jemandem geschrieben worden ist, so'n Erlebnisbericht oder so was, wird das schon drin vorkommen. (K05)
(*I:* Well, I thought, if someone has written this thing, a kind of report of a personal experience, a word like this could occur)
(10) *then:* Dieses *then* kommt in Texten immer vor, diese Abfolge. (S17)
(*then:* This *then* always occurs in texts, this sequence)

Strategies related to *world* knowledge: The choice of a word is influenced by the informant's knowledge about specific aspects of the world related to text content.

(11) *man:* Vielleicht kommt 'n Mann drin vor, weil er vielleicht die Fliege fangen will. (K14)
(*man:* Maybe there is a man in the story, maybe because he wants to catch the fly)
(12) *tribe:* Weil sich *superstition* immer so mit Urvölkern verbindet. (S25)
(*tribe:* Because *superstition* is always related to primitive tribes)

Quite often, however, informants are unable to report on the reasons for choosing a specific word. The grammar school students are especially uncertain about why they have tried out a word:

(13) *when:* Einfach so, ist mir einfach so eingefallen. (K12)
(*when:* Just like that, just came to my mind like that)
(14) *has:* Ich weiß nicht, aus keinem speziellen Grund. (K05)
(*has:* I don't know, for no apparent reason)

We have not finished the quantitative analysis of the strategic behaviour of the grammar school group yet, some obvious differences could easily be perceived, however:

- In general, the number of different strategies is higher in the university students' group. Within the different strategy types strategies are also more diversified.
- Grammar school students show a marked preference for world knowledge strategies. These strategies play only a minor role in the strategic behaviour of the university students.
- Grammatical and semantic knowledge plays a much greater role in the strategic behaviour of the university students. This knowledge, which is language specific, appears highly diversified judging from the strategies reported.
- University students make more use of the formal cues displayed on the screen.
- University students are almost always capable of giving reasons for their choices. This is often not the case with the grammar school students.
- Quite unexpectedly, grammar school students employ a higher amount of textual strategies. Their textual knowledge is very complex. Textual knowledge, which in general is not language specific knowledge, is used less often by the university students.

Some of the differences can be explained in the following way: In the first stage of the reconstruction process, university students exploit the cues provided by the screen to a much greater extent than the grammar school informants. As soon as more of the text has become available, they increase the number of data-driven processing strategies. Grammar school students, on the other hand, continue to use more concept-driven strategies during the whole text reconstruction process. This seems to indicate that it is the different level of L2-specific declarative linguistic knowledge which leads to processing differences: Grammar school students are *forced* to employ more concept-driven (top-down) processing, whereas university students, due to the amount of explicit L2 knowledge available, can make more use of data-driven (bottom-up) processing.

In conclusion, we would say that STORYBOARD promotes the learner's awareness of his implicit declarative and procedural linguistic knowledge.

4.2 Story-writing with STORYBOARD: an Integrated Production - Reconstruction Activity

We have so far reported on the conventional use of STORYBOARD in the classroom. The focus has been on a language awareness activity. We would now like to take up a different kind of classroom activity with STORYBOARD, in which the text reconstruction exercise formed a minor, but integral part of a more comprehensive activity which we have called 'Story-writing with STORYBOARD'. We had a small group of learners write texts on the word-processor module of STORYBOARD. These texts were then used as reconstruction exercises by other groups.

Using STORYBOARD in this way was highly successful, as becomes evident from learner comments such as the following (excerpt from transcript):

B: Das macht richtig Spaß.	(This is really fun)
C: Hm, super.	(Yeah, super)
A: Voll.	(emphatic agreement 'indeed')

Spontaneous positive - sometimes even enthusiastic - reactions of this kind are fairly rare in the 10th grade foreign language classes in Germany. It comes as no surprise then that the teachers were generally impressed with the texts produced by their students. Even groups of learners who normally only reluctantly engage in the creative writing exercises felt stimulated and found it challenging to write a text for their fellow students.

The question that we have to go into now is why this activity has been so well received by the learners and what are the criteria that lead teachers to assess the pedagogic value of this activity in such positive terms. We are convinced that it is the integral force of three different factors that contribute to the overall success of the activity:
- the group work effect
- the computer effect
- the program effect

We will take up these aspects in turn.

4.2.1 The Group Work Effect: Type of Language Produced

The overall value of group work in the foreign language classroom has been commented upon in the literature and proved in actual practice again and again. We do not want to go into details as to the pedagogical arguments for group work such as quantity of language practice, positive affective climate, student motivation etc. But we would like to corrobate earlier findings as to the quality of the language produced from a psycholinguistic point of view.Before we can illustrate this point, though, we must draw attention to some crucial differences between our data and the group work data reported upon by other researchers. The following remarks may - at first sight - look like a fly in the ointment.

The assessments of the quality of the target language in group work - as described in the literature - usually refer to communication and negotiation processes between learners while being engaged in some kind of classroom activity (cf. [8]). It is also communication through the target language about courses of action and/or certain topics - occasionally also communication through the target language about the target language.

When we asked our learners to write a story in small groups which would then serve as a reconstruction exercise for other learners, their normal medium of communication was their mother tongue, no matter whether we explicitly asked them to speak English all the time or not. The reasons for the avoidance of the L2 while negotiating the text are fairly complex. Let us just mention a few:
- ability factors (beginners of English/lower aptitude students)
- (lack of) familiarity with group work, and closely related to this point,
- classroom conventions as regards L2 use outside teacher control.

The discussion of the learners did not just involve the target language on a metalinguistic level, but the aim of the activity was to produce a coherent L2 text. This meant that a lot of target language use was going on, and the most interesting aspect was the qualitative difference between L2 language used during the discussion or negotiation phase and the final product as keyed into the computer.

Before we comment on the type of target language used, we would like to point out that the various learner groups used completely different text planning strategies. Whereas some groups devoted much time to planning text type, overall topic etc. (global planning), others built up the text sentence by sentence and planned as they went along (local planning). And the way they dealt with their writing task, influenced the type and amount of target language used. This has to do with the fact that text planning and negotiation of content is mainly carried out in the L1.

4.2.1.1 Local Planning

Let us begin by illustrating the planning behaviour of learners who heavily rely on local planning. Here the learners build up their text sentence by sentence, and the thematic progression of the text is thus sentence-oriented. In these cases the group often thinks it can dispense with more global planning because they have implicitly agreed to stick to some everyday knowledge schema, and this makes global planning largely superfluous. There may, however, be other reasons.

As can be seen from Figure 4, there are three ways of introducing a new topic:
- through a very tentative general L1 proposal
- through a specific L1 sentence model which is to be translated into L2
- through a specific L2 sentence.

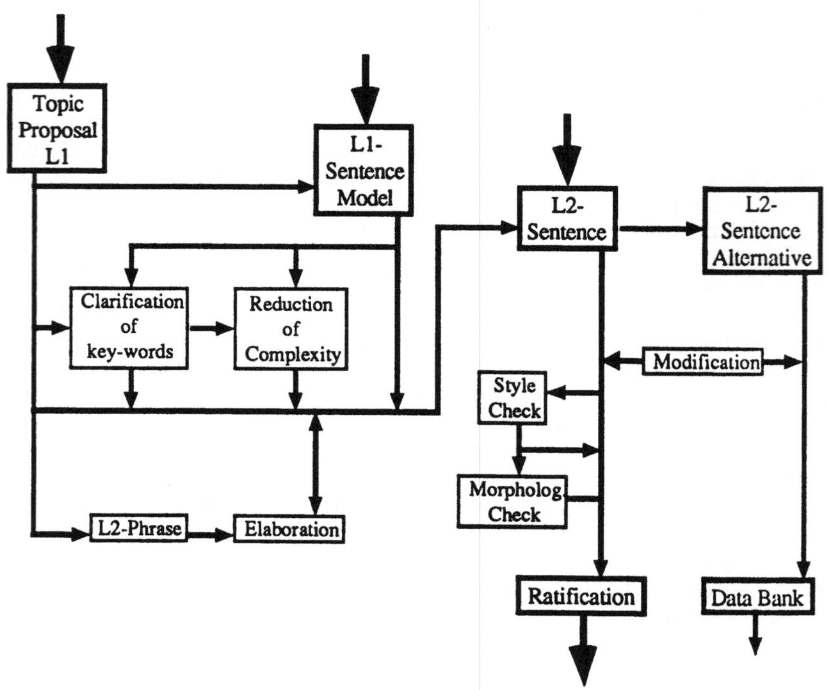

Figure 4. Sentence-oriented Planning Cycle (bottom-up)

However, since planning takes place generally in the L1, and planning cycles in these groups are sentence-bound, most topics are introduced in the L1.

When the topic is thus introduced through the L1, some kind of feasibility check is likely to follow. At this stage key words are clarified, and - if necessary - the complexity of a topic proposal is reduced.

Alternative L2 sentences put up for discussion, but which have not been selected at this planning cycle are then deposited in some kind of data bank, where they remain available for the next cycles.

The text THE SCHOOL below was produced mainly on the basis of local planning (cf. below). The learners from a Hauptschule had had about 4 1/2 years of English. What is characteristic of this learner group is the relatively late concern for the correct morphological endings. When discussing alternative L2 sentence proposals there is almost random variation as regards the third person singular -s or the plural endings. Before they finally ratify the product of their negotiations, their sentence undergoes a so-called 'polishing-up phase' in which most morphological endings are taken care of.

What we find amazing is the enormous amount of self-repair that goes on without the learners' correcting one another explicitly. Only rarely is a correct version of the negotiation phase changed into a deviant structure of the final version. Just compare the ratified text version as finally typed in and the various tentative suggestions discussed at an earlier stage:

THE SCHOOL

Final Version	*Tentative Suggestions*
Every morning we go to school. The bell rings at eight a'clock.	On the ring At eight a'clock the bell rings
After that the teacher and the pupils go into the class and	Teacher and pupils go together ...the teacher and the people come. / go in the class / the pupils come in the class
the lesson begins.	and the lesson begin.
The first break is at half past nine.	... at half past ten, and the pupils go out.
The most of the pupils eat their breakfast and drink something.	... eat her / his / the / they breakfast and drink a Coke.
The next two lessons begins at ten a'clock.	... begin ...
	Quarter past / to eleven ist Lehrerwechsel. A quarter to ten the teacher come. / When one of the lesson zuende ist
The second break is at half past eleven. Many of the pupils talk about the lessons.	Then comes the last lesson. Many pupils tell about...
The last hours begins. At half past one the school is out.	And then begins the last two hours / the last two lesson / At half past two the school were out

4.2.1.2 Global Planning

By contrast, let us have a look at a text in which global planning processes figured prominently. Planning depth is not restricted to a single sentence, but the individual sentences derive from an overall topic which the learners planned and agreed on beforehand. Compare the following excerpt from a story called 'Vampire' (Grammar School, 3 years of English):

C. Ja, hm, vielleicht sollten wir erstmal die Geschichte entwerfen. Ich mein ja nur so.
(Yes, perhaps we should first plan the story - I think.)

B: Ja, genau. Jetzt paß auf! Wir schreiben jetzt erstmal, was das für Typen sind, äh, wo die leben.
(Yes, indeed. Now listen. We first write what kind of people they are, where they live.)

Having discussed and ratified the global plan in the L1, learners can now focus on formulating individual L2 sentences. In other words, since planning and negotiation of content at the sentence level is reduced, sentence topics are to a much greater extent introduced in the target language.

The final text reads as follows:

VAMPIRE

Vampires are very dangerous. There was a vamp, called Lord Dracula. He lived in Transilvania. One night Peter Talk, a German reporter, arrived at Dracula's castle. He was very tired and hungry and he wanted to rent a room. He hadn't found a hotel yet. He hoped for the help of the strange Lord. Dracula was very friendly, because he looked forward to Peter's blood. Peter got a fine dinner and a bed. After the dinner he heard a noise. Suddenly Dracula stood in front of him. The Lord smiled and Peter realized his long teeth. He ran to the highest tower. But there was a dead end. Dracula followed him. As he wanted to bite him the sun came out. Dracula was gone.

A comparison between the final version and the tentative suggestions would again show the enormous amount of self-repair and implicit other-repair that has gone on in this group.

4.2.2 The Effect of the Computer and of Word Processing

What we have said so far has little to do with the computer and/or the STORYBOARD program, it is, however, directly related to language use and language learning. We would now like to focus on the function of the computer as such and the role played by the STORYBOARD idea, i.e., reconstructing a text from scratch.

- None of the groups had had any experience with computers, let alone with word-processing programs. This meant, on the one hand, that working with the computer had a certain fascination for most learners. The novelty value certainly increased their motivation. On the other hand, this might also have meant that they had to overcome keyboard problems and were possibly hampered by lack of experience with the word processor. However, this turned out not to be the case. Within no time the students had familiarized themselves with the STORYBOARD editing facility.
- Text production in small groups can, of course, also be done with paper and pencil. However, the computer - or rather the computer screen - offers a means to put the developing text equally well on view to all group members, thus making it easily accessible for any modifications. The computer also provides a central physical focus for the activity.

There has been a long debate in the literature whether or not the quantity and quality of the texts produced on a word-processor is significantly affected or not (cf. for example [10]). Our data do not allow any statements in this regard. All we can corroborate, though, is that revision work is generally slight and word-based. Text-based revisions do occur, although rarely. Another open question is whether the quantity and quality of the negotiation process between learners is significantly affected by the technology.

4.2.3 The STORYBOARD Idea

At the beginning we emphasized the importance of authenticity in the classroom and focused on purposeful communicative use of the target language. Authentic communicative situations, however, are intricately related to classroom activities which students can identify with, which they find meaningful and motivating.

The idea of producing a text which would then be the focus of a reconstruction activity turned out to be highly stimulating to most groups. In several groups the discussions return again and again to the purpose of their exercise, and the quality of the text is clearly influenced - and as we will illustrate below - also improved by the so-called STORYBOARD idea. However, some group discussions and texts gave no indication whatsoever as to whether or not the purpose of the task had played a major role in the text production. As a general tendency it can be said that the more laborious the task of writing a text in the foreign language is for the learners, the less they bother about the fact that their text will be used for a reconstruction exercise. Some learner groups seem to be entirely engrossed in filling the screen with English sentences, which absorbs all their cognitive energy and prevents them from directing attention to the overall purpose of the activity. This is, for example, generally the case with the groups from the Hauptschule.

Let us, by comparison, just have a closer look at the Vampire text. This text is heavily influenced by two concerns or strategic considerations, which are voiced throughout the process of text production by all the group members:

Strategy I: Avoid repetition of words or phrases, because this will facilitate reconstruction. Cf.

C: *He hoped for a, for a -*
B: Nee, *he wanted, he wanted* ; müssen wir ja nicht.
C: Nee, schon wieder *he wanted* .
C: Guck mal, wenn die dann schreiben *to want* , dann hab'n die schon zw-, dann hab'n die schon mehrere *want to* drin.
B: Wie, weiße was, eh, wir müssen noch mal dieses 'Peter Talk', das müssen wir noch mal machen. (?) die hab'n hundert *he* s, haben wir schon drinne.

Strategy II: Avoid everyday terms, find difficult words, because they will make the reconstruction task harder. Cf.

A: Nein, nicht *he* , sondern *Peter* .
C: *And he rea-, and Peter realized.*
B: *And Peter saw*
C. Ja, guck mal! *Realized*
B: Was heißt denn *realized* ?
C: 'Bemerken'
A: Ja, das hatten - Ja, klar, schreib!
B: Ja (?)
A: *Realized* . Weil - die müssen ja so wenig wie möglich Wörter wissen.

At times this group is even concerned that some of the phrases chosen might be too difficult for reconstruction.

B: Paß auf! *He he ran to the highest tower and* , äh, *in* , äh,
C: wieso *highest tower* ?
B: *in a, in a dead end room* , in einem, hm, hm, *room* . Eh, also in 'nem Raum mit 'nem toten Ende.

C: Häh?
B: Kennst du nicht? Mit 'nem - 'Einbahnstraße'! Nicht 'Einbahnstraße', äh, hinten Wendekreis.
C: Ja, 'Sackgasse' meinst du.
B: 'Sackgasse', genau.
C: Ja.
B: *Dead end*. So sagt man doch dazu, *dead end.*
A: Häh, Witz!.
B: Ja, das machen wir. *He ran through the highest tower, but there was a dead, dead end* .
B: So, was nehm'n wir dann. Äh, *but there was a dead end* haben wir gesagt.
C: Das kapieren die bloß nicht, ne?
B: Doch hatten wir. Wir hatten doch schon mal *dead end*. Ach, komm! Die werden das schon irgendwie checken.

It is student C who is particularly worried about the many words that he finds too difficult to reconstruct. (Cf. his remark: "Wer soll'n die Wörter suchen?") In addition to these linguistic considerations, there is also the concern about common or shared world knowledge. They hesitate to write about Count Dracula, because he is the best-known vampire and might be identified all too easily.

The following words have been deliberately included because of their assumed difficulty in the reconstruction phase:

(deviant) '*vamp*', proper name '*Peter Talk*', '*rent a room*', '*realize*', '*dead end*'.

They also tried hard to get rid of the allegedly easy phrase 'the sun came out'. However, they couldn't agree on the correct morphological form of the verb *to rise* , which they would have preferred.

These few examples will have to suffice in order to illustrate that for some learner groups the text reconstruction idea had a very decisive influence on the text production. In the great majority of cases the agreed-upon choices have not just made the task more difficult for the reconstruction groups, but have also improved the stylistic quality of the text. It might be argued that the tendency of some groups to prefer items that are hard to reconstruct could possibly distort the authenticity of the text. However, we think that at this stage of the learning process, when learners are still grappling with the limited textbook vocabulary, this danger should not be overestimated.

5. Conclusion

We have tried to show that students use different problem-solving strategies when trying to reconstruct a text from scratch. The more highly structured their declarative linguistic knowledge, the more heavily they resort to paradigmatic strategies. Reconstruction strategies of less advanced learners seem to indicate that their linguistic knowledge is largely stored in terms of lists of organized syntagmatic structures. Regardless of the type of strategy employed, working with STORYBOARD promotes language awareness. When the authoring module of the program is used as a tool in text production, learners make a special effort to improve the stylistic quality of their text in order to make the reconstruction exercise more demanding.

6. References

1. Börsch, S. (ed.): Die Rolle der Psychologie in der Sprachlehrforschung. Tübingen: Narr 1987
2. Criswell, E., Bryner, H. & Pfister, J.: Intelligent automated strategies of teaching foreign languages in context. This volume
3. Ellis, R.: Understanding second language acquisition. Oxford: Oxford University Press 1985
4. Ericsson, K.A. & Simon, H.A.: Verbal reports as data. Psychological Review 87, 215-251 (1980)

5. Ericsson, K.A. & Simon, H.A.: Protocol analysis. Verbal reports as data. Cambridge, Mass: The MIT Press 1984
6. Faerch C. & Kasper, G. (Eds.): Introspection in second language research. Clevedon: Multilingual Matters 1987
7. Frederiksen, C.H., Donin, J., Hoover, M. & Décarey, M.: Semantic discourse processing and tutoring systems for second language learning. This volume
8. Long, M. & Porter P.: Group work, interlanguage talk, and second language acquisition. TESOL Quarterly 19: 207-228 (1985)
9. MacWhinney, B.: The competition model and foreign language acquisition. This volume 1991
10. Piper, A.: Research into using the word processor with learner writers. Muesli News 2: 4-5 (1988)
11. Rumelhart, D.E. & Ortony, A.: The representation of knowledge in memory. In R.C. Anderson, R.J. Spiro & W.E. Montague (Eds.), Schooling and the acquisition of knowledge. Hillsdale, N.J.: Lawrence Erlbaum Associates 1976
12. Schank, R.C. & Abelson, R.P. (Eds.): Scripts, plans, goals and understanding: An inquiry into human knowledge structures. Hillsdale, N.J.: Lawrence Erlbaum Associates 1977
13. Swartz, M.L.: Issues for representing tutoring knowledge in foreign language intelligent tutoring systems. This volume
14. Zock, M.: Swim or sink: The problem of communicating thought. This volume

Learners' Intuitions, Misconceptions and Errors

Françoise Demaizière and Odile Blanvillain

UFRL - CNEAO, Université Paris 7, 2 Place Jussieu, Tour centrale 9e étage, 75005, Paris, FRANCE

Abstract : In this paper, we introduce elements from the research we have done in connection with the design and experimentation of many hours of "classical" computer-assisted language learning (CALL) tutorials. We try to rely on learners' spontaneous analyses and intuitions about language. We will show examples of learners' messages, in particular in answer to "open" questions and of the way they can, or cannot, be interpreted or technically dealt with easily. Some messages show inadequate personal interpretations, misconceptions, circular explanations, or inconsistencies (sometimes apparent). Some difficulties seem to be induced by previous teaching, usual terminology, or inadequate phrasing of the instructions or questions. Various aspects of possible reactions of the CALL materials to errors will also be presented. We think that learners often have very adequate intuitions about language but they approach it with their words, their logic, their lack of scientific experience. Their capacities are often underestimated, but one should never overestimate their ability to behave like trained scientists.

Keywords: CALL, English grammar, tutorials, misconceptions, errors.

1. Introduction

The ORDI[1] team belongs to the linguistics research department at Paris 7 University. Our research is connected to the design of computer-assisted learning (CAL) English courses. Over the past 20 years, nearly 100 hours of courseware have been experimented in various settings, in connection with research in linguistics and language teaching. One courseware package for beginners and one for intermediate learners are currently being developed for adults. So far, we have dealt with the basic linguistic concepts, operations, and structures of written English (future developments will include oral English).

In this presentation, we will try not to go into too much detail about the points and examples we have described and analyzed elsewhere [1-2-3]. We will focus on some elements we hope can be relevant to an artificial intelligence perspective and to language intelligent tutoring systems (ITS).

2. An Approach to CALL

2.1 Language Teaching and Learning

We chose an analytical approach to language teaching. This seemed appropriate for an exploration of the potentials of a CAL situation, since CAL provides good opportunities for reflexive, in-depth work and it can never be anything more than an artificial learning situation (as opposed to a natural acquisition environment).

---

[1] ORdinateur-Département Interdisciplinaire de Recherche sur l'Enseignement des Langues

NATO ASI Series, Vol. F 80
Intelligent Tutoring Systems for Foreign Language Learning
Edited by M. L. Swartz and M. Yazdani

2.2 Theoretical References

We were interested in linguistic analyses that stress the importance of the metalinguistic level at which one can work out the relationship between the linguistic forms, their values and the situations in which language is used. Relating forms to what is meant and understood by speakers and listeners is essential for the language learner. This is why we refer to the work done on enunciative operations by A. Culioli and others [4-5]. Language can be seen primarily as a meaningful representational activity. For us, teaching a language means relying on a system of representation rules that can be presented to learners in a structured way around a few basic operations and concepts.

2.3 Tutorials

Since we want learners to grasp a linguistic system inserted into a situation, we closely connect rules and explanations to situations by presenting whole stories, or small authentic texts rather than isolated sentences, for instance[1]. We also insist on aspectual or modal values, determination, the several points of view the speaker can choose in a given context or situation etc.

We have learners work with the rules or references and have them take part in their construction wherever possible. We want them to be active at all stages. This is what CAL should provide. Considering our perspective, we chose to design complex tutorials. We do not like the "traditional" type of tutorial, in which learners read rule 1 , then rule 2 , then rule 3... passively, and, then, in a different phase, have to do a whole block of application exercises or even tests working on isolated sentences and answering multiple choice questions or doing fill-in-the blank exercises with single words to be given.

For us, a tutorial is a way of intertwining a variety of presentations, explanations and applications in a way that will keep the learner active and involved (see [1]). More technically, it is also a tool that provides fairly rich answer analyses, different kinds of help, and follow-ups to learners' reactions. We have worked with various authoring languages that all provided good facilities for these activities.

3. Pedagogical Choices - Getting Learners Involved from the Start

We try not to group together all the rules or basic explanations at the beginning of a new lesson or sub-part. Various types of scripts can then be used. In a lesson on the present we introduce M. Dubois, a Frenchman, who does not speak very good English. He is at a meeting in England and he gets into trouble when he tries to answer a question asked by Mr Smith, by making a "classical" mistake, one many learners would also have made. (Mr Smith: *What do you do?* M. Dubois: *I listen to you.*) . We then help learners analyze what went wrong before going on to explain the aspectual value of *What do you do?* and then later on, showing the difference with *What are you doing?* In a lesson about various unusual ways of translating a French "imparfait" into English (viz. not with a preterit but with *would, used to* or a pluperfect), we work from a novel by G. Simenon and its translation into English (cf. Fig.1) . We show an excerpt with two "imparfaits" and ask learners how many possible combinations of English forms they think could have been envisaged by the translator: 2, 3 or 5 ? When they've been told that there are five possibilities, and that they will be able to give and understand them by the end of the lesson, we hope they will be better stimulated for what is to follow.

---

[1] See [12], this volume, for other examples of this approach.

Comment transposer l'imparfait en anglais

Ça m'a amusé de vous voir regarder les gens de travers avec l'air de les soupçonner tous... Remarquez que j'ai un cousin de ma femme qui *était* de la police aussi... Brigade des jeux ! ... [...] le plus marrant, c'est qu'il me *passait* des tuyaux [pour les courses de chevaux]... (p. 74)

It has been fun watching you coming and going since you got here yesterday... And above all seeing you looking at people as if you suspected them all... Mind you, I've got a cousin on my wife's side who [   ] in the police... The Gambling Squad... [...] the funniest thing of all was that he [   ] tips on to me ... (p. 54)

Il y a plusieurs "traductions" possibles pour chacun des deux imparfaits. Il y a donc plusieurs combinaisons envisageables.

A votre avis, combien ?

2
3
5

Désignez votre choix.

Figure 1. A sample multiple choice comprehension exercise for translating the French 'imparfait' into English.

Another similar way of having learners become aware of a linguistic phenomenon is by using a very simple question. For example, a yes-no question is introduced in a lesson about *may*. We start the part on the value of *may not* by asking learners whether they think that saying *You may not stay* is leaving the subject free not to stay. In such a case, if learners do not know the answer they will normally ask for help and go on to the next block where they will get the necessary explanations. The point is not to try and make them give a correct answer but to find a way of making them think about what is at stake. We think that it would be interesting to design similar procedures for the pedagogic module of a language ITS. These are examples in which we did little more than just try to help learners become aware of the problem. In other cases, we feel we can go further.

4. Relying on Learners' Spontaneous Analyses and Intuitions

We found out that in many instances an adequate technique was to start with a very open question, leaving it to learners to first phrase their own analysis[1]. Learners can then answer with one or

---

[1] Such techniques have also been experimented successfully in a classroom environment by various researchers and teachers in France (see [6] , [8]) and elsewhere (British language awareness experiments, see [9]).

more sentences, over one or several lines (when pre-testing the scripts on paper, we sometimes collected a whole written page).

4.1. How do learners phrase their analyses

We start a lesson on *say* and *tell* by showing a few examples and asking the learners to look at them and describe how *tell* is constructed. Here is a translation of some of the answers we got. (Our courseware is written in French.) These answers were recorded during a CAL session. Some of the French words used by the learner are in parentheses. (We won't try to translate the spelling mistakes in this paper.)

(1) "tell is followed by a complement that replaces one or several persons"
(2) "to tell is followed by a noun or a complement that reflects the persons"
(3) "tell is followed by a complement of persons (... un complément de personnes)"
(4) "tell is followed by one or several persons"
(5) "tell is used when relating to a person (... se rapporte à une personne)"
(6) "tell is often followed by a personal pronoun, it is used when one addresses a person or a group of persons"
(7) "after tell, one gets a person"
(8) "tell is followed by a noun of person (un nom de personne)"
(9) "tell is used in the case when one says something to somebody. So the verb is always followed by a personal pronoun or a noun that determines a person or a group of people"
(10) "tell for a person, say for an object, a thing"
(11) "after tell one finds a complement (complément d'objet) concerned with a person whereas for say there's a c. (c.o.) concerned with a thing (portant sur ...)"

In this lesson, we want learners to see that in the case of *tell,* the privileged relationship is between the persons involved, the subject and the person talked to. We then connect this to its construction ("tell somebody something", what is privileged comes first). Then, what is usually learnt by heart as a list of "expressions to be remembered" (tell a story, a lie, the truth vs say one's lessons, tables, prayers...) can be "logically" deducted from the basic values. Consequently learners are presented with a kind of problem solving exercise. They are asked to find by themselves which verb to use in each case, a good way of having them active and involved.

If one looks at the above answers, one can see that the learners spontaneously had an adequate perception of what was pertinent. They do not repeat a rule learnt at school, they make their own analysis. Very few learners referred to one of the traditional rules given in French textbooks, like "with *tell* the indirect object is constructed directly". But, of course, learners do not phrase their analysis the way we would have. They do not give a proper "scientific", general and unambiguous rule. They are often clumsy or inadequate in the choice of one or several terms, and they have their own way of "adapting" some usual grammatical terms (see "se rapporter à", "déterminer" in the examples presented above). Nevertheless, we feel that the effort they have made in order to construct their answer is positive and will help them to better grasp the "neater" explanation we will suggest later on. What is important here is to try and pick up the terms and references they used and to write comments that will help them connect their analysis to the final one we give.

4.2 Computer Analysis

4.2.1 What is easily done

When we work out the answer analysis for such a question, we always rely on a sample of actual answers (we try to get around 120). We use combinations of key elements. For the answers given above, finding *person, somebody* or *people* would be enough. In the courseware, the actual list corresponding to a "correct" answer contains 14 elements, some with wildcard characters, a "followed by" and a "not" operator are used too. If one introduces wildcard characters so as to group together *personne, personnes, personnage...* the problem is to make sure that *personal pronoun* is not confused with *person* .

Some learners say that *tell* is followed by a personal pronoun as a general rule even though they are shown examples with "...tell Henry...", "... tell his parents... that" . Giving a rule that only applies to one case or group of cases and that is not general enough is a common difficulty. It is commented upon specifically here. Our analyses usually include 10 to 12 different groups of key elements with a specific comment for each.

4.2.2 Problems - One word, several contexts

The technical difficulties we are faced with do not usually come from incorrect or complex syntactic structures but from words or roots that are used with various meanings depending on the context. Here, for instance, we had trouble with *subject* (sujet). A few learners said that *tell* is followed by a subject in a way that suggests they mean a person, while others talk about problems of agreement between the verb and the subject. Very few learners were involved with this error, so we decided to tell those who used the word that we would rather they didn't since we could not decide whether they were talking about what comes before or after *tell.* We usually are very cautious in such cases and do not try to pretend we understand everything in the learner's answer.

Could such problems be avoided more easily with more sophisticated language analysis? But, then, wouldn't one have trouble with the clumsiness or inappropriate use of some words we mentioned earlier? (Also see 4.3. below.) Clearly more work has to be done in order to understand learners' verbalisations [1].

4.3 Consistency and Reference to Familiar Grammatical Analyses

Here is another example of a very open question. In the second lesson of a courseware package for beginners we deal with *the* . We introduce Harold and Maud who are very fond of astronomy. They have gone out on the balcony in order to observe the sky. Maud first asks Harold "Bring a chair, please, Harold !". Later on, Harold has brought what Maud wanted. Harold says " Take the chair, Maud ! ". The question is "When Harold says *the chair* , it is not any chair but a located element (un élément repéré). Why?" Learners saw earlier that *a* indicates that one talks about any single element from the class concerned.

Most learners, when asked, give an explanation that can be analyzed adequately. We had trouble with the word "désigne" (designate, indicate) the same way *subject* was a problem. Some learners say that "*the* designates the definite article" and others that "Harold designates the chair". Here is an English translation of an answer we collected from a pupil in the fourth year at secondary school: "It is a located element because Maud already talked about the chair when she asked for a chair at random. Harold brought the chair that was asked for, hence the chair is

---

[1] See [7, 13], this volume, for an ITS approach of what can be done for an analysis of learners' written productions.

specified (précisée). He tells her to take the chair which is in his hands so it is no longer a determined chair but a *specific* (précise) chair."
The learner has very adequately felt that *the* could be explained in two ways here, either because it is the same chair Maud talked about before (contextual explanation), or because Harold is holding the chair, or it is the only chair around... (situational explanation). Of course, learners will receive different presentations later on, depending on the explanation they first gave.

It is to be noted that it is impossible to decide whether the learner in the above example is making a link between the two different explanations she is giving. We talked about *a* referring to any element. She uses *at random* which is an adequate rephrasing. Thus she has appropriated the explanation we introduced. But what is a real problem here is the way *déterminée* (determined) is opposed to *précise* (specific). Both words are often used in grammatical explanations. They obviously create confusion here. We regularly come across such difficulties (cf. 4.4.4. below).

Previous teaching has often created problems that cannot be overlooked (teaching of the mother language and of other foreign languages). Too often, learners repeat terms in a parrot-like and meaningless fashion. They are so used to not understanding a lot of what is said at school anyway. What has been taught has obviously not been integrated into the learners' conceptual and linguistic systems. It is ignored or creates erratic behaviour. This is why we always pay great attention to the explanations and terms we choose and try to have learners work with them. Such problems are, we think, quite relevant to an ITS at the level of explanations or diagnosis of the learners' difficulties.

4.4 Inadequacies and Misconceptions

Let's now have a look at other problems that can come up when asking open questions.

4.4.1 Inadequate personal interpretations

Here are two other English versions of answers concerning *the* and Harold and Maud.

- "Because that chair is the closest to the place where he is.
  Because it may have something specific adapted to the thing he wants to do."
- "Harold says " the chair " because he is holding it out to Maud. Here it is a located and determined object because they often use it since they are keen on astronomy. "

Here again the learners have felt what was pertinent and sort of mix it with something that is not. They go beyond what can be understood from the English words. Such very personal interpretations are rare enough in our samples. Of course, all we could do here was to spot the pertinent elements and go on from there.

In the second explanation one can see another example of a major problem when trying to construct a logical connection between arguments. The first part is perfectly correct. The learner has associated *located*, the new term we have introduced, to *determined*, a more classical term, quite adequately. However, things go wrong with the second point she wants to make. The first learner had more safely created an implicit coordination or alternative between her two points.

Other examples of similar problems are :

- "Because he must be demonstrating the chair and it is that chair he wants and not another one (parce qu'il doit démontrer la chaise)."

This learner obviously confuses *montrer* (show) and *démontrer* (demonstrate). We did not take the risk of considering the two words as synonyms in our analysis.

- "Harold must be looking at a single object there is no copy of."
  (Harold doit regarder un objet unique qui n'existe en aucun exemplaire.)

At first sight, this learner has only forgotten the word *other* she meant to use. In fact, she makes the same mistake again when she answers the next question. She seems not to be able to make the difference between *aucun* (none) and *qu'un* (only one). Similar phonetic confusion may have caused the inadequate use of *déterminé* we mentioned above: *un déterminé* (a determined element) and *indéterminé* (undetermined) sound exactly the same. We always try to establish a clear distinction between opposites by using phrases like *absence de* rather than a prefix like *in-* . An elaborate phonetic fuzzy matcher might help to process messages of that kind.

4.4.2 Circular explanations

Learners also produced a few answers like the following :

- "because the determiner *the* is used to indicate a located element"
- "because *the* is a definite adjective".

Such a circular answer can correspond to the way learners try to say or write something when they cannot think of any answer or do not understand the question asked. Repeating the questions or any other element that has just been seen is a well-known way out.

Other similar messages may reflect the fact that learners did not connect a new term introduced to their usual terminology, for instance:

- "because it is a definite article".

4.4.3 Pertinent but unwanted answers

These are answers that the CAL designer is sorry to find. They are, for instance, answers that talk about the way a negative sentence is constructed in English for the question about the negation of *must*. We were interested in negating, in the difference between *mustn't* , *needn't* , " tu ne dois pas" ... and not primarily in where to put *not* in the sentence. We kept the question about negating because most learners did think about one of the points that was to be analyzed in detail. However, it is very important to phrase the question so as not to lead to such answers. Here again, experimenting is essential. Learners regularly have unexpected reactions or take initiatives that nobody in the designing team can predict.

4.4.4 Misconceptions

Beginning with open questions is also a way of having misconceptions come up and be corrected immediately. When we worked on *must* and its negation, we gave paper pre-tests. We found that 4.5% of the learners associated *mustn't* to the conditional, 4.5% to an imperative, 4.5% to eventuality (éventualité), 4.5% to an opinion, 21% to advice. For *must* , 7% talked of an order, 3.7% of possibility, 3.7% of permission. A test of this question in the courseware (see 4.3. above) also showed that some learners said that with a negative, as compared to *must* , there would be stronger or weaker, more or less insistent pressure... (we got both interpretations for the same form).

It is, of course, difficult to decide what is a misconception (talking of "possibility") and what is only a concept that can be connected to the point studied but is not adequate at that moment because it will lead to confusion (associating *mustn't* to "advice", for instance). The open question in the courseware will try and provide comments that will help learners spot what is incorrect or not quite adequate in what they say.

In the lesson about the "imparfait" , an open question will help learners see that they are wrong when they think that an "imparfait" expresses an action that is "long", "that lasts"... , whereas a "passé simple" corresponds to something brief, sudden... The example to be analyzed is "... Le panier à salade sortit vers deux heures... D'heure en heure ou de deux heures en deux heures... le brigadier Lucas... arrivait..." (... left around 2 o'clock... would come in...). This is a clear example of the negative impact of previous grammatical habits. Learners inadequately apply what they have learnt about an "imparfait", referring to a single action that is underway (usually *was -ing* in English) to the case of repetition. The first obvious distinction should be between a single and a repeated action here.

We think that opposing what is "long" to what is brief is a very inadequate distinction from a pedagogical point of view. Making learners try to objectively quantify what is expressed is very dangerous when what matters is the point of view of the speaker. This kind of distinction may look simple and easy to understand and it may be necessary for computational linguistics but we think that priorities should be different when one looks at the consequences on learners.

4.4.5 Summary - Starting with learners' intuitions

We would like to integrate learners' intuitions into a CAL "dialogue" for the reasons we just mentioned: learners are more active from the start; they are given the opportunity of comparing their analysis to the one that is suggested; they can have a better chance of connecting their terms to ours. They can do it at the beginning of a new learning phase, i.e. at a point when there still is plenty of time to get used to new elements and forget or correct what should be forgotten or corrected (which always is much more difficult). The effectiveness of this approach seems to be confirmed by the experimental results and the comments we received about our materials (see [9]). We think one could refer to what ITS specialists call a collaborative approach (see [10]) and say that we thus try to create some form of collaborative work within the limits of a classical tutorial approach.

5. Learners' Errors

Let's now consider the problem of learners' errors when they use the foreign language[1] .

5.1 Genuine errors and not so genuine ones

Experience and experimentation have shown us that one must be very cautious before labelling any answer, other than the right one(s) expected at first, as "wrong" or as errors reflecting an erroneous linguistic rule in the learner's interlanguage.

5.2 Causes for errors

Sometimes what looks like an obvious mistake is in fact due to a misleading way of presenting the question or activity, or to the fact that the learner is just not doing what he was supposed to. For instance, he is still trying to answer the previous question or doing the previous exercise.
One should never forget that many "guided" activities require successful answers to the following questions:

- What rules, references, explanations... am I to apply here?
- Which examples, vocabulary... am I to use as a model or to construct my answer?

---

[1] For more detail and examples about paragraphs 5 and 6, see [2] chapter 8, and [3].

- Where are the instructions or the question?
- What do they ask me to do?

Failure in answering one of the above questions will sometimes be enough to create an unacceptable answer which, however, does not indicate that the learner cannot achieve what the teacher or courseware designer wanted him to do.

5.2.1 Instructions

The phrasing of instructions must convey as unambiguously and as simply as possible what is to be done. This is not easy: short and simple instructions are often ambiguous.

If you want to check that learners know the interrogative *where* and ask them to "make up a question about a place", a rather nice, "open" activity, you will probably get answers like *what's the capital of France?* , *Is this your home?* We did. An unambiguous instruction is very difficult to imagine here.

5.2.2 Technical terms

Technical terms are also a major difficulty in the dialogue with the learners (also see 4.3. above). For instance, some terms may appear to be common knowledge and need not be defined when they are in fact used in a specific way (negation, verb...). In other cases, a technical term may not be understood as such. If an answer * *Eliza are writing a letter* receives feedback like "that is not the right person", the next answer may well be * *Paul are writing a letter,* instead of the expected third person, singular form.

5.2.3 Model examples, vocabulary, environment

It is very important to realize that explanations, references and the various pedagogical activities are surrounded with texts, examples, schemas, etc. that can all influence the way they are perceived. Learners regularly misunderstand the vocabulary used in a model example or in the sentence to be completed. This will lead to very inadequate feedback if it has not been anticipated. *We must hurry up* can be understood as *We are happy* (all the more so if capital letters are used) or as *We must get up*. When they have to make up an interrogative sentence from *She likes T-bone steak* , some learners think that *T-bone steak* is the nickname of some person and produce *Who does she like?* instead of the expected *What does she like?* The fact that the courseware introduced Calamity Mimi riding her horse called Jolly Drinker obviously didn't help here.

If you want learners to produce *He writes novels* from *He is a novelist,* some errors may be very dependent on the model shown. If it is *He writes poems. He is a poet,* you will probably get few problems with the verb to be used. We chose *He teaches geography. He is a geography teacher* and we collected answers like **He lists a novel* or **He novelizes* , which we hadn't anticipated ourselves (cf. Figure 2). Of course, with *He cooks well* , we didn't need the test to think of **He is a well cook* or *He's a good cooker.*

6. Dealing with Errors - Feedback

We think that a few points in our approach may be worth mentioning here.

Si l'on veut éviter tout malentendu, lorsque l'on s'adresse à quelqu'un comme M. Dubois, par exemple, on pourra insister ainsi:

Mr Jones — I teach geography. I am a geograph y teacher.

Imaginez maintenant que la conversation porte sur un romancier et complétez sur le même modèle.

Mr Smith — He is a novelist.

Figure 2. A transformation exercise used to reveals learners' misunderstanding of *He writes novels*.

6.1 A descriptive approach

In most cases, it is important to first describe the error. The learner must clearly know there is an error and where it is. Many comments that do not start with this are totally misunderstood and can lead to "corrections" that add a second, often worse, error to the first one (see [3]).

6.2 A prospective approach

A comment presented to the learner should not only spot the error but give some help in order for the learner to be able to find a "right" answer at a/the next try. It is essential to realize that from the point of view of the learner, during a CAL session, what is often important is the answer to give next rather than the one already given (the researcher's perspective is different). We try to establish feedback as a positive and collaborative process that will help the learner to go ahead and not just remind him of what went wrong.

A "prospective" approach is also a way not to focus too much on the diagnosis of previous errors. We often prefer not to say too much about why an error was made. We are too aware of the distance between our interpretations and formulations and the learners' . If the diagnosis is not correct or is not understood, the learner may be at a complete loss as to what is happening and what to do next. Spotting the error, describing it (without explaining it with too much detail), describing the characteristics of a correct message and leaving it to the learner to compare what he did to what should be done often seems to us a safe way of leaving some initiative to the learner.

6.3 An impressionistic approach

From a pedagogical point of view, it can sometimes seem inappropriate to give a well structured, "cartesian", but long and tedious explanation about the error or errors made. A learner will not always be ready to read a comment that is 10 lines long if she is in trouble, has made mistakes, and wants to try and give other answers. The necessary balance between helpful comments or reminders and overwhelming explanations has to be kept in mind. Diagnosing errors and helping learners correct them is a tricky task and too much detail may be undesirable. If there are more than one or two errors in a message, it may be more effective to correct only what will look more important and related to the objective of the session. If an error cannot be explained without referring to technical concepts and terms that have not been introduced yet, if a mistake is still made when it has already been corrected several times, it may be appropriate to try a nontechnical explanation, to use humour, to be less "scientific" but more accessible or more "striking".

6.4 An adaptative approach

Since we deal with each question and answer separately, we can afford to adapt our feedback to the context of the question as well as to the learner's type of error. We can tailor the comments to each example treated and adapt the general rule that is involved to any specific situation presented. We can thus comment on an error in reference to the general rule and to the specific context at the same time. This is, of course, especially helpful when we deal with "real" examples. For instance, in a lesson on the present tense, we work on a newspaper article (cf. Fig. 3). Learners must find what the journalist wrote: "A language centre for Scottish industry and commerce ... at Glenrothes, Fife. That was disclosed to Fife Education Committee yesterday when...". Here is an English version of part of the comment given to the answer *is planned*: : "... a state would suggest that the project has been well known for a long time, that it is a permanent characteristic of Glenrothes to be the site where a centre is to be. But the news was only announced yesterday, the speaker focuses on the present situation, with an -ing present".

The Times

From our correspondent.
Kirkcaldy.

A language centre for Scottish industry and commerce__________________at Glenrothes, Fife. That was disclosed to Fife Education Committee yesterday when it approved a £ 300,000 project to make Ballinnie house into a centre for intensive language learning courses.

Le verbe est **plan.**

Figure 3. A cloze exercise for verb conjugation in English.

7. Conclusion

After experimenting with a large number of pedagogical scripts and being confronted with many learners' reactions, we are convinced that several elements cannot be overlooked. No research on teaching or learning can bypass the importance and specificity of the pedagogical situation. A. Culioli says that comprehension is but a specific instance of misunderstanding. It is all the more true in the case of a learner trying to communicate with a teacher or a piece of courseware. Learners can be trusted to have a lot of very adequate intuitions about the language they are studying and about language in general. One should not forget that they master language through their use of their mother tongue. They have a lot to say by themselves and they usually enjoy doing it. But they will approach everything their way, with their interpretations, their words, their logic, their lack of scientific experience.

Researchers designing teaching/learning materials should neither underestimate the capacities of their target audience nor overestimate their mastery and experience of what actually is very specialized. Any second language learner is a native speaker of his mother tongue, he is not a trained linguist, scientist, or teacher. Cognitive and linguistic studies, artificial intelligence and intelligent tutoring systems, will perhaps help bridge the gap, leaving learners as autonomous as possible while establishing the right communication level with them. The other chapters in this book show the progress that has been made to date.

References

1. Demaizière, F. & Gandilhon, N.: Potentials of CAL in higher education curricula, English grammar courseware. In: Higher education and new technologies (H. Oosthoek, T. Vroerijenstijn eds.), pp. 157-168, Oxford: Pergamon Press 1989
2. Demaizière, F.: Enseignement assisté par ordinateur, Paris : Ophrys 1986
3. Demaizière, F.: Erreur et EAO. In : Les langues modernes, n° 5, pp. 48-53 1987
4. Culioli, A.: Representation, referential processes, and regulation. Language activity as form production and recognition. In: Language and cognition (J. Montangero, A. Tryphon, eds.), Cahier n°10, pp. 97-124, Geneva : Fondation Archives Jean Piaget 1989
5. Bouscaren, J. & Chuquet, J.: Grammaire et textes anglais. Guide pour l'analyse linguistique. Paris : Ophrys 1987
6. Bailly, D. : Eléments de didactique des langues. L'activité conceptuelle en classe d'anglais. Paris : APLV 1984
7. Chanier, T., Pengelly, M., Twidale, M. & Self, J.: Conceptual modelling in error analysis in computer-assisted language learning. This volume
8. Charlirelle: Behind the Words, classes de 6e, 5e, 4e, 3e. Livres de l'élève et livres du maître, glossaire linguistique. Paris: OCDL. Diffusion M.D.I. (1975-1981)
9. Hawkins, E.: Awareness of language: An introduction. Cambridge: Cambridge University Press 1984
10. Basuyau, B., Demaizière, F., Hargrove J. & Trevise, A.: Grammar and CALL methodology. Experimenting ORDI courseware. In: Proceedings of the International CALL Conference. Rostock 1990
11. Self, J.A. : Bypassing the intractable problem of student modelling. In: ITS 88, Montréal, pp. 18-24. 1988
12. Swartz, M. L.: Issues for tutoring knowledge in foreign language intelligent tutoring systems. This volume
13. Tasso, C., Fum, D. & Giangrandi, P.: The use of explanation-based learning for modeling student behavior in foreign langauge tutoring. This volume

Section Two

Computational and Theoretical Bases for ITS: Grammars, Lexicons, Parsers, and Discourse Models

Appropriate representations of linguistic knowledge are crucial in the development of two of the knowledge bases in a foreign language ITS: the expert and learner models. We also need computational linguistic formalisms to give the computer the ability to process natural language in a learning scenario. At first glance, we might expect to use formal, computationally tractable linguistic theories for developing the expert and learner models in an ITS. However, language learners are not taught formal grammars of the type theoretical linguists study. These formal grammars are primarily used to describe language competence in a native language, not learners' competence as defined by linguistic production skills in a foreign language (language performance). What we need then, is to construct a pedagogical grammar for the ITS models that specifies that portion of the grammar we wish to teach.

In this section the papers address the issue of developing computational bases for ITS development that are robust enough to formally represent and parse a real language, yet are constructed according to appropriate pedagogical principles and theories of foreign language acquisition. Chapter 3 opens this section with a model for foreign language acquisition that was constructed from numerous crosslinguistic studies. The author lays out a psycholinguistic account of features such as linguistic cues and form-function mappings that learners encounter and must master when acquiring a new language. This model describes Ll - L2 transfer, learner strategies, and a set of pedagogical principles that can be used to guide the Ll - L2 remappings that occur as a new language is learned.

Chapter 4 presents work that attempts to reconcile the dilemma surrounding the adequacy of computational formalisms required for a foreign language ITS. The authors propose use of a systemic grammar representation because of the emphasis on the functional aspects of language proffered by systemic theory [5]. We are shown how two types of grammar representations are needed in an ITS to adequately represent a language (formal grammar) yet are appropriate for dealing with the pedagogical reality of learners' limited competencies (naive grammar).

Many recent linguistic theories are emphasizing the lexical phenomena associated with aspects of language thought previously to be purely syntactic. As a consequence, grammatical formalisms and theories are being developed that can be termed 'lexicalized'. The next two chapters discuss current research on lexical grammars and lexical knowledge representations for foreign languages. Chapter 5 presents a computational formalism used to construct a lexical grammar in French and English. This formalism espouses the viewpoint that syntactic rules are not separated from lexical items. The author describes a grammar that consists of a lexicon where each word is associated with a finite number of elementary syntactic structures. These lexical items and their associated structures make up a Tree Adjoining Grammar (TAG) that describes both syntactic and semantic features for these linguistic units. We are shown how a parser is used for analyzing sentences input by the learner within the TAG to join elementary tree structures into larger constituents. The author then makes recommendations for the use of the TAG formalism in an ITS to illustrate the structural components of well-formed sentences as well as meaning to the learner.

NATO ASI Series, Vol. F 80
Intelligent Tutoring Systems for Foreign Language Learning
Edited by M. L. Swartz and M. Yazdani

Chapter 6 continues to look at lexical knowledge, but focuses more on a psychological model to represent word organization in memory. The authors describe the development of an on-line lexical database that uses different semantic relations to organize nouns, verbs, adjectives, and adverbs into an associative network. We are shown how these lexical relationships fit in a matrix that defines the association between a concept and its lexicalization in a language. This method is used to explain the organization of the semantic network model that underlies the database, WORDNET. The paper closes with some recommendations for using this on-line semantic network to learn words in a L2.

We know that language learning involves more than isolated vocabulary learning; words must be learned in the context of larger units, idioms, phrases, discourse. While the papers in this section have described different theoretical bases for representing grammars and the lexicon, we still need some way of representing language in larger linguistic units. The last chapter in this section describes such a formalism as well as a parser for understanding L2 discourse. The representation uses a propositional network [6] as a semantic model for L2 discourse. The authors describe how their system interface is designed to access the linguistic information as learners construct sentences. This model is based on a suite of psycholinguistic studies carried out by the authors to examine how learners process discourse in L2.

The Competition Model and Foreign Language Acquisition

Brian MacWhinney
Department of Psychology, Carnegie Mellon University, Pittsburgh, PA 15213, USA

Abstract: This article explores the application of the Competition Model [23] as an account of foreign language acquisition. The model is discussed in terms of the constructs of cue validity, cue cost, and form-function mappings. The model predicts certain types of transfer in phonological, syntactic, and lexical learning. In the attempt to maximize transfer of L1 structures the learner uses a variety of complex learning strategies. Tutoring systems for foreign language instruction need to recognize the use of these transfer strategies and correct the errors which they produce.

Keywords: Psycholinguistics, foreign language learning, sentence comprehension, grammatical devices, online processing, reaction times, transfer, intelligent tutoring systems, hypertext, semantics, cue validity, competition model, language universals, lexical learning, language learning, agreement, syntactic accent, critical period, fossilization.

1. The Competition Model

Psycholinguists have tended to focus their energies on the study of first language acquisition and processing. Unfortunately, this first language focus has resulted in a neglect of the equally important area of second language acquisition. When the subjects have been adults, they have usually been English speakers, largely freshmen college students in introductory courses in psychology. Similarly, the first language learners have often been the children of English-speaking developmental psycholinguists. Generalizations based on these limited populations are, of course, bound to lead to misleading, anglocentric views of the language-making capacity. Fortunately, the scope of psycholinguistics has been broadening in recent years to include a progressively wider array of monolingual subjects. Much of this new crosslinguistic first language acquisition research is discussed in Slobin [35]. An even newer line of research, which examines adult sentence processing crosslinguistically, is presented in MacWhinney and Bates [23].

This paper will examine a model which has arisen within the context of this new line of crosslinguistic research. The Competition Model was first formulated as an approach to crosslinguistic developmental research [2; 3; 18; 19; 23]. In the research presented in MacWhinney and Bates [23] the model was generalized to a wider array of crosslinguistic data, including adult sentence processing, language in aphasia, and second language learning. Although the Competition Model was not originally based on data from second language acquisition, its crosslinguistic developmental orientation seems to make it well-suited for use in this area too. At the same time, it is clear that data on the learning of foreign languages can play an important role in the testing and elaboration of the Competition Model.

The basic idea underlying the Competition Model is simple and rather traditional. The model takes as its starting point the Saussurean vision of the linguistic sign as a set of mappings between cues and functions. *Cues* are external phonological and word order

NATO ASI Series, Vol. F 80
Intelligent Tutoring Systems for Foreign Language Learning
Edited by M. L. Swartz and M. Yazdani

patterns which can be detected during the process of comprehension. *Functions* are underlying communicative intentions or meanings. In the Competition Model, each lexical item or syntactic structure can be understood as a cue-to-function mapping. For example, the meanings underlying the word "bat" are activated when the phonological cues contained in the sound sequence /bAt/ are detected. On the syntactic level, a similar relation holds. When the cues of preverbal positioning or verb agreement marking are activated, the functions corresponding to the "subject" are also activated. These functions include agency, topicality, perspective, first mover, causer, volitional agent, and so on.

In addition to the *correlations* between sets of cues and sets of functions, there are also correlations between functions and between cues. We can call these function-function correlations and cue-cue correlations. On the functional level, it is generally true that topics are also given, animate, definite, and so on. These correlations derive from real correlations between properties of the world in which we live. The highly correlated nature of language makes it so that no single cue expresses any single meaning and the relation between cues and functions is both fluid and robust. There are also important correlations on the level of cues. For example, words that take the article "the" also usually allow the plural suffix, and so on.

We speak of these various mappings as correlations because we know that all categories are imperfect and subject to category leakage [20]. For example, the correlation between preverbal positioning and agency in English breaks down in the passive and the imperative. Similarly, the correlation between plural marking and semantic plurality breaks down with words like "pants" or "faculty."

The interaction of cues such as preverbal positioning, animacy, case-marking, and subject-verb agreement has been modelled mathematically in the Competition Model using maximum likelihood techniques [28]. The data modelled in these studies come from experiments with real subjects in many languages and at many age levels using sentences in which the various cues are placed into "competition" with each other in an orthogonalized ANOVA design. The maximum likelihood techniques make it possible to estimate the *cue strengths* of particular cues. For example, in our studies of sentence processing in English, Italian, German, French, and Hungarian, we have been able to estimate the relative strengths of preverbal positioning, subject-verb agreement, and animacy as cues to the function of "agency." We have found that, in English, the preverbal positioning cue is extremely strong and that the agreement and animacy cues are only of any importance at all when there is no preverbal noun, as in VNN sentences. In Italian, on the other hand, the agreement cue is far stronger than the word order cue. Although both English and Italian are described as SVO languages, the actual strengths of the basic cues to sentence interpretation in these two languages are radically different.

Perhaps the most important empirical claim of the Competition Model is that cue strength in the adult native speaker is directly proportional to *cue validity*. What is crucial about this claim is that our cue validity measures are taken from actual text counts based on spoken or written discourse, whereas our cue strength measures are derived from experiments. This way of understanding the relation between the learner and the environment avoids the circularities often found in mathematical modelling in psychology. The idea is that, during language learning, the child comes to appreciate the relative order of cues in his language and to tune his cognitive system so that it correctly mirrors the environment. At first, the child picks up cues just on the basis of their *overall availability*. At this early period, the English-speaking child is already paying more attention to word order than his Italian counterpart. In Hebrew, if there are two ways to mark reflexivity, the child will first start to use the one that is more generally used or more frequent. In this early period, the child will also be strongly influenced by *cue detectability,* since it is difficult to pick up cues that are hard to perceive. For example, the Turkish child picks up accusative marking earlier than the Hungarian child, largely because of the clearer phonological status of the Turkish accusative suffix.

As development proceeds, the learner focuses more and more on the *reliability* of the cue, rather than simply its overall availability. In particular, the learner wants to know which cue to bet on when there is a head-to-head conflict between cues. For example, the preverbal positioning cue is highly available and fairly reliable, but when it comes into direct conflict with the case-marking cue on personal pronouns, the case-marking cue always wins. In the end, it is this *conflict reliability* which determines the final strength value of the cue in the language.

There are aspects of language for which the simple correlation between cue strength and cue validity tends to break down. These exceptions to the basic rule occur whenever a cue places a particular strain on the processing mechanism. For example, we have found that young Italian children take a long time learning to make use of the highly reliable cue of subject-verb agreement [8]. The problem seems to be that the variable word order of Italian requires the listener to process long-distance dependencies between separate words. By way of contrast, the marking of case in Hungarian only requires the listener to detect the presence of an accusative marker placed directly on the noun. Another set of divergences from simple cue validity occurs in relative clause processing where the piling up of nouns without verbs in an SOV language like Hungarian [25] can lead to delays in processing. The Competition Model refers to these various processing factors as *cue costs*. We do not consider cue costs as noise factors to be swept under the theoretical rug. On the contrary, they provide us with important glimpses into those aspects of the language processor which determine language universals. The Competition Model seeks to quantify *language particulars* in terms of cue validities, whereas it seeks to quantify *language universals* in terms of cue costs.

The interplay between cue validity and cue costs is one of the factors which leads to delays in the acquisition of particular grammatical patterns. The child must focus on strengthening those cues which are subject to high cost restrictions. In addition to late acquisition of high cost cues, the final stages of language acquisition also focus on the tuning of cue weights so that conflicts between cues can always be resolved in the favor of the cue with the highest conflict validity [26].

2. Transfer

There was a time when people thought that the learning of L2 was based on transfer from L1. However, with the demise of behaviorism, the theory of transfer was locked into the behaviorist dungeon. Slowly, that old ghost has been emerging as an important component in modern accounts of second language learning [6; 10; 12; 30; 31]. In the early 1970's the established wisdom was that the predictions of contrastive analysis for second language learning were largely incorrect and that simple behaviorist models of transfer were simply wrong. However, the psychological theory of transfer has now been reformulated within the richer framework of problem-solving theory [34] and analogical theory [32; 39]. The problem is that these newer cognitive models have not yet been brought to bear on the problems of second language acquisition. In this section, I wish to explore some of the ways in which the Competition Model can be used to understand aspects of positive and negative transfer in the early stages of second language learning.

2.1 Phonology

How can we conceptualize transfer within the framework of the Competition Model? The easiest place to begin is with phonological transfer. MacWhinney [21] proposed a Competition Model view of phonology based on a connectionist network. This network learns to auto-associate a set of auditory units to a set of articulatory units. Presumably, these associations are built up and solidified during the first two years of life. Of course, we know that not all articulatory patterns are learned with equal ease. Phonological processes [36] force certain patterns to have a higher cue cost. However, as the system matures, the strength of the various cues comes to approximate their true validity in the language. When the language learner begins acquiring vocabulary in L2, he simply treats these as additional words of L1 composed of sounds that match most closely to auditory and articulatory items already in his repertoire. Odlin [30] reviews dozens of studies which illustrate transfer of this type in both segmental and supersegmental phonology. In some cases, this transfer is fairly successful and goes unnoticed. For example, the places of articulation of nasal consonants are often similar between languages and even stop consonants often have similarities. However, the exact amounts of voicing of stop consonants or the exact forms of articulation for vowels seldom transfer without producing some accent. Some of the negative transfer also affects audition, where Chinese speakers may confuse "rice" and "lice," because of the absence of the /r/-/l/ distinction in Chinese.

The Competition Model does not assume that all L2 phonological learning is based on transfer. There are two additional factors which determine the shape of the learner's system: cue costs and L2 generalizations [10]. Cue costs express language universal phonological processes such as devoicing, vowel harmony, and other neutralizations. These processes can be expressed in terms of universal markedness theory. However, their real basis surely lies in the mechanisms of auditory and articulatory processing. In the early stages of L2 acquisition, L2 generalization plays only a minor role. However, as learning progresses, the L2 phonological auto-associative net begins to have a structure that is at least partially independent of the L1 net. As that network grows, we see the emergence of phonological overgeneralizations that match in part those exhibited by L1 learners.

How can we predict which of these three factors will be operative in a given stage of L2 phonological learning? The Competition Model prediction is that L2 learning will begin with massive transfer from L1 within the limitations set by cue costs or phonological processes. Here we expect some individual differences. Learners who have a richer array of auditory and articulatory patterns in L1 will be able to transfer somewhat more fine-grained patterns and show somewhat less negative transfer. These same speakers will also have succeeded more fully in overcoming cue cost limitations in L1. When they come to L2, they will also be able to overcome cue cost limitations. When L1 is close to L2, transfer will also be more clearly positive.

After a period of initial massive transfer from L1 to L2, we expect to see a long period in which the system tries to deal with the fact that its articulatory output does not correctly match the L2 target. Learning at this stage is promoted most strongly by correct registration of the phonology of the L2 target lexical items. If the target forms are passed through an L1 filter, the learner will never be able to detect a mismatch [17] between his own forms and the correct target forms. Without the detection of error, the L2 auto-associative network will not develop. The learner must be encouraged to perceive the mismatch between his output forms and the correct input forms. It would seem that the best way to bring this about would be through a process in which learners attempt to match their own productions to computer-controlled digitized speech. Such a procedure should be particularly helpful in acquiring intonational contrasts.

2.2 Lexical learning

During the initial stages, much of the work of second language learning involves lexical acquisition. Within this domain, there is a fairly massive conceptual transfer from L1 to L2. Consider the learning of the Spanish word /mesa/ by an English speaker. The speaker has already acquired a set of function-function correlations between the various meanings underlying the concept of "table." On the phonological level, the learner maps the sounds of /mesa/ onto already existing English segmental units. The only new learning that has to occur is in the mapping between the new sound string and the old meaning set. In this case, the transfer of old units and correlations is essentially positive. Of course, the actual phonological units used to represent /mesa/will be English-based, but the learner is able to use this simple transfer process to express a meaning easily and with a minimum of new learning. For common concrete nouns like "table" and "salt," the process of lexical learning may proceed with minimal error. However, abstract nouns, verbs, and adjectives may have subtle meanings that will have to be relearned in L2.

Using a *one-to-one* lexical mapping strategy, we find learners producing sentences such as, "*Ich wurde möchte zu gehen in das Geschäft," which derives apparently by word-for-word conversion from the English sentence, "I would like to go into the store." Or, to take an example from an English speaker's early Spanish, we find, "Yo soy hablando," derived from English "I am speaking." The corresponding German learner form would be "*Ich bin sprechen."

What happens when a simple type of transfer is blocked? When this occurs, the learner utilizes a secondary path of transfer to go around the barrier. For example, when confronted with the failure of one-to-one mapping, the learner can attempt a *many-to-one* mapping. For example, he can translate the German word "möchte" by the English phrase "would like to." At this point, his translation of "I would like to go into the store" would be "*Ich möchte gehen in das Geschäft." In general, we can view transfer not as a simple uniform process, but as a general approach to language learning in which the learner is exploring all possible *paths of transfer*. When a particular path of transfer is blocked, the learner explores another path. When all transfer paths are blocked, the learner either gives up or waits for new information. According to this account, the beginning learner always attempts to construct an L1-based interpretation of L2 structures.

The reader may object that any reasonable approach to L2 learning will keep the learner from even attempting simple lexical translation schemes of the type discussed here. The whole point of functional language training is to avoid simple translation and to have the student thinking and speaking directly in L2 from the beginning. However, the analysis I am offering is not in disagreement with this position. The Competition Model holds that these simple mappings can be corrected without requiring that the learner produce errors overtly. How can this be? As MacWhinney [17] and Berwick [4] have noted, errors in syntactic processing can often be corrected on the basis of data derived from "failure to parse." If the comprehension system is unable to find a one-to-one map from German "möchte" to a single English lexical item, it can still attempt a many-to-one mapping. The learner simply realizes that the input form "möchte" maps onto the string "would like to." In general, the learner will either discover such mappings for himself or perhaps acquire them from the textbook. In this way, many of the most obvious transfer errors will never actually occur in production. This is particularly true if the classroom emphasis is on listening to L2 forms and the learner is not required to produce forms which he does not control [14].

The learner's lexical transfer strategies need not stop with one-to-one and many-to-one mappings. There are several additional strategies that can be used that still depend on a mapping from L2 to L1. These strategies are more abstract and less general than the simple strategies of one-to-one and many-to-one mapping. For that reason, we would expect that structures that require these elaborate remappings would be relatively more difficult to acquire. In *discontinuous mapping*, the learner picks up new lexical items that have discontinuous mappings onto L2 forms and vice versa. Here, again, it is the initial "failure to parse" that leads the learner to invoke the strategy. For example, the German word "keinen" can be mapped onto the English sequence "not .... a ..." This will allow the learner to formulate the English sentence "He has not seen a man" as the German sentence "Er hat keinen Mann gesehen." Yet another strategy involves the *analysis* of pieces of L2 words. Using this strategy, the learner can identify the Spanish conditional suffix /ri/ with the English word "would." Thus, the Spanish phrase "habría visto" can be analyzed in

English as "have-would-I seen." At the same time, the learner can parse new strings such as "hablaría" or "comerían" always by pulling out the /ri/ from the surrounding material. This strategy is more analytic than a simple one-to-many mapping.

2.3 Automatization

So far, all of the strategies we have discussed involve ways of structuring the mapping between an L2 phonological string and an L1 conceptual or semantic representation. The mappings produced by these transfer strategies are not as direct as the corresponding native language mappings, because they use both L1 and L2 representations. Over time, the learner will attempt to restructure his representations so that true L2 phonological forms are mapped directly onto true L2 semantic forms. Instead of accessing the word "mesa" through the English word "table," the learner will access "mesa" directly. Increasing the speed of access involves processes which cognitive psychologists generally refer to as "automatization." However, in the case of L2 acquisition, one needs to differentiate two ways in which automatization can be achieved. These are "proceduralization" and "compilation" [22]. Proceduralization leads to the smoother and faster L2 functioning without major reorganization. Compilation, on the other hand, attempts to restructure processing so that processing goes directly from meaning to sound within L2. In many learners, these two forces work against each other. If a particular mapping using L1 transfer to L2 becomes highly proceduralized or automated, it becomes difficult to restructure it. In such cases, learners can end up blocking the "recompilation" of their processing system into more native-like systems.

2.4 Syntactic learning

Within the Competition Model [19], syntactic learning involves the formation and restructuring of the argument frames of particular lexical items, as well as the generalization of these frames across groups of lexical items. Some aspects of L1-to-L2 transfer involve the argument frames of particular lexical items. In general, when a new L2 word is learned, the complete argument frame of the L1 analog is transferred. In some cases, no error will results. However, for most closed class lexical items, there will be problems. For example, French and Spanish locative prepositions do not code directionality, whereas their English equivalents do. Direct translation of the English word "into" as French "en" will lead to errors such as the French sentence "*Je suis allez en la magasin" for "Je suis entrez dans la magasin" on the basis of English "I went in the store." In French, the verb that expresses the motion must also express the nature of goal. The correction of these mismappings involves more than simply lexical learning. It requires that the learner to restructure argument frames [19] for each new closed class lexical item and for many new verbs. This *frame restructuring* requires the learner to make a clear distinction between the L1 analog and the L2 form, thereby exerting a pressure toward the separation of the two languages.

Other forms of syntactic learning involve general patterns across constituents. Within the Competition Model, these general patterns are viewed as emerging from networks that correlate the semantics of lexical items to particular argument frames. Not all patterns are fully predictable from simple semantic patterns. However, the connectionist networks used in the Competition Model can handle the "abduction" of form classes from semantic-syntactic correspondences. Just as the learner transfers individual lexical frames from L1 to L2, so the learner can also transfer general patterns. For example, the English learner of Spanish initially assumes that the adjective precedes the noun. However, this rule is immediately subjected to massive negative evidence, as soon as the learner begins to hear Spanish noun phrases. At first, the learner may attempt to handle this through a process of *shuffling* in which a constituent is moved from its normal position to another position in the sentence. This strategy is used when formulating "Ella es una niña bonita" on the basis of "She is a pretty girl." The shuffling strategy allows the learner to preserve the basic lexical transfer strategy. Shuffling can also reorder major constituents. Initially, the Spanish learner of English uses Spanish-based patterns to produce "*Come here all my friends" on the basis of Spanish "Vienen aquí todos mis amigos." However, the learner soon realizes that English requires the subject to precede the verb. These shuffling strategies are only crutches along the pathway toward real control of L2 syntactic patterns. Eventually, the learner is able to use a syntactic network in L2 to order constituents directly without reference to L1 patterns and without shuffling.

The learner also has to pick up patterns of *omission* and *agreement* marking through initial reference to L1 structures. For example, the English learner of Spanish may initially say "Yo tengo un libro" for "I have a book." This use of the personal pronoun "yo" is not an error, but it implies some pragmatic contrast. At first, the learner must overtly delete the subject pronoun. Over time, he drops his reliance on the omission strategy as a way of correcting L1 transfer errors and directly produces sentences with pronouns omitted.

3. Cue Strength Transfer

Within the framework of the Competition Model there are now eight studies that investigate a particular type of L1 influence on L2 learning. This is the transfer of the specific strengths of the cues to subject identification from L1 to L2. Beginning with a study of German-English and Italian-English bilinguals [1], we have found repeatedly that L2 learners have what we have come to refer to as a "syntactic processing accent." This research is summarized in a special issue of the journal "Applied Psycholinguistics" in 1987 and in Kilborn and Ito [13]. To give an example of a typical finding, we observed that Germans listening to English NNV sequences assume that the first noun is the subject, whereas English monolinguals assume exactly the opposite. Similarly, Italians learning English pay attention to agreement cues and place little reliance on the preverbal positioning cue, whereas English monolinguals do exactly the opposite. This type of L1 to L2 transfer of cue strengths is exactly the pattern that would be predicted by the Competition Model.

McDonald and MacWhinney [28] and McDonald and Heilenman [27] have constructed mathematical models of the cue strength interactions in our experiments with bilinguals and L2 learners and found that the strength of cues at various points in learning are well-predicted by the various cue validity measures in the Competition Model. In general, the results to date have supported the Competition Model. There are two areas in which the simplest predictions of a model based only on transfer driven by cue validity have not been supported. Gass [9] suggested that the semantic cue of animacy seems to have a certain universal prepotency in both L1 and L2 learning. Within the Competition Model framework presented earlier, we can think of the prepotency of the animacy cue as involving a particularly low cue cost. In particular, Gass found that English learners of Italian are quick to drop their strong dependency on the preverbal positioning cue of English and pick up the reliance on animacy as a cue to subject that we find in monolingual Italians. A variety of additional evidence suggests that animacy may have the kind of prepotency suggested by Gass, although further work will be needed to understand the exact nature and size of this effect.

Another challenge to the Competition Model in its simplest form is the finding by Kilborn and Ito [13] that English learners of Japanese attempt to make rigid use of SOV order as a cue to sentence interpretation, much as they have made rigid use of SVO order in English. Indeed these English-speakers relied much more on SOV than native speakers of Japanese. Of course, the system of case-marking in Japanese has aspects that may be difficult for learners and this may have led to a tendency to rely most heavily on the simplest cue, even though its actual cue validity is comparatively lower. But the point is that English speakers seem to be particularly interested in trying to find some cue that will look maximally like the preverbal positioning cue they have come to know and love in their native language. In other words, they seem to be exploring a secondary *path of transfer* that looks for something close to their major L1 cue, since it is clear that the exact preverbal cue of L1 is not used in Japanese.

4. Functional Restructuring

So far, we have assumed that L2 acquisition involves an absolute minimum of functional restructuring. However, there is good reason to believe that, after the earliest stages, L2 learners are spending a great deal of time creating a new set of grammatical categories. A prime example of this type of restructuring might be the foreigner's attempts to pick up the category structure underlying the two major verbal conjugations of Hungarian. The intransitive conjugation is used not only when the verb is intransitive, but also when the direct object is modified by an indefinite article or by no article at all, when it is in the first or second person, when the head of the relative clause is the object within the relative clause, when the direct object is quantified by words like "each," "no," and so on. For example, the "intransitive" conjugation is used when a Hungarian says "John runs," "John eats an apple," "John eats your apple," and "John eats no apple." On the other hand, the transitive conjugation is used when the object is definite, when it is modified by a third person possessive suffix, when it is possessed by a third person nominal phrase, and so on. Thus, the "transitive" or "definite" conjugation is used when the Hungarian wants to say "John eats the apple" or "John eats Bill's apple." There are some 13 conditions which, taken together, control the choice between the transitive and intransitive conjugations [20]. There is no single principle that can be used to group this 13 conditions. Instead, both transitivity, definiteness, and referential disambiguation all figure in as factors in making this choice. This way of grouping together aspects of transitivity, definiteness, and possession is extremely foreign to most non-Hungarians. Not surprisingly, L2 learners of Hungarian have a terrible time marking this distinction; errors in choice of the conjugation of the verb are the surest syntactic cue that the learner is not a native Hungarian.

In order to acquire this new category, the L2 learner begins by attempting to transfer from L1. To some degree this can work. The learner attempts to identify the intransitive with the English intransitive. However, the fact that many sentences with objects also take the intransitive if the objects are somehow "indefinite" tends to block the simple application of this conceptual structure. In the end, no simple transfer will succeed and the learner must resign himself to picking up the pieces of this new category one by one and welding them together into a connected system. Here is an area where attempts at linguistic analysis on the learner's part only make matters worse. If the learner had proceeded like a Hungarian child [16], he would have learned the conjugations by generalizing from a few key collocations and phrases. The adult needs to amplify this case-based approach to learning with a way of focusing on contrastive structures in which cues are competing. Zock [40] presents a system which instructs the learner on the basis of errors and correct examples. For the adult, such focusing on particularly difficult parts of a grammatical system will increase the efficiency of acquisition.

In many cases, the transfer of syntactic patterns from L1 to L2 is structurally correct, but semantically inaccurate. For example, Trévise [38] observes that French speakers make excessive use of topicalization structures in English in the form of structures corresponding to left-dislocation, right-dislocations, and "c'est .. que" in French. Although these structures are all permissible in English, the actual conditions on their usage are far more restrictive than in French. Similarly, Seliger [33] notes that Hebrew learners of English tend to systematically underuse the passive. He attributes this underusage to the relatively tighter, genre-dependent conditions on the use of the passive in Hebrew. In general, it is clear that simple transfer of an L1 structure to L2 is not sufficient to guarantee correct usage, since both underutilization and overutilization can occur until the full conditions governing the use of a construction in L2 are learned.

5. Fossilization and the Critical Period

In his seminal analysis of the biological bases of language, Lenneberg [15] argued for a critical period for language acquisition. It is clear that, past a certain age, at least some aspects of a second language become more and more difficult to acquire. The most obvious problems are in the area of phonological learning. How does the Competition Model account for these apparent problems in later acquisition? The basic account is that increased automatization of the L1 system makes the addition of new auditory, articulatory, and semantic contrasts progressively more difficult. The more automatized a system becomes, the less it is available for restructuring. If the learner has not been exposed to a wide variety of phonological contrasts before puberty, the decreased plasticity of the brain will make it progressively more difficult to acquire new articulatory patterns, since these patterns will be driven by the ability to code auditory contrasts. There are apparently important individual differences in the nature of early experiences and the extent to which they leave some residual plasticity for later learning, since some adults are able to pick up second languages with only some difficulty and other find full acquisition of L2 virtually impossible.

There is a second important difference between L1 and L2 learning that tends to produce critical period effects. This is the fact that L2 learning relies on a massive amount of top-down constructive processing. The L2 learner can often pull one or two words out of a conversation and know pretty much what is being discussed. This form of processing is not available to the child. Unfortunately, constructive processing of this type tends to bypass some of the basic processes of lexical analysis and acquisition which may be crucial for acquisition of full native-like control of the language [11]. The L2 learner who is able to maximize top-down comprehension processes and who is able to utilize simple transfer processes to acquire some moderate ability to produce sentences may find himself in a position where the remaining amount of easily detected error is insufficient to force a full reorganization of a decidedly non-native system. To make further progress, the learner would have to refocus attention on the details of phonological form and argument structure, rather than on the actual process of communication. Unless he diverts attention to these secondary concerns, the learner's control of L2 will tend to fossilize.

6. FLITS and the Competition Model

What sort of FLITS pedagogical treatment is most in accord with the Competition Model approach? Swartz [37] cites ten principles that are clearly important.

1. Language behavior is learned through experience.
2. Present language in context.
3. Present language in its natural order (receptive to productive).
4. Teach the most frequent, high utility items first.
5. Teach simple to complex
6. Teach grammatical form through patterns in the language.
7. Support instruction with declarative explanation.
8. Repeat language behavior at appropriate intervals.
9. Vary practice exercises to internalize patterns.
10. Exploit communicative situations.

These principles focus on the contextual basing of instruction and the flow from simple forms to more complex forms. In addition to these considerations, the Competition Model points toward several additional pedagogical principles.

1. Early training should focus on the restructuring of the *phonological* system in the context of computer-controlled exercises encouraging the learner to match his own productions to clear L2 samples. Phonological training should be done in the context of the acquisition of new lexical items in simple syntactic frames.
2. Since *transfer* is inevitable, instruction should be designed to maximize the positive effects of transfer and minimize the negative effects.
3. Early in learning, there is an important role of *rote* acquisition of forms. Later in learning, such rote learning should be deemphasized.
4. Ideally, new *lexical* items should be acquired in the context of syntactic groupings which fully display their alternative argument frames [40]. Implementation of a HyperText system for lexical frames can allow the student to learn syntax in terms of operations on particular lexical groups. The instructional process does not need to specifically teach transfer or remapping strategies, since students will automatically apply them. However, errors produced by the transfer of L1 lexical frames need to be clearly presented in terms of HyperText systems.
5. Inevitably, the simplest transfer strategies will produce errors. However, it is better to focus on allowing the student to first deal with difficult materials in *comprehension*, rather than attempting, initially, to generate, detect, and correct errors in production. This is essentially an amplification of point 3 from Swartz.
6. As the student advances, the goal of instruction should be to progressively sharpen attention to those aspects of language which had previously been ignored and where the student is likely to make the largest numbers of errors. This can be done most effectively by increasing emphasis on *error detection* and *error correction* in later stages of L2 learning to prevent the fossilization of forms and mappings. This emphasis is in accord with the views of Demaizière and Blanvillian [7]. This type of training should focus on *functional restructuring*.

In order to implement points 3 through 6 above, we will need to build an FLITS system that provides two basic sorts of challenges to the learner. One challenge will be the challenge of lexical acquisition. The learner should be acquiring new words at a rapid pace, but within a context that is rich syntactically, pragmatically, and situationally. Semantic nets of the type discussed by Miller [29] or of the type implemented by MacWhinney and Hill (in preparation) will be relevant. However, the positive acquisition of new lexical structures is not enough. A complete FLITS system [5] will have to have rich tools for error detection that provide the learner with specific instruction designed to correct each error type. In accord with the Competition Model, error-driven instruction should focus on the presentation and elaboration of the L2 pattern that should compete with the learner error. For example, if the learner produces a gender error in German in a particular case, there should be instruction to correct this error that illustrates the particular form in the context of others that are phonologically similar and which have the same gender [24].

The generation of errors and the use of tools for correcting these errors can provide us a way of gaining new psycholinguistic data on learner strategies and the relative efficacy of different instructional methods. The current top priority for research in foreign language learning should be the acquisition of new empirical data of this type. Using structured methods such as fill in the blanks, matching, question-and-answer, dictionary exercises, translation, error detection, and multiple choice, we can ellicit similar responses in a group of learners which can be tracked within the program. It will then be possible to conduct psycholinguistic experiments within the context of the tutoring system itself. These data will allow us to elaborate increasingly refined models of the learner and will also facilitate development of the Competition Model for second language learning.

7. Summary

Research within the context of the Competition Model is now focusing increasingly on L2 acquisition. The model views L2 learning as a process of cue acquisition which relies initially on transfer from L1 to L2. Cues with the strongest strength have the strongest transfer, although there is fairly general transfer across particular well-worn paths, such as the path with allows the transfer of the meanings underlying L1 words to L2 words. In some cases simple transfer is blocked and the learner developes a set of strategies to get around this blockage by postulating more complex remappings from L1 to L2.

The learner's attempt to proceduralize the mappings from L1 to L2 runs counter to attempts to restructure the L2 to avoid reliance on L1. In order to prevent fossilization and to facilitate functional restructuring, it is important to expose the learner to precisely those structures that differentiate true L2 strategies from transferred L1 strategies. Because transfer is inevitable, there is no sense trying to defeat it. Instead emphasis should be placed on moving the learner through the period of transfer into a period of functional restructuring.

References

1. Bates, E., & MacWhinney, B.: Second language acquisition from a functionalist perspective: Pragmatic, semantic and perceptual strategies. In H. Winitz (Ed.), Annals of the New York Academy of Sciences conference on native and foreign language acquisition. New York: New York Academy of Sciences (1981)
2. Bates, E., & MacWhinney, B.: Functionalist approaches to grammar. In E. Wanner, & L. Gleitman (Ed.), Language acquisition: The state of the art. New York: Cambridge University Press 1982
3. Bates, E., & MacWhinney, B.: Functionalism and the Competition Model. In B. MacWhinney, & E. Bates (Ed.), The crosslinguistic study of sentence processing. New York: Cambridge University Press 1989
4. Berwick, R.: Parsability and Learnability. In B. MacWhinney (Ed.), Mechanisms of Language Acquisition. Hillsdale, N.J.: Lawrence Erlbaum 1987
5. Chanier, T., Pengelly, M., Twidale, M. & Self, J.: Conceptual Modelling in Error Analysis in Computer-Assisted Language Learning. This volume
6. Dechert, H., & Raupach, M. (Ed.).: Transfer in language production. Norwood, NJ: Ablex 1989
7. Demaizière, F. & Blanvillain, O.: Learners' Intuitions, Misconceptions and Errors. This volume
8. Devescovi, A., D'Amico, S., Smith, S., Mimica, I., & Bates, E.: The development of sentence comprehension in Italian and Serbo-Croation: Local versus distributed cues. NICHD, NICHDS. Unpublished manuscript 1990
9. Gass, S.: Sentence interpretation in L2 learning. 8, 329-350 (1987)
10. Gass, S., & Selinker, L. (Ed.).: Language transfer in language learning. Rowley, MA: Newbury 1983
11. Johnson, J., & Newport, E.: Critical period effects in second language learning: the influence of maturational state on the acquisition of English as a second language. Cognitive Psychology, 21, 60-99 (1989)
12. Kellerman, E., & Sharwood Smith, M. (Ed.).: Crosslinguistic influence in second language acquisition. New York: Pergamon Press 1986
13. Kilborn, K., & Ito, T.: Sentence processing in Japanese-English and Dutch-English bilinguals. In B. MacWhinney, & E. Bates (Ed.), The crosslinguistic study of sentence processing. New York: Cambridge University Press 1989
14. Klein, W., & Perdue, C.: The learner's problem of arranging words. In B. MacWhinney, & E. Bates (Ed.), The crosslinguistic study of sentence processing. New York: Cambridge University Press 1989
15. Lenneberg, E. H.: Biological foundations of language. New York: Wiley 1967
16. MacWhinney, B.: How Hungarian children learn to speak. University of California, Berkeley: Ph.D. Thesis 1974
17. MacWhinney, B.: The acquisition of morphophonology. Monographs of the Society for Research in Child Development, 43, Whole no. 1, (1978)

18. MacWhinney, B.: Hungarian language acquisition as an exemplification of a general model of grammatical development. In D. Slobin (Ed.), The cross-cultural study of language acquisition. Hillsdale, NJ: Lawrence Erlbaum 1985
19. MacWhinney, B.: The Competition Model. In B. MacWhinney (Ed.), Mechanisms of language acquisition. Hillsdale, NJ: Lawrence Erlbaum 1987
20. MacWhinney, B.: Competition and lexical categorization. In R. Corrigan, F. Eckman, & M. Noonan (Ed.), Linguistic categorization. New York: Benjamins 1989
21. MacWhinney, B.: Connectionism as a framework for language acquisition theory. In J. Miller (Ed.), Progress in research on child language disorders. Baltimore, MD: University Park 1990
22. MacWhinney, B., & Anderson, J.: The acquisition of grammar. In I. Gopnik, & M. Gopnik (Ed.), From models to modules. Norwood, N.J.: Ablex 1986
23. MacWhinney, B., & Bates, E. (Ed.): The crosslinguistic study of sentence processing. New York: Cambridge University Press 1989
24. MacWhinney, B., Leinbach, J., Taraban, R., & McDonald, J.: Language learning: Cues or rules? Journal of Memory and Language, 28, 255-277 (1989)
25. MacWhinney, B., & Pléh, C.: The processing of restrictive relative clauses in Hungarian. Cognition, 29, 95-141 (1988)
26. McDonald, J.: The acquisition of cue-category mappings. In B. MacWhinney, & E. Bates (Ed.), The crosslinguistic study of language processing. New York: Cambridge University Press 1989
27. McDonald, J., & Heilenman, K.: Determinants of cue strength in adult first and second language speakers of French. Louisiana State University. Unpublished manuscript 1989
28. McDonald, J., & MacWhinney, B. : Maximum likelihood procedures in sentence processing research. In B. MacWhinney & E. Bates (Eds.), The crosslinguistic study of sentence processing. New York: Cambridge University Press 1989
29. Miller, G. & Fellbaum, C.: Wordnet and the Organization of Lexical Memory. This volume.
30. Odlin, T.: Language transfer: Cross-linguistic influence in language learning. New York: Cambridge University Press 1989
31. Ringbom, H.: The role of the first language in foreign language learning. Clevedon: Multilingual Matters 1987
32. Rumelhart, D., & McClelland, J.: Parallel Distributed Processing. Cambridge, MA: MIT Press 1986
33. Seliger, H.: Semantic transfer constraints on the production of English passive by Hebrew-English bilinguals. In H. Dechert, & M. Raupach (Ed.), Transfer in language production. Norwood: NJ: Ablex 1989
34. Singley, K., & Anderson, J.: The transfer of cognitive skills. Cambridge, MA: Harvard University Press 1989
35. Slobin, D.: The crosslinguistic study of language acquisition. Hillsdale, N. J.: Lawrence Erlbaum 1985
36. Stampe, D. : A dissertation on natural phonology. University of Chicago 1973
37. Swartz, M. L.: Issues for Tutoring Knowledge in Foreign Language Intelligent Tutoring Systems. This volume
38. Trévise, A.: Is it transferable, topicalization? In K. Kellerman, & M. Sharwood Smith (Ed.), Crosslinguistic influence in second language acquisition. New York: Pergamon 1986
39. Vosniadou, S., & Ortony, A. (Ed.): Similarity and analogical reasoning. New York: Cambridge University Press 1989
40. Zock, M.: SWIM or Sink: The problem of communicating thought. This volume

Naive vs. Formal Grammars: A Case for Integration in the Design of a Foreign Language Tutor

Danilo Fum [1], Bruno Pani [2], and Carlo Tasso [2]

[1] Dipartimento di Psicologia - Università di Trieste, via dell'Università 7, I-34123 Trieste (Italy) - fum@uts882.units.infn.it.bitnet

[2] Laboratorio di Intelligenza Artificiale - Università di Udine, via Zanon 6, I-33100 Udine (Italy) - tasso@uduniv.infn.it.bitnet

Abstract: The relationship between formal and naive (i.e., used for didactic purposes) grammars in foreign language teaching is dealt with in the paper which presents, as a case study, an attempt to integrate the two approaches within an intelligent tutoring system. This work has been carried on in the framework of the ET *(English Tutor)* project whose long term goal is the development of a tutoring system aimed at helping Italian students master English verb tenses. Within the project, a prototype system based on a naive approach to the grammar of tense has been built. The experimentation performed with the prototype provided the motivation for a critical re-evaluation and revision of some of the assumptions which it was grounded upon. The possibility of integrating some naive intuitions into a systemic representation of grammatical knowledge is discussed in the paper, and a new version of the domain expert module exploiting the systemic approach to tense selection is illustrated.

Keywords: intelligent tutoring systems, foreign language teaching, systemic grammar.

1. Introduction

One of the most distinguishing features of an intelligent tutoring system (ITS) - at least in comparison with the traditional computer-aided instruction programs - is constituted by the explicit representation of the domain knowledge it utilizes. This knowledge does not represent only a description of the concepts and skills to be taught, but often makes up a runnable model which allows the system to generate answers and explanations, and to execute the tasks and exercises presented to the student. As for systems working in the domain of foreign languages, this knowledge is represented basically by grammatical knowledge. The so-called *domain expert* module of such systems represents therefore a model of the grammatical competence the student is intended to acquire.

A problem that must be dealt with in order to build an ITS in the domain of foreign language teaching is that of establishing what kind of grammatical knowledge has to be included in the Domain Expert module. At first sight, two distinct options are possible:
a) to utilize the knowledge contained in textbooks and school grammars;
b) to adopt some of the formal grammars developed by theoretical and computational linguists.
Both these solutions have their shortcomings.

A lot has been said about the grammar which is taught in schools and the textbooks utilized for such teaching. Traditional grammar textbooks (see the discussion, for example, in [2, 4, 25]) have serious drawbacks which concern both their content and the way it is presented to the student (conceptual descriptions framed on classic languages, definitions and explanations that are often incoherent and grounded upon heterogeneous criteria, overly focused attention to written language, morphologic problems and 'exceptions', etc.). The introduction of the notional syllabuses and the almost general adoption of the communicative approach [14, 28, 29] have somehow changed the general attitude and the strategies utilized in foreign language teaching, but even the grammars that follow these methodologies do not overcome the most severe limitation of what we call the *naive* approach to the representation of linguistic knowledge, i.e., the incapacity to provide a global and coherent model of language.

NATO ASI Series, Vol. F 80
Intelligent Tutoring Systems for Foreign Language Learning
Edited by M. L. Swartz and M. Yazdani

The formal grammars developed by linguists, on the other hand, show their shortcomings when we try to use them directly for didactic purposes. The point is that these grammars have been developed to pursue goals that are different from those of school grammars. Theoretical linguists are in fact interested in providing mathematically well defined descriptions of a language which capture the competence of a native speaker. Computational linguists are interested in discovering computationally effective models of the processes that allow the speaker to utter or to understand a sentence in that language. Both kinds of descriptions are mostly centered around the syntactic properties of the language. Considered from the point of view of a foreign language teacher, these formal descriptions are generally useless since the (meta)language in which they are framed and the concepts which they are grounded upon are different from those utilized in daily teaching. Moreover, syntactic descriptions are not enough: learning a language means not only to become aware of the set of structures available in the language but also to realize how and when such structures could (and should) be used, and which contribution they provide to the communication process [15].

Such a situation, in which scientific research and teaching practice go along parallel roads, without mutual exchanges and influences, presents several disadvantages. On one hand, the naive grammars utilized in schools support an empirical kind of teaching that is not rooted in linguistics research. The theoretical basis of such a teaching is in fact generally fragile, the concepts and the principles it relies upon are often unsystematic and badly defined. On the other hand, the elegant formal descriptions developed by linguists are not immediately usable in practice. The main issue concerning the relationship between formal and naive grammars is still that pointed out by Saporta: "A central question in the application of linguistics to the teaching of foreign languages involves the conversion of a scientific grammar into a pedagogical grammar" [26]. Such a conversion, as far as the ITS development is concerned, requires the following steps:

- to choose, among the different formal linguistic theories, the one which appears particularly promising from a pedagogic point of view;
- to develop, within the chosen theoretical framework, an explicit description of the language subset we are interested in teaching;
- to fit such a description into a computationally adequate and pedagogically reliable form.

The relationship between formal and naive grammars in foreign language teaching is dealt with in this paper which presents, as a case study, an attempt to integrate the two approaches within an intelligent tutoring system. The work has been carried on in the framework of the ET *(English Tutor)* project whose long term goal is the development of a tutoring system aimed at helping Italian students master English verb tenses. Within this project, ET-1, a prototype system based on a naive approach to the grammar of tense (described in [5]), has been built. The experimentation performed with ET-1 provided the motivation for a critical re-evaluation and revision of some of the assumptions which the prototype was grounded upon. The possibility of formulating some naive intuitions into a systemic representation of grammatical knowledge is discussed in the paper and a new version of the domain expert module exploiting the systemic approach to tense selection is illustrated. The following section presents our previous naive approach to a grammar of English verb tense, describes how the grammatical knowledge has been utilized by the domain expert module of ET-1, and clarifies why such an approach has been found in the long run unsatisfactory. Section 3 illustrates the reasons why, among the different formal descriptions, the systemic approach to tense developed by Halliday [8] and Matthiessen [16,17] has been chosen, while section 4 illustrates its main features. Section 5 presents our original contribution showing how the naive approach has been integrated into a systemic framework and which changes to the original formulation have been made. Section 6 presents some evaluation criteria for the present proposal and suggests guidelines for future research.

2. A Naive Approach to Verb Tense Selection

The basic goal pursued in constructing the domain expert module - called Verb Generation Expert - of ET-1 has been that of building a glass-box model of the competence underlying the choice and conjugation of an English verb tense. One of the main concerns in designing the knowledge base for this module has been that of using the same (meta)language and the same concepts found in the naive grammars which we referred to [3, 7, 19, 22, 27].

The following explanation - concerning some subtle meaning distinctions that are possible to express through the use of the present continuous tense - is typical of what we mean by a naive approach.

> ***164.*** *Other possible uses of present continuous:*
> ***a.*** *With a point in time to indicate an action which begins before this point and probably continues after it [...]*
> *The present continuous is rarely used in this way except in descriptions of daily routine and in dramatic narrative [...]*
> ***b.*** *With* ***always*** *for a frequently repeated action, often one which annoys the speaker or seems unreasonable to him [...] Sometimes, especially when used with the first person,* ***always*** *with the continuous tense implies that the action is accidental, while* ***always*** *with a simple tense would imply a deliberate action. [27 , pg. 95]*

This explanation utilizes some intuitive and informal concepts that exploit the student analysis capabilities and rely on his linguistic insights. In fact, it is difficult to realize how it is possible to formally establish that an action constitutes a daily routine, that it can annoy the speaker or that the text represents a dramatic narrative. These ideas, however difficult to express in a computational form they may be, have, however, deep pedagogic value since they form part of the teachers metalanguage and are utilized to talk about and to explain the object language.

It is possible to provide other examples of naive explanations that involve intuitive concepts like the formal or informal register:

> ***Be going + infinitive*** *is commonly used to express the future in informal speech [30, pg. 46]*
> ***Be to + infinitive*** *can be used to refer to a future plan or programme. This is a fairly formal way of expressing the future and is used more often in written than in spoken English [30, pg. 61]*

or that refer to some complex psychological states:

> *The problems of future tense in English involve not only aspects of activity and time but also mood, i.e. the certainty, hesitation, willingness, determination, hope, sense of obligation or of prohibition, or pure neutrality, with which the speaker views what is to come [...] Each expression of futurity is often complicated by subjective attitudes on the part of the speaker and his audience ... [3, pg. 96]*

In designing the Verb Generation Expert for ET-1 we wanted to maintain the wealth of ideas and intuitions existing in the naive account of tenses while developing at the same time a computationally tractable model of the tense selection process.

In ET-1, the Verb Generation Expert module [6] is devoted to generating the right answers to the exercises presented to the student. Usually the exercises are constituted by one or two sentences in which some of the verbs *(open items)* are given in the infinitive form and have to be conjugated into the appropriate tense. The Verb Generation Expert is therefore able:

- to select the grammatical tense for each open item of the exercise in order to correctly describe the status of the world the sentence is intended to represent;
- to appropriately conjugate the verb according to the chosen tense.

Besides these basic functionalities, the tutoring environment in which the domain expert operates imposes a further requirement, i.e., the Verb Generation Expert should be able:

- to explain to the student how the solution has been found, which kind of knowledge has been utilized and how.

In order to build the Verb Generation Expert, we started by examining the explanations about tense usage given in the reference grammars and by extracting a set of *tense features* representing the ideas and concepts which were utilized in providing such explanations. Some of these features were strictly syntactic and referred, for instance, to the clause kind (main or secondary clause at various levels of subordination) or the clause mood (affirmative, negative, interrogative, interrogative-negative). Other features dealt with the functional properties of the sentence constituents. Still others referred to semantic and contextual aspects, such as the kind of action described in the clause, the temporal length of the action described in the clause, the register (formal vs. informal) of the utterance, etc. Each exercise was then described according to these tense features.

To give a more concrete idea of what the descriptions looked like, we report here the (simplified) representation of the exercise:

Yesterday, when I (arrive), Tom (talk) on the telephone.

```
(defexercise ex5
    (text (Yesterday when I (arrive) Tom  (talk) on the telephone))

(structure ex5 (clauses (c1, c2)))

(defclause c1
    (text (when I (arrive)))
    (in-exercise ex5)
    (open-item (arrive))
    (clause-kind (subordinate  temporal))
    (superordinate (c2))
    (clause-form affirmative)
    (open-item-time-interval t1)
    (fact-kind (action single))
    (aspect (action  completed))

(defclause c2
    (text (Yesterday Tom (talk) on the telephone))
    (in-exercise ex5)
    (open-item (talk))
    (clause-kind (main))
    (subordinate (c1))
    (previous-coordinate nil)
    (clause-form affirmative)
    (open-item-time-interval t3)
    (time-expression ((yesterday) t2))
    (fact-kind (action single))
    (aspect (action uncompleted)))

(deftemporalrelations ex5
    (before t2 now)
    (during t1 t2)
    (during t1 t3)
    (during t3  t2)))
```

An exercise is described basically through lists of attribute-values pairs, one for each exercise clause. The first member of the pair indicates a tense feature, the second member the value the feature receives in the clause. The exercise description comprises also a list of *temporal relations* expressing the relationships that exist between the time intervals mentioned in the sentence. These time intervals are associated with the situations (states and/or events) described by the sentence verbs and with the temporal expressions occurring in the sentence, and are represented through the symbols *t1 .. tn*. In our exercise, for example, we find two verbs (both open items) and one temporal expression, therefore three time intervals are utilized to describe the exercise. The time interval *t1* is associated with the state indicated by the verb *to arrive*, the time interval *t2* with the temporal expression *yesterday*, and so on. The temporal relations specify the relationships existing between these intervals so, for example, *(during t1 t2)* states that the time interval *t1* is included within the interval *t2* : the verb *to arrive* indicates thus an action that happens within the time interval represented by *t2* (i.e., *yesterday).* A special time interval is represented by the symbol *now* which stands for the *speaking time*, i.e., the interval during which the sentence is being uttered.

Since the number of the potential temporal relations holding between the time intervals contained in the sentence could be quite large, only the relations directly derivable from the exercise text are explicitly represented in the description. At the beginning of its operation, the Verb Generation Expert deduces therefore from the stated temporal relation all the possible relations holding between the various time intervals. In doing this, it applies a set of inference rules that implement a reduced version of Allen's temporal logic [1]. Thus, for example, since *t2* (i.e., *yesterday)* by definition comes before the speaking time *now* (i.e., *(before t2, now))* and since it is asserted in the exercise description that *(during t1 t2)*, it is possible to infer that *(before t1 now*), i.e., that the action described by the verb *to tell* refers to a time interval *(event time)* that comes before the speaking time. The same rule allows the inference that *(before t3 now)* i.e., that the action indicated by the verb *(talk)* happened in the past too.

In order to be able to choose the tense for a sentence clause containing an open item, it is generally necessary to know not only the relation between the time in which the sentence is uttered and the time of the events described in the sentence, but also the relation which holds between the event time and the so called *reference time*, i.e., the interval of time the situation described in the clause refers to. So, for example, in the sentence:

By the end of next month I shall have finished my thesis.

the speaking time is *now*, the event time is given by the time interval associated with the action *to finish the thesis* and the reference time is constituted by the time interval indicated with *by the end of next month.*

In some clauses the reference time may be absent and, in such cases, the only temporal relationship involved in the choice of the tense is that which holds between the speaking time and the event time.

In the following operation step, the Verb Generation Expert computes the reference time (if it exists) for every exercise clause through a series of production rules. In our case the following rules applies:

IF *the clause is a main clause,*
there is a subordinate temporal clause related to it,
the event time includes the event time of the subordinate temporal,
THEN *set the reference time to the event time of the temporal subordinate clause.*

and

IF *the clause is a subordinate temporal,*
the event time is included in the event time of the main clause,
there is at least a temporal expression in the related main clause,
THEN *set the reference time to the most specific time expression of the main clause.*

The first rule asserts that the main clause *c2:*

Yesterday Tom (talk) on the telephone

has as its reference time *t1*, i.e., the time interval represented by the event time of the subordinate temporal *c1*:

when I (arrive)

This clause, on the other hand, has as its reference time the time interval represented by the most specific time expression of the related main clause *c2*. In our case it is *t2*, i.e., *yesterday* , whereas in a sentence like

Yesterday, after the Geography lesson, Tom (talk) on the telephone

the reference time would be represented by the temporal expression *after the Geography lesson.*

Once the reference times for the exercise clauses have been computed, it is possible to choose the tense for each open item. To do this, a set of tense selection rules are used. The antecedent of these rules is constituted by some conditions concerning the tense features that must hold in the clause description, while the consequent indicates the tense that has to be assigned to the open item. In our example, the following rules are utilized for the clauses *c1* and *c2*, respectively:

IF *the clause describes a past event,*
the reference time is past,
the event is completed
THEN *use the simple past tense.*

and

IF *the clause describes a past event,*
the reference time, if defined, is past and it is included in the event time,
the event is not completed
THEN *use the past continuous.*

According to our rules, therefore, the tense that is chosen for *to arrive* is the simple past while *to talk* has to be conjugated into the past continuous.

The last step to be carried out at this point is the conjugation of the verbs into the chosen tenses. For the regular verbs a set of conjugation rules are exploited, whereas the conjugation of the irregular forms is performed by a simple dictionary look up.

Leaving aside some computational complexities deriving from the need of drawing the logical temporal inferences and of computing the reference time for each exercise clause, the process performed by the Verb Generation Expert relies on the same concepts and rules described in the naive grammars. However, the adoption of the naive approach has its problems, as we realized by experimenting with the prototype.

First of all, the translation of a naive grammar into a computationally suitable form is not straightforward. The explanations given by the naive grammars - the 'tense selection rules' that are derived from the textbooks - are in fact incomplete and even inconsistent. As a result, ET-1 was sometimes incapable of solving a given exercise since the rules of the grammar did not cover that particular case. In other instances we found the opposite to be true, i.e., we obtained multiple incompatible solutions for the same exercise since several rules could be legitimately applied to the case at hand. The computational application of the naive grammars, in other words, disclosed some deficiencies and incongruities that went unnoticed in the original formulation.

Second, the informal concepts used in the naive grammars and utilized in ET-1 to express the tense features have generally no well stated definition. This means that it is difficult to attribute unequivocally the value to the temporal features describing an exercise since a lot is left to the insight of the exercise coder. Different implementers can thus describe the same exercise in a different way and obtain therefore different, often incompatible, solutions.

From the experimentation performed with the prototype, and from an analysis of its limitations, the need of a theoretically sound formulation of the grammatical knowledge, keeping as far as possible the 'cognitive transparency' of the naive grammar, has arisen.

3. The Reasons of a Systemic Choice

Systemic grammar, a theory originally formulated by the linguist M.A.K. Halliday (for a general introduction, see [9] and also [13, 18) has been chosen as the formal grammar to be utilized by the Verb Generation Expert module of the new version of ET. Systemic theory puts a strong emphasis on the functional aspects of the language: grammar, according to this approach, is a description of the resources which a speaker can rely upon in order to convey a given meaning. The most important concept of systemic grammar is that of *system* i.e., a mutually exclusive set of classes which express the options from which a speaker can choose in planning an utterance. Thus, for example, the system for the clause mood presents the speaker with a choice between an indicative and an imperative clause: the two options are alternative. Or, to make another example, in deciding the person of a pronoun, the speaker can select among first, second, and third. A particular choice, however, is not always applicable; thus some sort of context must be introduced to determine when a given set of choices becomes relevant. In systemic grammar, context is defined in terms of other choices: systems, in other words, are hierarchically ordered according to entry conditions in the so called *system networks*. To take our example a step further, if the speaker chooses to utter an indicative clause, he can select between a declarative and an interrogative. If the latter is the case, he can decide between a wh- or a polar (yes/no) kind of question.

Systemic grammar interprets a language as being a huge network of meaning potentials. The task of the grammar is to specify, through the net of systems, the total grid of options available to a speaker of the language. The introduction in the systemic grammar of this semantic functional dimension reflects the thesis that language is a social activity taking place in a situational context and fulfilling a number of social (meta)functions. More particularly, language can be used to communicate ideas (and the logical relationships existing among them), to organize the text into a relevant and coherent discourse fitting into the communicative situation, to establish and maintain social relations, to influence people's behavior, to express the speaker's feelings, attitudes and opinions, etc. A systemic description would include an understanding of the way grammatical structures and constituents contribute to one or more of these (meta)functions.

This view of grammar as a set of resources from which to choose and the focus on the social role of language are two of the reasons that support systemic grammar as a candidate formalism for pedagogic utilization. It is evident, in fact, that the notion of choice, the concept on which such grammars are based, is more familiar to teachers and students than other abstract principles (e.g., unification) which other formalisms rely upon. The emphasis on the functional organization of the language - how it presents speakers with systems of meaningful options as a basis for communication - makes systemic grammar in keeping with modern approaches to language teaching. But there are other reasons that support such a choice. Among these we mention:

- the fact that the grammar of tense, the subset of language dealt with in the ET project, is well documented in the systemic approach through papers by Halliday himself [8] and, from a computational point of view, by Matthiessen [16, 17];
- the interest shown by Halliday for the issues related to teaching, and the fact that much of his writing has been aimed at this topic (see, for example, [10]);
- the fact that the systemic approach provides us not only with a static description of linguistic structures but, especially in the computational application of Matthiessen, with a runnable model of language;
- the fact that it is possible to translate the systemic approach into rigorously formal terms [21] and to express it into a notation that is compatible with the formalisms, like functional unification grammar, currently used in computational linguistics [12].

For all these reasons, the systemic approach has been judged particularly suitable to serve as the conceptual ground for an intelligent tutoring system devoted to foreign language teaching. At the best of our knowledge, this is the first time that a (subset of) a systemic grammar has been utilized as part of an ITS.

4. The Systemic Approach to Tense Selection

In this section the systemic approach to the problem of tense selection is briefly described. What follows is based on the work of Halliday [8] and, in particular, of Matthiessen [16, 17].

According to the systemic approach, two assumptions are made concerning the grammar of the English tense. These assumptions are:

a) *Tense opposition:* the tense in English is considered as a three term opposition. From a linguistic point of view, it is an opposition of past vs. present vs. future; from a semantic point of view, as we will see below, it is interpretable as a precedence relation between two temporal variables.

b) *Seriality:* complex tense combinations can be constructed by repeatedly selecting among the three term opposition.

As far as the first assumption is concerned, it should be noted that not all the linguists agree with the idea of English as a three-tense language. Some scholars claim in fact [20, 24] that in English it is possible to distinguish only between present and past, the future being a modal form of the present.

The second assumption reduces the process of tense selection to a series of iterative choices concerning the three term option. In other words, a tense combination like *'is going to have built'* is chosen by picking up the first time *(primary tense)* the present, then *(secondary tense)* the future and finally *(ternary tense)* the past. The name for a tense combination in the systemic approach is determined by considering the inverted order of the choices: in our case the tense combination is a *past in future in present.*

An important point concerns which possible tense combinations are allowed. It should be noted that, according to Halliday, up to quinary tenses (like: *'will have been going to have been taking'*: a present in past in future in past in past) are admissible in English. Some tense combinations, however, are not allowed; in English, for instance, there is no future in future in present and the following sentence is considered ungrammatical:

* *Henry is going to be going to cook dinner*

The restrictions that the English grammar puts on the possible tense combinations are called 'stop rules' by Halliday and can thus be paraphrased:

1. The present can occur only at the ends of the tense sequence (as a beginning or final choice).
2. Except in the last and penultimate place, the same tense cannot occur in two consecutive positions.
3. The future can occur only once, apart from the last position.

These rules define whether a tense combination is legitimate but they do not indicate *how* a given tense combination is selected. To this end a significant contribution has been given by Matthiessen with his notion of *chooser.* To each option concerning the tense, and represented in the grammar through a system, Matthiessen assigns a chooser "that states how the selection among the options specified is controlled. A chooser is a procedure that consists of steps that ascertain conceptual distinctions and make grammatical choices according to the conceptual distinctions." [17, pg. 1].

According to this point of view, a verb tense essentially indicates the temporal relation which holds between the speaking time and the event time, and the tense selection process is determined by such a relation. More particularly, for each iteration step, the choosers take into account a relation of precedence (anteriority) - that we symbolize through '<' - between two different temporal variables (let us call them Tx and Ty) and:

- if Tx come after Ty $(Ty < Tx)$, then the past is chosen;
- if Tx comes before Ty $(Tx < Ty)$, then the future is chosen;
- if none of the above alternatives holds, then the chosen tense is present.

The tense selection process can be expressed through the following algorithm:

```
Tx := Ts;
repeat
 find the value for the comparison time Tc;
 Ty := Tc;
 if Ty < Tx
      then Tense := past
      else if Tx < Ty
             then Tense := future
```

else Tense := present;
Tx := Ty
until Ty matches Te

The process, in other words, starts by setting the time variable *Tx* to the speaking time *Ts* and by looking for the *comparison time Tc,* i.e., the time interval the speaking time is related to. This is the time that is assigned as a value to *Ty*. At this point it is possible to choose the primary tense according to the relation which holds between *Tx (= Ts)* and *Ty (=Tc)*. If the comparison time matches the event time *Te,* then the temporal relation holding between *Ts* and *Te* has been found and the resulting tense combination consists only of a primary tense (a simple present or a simple past or a simple future). If, on the other hand, the comparison time is different from the event time, the process cannot terminate since no temporal relationship has been established between the speaking time and the event time. A new iteration cycle starts by assigning the old *Tc* to *Tx* and by looking for a new comparison time *Tc* to be assigned to *Ty*. The choice of the secondary tense is made again according to the relation holding between *Tx* and *Ty* and the process terminates if *Tc* matches *Te*. If this is not the case, the process goes on according to the same modalities with a tertiary, quaternary or quinary tense, until a link between the speaking time and the event time will be found.

From the above description it is evident how complex tenses arise from the pairwise comparison of times. Each order of tense (primary, secondary, tertiary, etc.) has its own reference time, the *Tx* of each *Tx-Ty* pair. The first reference time is *Ts,* the speaking time, while each subsequent reference time is the comparison time related to the reference time of the previous tense. Given a reference time *Tx*, it is necessary to establish what time is to be related to it through a tense selection, i.e. it is necessary to establish the *Tc* to be assigned as a value to *Ty*. This is a question that ultimately concerns text planning: the choice of the temporal relations among different times depends in fact on the meaning a given utterance is intended to convey.

The identification of the comparison time for each iteration step is based on an interaction between the tense choosers and the so called *environment*, i.e., the non-linguistic part of the system "where conceptual information resides, for instance the knowledge base and text plans" [16, pg. 3]. It is useful to think of this interaction as a dialogue, with the choosers presenting inquiries and the environment responding. The choosers act thus as an interface through which semantic/pragmatic considerations can be brought to bear on choices in the grammar. It is the task of each chooser to select grammatical features according to the conceptual distinctions that exist in the environment. The identification of the comparison time for each iteration step is based therefore on the answer the environment provides in response to a specific chooser question concerning what time is to be directly related to *Tx*. This inquiry is obviously compulsory for primary tense. Since there is always a primary tense in a temporal clause, a time to be related to *Ts* has to be determined. The situation is different for the other tenses (i.e., secondary, tertiary, etc.) being that the identification of a new comparison time is dependent on whether a link between the speaking time and the event time has already been established or not.

Two points should be emphasized at the end of this description of the systemic grammar of tense. The first concerns the fact that, in the Matthiessen's approach [16, 17], the identification of the comparison time - which represents, according to our point of view, the most critical step in the tense selection process - is a process that falls outside the grammar since it is ultimately based on the speaker's plans and goals and takes into account those semantic/pragmatic factors that form part of the environment. This will represent, as we shall see below, a critical issue in our systemic treatment of tense.

The second point concerns the semantics of tense. According to Matthiessen, the verb tense expresses a temporal relationship between two times: the speaking time and the event time. These two times are directly linked in the case of a primary tense; they are connected through the mediation of one, two, three, or four intervening times in the case of secondary, ternary, quaternary and quinary tenses, respectively. The fact that no tense exists beyond the quinary depends on reasons of meaning and text planning, not on grammatical motives. As Matthiessen puts it,"constraints on communicative complexity lead to constraints on semantic and grammatical complexity" [17, pg. 131]. Other approaches (among these the classic account of [23], see also [11]) claim that the temporal structure is restricted to three elements, i.e, the speaking time, the event time, and *one* reference time. According to the latter point of view, tense is always a function of three variables *(Ts, Te, Tr)* whereas in the former it is an *n-ary* function (with *n* varying from 2 to 6).

5. Combining the Naive and Systemic Approaches

Two main problems have been dealt with in applying the systemic model to the representation of the grammatical knowledge for the new Verb Generation Expert:
- the first deals with the treatment of the tense features utilized in the naive grammar according to the systemic approach;
- the second concerns the construction of the choosers for selecting the appropriate tense combination.

5.1 The treatment of the tense features

In the first version of the ET prototype, the process of tense selection was performed through a group of production rules exploiting a set of (sometimes fuzzily defined) tense features derived from the naive grammars. Some of these features (mainly of morphological and syntactic nature) are indeed compatible with the systemic approach and it has been easy to put them directly into the systemic network. So, for example, the features referring to the clause kind, the clause mood, the case roles etc. are immediately translatable into systemic terms. Other features, however, refer to properties that depend on word sense and discourse context. To establish, for example, the time required by an event or whether an action is performed voluntarily or whether it is habitual demands some general world knowledge and the knowledge of the context in which the communication occurs. It is difficult therefore to assign a value to the features which are not directly expressible in systemic terms but which are, however, explicitly mentioned in the naive grammar and utilized by the tense selection rules.

In the new version of the Verb Generation Expert these features appear as dictionary attributes. In other words, the dictionary reports the value these features assume for each lexical item. Thus the information that *to be born* and *to die* are actions that cannot be iterated, that *inadvertently* and *thoughtless* express the idea that something is done without any conscious intention, or that *daddy* is a word that is used only in an informal context whereas *Sir* represents a formal way to address someone is contained in the dictionary.

An interesting point concerns the way these features influence each other. The tense features associated, for example, to a verb definition can thus be reinforced or contradicted by the occurrence in the sentence of other words (for instance adjectives or adverbs) whose features agree with or differ from those of the verb. Let us consider for example the following sentence:

(Due to a timer malfunctioning) the light flashed all through the night.

The verb *flash* generally expresses an action that is short, almost instantaneous; the event described in the sentence is, however, long since the real temporal length of the action is expressed not by the feature *event-duration* of the verb but by the temporal expression *all through the night*. Instead of a single instantaneous event, therefore, the sentence indicates an iterated action that occurs within a rather extended period of time.

To manage these cases, a series of heuristics have been developed which state how the tense features of the modifiers take over the features of the modified words. As it is the case for all the heuristics, ours also have no absolute value. They work satisfactorily for the exercises the system is capable of solving even if it is always possible to find some counterexamples in which the setting of the values to the tense features is wrong. The rationale behind the heuristics is different, however. They represent an attempt to implement the hypothesis that a speaker is capable of assigning the right value to the tense features by relying on the sense of the words which occur in the sentence and by computing the meaning the words assume in the context of discourse. By using these heuristics the assignment of the values to the tense features is made computationally feasible, and the values of the features irreducible to a systemic approach results not from a subjective judgment of the exercise implementer, but from an effective procedure - even if it is based on heuristic criteria.

5.2 The construction of the tense choosers

A second, and more important problem, concerns the construction of the tense determination rules (choosers) capable of establishing in a cognitively transparent way (i.e., using as much as possible the ideas and concepts of the naive approach) a tense combination according to the assumptions of seriality and opposition of the systemic approach. Adopting these assumptions led to a complete change of the original verb generation strategy which was based on the direct choice, in a single step without iteration, of the verb tense according to a heterogeneous set of features taken into account by the rule antecedents.

Solving the problem of tense determination according to the systemic approach requires finding the solution to the following subproblems:

- how to choose the tense in each iteration step;
- how to stop the iteration process.

We have examined in a previous section Matthiessen's proposal [16, 17]. His procedure for choosing the tense in each step is based on successive comparisons between the reference and the comparison time, while the termination procedure is based on a match between the current comparison time and the event time.

The burden of the whole process falls primarily on the identification, in each iteration step, of the appropriate comparison time, and this is performed through a dialogue between the choosers and an environment representing the semantic and pragmatic factors influencing the choice of the tense. These factors are, however, hidden from the choosers which simply receive from the environment the answers to their inquiries. In other words, the choosers work by exploiting only the temporal relations between the different times, while the semantic and pragmatic factors play a covert role in the identification of the comparison time the choosers receive as input.

According to our point of view, it is possible to make explicit the criteria underlying the determination of the tense and build cognitively adequate choosers that utilize them directly. In our new approach, this is done by dividing the features used by the tense selection rules of the naive grammar into two classes: the first class comprises those features which express the temporal relations among the time intervals occurring in the exercise sentence; the second class comprises the features of morphological, syntactic, semantic, and pragmatic information. These two classes play a different role in determining a tense combination. More particularly, the temporal features are utilized by a first type of chooser which discriminates in each iteration step between past vs. present vs. future *(selection choosers)*. The remaining features are utilized by a different category of choosers whose task is to establish whether the tense selection process should be iterated or not *(termination choosers)*. Differently from Matthiessen, however, the decision of the termination choosers is not based on a simple matching procedure which checks whether a link between the speaking time and the event time has already been established.This decision instead exploits a series of more complex factors through which the criteria underlying the determination of a tense combination in a given language are made explicit.

Let us clarify this new approach, which integrates the systemic treatment of tense with the use of the features found in the naive grammars, by reconsidering, as an example, the exercise presented in section 2:

Yesterday, when I (arrive), Tom (talk) on the telephone.

The solution to this exercise requires the use of the (simple) past for the first verb and the present in past (or past continuous) for the second open item. While in the previous version of the Verb Generation Expert these solutions were chosen through appropriate rules that directly established the correct tenses, according to the systemic theory the tense determination process is iterative. In other words, the first tense is determined by choosing past for the primary tense and halting the process. The second tense is determined by choosing past as the primary tense, iterating the selection process for the secondary tense in which present is chosen, and then stopping.

In order to perform such a process, both the selection and termination choosers are needed. In our case, the following chooser applies:

IF   *the clause describes a past event,*
the reference time is past,
THEN   *set the primary tense to past.*

This chooser is very similar to the naive tense selection rule utilized to establish that a given verb should be conjugated into the simple past: it has been obtained, in fact, by withdrawing from that rule the condition concerning an aspectual feature (the event is completed). The selection choosers work thus by exploiting only the temporal features, and the choice among past vs. present vs. future is performed by taking into account only the temporal relations among the states and events described in the sentence. This chooser allows the identification of past as the primary tense for both the open items of the exercise. As for the first open item, after the primary tense has been selected, a termination chooser can be applied:

IF   *the primary tense is past*
the clause contains an explicit time expression
the action described in the clause has been completed
THEN   *stop.*

The termination choosers work by exploiting features of morphological, syntactic, semantic, and pragmatic information. While the tense selection choosers take into account the temporal aspects of the tense determination process, the termination choosers represent an interface between the tense system of a particular language and the relationships among the states or events described in a sentence the speaker intends to convey through the usage of a given tense.

In our case, the first condition determines the applicability of the chooser (it represents one of the termination choosers for the (simple) past), while the remaining conditions put forward two of the criteria that establish when the simple past represents a necessary and sufficient tense combination for expressing a given meaning: i.e.. when the action described in the sentence has been completed in the past at a definite time.

No termination choosers are applicable to the second open item which therefore resorts to a secondary tense selection. The following selection chooser applies:

IF   *the clause has a definite reference time,*
the event time is equal to or includes the reference time
THEN   *set the secondary tense to present.*

As a result of the action performed by the chooser, the secondary tense is set to the present. After the secondary tense has been determined, the following, very simple, termination chooser applies:

IF   *the primary tense is present,*
the secondary tense is past
THEN   *stop.*

According to the systemic grammar of English tense, in fact, no further tenses are possible after a combination of present in past has been chosen.

6. An Evaluation of the Integrated Approach and Future Developments

In the paper a new approach to the problem of determining the tense combination for an English sentence has been proposed with integrates the treatment of tense in a systemic grammar with the naive approach in school grammars. The systemic theory provides general assumptions (i.e. three-tense opposition and seriality) which the tense selection process relies upon, while the naive features provide the criteria for terminating the selection process. The integration of the naive approach into a systemic framework can be evaluated according to three different perspectives:

- *Computational.* How effective is the proposed theory? What is its coverage? How general is it?
- *Pedagogical.* Is it possible to utilize such a theory to really teach the English verbs? How efficient is such an approach in comparison with the traditional one?
- *Psychological.* To which extent does the serial theory of time mirror the real processes that occur in the mind of a speaker ?

The ongoing research tries to answer these questions. A series of computational experiments with the new Verb Generation Expert, implemented in PROLOG on a MacII, is under way with the goal of establishing the reliability of the proposed approach. The construction of a new Tutor aimed at teaching the serial theory of time is under development. Finally, a series of psychological experiments concerning the cognitive validity of the systemic treatment of tense are being planned.

References

1. Allen, J.F.: Towards a General Theory of Action and Time. Artificial Intelligence, 23, 123-154 (1984)
2. Berretta, M.: Linguistica ed Educazione Linguistica. Milano: Einaudi 1977
3. Close, R.A.: English as a Foreign Language (3rd ed.). London: Allen & Unwin 1981
4. Francis, W.N.: Revolution in Grammar. In: Readings in Applied English Linguistics (H.B. Allen, ed.). New York: Appleton Century Croft 1964
5. Fum, D., Giangrandi, P., and Tasso, C.: ET: An intelligent tutor for foreign language teaching. Proceedings ITS-88, Montreal, pp. 462-468, 1988
6. Fum, D., Giangrandi, P. and Tasso, C.: Tense Generation in an Intelligent Tutor for Foreign Language Teaching: Some issues in the design of the verb expert. Proceedings of the 4th Conference of the European Chapter of the Association for Computational Linguistics, Manchester, pp. 124-129, Association for Computational Linguistics 1989
7. Graver, B.B.: Advanced English Practice. Oxford: Oxford University Press 1986
8. Halliday, M.A.K.: The English Verbal Group. In: Halliday: System and Function in Language (G.R. Kress, ed.). Oxford: Oxford University Press 1976
9. Halliday, M.A.K.: An Introduction to Functional Grammar. London: Edward Arnold 1985
10. Halliday, M.A.K., McIntosh A., and Strevrens, P.: The Linguistic Sciences and Language Teaching. London: Longman 1964
11. Hornstein, N.: The Study of Meaning in Natural Language: Three approaches to tense. In: Explanation in Linguistics: The Logical Problem of Language Acquisition (N. Hornstein and D. Lightfoot, eds.). London: Longman 1981
12. Kasper, R.: Systemic Grammar and Functional Unification Grammar. Information Sciences Institute Research Report 87-179, University of Southern California, Marina del Rey, CA, 1987
13. Kress, G.R. (Ed.): Halliday: System and Function in Language. Oxford: Oxford University Press 1976
14. Leech, G. and Svartvik, J.: A Communicative Grammar of Contemporary English. London: Longman 1975
15. Legenhauser, L. and Wolff, D.: Storyboard and the Communicative Language Learning, this volume.
16. Matthiessen, C.: Choosing Primary Tense in English. Studies in Language 7, 369-429 (1983)
17. Matthiessen, C.: Choosing Tense in English. Information Sciences Institute Research Report 84-143, University of Southern California, Marina del Rey, CA., 1984
18. Morley, G.D.: An Introduction to Systemic Grammar. London: Macmillan 1985
19. Murphy, R.: English Grammar in Use. Cambridge: Cambridge University Press 1985
20. Palmer, F.: The English Verb. London: Longman 1974
21. Patten, T. and Ritchie, G.: A Formal Model of Systemic Grammar. In: Natural Language Generation (G. Kempen, ed.) Dordrecht, The Netherlands: Martinus Nijhoff Publ. 1987
22. Quirk, R., Greenbaum, S., Leech, G. and Svarvik, J.: A Grammar of Contemporary English. New York: Seminar Press 1985
23. Reichenbach, H.: Elements of Symbolic Logic. New York: MacMillan 1947
24. Riviere, C.: Tense, Aspect and Time Location. Linguistics, 18 (1980)
25. Roulet, E.: Théories Grammaticales, Description et Enseignement des Langues. Bruxelles: Editions Labor 1972

26. Saporta, S.: Applied Linguistics and Generative Grammar. In: Trends in Modern Language Teaching (A. Valdman, ed.). New York: McGraw-Hill 1972
27. Thompson, A.J. and Martinet, A.V.: A Practical English Grammar (2nd ed.). Oxford: Oxford University Press 1969
28. Widdowson, H.G.: Teaching Language as Communication. Oxford: Oxford University Press 1978
29. Wilkins, D.A.: Notional Syllabuses. Oxford: Oxford University Press 1976
30. Woods, E. and McLeod, N.: Using English Grammar: Meaning and form. New York: Prentice Hall 1990

A Lexicalized Tree Adjoining Grammar for French and its Relevance to Language Teaching

Anne Abeillé*

LADL & UFRL, University of Jussieu-Paris 7, 2 place Jussieu, 75005 Paris, France, abeille@franz.ibp.fr

Abstract: We present a computational grammar for French written in the formalism of lexicalized Tree Adjoining Grammars. This can be viewed as a data-base consisting of both a sizable lexicon (3000 words) and the corresponding syntactic structures. A parser has also been designed which is currently being used for analysing and disambiguating a large range of French sentences provided by the user. A similar lexical grammar has been designed for English with approximately the same linguistic coverage. We are currently working on a transfer system that matches the corresponding entries in both languages. Although we do not present any proper educational tool, we aim at exploring the possible uses of our system for teaching French to English speaking students.

Keywords: French, idioms, lexicalization, language teaching, parsing, TAGs.

1. Designing a lexicalized grammar for French

Most current linguistic theories give lexical accounts of several phenomena that used to be considered as governed by structural rules only. The information put in the lexicon has been increased both in amount and complexity and is the major component of such grammatical theories as Lexical Functional grammar (LFG), Head-driven Phrase-structure grammar (HPSG) or Lexicon grammars [16]. Tree Adjoining grammars (TAG), originally defined by Joshi et al. [21, 22], enable one to generalize this position and to define "lexicalized" grammars.

A lexicalized TAG, as defined in [31], consists of a finite set of elementary trees associated with lexical items anchoring them in the lexicon. These elementary trees can be of two types : initial trees (noted α) and auxiliary trees (noted ß). They are combined together by two operations : substitution or adjunction.

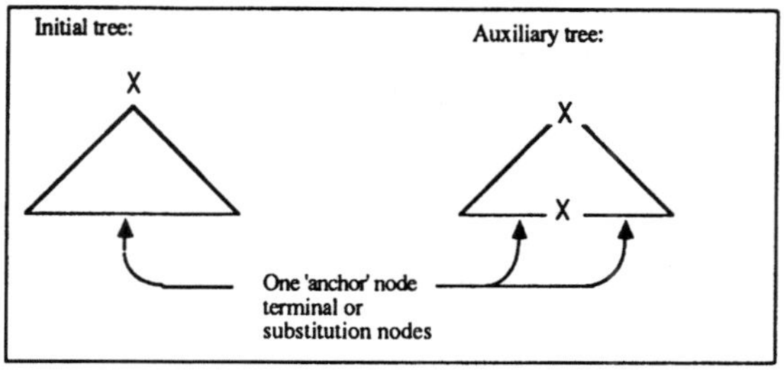

Figure 1. Schematic initial and auxiliary trees

* The work presented here partially results from a collaboration between the University of Jussieu-Paris 7 and the University of Pennsylvania (Philadelphia).

NATO ASI Series, Vol. F 80
Intelligent Tutoring Systems for Foreign Language Learning
Edited by M. L. Swartz and M. Yazdani

All elementary trees are required to have at least one leaf node bearing a lexical terminal. This lexical head can be arbitrarily distant from the root node (s) of the tree. Auxiliary trees have a special constraint : one of their leaf nodes must be of the same category (x) as that of their root node. This leaf is called "foot node" and is used for adjoining the auxiliary tree (See Figure 1).

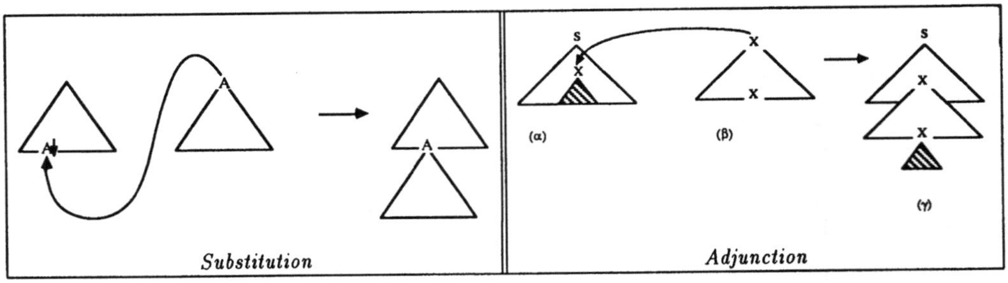

Figure 2. Operations of substitution and adjunction

Substitution is used to combine an initial tree at a leaf of any other tree, while adjunction is used to insert an auxiliary tree at any node of another tree. In case of an adjunction, the subtree dominated by the node where the adjunction takes place is pushed down and copied under the foot node of the auxiliary tree (See Figure 2). Feature structures can be associated at each node in an elementary tree and constraints on combining trees can be expressed in terms of success or failure of unification [38, 9].

Combinations of elementary trees result into two different kinds of structures: a "derived tree" (noted γ) which is the fully expanded syntactic tree that results, and a "derivation tree" which illustrates how the derived tree has been obtained (by combining which elementary trees together at particular nodes). Because of the operation of adjunction, TAGs are more powerful than context-free grammars but only mildly so [35].

An extension of TAGs has been defined which is called Synchronous TAGs. This extension allows one to consider more than one grammar at a time and to define links between elementary structures of each grammar. Two sentences are equivalent if such links between their elementary trees are kept throughout their derivation. They are thus to be built "synchronously": if a node A in a tree of the first sentence is linked with a node B in another tree of the second sentence, for any adjunction or substitution taking place at node A, the similar combination of an equivalent elementary tree has to take place at node B. This system is currently being used for matching English syntactic structures with logical form expressions [34] and for machine translation [6].

Lexicalized TAGs have been used to write two sizable grammars: one for French [2,8], one for English [4, 5, 25]. Several parsers have been designed [32, 37], based on algorithms similar to those existing for context-free grammars. We now present the internal organization of the French grammar.

1.1 Elementary structures

A lexicalized TAG has been defined for French [8]. Elementary structures have been defined for French and each of them is selected by at least one lexical item serving as its head (or 'anchor') in the lexicon. Elementary structures correspond to complete predicate argument structures. For a given predicate, these structures comprise the nodes at which to attach all its arguments. For a given modifier, they comprise a node (the foot node) corresponding to the category it modifies. Nodes for subjects and complements thus belong to the elementary trees of their predicates, as well as nodes for corresponding fillers and gaps. These elementary trees form the syntactic and semantic units of the grammmar.

A predicate yields an initial or auxiliary tree, depending on whether or not it takes sentential complements. An argument yields an initial tree, and an adjunct an auxiliary tree rooted in the category of the elements it modifies. Examples of arguments are names (e.g., "Jean") and nouns (e.g., "femme": woman). Examples of adjuncts are determiners (e.g., "un": a), adjectives (e.g., "joli" : pretty), adverbs (e.g., "souvent": often) or modals (e.g.,"pouvoir": can). Examples of predicates with nominal arguments are the verbs "dormir" (sleep) or "manger" (eat), while a predicate with a sentential complement is exemplified by "penser que" (think):

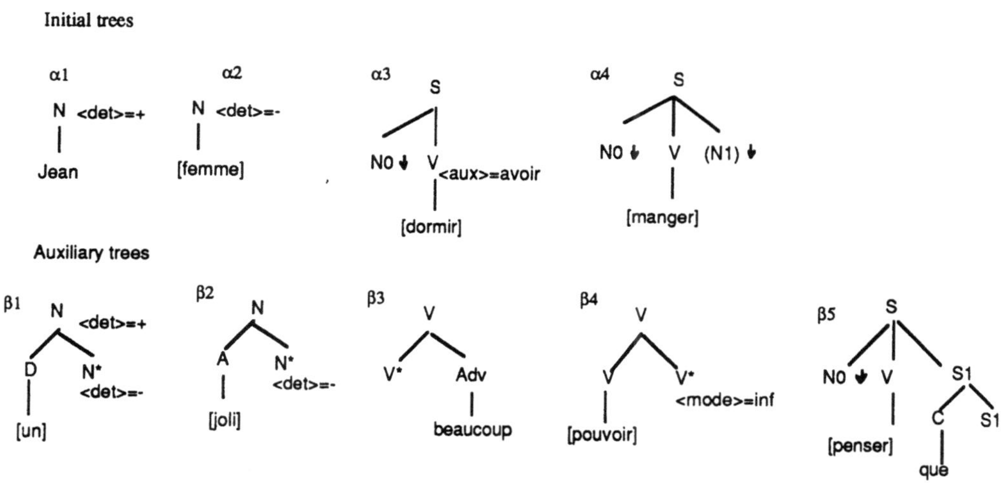

Figure 3. Elementary trees for some French predicates, arguments and modifiers. We use ↓ for substitution and * for the foot node of the auxiliary trees. The symbol 'X' means that the node X and its subtree are optional. The index 0 is used for the subject; the following indices correspond to the complements. Not all features are shown here.

Substitution is always obligatory at a node and performed only once, while adjunction is usually optional and can be reiterated (explicit constraints on adjunction can make it compulsory or rule it out). The former corresponds naturally to the predicate-argument relation, while the latter is used to insert modifiers. Examples of substitution or adjunction for the elementary trees seen above are as follows in Figures 4 and 5:

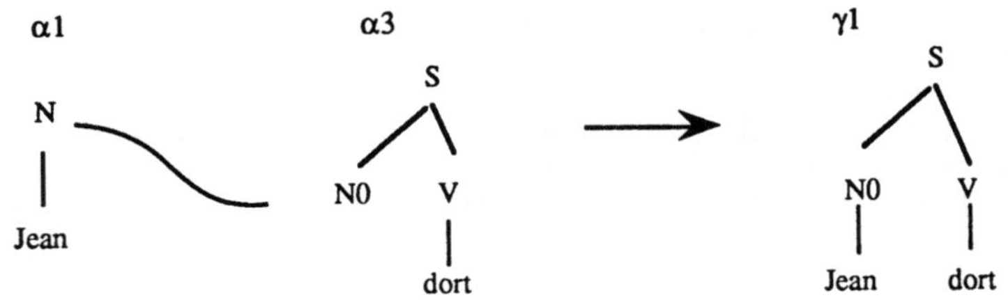

Figure 4. Example of substitution : *Jean dort.* γ1 illustrates the derived tree.

Notice that the category of a word in the TAG lexicon is not reduced to its traditional part of speech. Its part of speech is only the first node dominating this word in the elementary tree associated to it and this elementary tree is properly speaking the category of this word. Notice also that an elementary tree defines an extended domain of locality which would be equivalent to a set of phrase structure rules. For example, the phrase structure rules for the tree α5 would be:

S -> N0 V S'1
V -> penser
S'1 -> C S1
C -> que

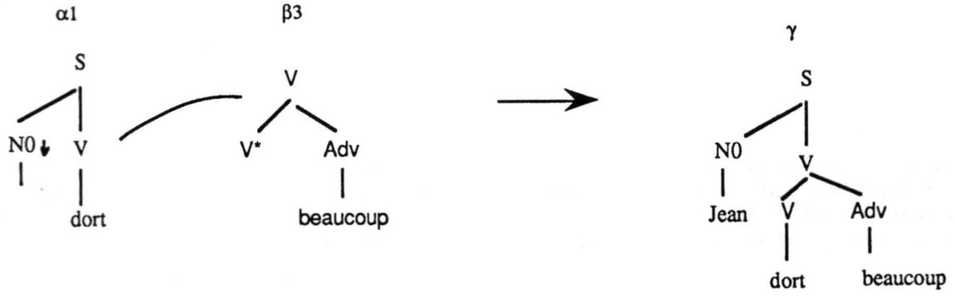

Figure 5. Example of adjunction: *Jean dort beaucoup*

Because the units of the grammar are trees and not rewrite rules, TAGs have a larger domain of locality than formalisms based on phrase structure rules. Thus less features and less feature passing between nodes are necessary. For example, we do not need a special feature for complement subcategorization. The subcategorization frame of the verb is apparent in the structure of its elementary tree. For example in Figure 6, verbs such as "dormir", (sleep), "aimer" (love) and "donner" (give) are associated with the following elementary trees in the grammar (among others):

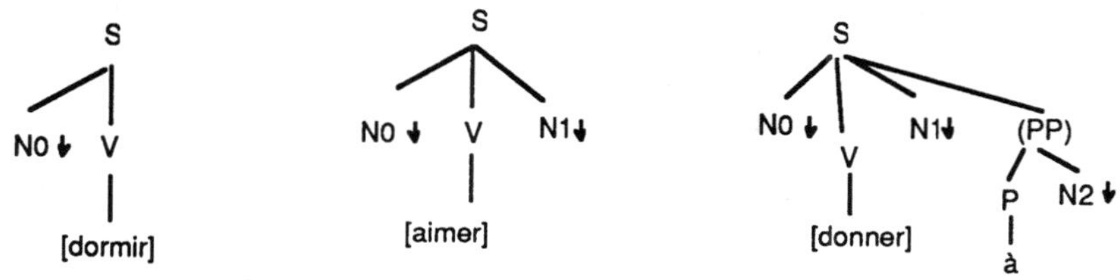

Figure 6. Elementary trees for *dormir* (sleep), *aimer* (love) and *donner* (give)

"Dormir", which is an intransitive verb, has only one substitution node (corresponding to its subject), while "aimer" has two (one for the subject and the other for its direct complement) and a ditransitive verb like "donner" has three. Similarly, we don't need a feature to differentiate post-posed adjectives from preposed ones (See Figure 7), since their position is encoded in their tree structure:

Figure 7. Trees for the adjectives *grand* (big) and *bleu* (blue)

We thus have:

Une maison bleue (a blue house)
* *Une bleue maison*
* *Une maison grande*[0] (a big house)
Une grande maison

But we do need features to distinguish those adverbs which can take a degree modifier and those that cannot, since these modifiers are not part of the tree structure of adverbs. We have thus souvent (often) and récemment (recently) which are marked <deg>=+, whereas dernièrement (lastly) and demain (tomorrow) are marked <deg>=-:

très souvent (very often)
très récemment (very recently)
* *très dernièrement* (very lastly)
* *très demain* (very tomorrow)

---

0 Allowed in fact in certain contexts such as coordinations : une maison grande, claire et bien meublée.

1.2 Complex predicates and semi-compositional phenomena

Non-compositional phenomena create all sorts of difficulties for natural language processing, especially for machine translation if one tries to translate them in a compositional way. The French expression "prendre une veste" for example, which means "to be put down" cannot be translated literally : "to take a jacket". Such expressions are difficult to handle automatically since they can occur in various forms and often exhibit the same syntactic flexibility as compositional expressions of the language.

We consider the following combinations as complex predicates: copula-adjective combinations, light-verb constructions and various idiomatic and metaphoric expressions. For such constructions more than one lexical item is considered as the head of the structure and the associated elementary trees are usually more expanded than those for simple predicates.

Copula-adjective combinations yield sentential trees where the node for the subject is directly accessible to the adjective: agreement and corestriction between them is thus easily expressed. It is thus easy to differentiate adjectives that might qualify sentences from adjectives qualifying nominals only[1].

Light verb constructions described for French [17, 14, 15] are other examples of non compositional phenomena. They comprise of a predicative nominal and an associated verb which is semantically empty. Which light verb is associated with each predicative noun is not entirely predictible and there are numerous language-specific idiosyncrasies. We thus consider these combinations as one semantic unit and one elementary tree (see [1] for more details). A combination such as "N0 prendre la décision de/que S" is thus considered as one lexical entry and one elementary structure (which is equivalent to "N0 décider de/que S"; to decide upon something), and similarly for "N0 commettre une agression contre N1" (equivalent to "N0 agresser N1"; to attack someone) or "N0 faire une gaffe" (= "N0 gaffer"; to blunder).

Idioms are other examples where expanded lexical structures are needed. As has been shown by Gross' extensive studies [18, 20], French idioms are syntactically much more flexible than is usually thought (adverb insertion, nominalization, passive and most syntactic rules may apply to them). We thus assign them an internal syntactic structure and make them fall into the same grammar as non-idiomatic constructions [3]. The only specificity of idioms in our representation is that they are selected by several lexical items (forming a multicomponent head) and assigned elementary trees which are more extended than for non-idiomatic constructions. Figure 8 shows three examples.

The lexical anchors of such elementary structures are respectively [prendre], "une" and "veste" for $\alpha 1$, [tomber], "à", "l'" and "eau" for $\alpha 2$, and [prendre], "en" and "compte" for $\alpha 3$.

1.3 Tree Families for syntactic rules

There are no separate grammar rules in our grammar, the only "rules" being those of substitution and adjunction which combine the lexical structures together. Traditionnal lexical and syntactic rules such as passive or wh-movement are encoded with additionnal tree structures associated to the different predicates.

---

1 The distinction is not a mere semantic one since some adjectives qualify abstract terms but not corresponding sentential forms:

Ce voyage est cher

? Faire ce voyage est cher

** Que l'on fasse ce voyage est cher*

For more details see Abeillé [8].

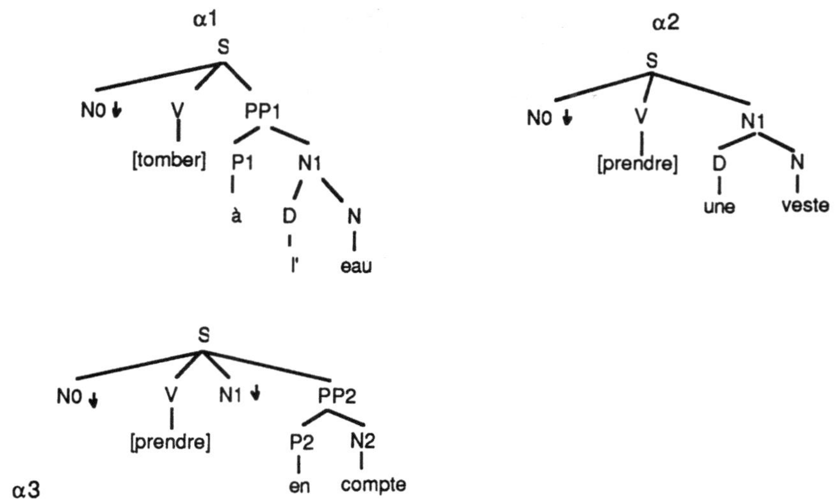

Figure 8. Elementary trees for *N0 prendre une veste* (to be put down), *N0 tomber à l'eau* (to go to the dogs) and *N0 prendre N1 en compte* (to take something into account).

Different surface realizations of arguments of a given predicate (whether due to movement or to change of grammatical function) are captured by having several elementary trees associated to this predicate. These different elementary trees are gathered into what we call Tree Families. Figure 9 shows examples of such trees associated with the verb "aimer"[2]. Notice that these different structures are part of an equivalence class. We can thus present various types of sentences to exemplify the frame (and the possible meaning) of a given verb, without having to consider one (e.g. the declarative construction) more important than the others. We have thus represented passive, cleft extraction and wh-movement, extraposition, ergative and symetry alternation.

Tree families are similarly associated with complex predicates and idioms (See Figure 10) and adverbs and prepositional adjuncts (See Figure 11) are shown. These sets of trees can be viewed as exemplifying general syntactic rules of the language, e. g., for question formation, (the verbal head serving as an example). They can also be used to show how these rules are in fact sensitive to certain lexical items, such as idioms [7].

---

2 The coindices associated to arguments stand in fact for links between the leaf nodes of the following trees.

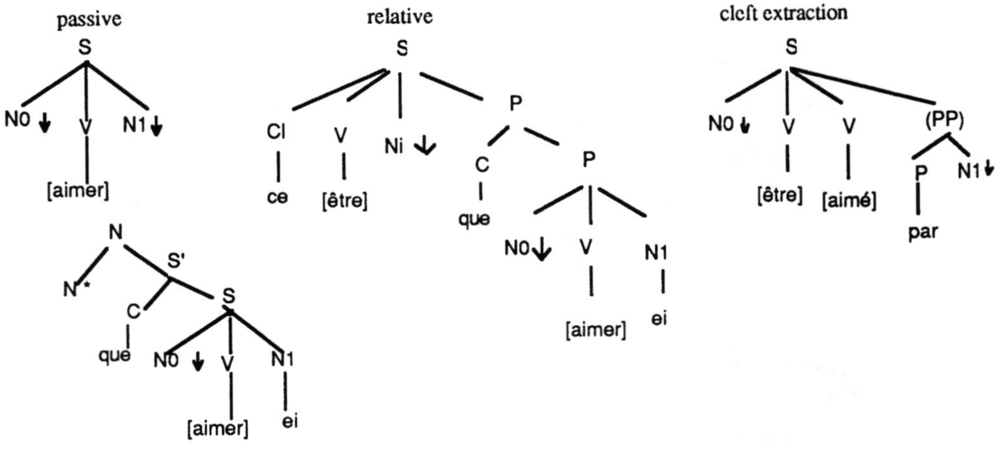

Figure 9. Elementary trees for the transitive verb *aimer* (love).

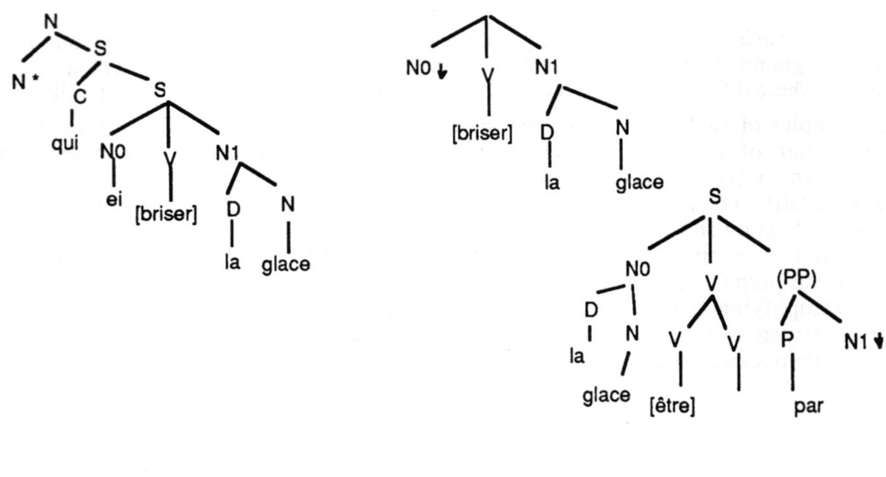

Figure 10. Examples of elementary trees associated with the idiom *N0 briser la glace* (to break the ice).

Tree families for adverbs and prepositional adjuncts are also defined:

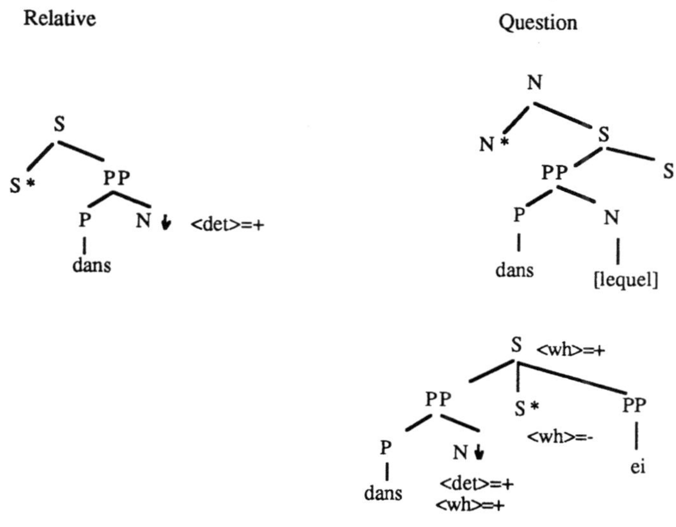

Figure 11. Elementary trees associated with the preposition *dans* (in).

1.4 Analysing or generating sentences

As most unification-based formalisms, Lexicalized Tree Adjoining grammars are not parsing-or generation-oriented. They can be used both ways and our French grammar is "reversible". Elementary structures in a TAG correspond to linguistic units of both syntactic and semantic relevance. When such units are combined together into a sentence, their corresponding semantics is being combined as well. This ensures the strict monotonicity of our formalism, which is desirable both from a computational and a psychological point of view.

Sentences when analysed (or produced) with a TAG are associated with two different types of results: a derived tree and a derivation tree (actually more than one if the sentence is ambiguous). A derived tree is the tree resulting from the combination of different elementary trees. It is similar to standard phrase structure analyses yielded by context free-based formalisms. A derivation tree, on the other hand, expresses how the proper elementary trees have been combined together to form the corresponding derived tree.

These two outputs are a specificity of TAGs, as opposed to context free-based grammars. The basis for semantic interpretation in a TAG is the derivation tree, not the derived tree (which corresponds to syntactic properties). For example, in the case of unbounded dependencies, the fronted element can be located indefinitely far ahead of its matrix verb in the derived tree (consistently with the order of the words in the string), but will be adjacent to it in the derivation tree[3].

Syntactic ambiguities show up in both derived trees and derivation trees. For example a sentence such as "Jean attend la nuit" where the NP "la nuit" can be either a verb complement (= he's waiting for the night) or a temporal adjunct (= he's waiting (for something) during the night) is associated two derived trees and two derivation trees as shown in Figure 12:

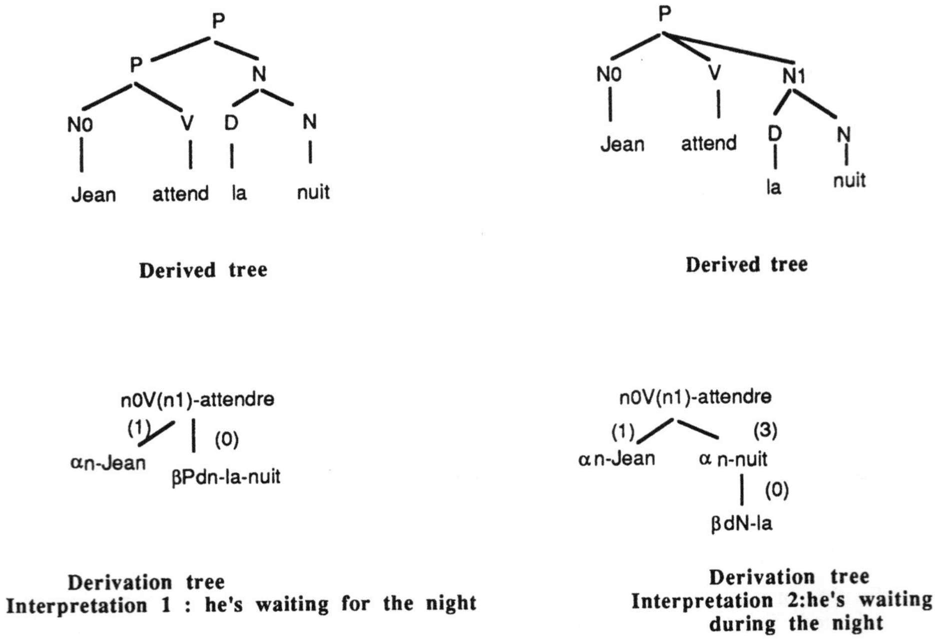

Figure 12. Analyses of the ambiguous sentence *Jean attend la nuit.*

Semantic ambiguities show up mainly in derivation trees. TAGs are thus a fruitful formalism for exploring discrepancies between syntax and semantics. French idiomatic (or semi-idiomatic) expressions are clearly of this kind: their syntax is regularly compositional while their semantic is not. Figure 13 shows that their derived trees are the same as those of non idiomatic constructions, but their derivation trees are different.

---

[3] Unbounded dependencies such as: ***Qui** pensez-vous que **Jean aime**?* are derived from the adjunction of the auxiliary tree corresponding to the matrix clause "pensez-vous que S?" into the tree of "Qui Jean aime". This representation allows one to localize unbounded dependencies such as wh-movement, or topicalization [25].

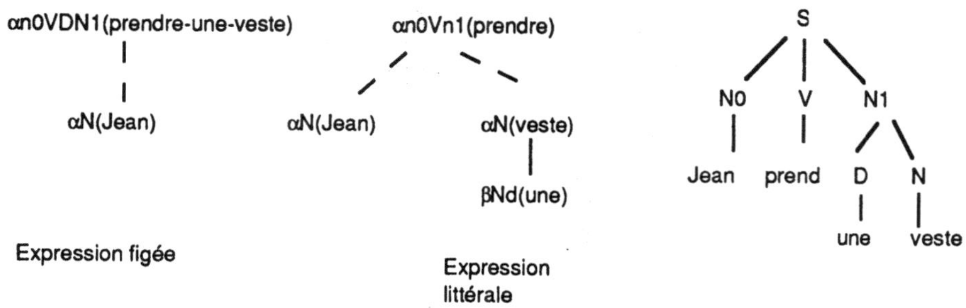

literal derivation **idiomatic derivation** **unique derived tree**

Figure 13. Analyses of the ambiguous sentence *Jean prend une veste.*

The first derivation tree corresponds to the literal interpretation (Jean takes a jacket): four elementary trees have been combined, one for "Jean", one for "prend" (takes), one for "une" (a) and one for "veste" (jacket). The second derivation tree corresponds to the idiomatic interpretation (Jean is put down): only two elementary trees have been combined, one for "Jean" and one for "prend une veste" (is put down).

The reverse situation also holds. When two sentences are quite different syntactically but similar semantically (e.g., an active sentence and its passive counterpart), they are associated with different derived tree but equivalent derivation trees. This kind of equivalence holds, for example, between active and passive sentences and is provided by Synchronous TAGs [35]. Links are defined between semantically equivalent lexical trees (and between some of their nodes). Elementary trees belonging to the same Tree Families are linked according to this principle. The two sentences "Jean aime Marie" and "Marie est aimée par Jean" can thus be built up synchronously. They will have different derived trees but equivalent derivation trees.

2. Advantages in a teaching perspective

In parallel to the increasing role played by lexical issues in linguistic theories, there has been more and more emphasis on lexical learning in the field of language acquisition [30]. McWhinney [26] explores the extent to which acquisition of grammar can emerge from the mere acquisition of lexical items. Such developements obviously converge with long-time practice in second language learning (computer-aided or not) which has always emphasized the learning of words (even in such simplistic form as vocabulary lists). Our representation also makes language learning crucially dependent on lexicon learning, but with the possibility of considering more structured units than single word forms. Often these units consist of several lexical items.

2.1 A sophisticated French computational dictionary

Our grammar consists of two lexicons: one morphological dictionary giving all the inflected forms for the corresponding lemma (which is not specific to TAGs) and a "syntactico-semantic" one which is our main component. This syntactic lexicon currently consists of approximately 3000 words, which are the most common for French according to the frequency lists of Juilland et al.

[24]. It subdivides as follows: 1000 verbs, 1500 nouns, 400 adjectives, and 100 adverbs, prepositions and determiners (for more details, see [2, 8].

All entries have the same format[4]:
[word1], preterminal category; word2, preterminal category ...: tree structure(s) {feature constraints}.

Examples:

[abandonner],V : n0V{N0:<hum>=+}.
[abandonner],V;à,Prep: n0Vn1(pn2){N0:<hum>=+}.
[abandonner],V: n0Vn1{N1:<hum>=+,N0:<hum>=-}.
[abime],N : aN{N.b:<Det>=-}.
[abime],N; [de],Prep;[un],Det: ßn'DNP {N*:<Det>=-;N*:<abs>=+, N'.b:<Det>=+}.
[abri],N; (contre,Prep): aN(Pn1){N.b:<Det>=-}.
[absence],N; ([de],Prep): ßN(Pn1){N*:<Det>=+/N*<num>=+}.
[absence],N; [avoir];N: n0VdN1 {N0:<hum>=+; N1.b:<Det>=-; N1.t:<Det>=+}.
[accepter],V; [que]/[de],Comp: n0Vn1 {N0:<Det>=+; N1:<Det>=+}; n0Vs1{N0:<Det>=+; S1:<mode>= inf/subj}.
[accepter],V: n0Vn1pn2 {N0:<hum>=+; P:<loc>=+}

Linguistic notations and symbols are in English. This is a compact notation, and from a teaching point of view it would be better to display directly the tree graphics associated with the entries. No explicit syntactic or semantic vocabulary[5] are needed in order to explain such notions as predicative, idiomatic, transitive, etc... since they are shown by the tree structures themselves. The learner only needs to know standard parts of speech, such as: V, Prep, Det, Noun and phrases such as sentences (noted S) or prepositional phrases (noted PP) in order to understand the internal nodes of a tree graph.

This syntactic dictionary can be used as a sophisticated data-base to be directly queried by the learner, or called upon in the context of more specific exercises (see sentences construction exercises [36, 39], this volume, as examples). The knowledge provided by this dictionary puts an emphasis on three aspects of language learning:
a) *Importance of subcategorization frames.* This domain exhibits one of the crucial differences between first and second language learning. Whereas children make strikingly very few mistakes of subcategorization in learning their mother language [27], these kinds of mistakes are very frequent in second language acquisition and typical examples of transfer errors. Since subcategorization frames play a crucial role in the syntax-semantic interface, learners tend to assign to foreign verbs the subcategorization frame of their equivalents in their native language. A French learner of English will often say *"I approve this plan" or *"I'm waiting you" because "approuver" (approve) and "attendre" (wait) are both transitive verbs in French. This kind of mistake could be reduced if learners are always taught verbs with their complete subcategorization frame(s).
b) *Importance of idiomatic (or semi-idiomatic) expressions.* These expressions are very frequent in standard oral and written French. Any realistic natural language application cannot ignore them [19]. The Dutch school system which presents the students with lots of English idioms to learn has proved one of the most efficient ones for second language teaching.

Learners of a language (first or second language in a natural environment) exhibit a striking capacity to memorize long sequences of words which they use as compounds, and learn how to decompose them only gradually as their knowledge of the language increases. However, they are usually at a loss (no matter how advanced they are) for identifying which among these sequences

4 We note lemmas (i.e. sets of inflected forms) with square brackets.

5 Mastering theoretical linguistic terms cannot be expected from the learner and requires the design of specific exercises [see 13].

are true compounds (or collocations) and which ones are not, since they don't know well enough which combinations are productive and which are not. This is why it is especially important to teach learners compounds and collocations as such. Light verb constructions are a good example of such expressions which are usually easy to understand but with which most foreigners have trouble when it comes to use them. Native English speakers learning French usually transfer the light verb of their own language attached to a given predicate. With "décision" (decision), for example, they make up the expression *" faire une décision" which is erroneous (instead of the correct "prendre une décision") because of the English "make a decision". Similarly, one often hears English-speaking persons say *"demander une question" ("ask a question") instead of the correct "poser une question" (see Danlos [12] for a systematic study of mismatches of light verbs between French and English). TAG's extended domain of locality is especially suitable to present such multi-word units.

c) *Importance of ambiguity*. Coping with the pervasive ambiguity of natural language is one of the most important problems in applications in Artificial Intelligence. For example, the systematic classification of French verbs done by Gross' team has shown that each verb has on the average more than two meanings, and the average is about 5 for more frequent verbs [16][6]. However, these ambiguities are often overlooked in computer-assisted language learning and language teaching in general.

Linguists usually distinguish different kinds of ambiguities (lexical, structural, semantic). An interesting aspect of our formalism is that most ambiguities show up in our lexical representation. If several adverbial attachments are possible, for example, there will be as many tree structures associated with the adverb as there are different types of categories it can be attached to. In general, we rely mostly on different tree structures for most lexical disambiguation, thus avoiding the need for an explicit semantic representation.

French words are thus disambiguated in several ways:

- depending on their subcategorization frame. The French verb "voler" for example, has two very different meanings: to steal and to fly. They correspond to two distinct tree structures: one for "N0 voler N1 à N2" (to steal) and one for "N0 voler (Loc N1)" (to fly).
- depending on the features of their arguments. Less frequently, a French verb is disambiguated on the mere basis of such features. For example, two meanings of the verb "aller" (among lots of others) both correspond to a prepositional complement structure: "N0 aller Loc N1" (to go) and "N0 aller à N1" (to fit). But in the first one, the subject has to be animate, the object being a locative; while in the second one, the subject is animate and the object animate:

Jean va à la plage (Jean is going to the beach)
Cette chemise va à Jean (This shirt fits Jean)

- depending on the other items they are associated with to form an idiomatic phrase. A verb like "casser" (to break) does not seem to be very ambiguous on the face of it. Nonetheless, it is part of numerous idioms that are quite heterogeneous semantically: "casser sa pipe" (to kick the bucket), "casser du sucre sur le dos de'quelqu'un" (to criticize someone behind his back), "casser les pieds à quelqu'un" (to get on somebody's nerves), "casser les oreilles à quelqu'un" (to deafen someone) etc... Notice that in our representation, the verb "casser" is not itself ambiguous. It is the different idiomatic phrases (with all their different lexical items) which are presented as distinct lexical entries : they are thus distinct semantically.

Our grammar presents the learner with the complete argument structure (with appropriate features) of the entry, and also presents all lexical items making up one entry. It thus helps for much disambiguation which is a source of major difficulty in the learning of foreign words. We think that it is better to present the learner with all the different meanings (among the frequent ones)

---

[6] Miller and Fellbaum [28] report similar results about the ambiguity of English words.

of a word, and some of the common idiomatic phrases it is part of, from the start instead of teaching him or her a privileged meaning (without any clear basis upon which to define it) and in a second step teach him or her the others.

2.2 Teaching meaning via some lexical semantic relations

Notice that we do not have any explicit semantic representation in our system. There are different possibilities for the learner to guess the word meaning(s). We can use our syntactic lexicon in order to generate example sentences at random involving a certain predicate[7]. More specific software may supplement appropriate sentential or graphic contexts in the course of particular exercises (see [36, 39] this volume, as examples).

We are also currently exploring the construction of a semantic network out of our syntactic lexicon. The idea is not to build a semantic dictionary on top of the syntactic one but simply to express relevant semantic relations among our syntactic entries. This is an approach to lexical semantics which is close to Wordnet's (see [28], this volume) in the sense that word meanings are considered more relational than decompositional. For the moment, we have only considered a similarity relation, which is a little bit larger than usual synonymy, but others such as antonymy or entailment could be added. One difference with Wordnet is that our lexical units are expanded and structured as trees: we can thus easily express relations not only between predicates (say two verbs) but also between their arguments and even between the adjuncts which may modify them. Multi-word units are also easily defined as lexical entries. Another difference is that we aim at computing semantic relations between sentences.

Our semantic relations, consistent with the idea of synchronous TAGs [35] are expressed as links between nodes in elementary (i.e., lexical) trees. For example, one might want to relate sentences *Jean a peur de Marie* with *Jean craint Marie* or *Marie effraie Jean* which are different paraphrases for the notion of Fear. One difficulty is that they do not comprise the same number of words : "avoir peur de" has three (besides Jean and Marie) whereas "craindre" has one. Another difficulty is that the order of the arguments (and their syntactic functions) vary : Jean is in the subject position with "craindre" but in the object position with "effrayer". Tthe elementary trees defined in the TAG grammars make all these differences quite explicit. Figure 14 shows the corresponding arguments linkages in the following way:

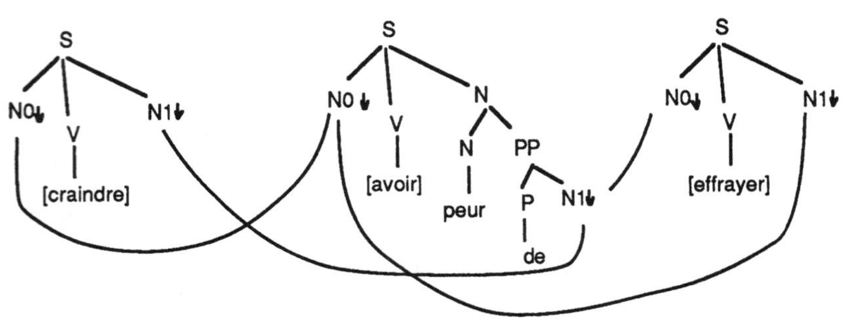

Figure 14. Correspondencies between the trees for *craindre* (to fear), *avoir peur de* (to be afraid of), and *effrayer* (to frighten).

7 A generation system using lexicalized TAGs is currently under development [23, 34].

The trees for "Marie" and "Jean" are linked to themselves and the derivations of the above sentences are considered "synchronous", that is to say semantically equivalent.

Interestingly, words of different categories can be sematically similar in particular contexts. We have concentrated so far on morphologically related items such as femme-féminin (Noun-Adjective), aveugle-aveuglément (Adjective-Adverb), arriver-arrivée (Verb-Noun). These items will be considered as possible semantic equivalents and the corresponding trees will be linked. If one takes a verb like déplorer, which either takes a nominal or a sentential complement, the equivalence between the sentential tree of "arrêter" and the nominal tree for "arrestation" will be activated in the course of the derivation but not otherwise. The following sentences will thus be "synchronously" derived and considered semantically equivalent.

Paul dépore que la police ait arrêté Jean.

Paul déplore l'arrestation de Jean par la police.

In certain contexts, the verbal node (receiving adverbial modifiers) and the node of the first complement (which receives adjectival modifiers) will be linked. The possible equivalence between the adjective "simple" and the adverb "simplement" will thus be activated and the following sentences will be derived synchronously :

Paul a une simple grippe (Paul has a simple flue)
Paul a simplement une grippe (Paul simply has a flue)

As in Wordnet, showing which entries are related also helps for disambiguation purposes. Going back to the two different verbs "aller" mentioned above (section 2.1), they have quite different synonyms. "N0 aller Loc N1" (=go) is linked to "N0 se rendre Loc N1" (=gain). "N0 aller à N1hum" (=fit) is linked to "N0 convenir à N1". A similar disambiguation holds when one considers semantic relations involving morphologically related items. Linguistic studies on derivational morphology have often noticed that a derived item often has a much more restricted meaning than that of the word it is derived from. For example, the verb "arrêter" is several times ambiguous and has different derived nominals and light verb constructions depending on which of the verb's senses is involved:

N0 arrêter N1hum = N0 procéder à l'arrestation de N1 (=to arrest someone)
N0 s'arrêter Loc N1 = N0 faire un arrêt Loc N1 (to make a stop somewhere)

The French verb "arrêter" when it means to arrest is linked with the noun "arrestation" (and not with the noun "arrêt"). When it means to make a stop, it is linked with the noun "arrêt" but not with the noun "arrestation". Enriching the learner's vocabulary with derived verbs or synonymous collocations thus implies that word senses have been carefully distinguished first.

Notice that our links are not labeled and roughly mean "semantically equivalent". They could be labeled with finer grained relations, and an inheritance system would have to be constructed in the case of sentences involving items with different kinds of links. Contrary to Wordnet, our equivalence system is not fully implemented yet, and we do not have the proper software to search it.

2.3 Teaching some bilingual correspondencies

Another possibility for learning French words is to match them with their equivalent in the learner's own language. A lexicalized Tree Adjoining Grammar for English has been built along the same lines as the French one [4, 5]. The idea of connecting both grammars together has emerged first in a machine translation perspective [6] but could be used in a tutoring system for English-speakers learning French (or vice versa) as well.

Matching such complex units as our elementary trees (with annotated nodes and leaves filled with lexical items) leads to a very specific kind of bilingual dictionary. The lexical items anchoring the trees are matched to one another (as is the case in standard bilingual dictionaries and in most translation systems), but also other nodes of these trees can also be matched with one another. For that purpose, we use the notation of Synchronous TAGs [35] which defines such complex links between tree units. Let us take three examples of such links shown in Figure 15 to 19. 1) The simplest case is when both entries consist of the same number of lexical items and have the same tree structure associated to them[8]:

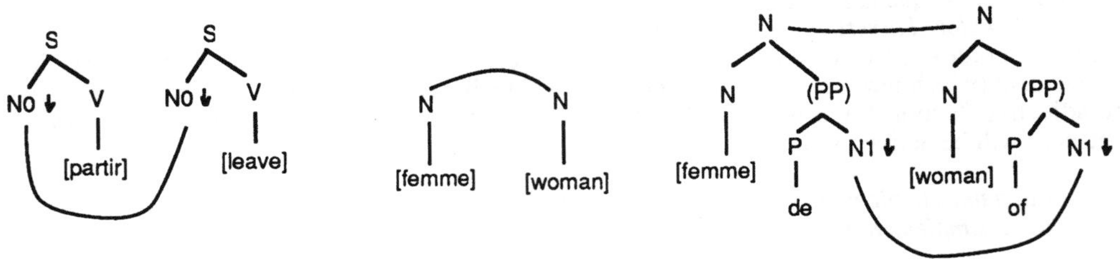

Figure 15. English TAG translations of the French *partir* and *femme*.

The verb "partir" matches the English "leave" (in its intransitive construction) and they have the same tree structures. The noun "femme" is disambiguated depending on whether it takes a prepositional complement (=wife) or not (=woman). The matches between such trees can be many to one when a lexical item has several equivalent translations. Notice also that the way the different nodes are matched is not always the same. For example, the two verbs "rappeler" and "remind" have a similar argument structure but the order of their arguments is mismatched. The first complement of "rappeler" corresponds to the second complement of "remind" and vice versa: "N0 rappeler quelquechose à quelqu'un" = "N0 remind someone of something".

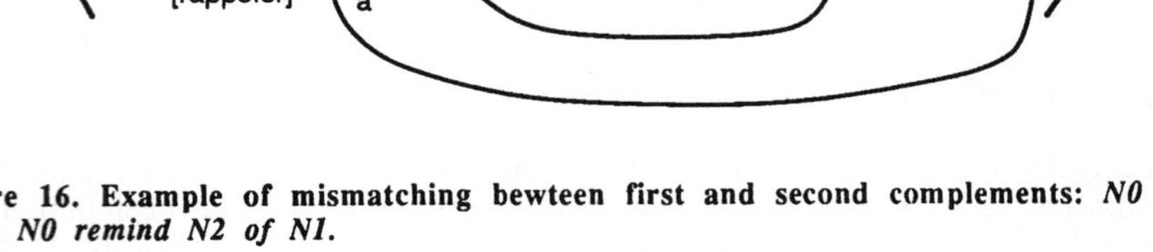

Figure 16. Example of mismatching bewteen first and second complements: *N0 rappeler N1 à N2 = N0 remind N2 of N1.*

8 We are dealing here only with sets of inflected forms which are matched as wholes without further specifications. In the sentential context shown, only the right forms will be selected.

2) One lexical item in French may correspond to several in English (or vice versa), thus exhibiting a different internal structure. This is especially true for French reflexive verbs, English verb-particle combinations, and complex predicates in both languages. The matching process follows the same lines, each tree structures being considered as a whole (See Figures 17 and 18).

3) In a number of cases, there are several lexical items involved in each language, exhibiting different internal structures. The number of items, as well as the tree shapes, may be the same in each language or not. The extended domain of locality of TAGs helps matching the relevant semantic units in every case (See Figure 19).

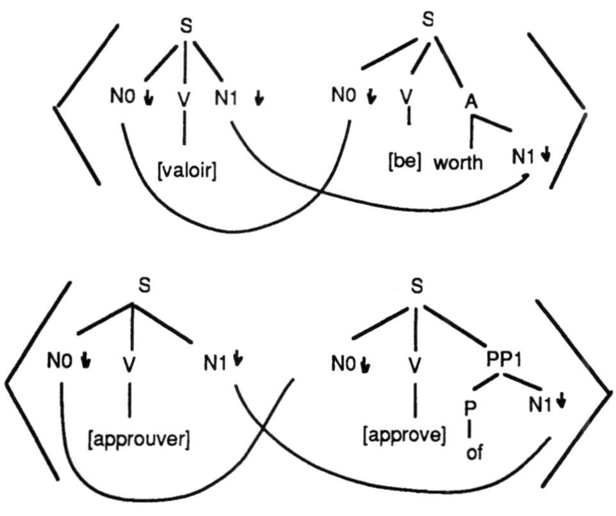

Figure 17. English equivalents for *N0 valoir N1* and *N0 approuver N1* . One lexical item in French = several lexical items in English.

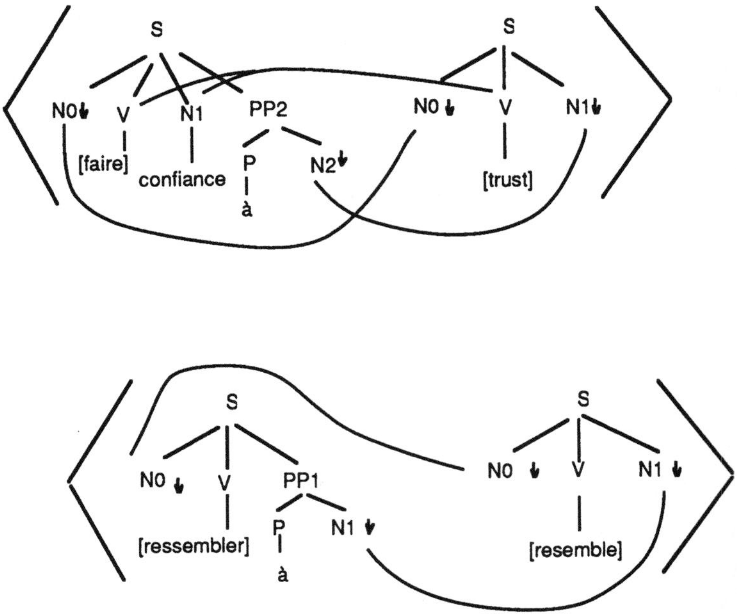

Figure 18. English equivalents for *N0 ressembler à N1* and *N0 faire confiance à N1*. Several lexical items in French = one lexical item in English.

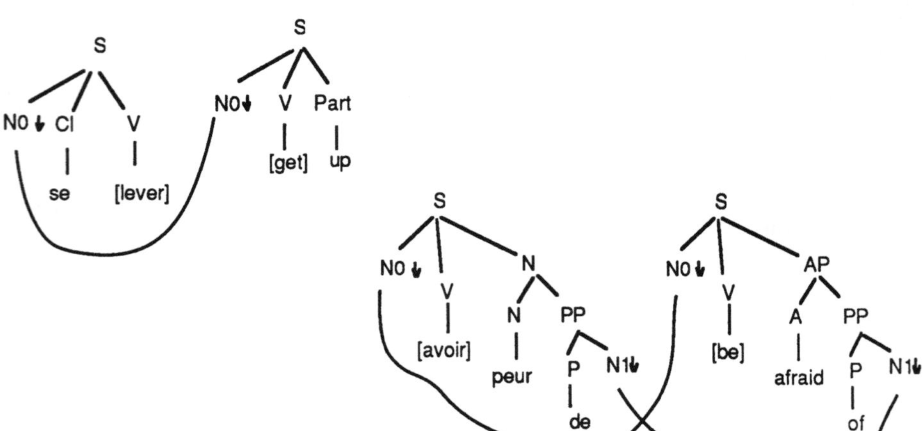

Figure 19. English equivalents for *N0 se lever* and *N0 avoir peur de N1*.

A pronominal verb such as "se lever" in French is thus matched to a verb-particle combination in English : "to get up". Similarly, the light verb construction "N0 avoir peur de N1" is matched with a be-adjective combination in English. The number of lexical items involved is the same but their category and the tree structures of their entries are quite different.

2.3 Further applications

Generation. We intend to explore generation to show how complex sentences are built out of simple ones. A generation system using lexicalized TAGs is currently under development [23, 34]. But we can also have the learner actually generate the sentence by manipulating the trees him- or herself. Adjunction or substitution are dynamically performed and checked by the TAG editor[9]. Thus learners could select words from some menu interface (see Figure 20) and get to see the various operations displayed on the TAG editor (see Figure 21):

Enter word: arrivera		Menu Show morphological entries Show syntactic entries

Morphological Lexicon arrivera:[arriver],V{<mode>=ind,<pers>=3,<num>=sing,<tense>=fut}. arriver:[arriver],V{<mode>=inf}. arrive:[arriver],V{<mode>=ind/subj,<pers>=1/3,<num>=sing,<tense>=pres}. arrives:[arriver],V{<mode>=ind/subj;<pers>=2,<num>=sing,<tense>=pres}. arrivent:[arriver],V{<mode>=ind/subj;<pers>=3,<num>=pl,<tense>=pres}. arrivé:[arriver],V{<mode>=ppart,<num>=sing,<gen>=masc}.

Syntactic Lexicon [arriver], V : n0V(pn1){p:<loc>=+}. %to come %= arrivée [arriver], V;que,C : s0V{s0:<mode>=subj, extrap=+}. %to happen [arriver], V;à,P : n0Vps1{s1:<mode>=inf}. %to succeed	Menu Show elementary trees Show related French entries Show related English entries Show example sentences

Figure 20. Lexicon menus

9 This TAG editor exists in two versions: one for Symbolics machines, the other for Suns and Unix machines [29]. The same for the TAG parser.

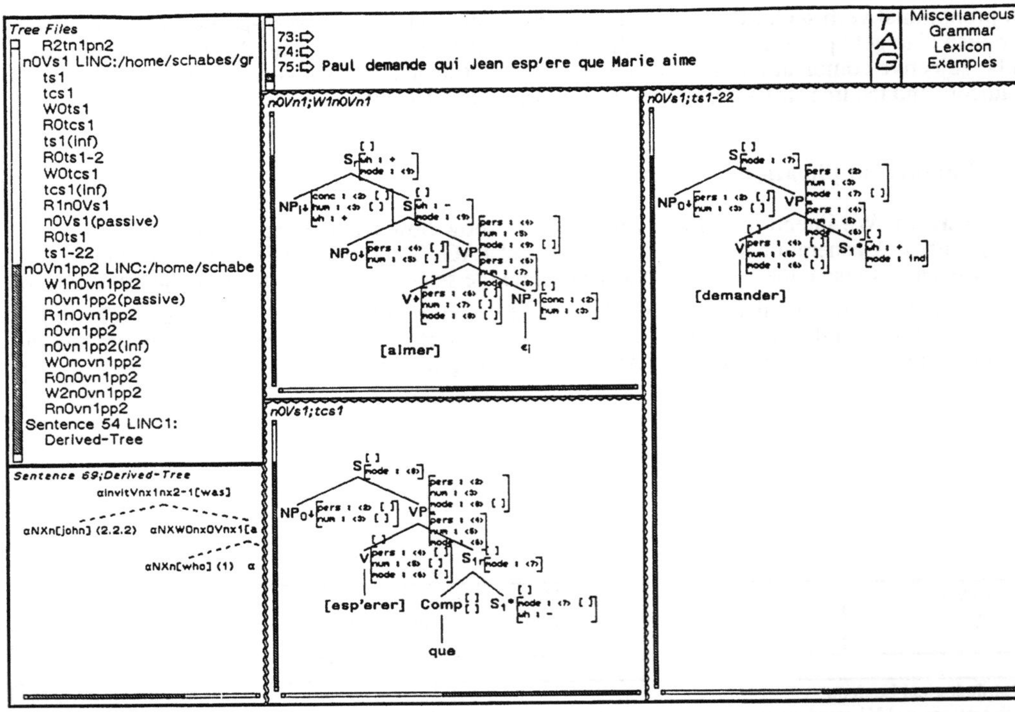

Figure 21. The TAG editor

The learner types an inflected form and can access both the morphological file or the syntactic file. If he chooses the morphological file (*show morphological entries*), he is shown the different lemmas corresponding to the form he has entered; if there is only one, he is shown some other inflected forms as well for the same lemma. If he chooses the syntactic file (*show syntactic entries*), he is shown the different entries corresponding to the lemma of the form he has entered. He can then click on a syntactic entry and access another menu for displaying either some trees corresponding to this entry (*show elementary trees*), some example sentences, some paraphrastic entries (*show related French entries*) or some English possible translations (*show related English entries*).

The TAG editor is a multi-window system which displays tree structures as well as excerpts from the lexicon file. It is interfaced with a parser and the upper window is for typing a sentence to be parsed. The window down to the left shows a derivation tree corresponding to an input sentence and the corresponding derived tree will be shown if the user asks for it. The other windows shown here display elementary trees from the data-base, the upper right window lists some tree files (tree families) from this data-base. A menu is associated to each tree window, the user can thus perform substitutions or adjunctions between the trees displayed and the resulting derived tree will show up dynamically in another window.

The interesting aspect of TAGs is their extended domain of locality which ensures that the learner always manipulates syntactic units of semantic significance. Combinations of such elementary trees can be ruled out either by the shape of the tree itself (if there is no match between the categories of the nodes in contact) or by some other incompatible features of the nodes in contact. In the complete version of the grammar, there are features which are quite elaborate linguistically and might be difficult to explain to a learner. But in a simplified version, only "intuitive" features could be used: agreement features (number, person, gender), mode of the verb for finite or embedded clauses and human/ non human features for selectional restrictions on subjects or complements.

When our semantic network is done and a parser for synchronous TAGs fully implemented, our system will be able to generate some possible paraphrases of a given sentence. It could be called upon by the learner who has not understood a given sentence or to help learners who want to write or express themselves in a richer French.

Parsing. Our French grammar has been interfaced with a specific parser for Lexicalized TAGs fully described in [33]. This parsing system can be used as such in order to check the learner's inputs (when answering questions for example). As for now, the parser gives only the result "correct" or "uncorrect" and some software would have to be added in order to explain what kind of ill-formedness is involved.

In order to take full advantage of the lexicalization of the grammar, the parser follows the off-line parsing strategy defined by [31]. It first scans the input string, loading the corresponding subset of the grammar and attaching the elementary trees with their lexical heads. It then parses the sentence in a standard way. An on-line strategy could also be designed [33]. Standard techniques defined after [10] for robust parsing could also be adapted if one wants to use our grammar in a more "communicative" perspective.

More sophisticated forms of computer dialog could be designed if the grammar (together with the parser and the generator) is connected to a knowledge-base of some domain with its own semantic representation. The learner would have to ask his or her queries in French (with possible corrections) and would be answered back in French as well.

3. Conclusion

Formalisms defined in computational linguistics can be difficult to use for teaching purposes. Unification-based formalisms for example are based on complex feature-bundles which may be difficult to grasp and manipulate for a naive learner (see [11], this volume). The risk is then to teach the learner the specifics of the formalism instead of teaching him or her the language to be taught. But if one wants to build up "intelligent" tutoring systems, and initiate a real dialogue with the user, one needs to use artificial intelligence techniques for natural language processing (for understanding the learner's input or to generate sentences corresponding to what the learner expects). One has thus to use formal linguistic representations of some sort.

We consider Lexicalized Tree Adjoining grammars to be a good candidate for several reasons:
- the formalism is quite flexible and completely lexicon-oriented. There is thus a natural match with exercises designed for enlarging the learner's lexical competence.
- the formalism is naturally "reversible" : it is not primarily parsing-oriented or generation-oriented. This is important for a dialog system.
- sizable grammars have been written for French and English over the past few years and are available for pedagogical experiments.

We have presented here this computational tree-based grammar for French. Numerous applications can be made for teaching purposes. The most immediate one is to use a sophisticated query-system linked to our lexico-syntactic data-base. This would be appropriate for advanced learners willing to check or extend their lexical knowledge. Another application would be to have learners build complex sentences out of simple ones by playing with the tree editor displaying some elementary structures in the language. This would be best adapted for beginners (although not limited to them). Further applications include robust parsing and game environments.

References

1. Abeillé A.: Light verb constructions and extraction out of NP in Tree Adjoining Grammar, Papers from the 24th Regional Meeting of the Chicago Linguistic Society, Chicago 1988
2. Abeillé, A.: Parsing French with a Tree Adjoining Grammar, Proceedings of COLING'88, Budapest 1988
3. Abeillé A., Schabes Y.: Parsing idioms with a lexicalized Tree Adjoining Grammar, Proceedings of the 4th European Conference of the Association of Computational Linguistics, Manchester 1989
4. Abeillé A., Bishop K., Cote S., Joshi A., Schabes Y.: Lexicalized TAGs, parsing and lexicon, Proceedings of the DARPA Speech and Natural Language Workshop, Philadelphia 1989
5. Abeillé A., Bishop K., Cote S., Schabes Y.: "A lexicalized Tree Adjoining Grammar for English", Technical Report, CIS Dept, Univ. of Pennsylvania, Philadelphia, march 1990
6. Abeillé A., Schabes Y., Joshi A.: Using lexicalized TAGs for machine translation, Proceedings of COLING'90, Helsinki 1990
7. Abeillé, A.: Lexical and syntactic rules in a Tree Adjoining Grammar, Proceedings of the 29th ACL meeting, Pittsburgh 1990
8. Abeillé A., Une grammaire lexicalisée d'arbres adjoints pour le français, PhD thesis, University of Paris 7, Paris 1991
9. Abeillé, A.: "L'unification dans une grammaire d'arbres adjoints: quelques exemples en syntaxe française", T.A. Informations, Bulletin de l'ATALA, Paris 1991
10. Carbonell J., Hayes P. : Coping with extra-grammaticality, Proceedings of COLING'84, Stanford, 1984
11. Chanier, T., Pengelly, M. & Self, J. Conceptual modelling in error analysis in computer-assisted language learning systems (this volume)
12. Danlos L.: Support verb constructions: linguistic properties, representation, translation, Journal of French Language Studies, Cambridge University Press (1991)
13. Demaizière, F. & Blanvillain, O. Learners' intuitions, misconceptions and errors (this volume)
14. Giry-Schneider, J.: Les nominalisations en français. L'opérateur Faire dans le lexique, Droz, Genève 1978
15. Giry-Schneider, J: Les prédicats nominaux en français. Les phrases simples à verbe support, Droz, Genève, 1987
16. Gross, M.: Méthodes en syntaxe, Hermann, Paris 1975
17. Gross, M.: Les bases empiriques de la notion de prédicat sémantique, Langages, n°63, Larousse, Paris 1981
18. Gross, M.: Classification des phrases figées en français, Revue Québécoise de Linguistique, Montréal 1982
19. Gross, M.: Lexicon grammar: The representation of compound words, Proceedings of COLING'86, Bonn 1986
20. Gross, M.: Les expressions figées en Français, Technical Report, LADL, University of Paris 7, Paris 1989
21. Joshi A., Levy L., Takahashi M.: Tree Adjunct Grammars, Journal of the Computer and System Sciences, 10:1 (1975)
22. Joshi, A.: Introduction to Tree Adjoining Grammar, in A. Manaster Ramer (ed), The Mathematics of Language, J. Benjamins 1987
23. Joshi, A.: The relevance of Tree Adjoining Grammar to generation, in G. Kempen (ed), Natural language generation: new results in AI, psychology and linguistics, Dordrecht, Kluwer 1987
24. Juilland A., Brodin D., Davidovitch C.: Frequency dictionary of French words: 5000 words, Mouton, The Hague 1970
25. Kroch A., Joshi A.: "Some aspects of the linguistic relevance of Tree Adjoining Grammar", Technical report, CIS Dept, University of Pennsylvania, Philadelphia 1985
26. MacWhinney B.: The competition model and foreign language acquisition (this volume)
27. Maratsos M., Chalkley M.: The internal language of children's syntax: the ontogenesis and representation of syntactic categories, in K. Nelson (ed), Children's language, vol 2, Gardner Press 1981
28. Miller, G.A. & Fellbaum, C. Wordnet and the organization of lexical memory (this volume)
29. Paroubek P., Schabes Y: Description of XTAG system, Technical Report, CIS Dept, University of Pennsylvania, Philadelphia 1991
30. Pinker S.: Language learnability and language developement, Harvard University Press 1984
31. Schabes Y., Abeillé A., Joshi A.: Parsing strategies with 'lexicalized' grammars: an application to Tree Adjoining Grammars, Proceedings of COLING'88, Budapest 1988
32. Schabes Y, Joshi A.: An Earley-type parsing algorithm for Tree Adjoining Grammars, Proceedings of the 26th ACL meeting, Buffalo 1988

33. Schabes Y., Joshi A.: Parsing lexicalized TAGs, in M. Tomita (ed), Current Issues in Parsing Technologies, Kluwer 1990
34. Shieber S., Schabes Y.: Generation and synchronous TAGs, Proceedings of the 3d International Workshop on generation, Pittsburgh 1990
35. Shieber S., Schabes Y.: Synchronous Tree Adjoining Grammars, Proceedings of COLING'90, Helsinki 1990
36. Swartz, M. L.: Issues for tutoring knowledge in foreign language intelligent tutoring systems (this volume)
37. Vijay-Shanker K.: A study of Tree Adjoining grammar, PhD Thesis, University of Pennsylvania, Philadelphia 1987
38. Vijay-Shanker K., Joshi A.: A Feature-based Tree Adjoining Grammar, Proceedings of COLING'88, Budapest 1988 (Journal of Computational Linguistics, 1991, forthcoming)
39. Zock, M. SWIM or sink: The problem of communicating thought (this volume)

WordNet and the Organization of Lexical Memory

George A. Miller and Christiane Fellbaum

Cognitive Science Laboratory, Princeton University, 221 Nassau St., Princeton, NJ 08540

Abstract: Mastering vocabulary is a major component of foreign language learning, and a better understanding of the mental lexicon should facilitate the development of better instructional strategies. A sampling of psycholinguistic research into the organization of semantic memory in bilinguals suggests that much more is involved in acquiring a second vocabulary than simply matching new words with concepts already lexicalized in the first language. The semantic relations among groups of words can be very different in two languages. How an accomplished bilingual maintains two different relational structures in semantic memory is not clear, but it is clear that learners need assistance in mastering semantic relations as well as semantic denotations. WordNet, an on-line lexical database for English based on psycholinguistic principles, provides a description of the goal for this relational part of the language learning task. It is suggested that semantic networks like WordNet would be valuable aids in teaching second language learners the semantic structures of an unfamiliar language.

Keywords: Lexical matrix, on-line lexical database, semantic network, semantic relation, vocabulary learning

1. The Importance of Vocabulary

The problems faced by people who set out to learn a foreign language vary depending on the language they start from and the language they aspire to, but one task is always daunting regardless of the language—the task of mastering a new vocabulary. There is general agreement that the most serious errors a novice can make are those that invite misunderstanding [5], and unfamiliar words are the surest source of such errors.

The English lexicon is so large—there are English dictionaries with half a million words—that vocabulary acquisition becomes especially critical for anyone learning English as a second language. The vocabulary of the average American high school graduate has been estimated at around 40,000 words [19], but that is only the beginning; learning new words is a lifetime preoccupation for anyone who remains intellectually active. Most other languages are less demanding. Hebrew or Arabic, for example, have a relatively small inventory of distinct word roots and make extensive use of morphology to derive new words. Learners report that they can acquire the vocabulary for these languages more easily than they can learn the vocabulary of languages like French or German, for example. But even in highly inflected languages, a learner must acquire the meanings of several thousand new words. If intelligent tutoring systems could provide significant help with this learning task, untold person-years of intellectual labor might be saved for more productive uses.

NATO ASI Series, Vol. F 80
Intelligent Tutoring Systems for Foreign Language Learning
Edited by M. L. Swartz and M. Yazdani

Considering its importance, it is regrettable that more is not known about the mastery of foreign vocabularies. A central question in research on the bilingual lexicon has been how two sets of words can be stored with respect to each other and to the concepts they express [9]. To learn a word is to make it a part of your mental lexicon, so the cognitive structure of your mental lexicon must have important consequences for the learning process. Some investigations have now begun to shed light on how expert bilinguals organize their lexical knowledge and gain access to it ([15], [18], [23], [26], [27]), but little is yet known about how novices build such bilingual knowledge structures or what methods of instruction would be most helpful.

Since the nature of the connections between two (or more) vocabularies poses a fundamental question for attempts to facilitate the word learning process, it is important to be explicit about its formulation. Consider first how lexical knowledge for a single language might be organized.

2. The Lexical Matrix

At least since Saussure [25] it has been recognized that *a word is a conventional association between a concept and an utterance that plays a syntactic role.* Since "word" is commonly used to refer not only to the union of concept and utterance, but also to the utterance itself or to the concept it can be used to express, it helps to avoid confusion if the utterance (or inscription) is referred to as a *word form* (or word image) and the associated concept is referred to as a *word meaning*. (In a similar vein, McWhinney, this volume, refers to the phonological and syntactic characteristics of a word as its "cues," and to its semantic and communicative properties as as "functions.") The word form and the word meaning are not independent things; they are like the outside and the inside of a single entity. That is to say, there are utterances (and inscriptions) that are not word forms, just as there are concepts that are not word meanings; a form becomes a word form, or a concept becomes a word meaning, by virtue of incorporation in a psychological unit that can be referred to simply as a *word.*

Although it is necessary to insist on the integrity of the word as a synthesis of sound and meaning, the starting point for lexical semantics is the conventional mapping between word forms and word meanings. A basic question for the theorist is how that mapping should be represented. One possibility is to draw a diagram. Psycholinguists frequently formulate their hypotheses about language processes as box-and-arrow diagrams that resemble the flow charts of computer science (except that it is often unclear what is flowing between psycholinguistic boxes). The mapping between word forms and word meanings can be represented in that manner. The diagram would have two boxes with arrows between them, one box labeled Forms and the other box labeled Meanings. The arrows would indicate that a speaker or writer might start with a meaning and look for appropriate forms to express it, or that a listener or reader might start with a form and retrieve the appropriate meanings. The value of such a box-and-arrow diagram is that it makes clear the distinction between morphology (the Form box) and semantics (the Meaning box)—between the form:form relations that characterize theories of word formation and the meaning:meaning relations that characterize theories of linguistic semantics. The trouble with such a diagram, however, is that it provides no help in describing how particular meanings are mapped onto particular forms. And it leaves the contents of the Meaning box unspecified.

Mappings are better thought of as matrices [19]. Table 1 is offered to make the idea of a lexical matrix more explicit. Word forms provide the headings for the columns of the matrix; word meanings are headings for the rows. An entry in a cell of the matrix indicates that the meaning in that row can be expressed by the form in that column. Thus, the entry $E_{i,j}$ indicates that word meaning M_i can be expressed by word form F_j. If there are two entries in the same column, that word form is said to be *polysemous*; if there are two entries in the same row, those two word forms are said to be *synonymous* (relative to a context). The mapping is many:many—some forms have several different meanings and some meanings can be expressed by several different forms. Thus, two difficult lexicographic problems, polysemy and synonymy, can be seen as complementary aspects of this mapping.

Table 1. Illustrating the Concept of a Lexical Matrix.
(F_1 and F_2 are synonyms; F_2 is polysemous)

Word Meanings	Word Forms F_1	F_2	F_3	. . .	F_n
M_1	$E_{1,1}$	$E_{1,2}$			
M_2		$E_{2,2}$			
M_3			$E_{3,3}$		
⋮				. . .	
M_m					$E_{m,n}$

The lexical matrix merely formulates the problem, it does not solve it. It is still necessary to characterize the morphological structure of a vocabulary in terms of rules that relate different columns of the matrix, and to characterize its semantic structure in terms of meaning relations between rows of the matrix (see [1] for an approach to this problem).

The question of how word meanings should be represented is still unanswered, however. One possibility, a simplification of standard lexicographic practices, has been adopted in WordNet and will be discussed below. For the moment, assume that some workable solution is available and consider instead the bilingual question: how can lexical matrices for two different languages be combined?

3. The Bilingual Lexical Matrix

A first question for bilingual lexicology is how words in two different languages are associated. How, for example, does a bilingual German-American know that *horse* and *Pferd* can be used to refer to the same animals? Different logical possibilities can be outlined. For example:

(1) *Independence*: bilinguals may have two independent lexical matrices, one for each language.

(2) *Word association*: bilinguals may have a single lexical matrix for their first language, plus a word:word mapping of new word forms onto the word forms of the first language.

(3) *Concept mediation*: bilinguals may have a single lexical matrix with a single set of concepts, but have an enlarged set of word forms that can be used to express those concepts.

All three possibilities have been endorsed in one form or another by different students of the bilingual lexicon.

Most researchers reject the first hypothesis—independent language-specific semantic representations—although some parts of the lexicon, particularly prepositions and modal verbs, are so difficult to translate that it is hard to believe that they would not be learned independently. Hypothesis (1) is probably incorrect for nouns that refer to concrete objects, although Kolers [15] found that bilinguals do give somewhat different word associations in their two languages, especially for words referring to abstractions or to emotions (unless the words are cognates, like the French-English *courage* [30]). The principal criticism of (1) is that it fails to account for the observation that most skilled bilinguals find it easy to translate words from one language to the other.

The second hypothesis would seem to follow from the conventional paired-associate method of teaching vocabulary. It is not clear, however, that anyone has defended (2) as a plausible characterization of expert bilinguals, although something like it might be attributed to McCormack [18], who argued that bilinguals have two sets of word forms that are "tagged" as belonging to one language or the other. The most obvious criticism of (2) is that many words in one language cannot be translated by a single word in the other language.

Most researchers have adopted some form of hypothesis (3). Experiments indicate that equivalent words in two languages are connected in a bilingual's or a learner's lexicon via one underlying nonlinguistic concept [23, 27]. Thus, if a word form F_1 in the speaker's native language is associated with a word meaning M_i that can be expressed by a word form F_2 in another language, the speaker will not associate F_2 with F_1 directly; the association between the two word forms will be mediated by the common word meaning M_i. In other words, the relation of the foreign language word to the concept it expresses is assumed to be the same as the relation of the corresponding word in the native language to the same concept; the two word forms are simply regarded as synonyms (relative to a context). Although (3) makes no explicit provisions for indicating which word forms belong to which language, presumably the language tag is provided by context, that is to say, by the different morphological relations and syntactic rules that apply to words in the two vocabularies. The principal criticism of (3) is that it is too simple; it it makes no allowance for structural differences between vocabularies.

This criticism raises a second question for students of bilingual lexicology: are words and concepts related to other words and concepts in the second language in the same way as in the speaker's native language, or does their organization as a lexical system differ between the two languages? Differences in the morphological relations between word forms in different languages are notorious, and pose major obstacles for second language learners. The possibility that semantic relations may also differ and may also pose learning problems has not been as widely recognized. But it is at least conceivable that two vocabularies could both contain word forms with similar morphologies, both expressing all the same word meanings, yet the semantic relations between word meanings in the two languages could be very different.

Most of the experiments that have involved relations between equivalent words in two languages have assumed implicitly that the position of a form-meaning pair in one lexical structure is the same as that of the equivalent form-meaning pair in the other lexical structure. For example, Kirsner et al. [14] found cross-language priming—in a lexical decision task, if bilinguals saw *horse*, say, it facilitated the subsequent recognition of either *cow* or *Kuh*—which indicates that these concepts are similarly related in the two languages. Further experiments reported by Smith [27] involved repetition priming with semantically related items; the results indicate that the priming that results from activating a word meaning will facilitate word-fragment completion in either language. Potter et al.'s [23] experiments with bilinguals involved matching an item to a superordinate term; no cross-linguistic differences were found. Bilingual tasks involving both category matching and the production of category names have also shown similar results for both languages [6, 26].

The results of these and other related experiments are suggestive but somewhat inconclusive; they support the notion that relations between word forms in different languages are conceptually mediated, but they do not seem to permit a firm answer to questions concerning the organization of the mental lexicon of multilingual speakers. How one relational structure can be combined with another relational structure is a far more complicated question than how two word forms might express the same concept.

Examination of a specific instance should make the importance of the relational structure of a lexical system more apparent. WordNet illustrates one way to represent such a structure.

4. WordNet

Psycholinguistic evidence collected over several decades points to an organization of lexical knowledge in terms of an associative network, where semantic and lexical relations link both word forms and word meanings. At Princeton University's Cognitive Science Laboratory a group of psychologists, linguists, and lexicographers have been exploiting psycholinguistic principles in order to construct WordNet, an on-line lexical database of English organized as a *semantic network* [2, 20]. The scope of this database, which presently contains some 54,000 different word forms that are mapped onto some 49,000 different word meanings, has raised new questions about the structure of the lexicon and led to modifications of previous assumptions based on experiments that tested only small samples of the lexicon.

WordNet is organized as a lexical matrix. Word forms are represented by English words written in standard orthography; the difficult question is how word meanings should be represented. The solution adopted in WordNet is to represent word meanings by sets of *synonyms*, or *synsets*—the set of words that can be used (in appropriate contexts) to express the concept. In other words, the word meaning M_1 in Table 1 can be represented by simply listing the word forms that can be used to express it: $\{F_1, F_2, \ldots\}$ in this example. This solution assumes that the database will be used by someone who has already acquired the concept and needs merely to identify it. These synsets will not suffice to enable a user to acquire a new concept. For example, someone who knows that the English word *board* can signify either a piece of lumber or a group of people assembled for some purpose will be able to pick out the intended word meaning from the synsets {*board, plank*} and {*board, committee*}. But someone unfamiliar with *board* could not easily discover its meanings from such cryptic pairings.

In WordNet, therefore, the lexical matrix is represented as a mapping between written word forms and synsets. Since English is rich in synonyms, synsets are often sufficient for differential purposes. Sometimes, however, an appropriate synonym is not available, and then the ambiguity may be resolved by a short gloss or definition. For example, the one-word synset {*board*, (a person's meals, provided regularly for money)} can serve to differentiate this sense of *board* from the others. A defining phrase serves much the same purpose as a synonym, except that it is not used as a column head and no one would know to look it up in the database.

Once synsets are available to represent word meanings, various other *semantic relations* can be represented by *pointers between synsets* [20, 21]. (However, synonymy, the fundamental semantic relation in WordNet, is indicated by the brackets "{" and "}" rather than by a labeled pointer.) Although a great variety of semantic relations can be (and have been) described, the following relations used in WordNet appear to be cognitive universals. That is to say, these semantic relations seem to be found in every language, although the particular words or word meanings that they relate will be language specific.

4.1 Synonymy: According to one definition, two expressions are synonymous if the substitution of one for the other does not change the truth value of sentences in which the substitution is made. By that definition, true synonyms are rare, if they exist at all. A weakened notion makes synonymy relative to a context. Two expressions are said to be synonymous in a context C if the substitution of one for the other in C does not alter the truth value. For example, *plank* and *board* are synonyms relative to most carpentry contexts, although in other contexts that substitution would be totally inappropriate.

The definition of synonymy in terms of substitutability makes it necessary to partition WordNet into nouns, adjectives, and verbs. If concepts are represented by synsets, and if synonyms must be interchangeable in a context, then words in different syntactic categories cannot be synonyms (cannot form synsets) because they are not interchangeable.

The definition of synonymy in terms of truth values seems to make synonymy discrete: two words either are synonyms or they are not. It is widely recognized, however, that synonymy is best thought of as one end of a continuum along which likeness of meaning can be graded. The gradability of *semantic similarity* is ubiquitous, but it is most important for understanding the organization of adjectival meanings.

4.2 Antonymy: Another familiar relation serving to organize word meanings is *antonymy*. Everyone recognizes antonymic pairs of words, but the relation is surprisingly difficult to define. The antonym of a word F is sometimes *not*-F, but not always. *Big* and *little* are antonyms, although something that is not big is not necessarily little.

Antonymy is a relation between words, not a relation between word meanings. For example, the meanings {*rise, ascend*} and {*fall, descend*} are conceptual opposites, but they are not antonyms; *rise/fall* are antonyms and so are *ascend/descend*. Few people would agree that *rise/descend* or *ascend/fall* are antonyms; Gross et al. [10] refer to them as indirect antonyms. The relation of direct antonymy is represented in WordNet by labeled pointers between the antonymous words. Antonymy provides a central organizing principle for adjectives in WordNet; adjectives having no direct antonym are entered as semantically similar to adjectives that do have.

4.3 Hyponymy: Noun concepts are organized largely by the *hyponymy/hypernymy* (otherwise known as the ISA relation, or subordinate/superordinate, or the subset/superset). A lexical concept represented by the synset $\{F_1, F_2, \ldots\}$ is said to be a hyponym of the concept represented by the synset $\{G_1, G_2, \ldots\}$ if native speakers accept sentences of the form, "An F is a (kind of) G." For example, both *fall* and *descent* are kinds of motions or movements, so a pointer labeled "hyponym" can be inserted from the synset {*motion, movement*} to the synset {*fall, descent*}.

Hyponymy is asymmetrical and transitive, and, since there is normally a single hypernym, it generates a hierarchical or taxonomic semantic structure. Such hierarchical representations are widely used in information retrieval systems, where they are called inheritance systems: a hyponym inherits all the features of its hypernym, plus at least one additional feature that distinguishes it from the hypernym and from all other hyponyms of that hypernym.

4.4 Meronymy: The semantic relation that reflects the part-whole relation is known as *meronymy/holonymy* (or the HASA relation). A concept represented by the synset $\{F_1, F_2\}$ is said to be a meronym of the concept represented by the synset $\{G_1, G_2\}$ if native speakers of English accept sentences constructed from such frames as "An F is a part of G" or "A G has an F as a part." The part-whole relation, relative to an object (or the image of an object), is hierarchical, but meronymy as a semantic relation is much more complex. A particular word meaning can be a meronym of many different holonyms; think, for example, how many things have handles as a part.

The semantic relation of meronymy is represented in WordNet by labeled pointers between synsets. Since the features of a concept are inherited by its hyponyms, all of the parts of a hypernym will also be parts of a hyponym. For example, having entered into the database that {*brim, rim*} is a meronym of *cup* and that *teacup* is a hyponym of *cup*, the fact that {*brim, rim*} is also a meronym of *teacup* need not be entered, but can be inferred from the relational structure. The interaction between hyponymy and meronymy in the noun lexicon can become very complicated.

4.5 Causal entailment: Semantic relations between active verbs rely heavily on *entailments*: the activity denoted by verb V_1 entails the activity denoted by verb V_2 if V_1 cannot occur without V_2 also occurring. For example, the activity of killing x cannot occur without x dying, so *kill* entails *die*. Thus, the semantic relation between *kill* and *die* is an example of causal entailment.

4.6 Troponymy: Another common entailment relation between verbs is *troponymy*. If V_1 is a manner of doing V_2, then V_1 is a troponym of V_2. For example, marching is a manner of walking, so *march* is a troponym of *walk*. Troponymy for verbs resembles hyponymy for nouns, although important differences make it inadvisable to use the same term for both [8].

Verbs exhibit the most complex semantic organization; in addition to causal entailment and troponymy, they are linked by other forms of entailment and by lexical opposition. The information about verbs that is coded in WordNet also includes "sentence frames" specifying the more important selectional restrictions and semantic subcategorization features [7].

These and a few other semantic relations serve to organize WordNet. The result is a complex network highly interconnected by labeled pointers. Knowing where a word's meaning is located in this network is a significant part of knowing the word. There is enough structure to hold each word meaning in its place relative to the others, yet there is enough flexibility for the network to grow and change with learning.

The most significant advantage of an on-line semantic network like WordNet over a conventional dictionary is that it links words by means of several relations other than synonymy and hypernymy. To the extent that such relational networks model the organization of lexical memory, it can be argued that they would be useful guides for language learners. The results reported in Swartz [28] with learners who had used her LEXNET-INSITU tutor indicate that an associative network representation for the lexicon is indeed an effective tool for vocabulary acquisition.

5. Matching Two Lexicons

If every language had the same morphological and conceptual structure, the conceptual mediation hypothesis would be sufficient to account for the bilingual lexicon: acquiring the vocabulary of a foreign language would be a simple matter of associating a foreign word form with the corresponding word meaning in the semantic network of the native language. In terms of WordNet, this would correspond to adding the foreign word form to the appropriate synset. This simple strategy does seem to work in some instances; the numbers 0 to 9, for example, where the underlying conceptual structure is the same in many different languages. Most of the psychological studies of the bilingual lexicon have used words for which this strategy is more or less plausible. Unfortunately, however, for any pair of languages L1 and L2, cross-linguistic comparisons will quickly reveal that many words in language L1 cannot be so simply matched with corresponding words in language L2, and vice versa. McWhinney [17] discusses the lexical mapping strategies learners employ to match the English and the German forms of the modal *would like to* in terms of his Competition Model. While his example involves syntactic differences between the two forms, we will concentrate here largely on semantic incongruities between the lexicons of two languages.

The following brief typology of the most common mismatches shows why the concept mediation hypothesis is insufficient, and why a single, multilingual semantic net would be difficult to construct.

5.1 Lexical Gaps: One type of lexical incongruence can be characterized as a one:zero mismatch, where one language has not lexicalized a given concept and lacks a corresponding word altogether. These *lexical gaps* (or lexical holes) constitute the most easily detectable differences between the lexicons of different languages; they have at times attracted the attention of anthropologists interested in cross-cultural categorization (the most celebrated but recently debunked example is the "snow" lexicon of the Eskimos [24]). In many cases, a language lacking a word that is lexicalized in another language can express the same concept by means of a modified superordinate term or a phrase. For example, Japanese, but not English, has distinct lexemes for older and younger sisters and brothers; English speakers must use such qualified noun phrases as *big sister* or *little brother*. There would be no node in a relational net of English to which these terms could be attached; they would have to be added as hyponyms of *brother* and *sister*. On the other hand, Japanese does not have a word corresponding to English *sibling*, so *brother* and *sister* would have to be attached directly below the concept {*family member, relative*}. These differences in the lexicons of English and Japanese would be reflected in a bilingual network in two ways: not all nodes would have labels both in English and Japanese, and the connections between nodes would not be valid for both languages.

Often, lexical gaps result from different lexicalization patterns, some of which can be shown to be quite systematic. For example, English has many more denominal verbs than German. That is to say, in English, nouns like *bank, floor, pocket,* and *toe* can also be used as verbs, whereas in German the corresponding words can be used only as nouns. To express the English verb concepts, German uses the superordinate verb plus an adverbial phrase; there would be no synset corresponding to this concept in a German net. (For a cross-linguistic survey of verb conflation patterns in general, see Talmy [29] and Levin and Rapoport [16].)

5.2 One:Many Matches: One:many matches constitute another common discrepancy between lexicons. In these cases, a speaker of L1 finds that a bilingual dictionary will return two or more words in L2 for one word in L1; looking up these several entries, the dictionary of L2 will in each case return the same one word of L1. An instructive example is provided by the verbs of throwing.[1] English has (at least) eight different verbs describing manners of throwing (*chuck, hurl, fling, toss, cast, sling, pitch, thrust*); some are very similar in meaning, others are not interchangeable in many contexts. The troponyms elaborate their

[1] We are indebted to Joe Psotka for stimulating discussions of these examples.

superordinate along different dimensions (propelling force, direction). The subtle meaning differences are partly manifested in different selectional restrictions; each troponym of *throw* co-occurs only with a subset of the semantic noun classes compatible with its superordinate. For example, you can *fling* yourself into a chair, *hurl* yourself in front of a bus, or *thrust* yourself into a crowd, but you cannot *chuck, toss, cast, sling,* or *pitch* yourself anywhere. In comparison, a German dictionary lists only two troponyms of *werfen*: *schleudern* and *schmeissen*. If one thinks of all the contexts in which the English verbs can be used, and compares them with all the contexts where the German verbs are appropriate, it becomes apparent that neither of the two German verbs can be simply matched with a subset of the English verbs; there is no common set of concepts that the two groups of troponyms express. The meanings of the eight English troponyms partially overlap with the meanings of the two German verbs. It would not be possible to add the German troponyms to the English synsets, or vice versa, because the relations linking the English verbs would not hold for the German verbs; adding the English verbs to the two verbs in a German synset would make it impossible to distinguish the meanings of the English verbs.

5.3 One:One Mismatches: In some cases, the meanings of a pair of words in L1 and L2 are quite close, but do not share all the same contexts, stylistic connotations, or subcategorization features. For example, English *eat* corresponds to the two German verbs *essen* and *fressen*. Whereas both German verbs translate as *eat* and could be regarded as synonyms, the verbs differ in their selectional restrictions: *essen* is reserved to denote people's food consumption; *fressen* refers to an animal's eating, or a meat-eating plant's ingestion. But *fressen* can also be used of human subjects if their eating manners are uncouth. *Fressen*, moreover, occurs with inanimate subjects in sentences like *Der Neid frisst ihn (Envy is eating him)*. In a single bilingual net, these stylistic and subcategorization restrictions that distinguish the two German verbs but that do not exist in English could not easily be accounted for under a single synset for *eat*, nor is there any obvious way to distinguish them as two hyponyms of *consume*.

5.4 Differences in Taxonomic Levels: Even if two languages lexicalize the same concepts, the semantic relations between them and other concepts in the same language may not be identical in both languages. Heltai [11], in comparing English and Hungarian noun taxonomies, notes that the hyponymic relations that hold between two words in one language do not necessarily hold between the corresponding two words in the other language. For example, English speakers generally judge the superordinate of *chicken* to be *bird*; in Hungarian, on the other hand, people will respond with the Hungarian term for *animal* when asked what the superordinate of *csirke (chicken)* is. So in Hungarian, a noun phrase like *chicken and other birds* would be infelicitous, but phrases like *chicken and other animals* are attested. Such discrepancies in the hierarchical position of two otherwise equivalent words could be problematic for a multilingual network.

These examples show why the lexicons of different languages cannot be mapped completely onto the same network. The simple strategy of adding onto an English synset all of the foreign language words that express the same concept is not feasible. Which leaves something of a puzzle. It is obvious that bilingual individuals do manage to maintain rather different semantic structures in one head, but it is equally obvious that psycholinguists do not yet understand how it is done. In that situation, it would be rash to try to build a bilingual WordNet to simulate the lexical knowledge of an accomplished bilingual individual.

This argument does not imply, however, that semantic networks like WordNet have no contribution to make to vocabulary instruction in a foreign language. Instead, the implication is that a learner who is trying to master a foreign vocabulary has much more to learn than the mere pairing of words in two languages, which prompts the suggestion that an opportunity to browse through a monolingual semantic net of the target language might be very profitable. The proposal, therefore, is that a semantic net similar to WordNet be constructed for second-language learners, who could use it to discover the relational structure of the unfamiliar lexicon as well as its translational equivalents.

6. Learning Words with an On-line Semantic Network

The following examples are intended to show, first, how the semantic and lexical relations coded in WordNet are superior to the information in a conventional dictionary, and, second, how a monolingual semantic network of for the target language would be preferable to a single multilingual net in helping a speaker of L1 acquire the vocabulary of L2. The examples are concentrated on the verb lexicon because the relations linking verbs are more complex than they are for other lexical categories. Most of the examples are drawn from German, a language familiar to the authors. Since German and English are closely related historically, the problems described here would surely be even worse for other languages.

6.1 Causation: The semantic relation of causal entailment links such English verbs as *raise* and *rise*, or *show* and *see*. In English, relatively few causatives are independently lexicalized. Instead, the analytic, or periphrastic, causative construction, with *cause to/make/have/get to*, is used productively, as in *She made/had him leave the room.* Some languages have virtually no lexicalized causatives and use only a causative morpheme. German resembles English in having some lexicalized causatives in addition to a productive auxiliary construction. But the causatives that are lexicalized in German are not always the same ones that are lexicalized in English. For example, German does not have a verb for (causative) *drop*, and uses a periphrastic causative, *fallen lassen (let fall)*, instead. When German speakers look up *drop* in a semantic network of English like WordNet, they will find a pointer labeled Cause from *drop* to *fall*, and so learn that English has a lexicalized causative here. Conversely, English speakers who look up the German (intransitive) verb *fallen* in a German net will not find a pointer to a German causative verb corresponding to English (transitive) *drop*, which will tell them that there is no lexicalized German causative in this case, and that causation must be expressed periphrastically. In a conventional dictionary, causatives and resultatives are not listed together, and a German user looking up intransitive *fall* would not, on the basis of his German lexicon, think of searching for an independently lexicalized causative, and so would not learn (in this instance) that English has one, *drop*.

English has a number of verbs that have both a transitive causative and an intransitive "anticausative" use. These verbs, which are mostly verbs of motion or change, include *grow, starve*, and *race*. In German, the corresponding class of verbs with both a causative and an anticausative meaning is much smaller; *wachsen (grow), verhungern (starve)*, and *rennen (race)* are intransitive, and cannot be used causatively. German speakers, when looking up the English equivalents of these verbs in WordNet, will find a pointer to a homographic verb with an anticausative meaning; they learn that they do not have to form a periphrastic causative. And English users of a German net, when searching for the German equivalent of a verb like *grow*, will not find a pointer to a German causative, enabling them to avoid using *wachsen* transitively, on the analogy with English.

6.2 Entailment: Many verb pairs in English are related by lexical entailment. For example, *snoring* entails *sleeping* because when one snores, one must necessarily sleep. Because no two languages lexicalize all the same verbal concepts, the net of one language will occasionally have an entailment pointer relating two synsets where another language is missing such a pointer, because either the entailed or the entailing concept is not lexicalized in one of the languages. For example, *ride* and *drive* are related by entailment in English; you cannot drive a vehicle without riding in it. In German, these two concepts are not distinguished; both are conflated in the verb *fahren*. A German learning English by browsing WordNet would be directed from one verb to the other by the entailment pointer, and so will learn both verbs and their semantic relation. English-speaking users of a German net will not find *fahren* to be related by entailment to another verb; they will be prevented from incorrectly using, say, *reiten (ride on the back of an animal)*, the German cognate of *ride*, because there will be no connection between *reiten* and *fahren*.

6.3 Troponymic and Opposition Relations: Of the several relations organizing the verb lexicon, troponymy, the manner relation, is the one most frequently coded in WordNet; many English verbs can be expressed as troponyms of other verbs. And English dictionaries define many verb meanings by giving a superordinate verb plus some modification. But if one tries to construct verb taxonomies with the troponymy relation, one realizes that verbs are not easily arranged into the same kinds of tree structures that nouns can be mapped into [7]. Verb hierarchies tend to have a more shallow, bushy structure where the number of hierarchical levels rarely exceeds four. Virtually every verb taxonomy shows a bulge, that is to say, a level far more richly lexicalized than the other levels in the hierarchy. The verbs of throwing, already considered, include at least eight troponyms of *throw*. Similarly, there are several dozen verbs denoting manners of walking, *hit* has some forty troponyms, and there are about 25 different verbs for manners of speaking. These troponyms in turn have very few troponyms of their own, and these are usually compounds rather than primary lexemes (e.g., *goose-step* is a troponym of *march*). Above the level of *walk, throw, hit,* and *speak*, the verb concepts usually define an entire semantic field (*move, touch,* and *communicate*).

The verb lexicons of other languages follow a similar pattern, with a single superordinate verb and a richly lexicalized level of troponyms. Moreover, the meanings of the verbs at the level of *move* and *walk* tend to be equivalent across languages, but the number and meanings of the troponyms differ considerably cross-linguistically. Comparing English and German verb hierarchies, we generally find that English has more troponyms; this is sometimes, but not always, due to the fact that English has both Germanic and Romance based words. The important point, however, is that the larger number of troponyms in English does not mean that there are more English synonyms to express the same number of lexicalized concepts as in German, where there are fewer but more polysemous verbs. Some English troponyms do not have a lexicalized counterpart in German, where their concepts must be expressed by the superordinate plus a qualifying expression. A German speaker using WordNet could learn the meanings of these English verbs, not only in relation to their superordinates, but also in relation to verbs with which they are in opposition.

In the class of change verbs, for example, English has more troponyms of *increase* and *decrease* than does German. Among these, the verbs *wax* and *wane* have rather limited uses, one of them being to refer to the phases of the moon. In German, the more general verbs *zunehmen* and *abnehmen* (corresponding to the superordinates {*gain, increase*} and {*lose, decrease*}) are used in this context. Here, the German superordinate verbs are more polysemous and have to cover a broader semantic area, where English has specialized hyponyms. Using WordNet, the learner of English would be pointed from *increase* to all its hyponyms, including *wax*. And *wax* would have an antonymic pointer to *wane*. A German who was learning English from dictionaries would have difficulty discovering these specialized antonyms; a conventional dictionary would not point the user from *wax* to *wane* or vice versa.

Browsing a semantic net for L2 and exploring hyponymic and antonymic relations between words can teach speakers of L1 the meanings of words they might otherwise use incorrectly due to interference from their native language. A case in point is the converse pair *borrow* and *lend*. Although German has two cognate verbs, *borgen* and *leihen*, these verbs are synonyms rather than converses; they express the concept of both *borrow* and *lend*, and a conventional bilingual dictionary lists both words with each of the English entries. To make the sense distinction in German, these verbs must be used in different syntactic constructions. Using a semantic net like WordNet, the German speaker who was learning English would be taught to distinguish the two English verbs, not as synonyms, but one as a hyponym of *give* and the other as a hyponym of *take*. As part of this information, WordNet tells the user that the syntactic frames for *borrow* and *lend* are the same as those of their respective superordinates, and thus differ from one another. Moreover, because converse verb pairs are linked by an opposition pointer in WordNet, the user would learn to associate these two English verbs as antonyms.

7. Conclusion

It seems apparent from these considerations that the acquisition of a bilingual vocabulary involves more than associating pairs of words from two languages, even when the association is mediated conceptually. The semantic structure of the second language poses additional problems for a learner, problems that cannot be resolved by consulting a standard dictionary, either bilingual or monolingual. Standard dictionaries do not prevent the learner from employing different paths of transfer [17], which will lead to incorrect L2 usage in many cases.

The proposal here is that much of the structural information omitted from conventional vocabulary instruction could be provided by semantic networks like WordNet. The question of how to teach vocabulary with associative networks has been discussed by Carter [5] and Comu [6]. Most teachers of foreign languages recognize the students' need for relational semantics. At George Mason University a group of linguists and English teachers have noted that teaching English vocabulary to foreign students is done more successfully when the new words are presented in semantically related groups. By their method of enriching vocabulary instruction [12, 13], adjectives are taught in clusters around antonymic pairs, nouns are taught as hyponyms of other nouns, and verbs are presented as groups of troponyms. Swarts [28] describes the preliminary use of an intelligent tutor for vocabulary learning based on an associative network. Their results indicate the effectiveness of such a model of lexical knowledge. The success of these various efforts lends some credence to the present suggestion that semantic networks designed along the lines of WordNet might be valuable aids in mastering the vocabulary of a foreign language.

Acknowledgements

Work on WordNet has been supported in part by contract N00014-86-K-0492, with funding provided by the Navy Personnel Research and Development Center and the Manpower, Personnel and Training Research Program of the Office of Naval Research; in part by contract MDA 903-86-K-0242 with the Army Research Institute; and in part by a grant from the the

James S. McDonnell Foundation. The views and conclusions contained herein are those of the authors and should not be represented as official policies or ONR, ARI, the McDonnell Foundation, or Princeton University.

References

1. Abeille, A.: A lexicalized Tree Adjoining Grammar for French and its relevance to language teaching. (This Volume)
2. Beckwith, R., Fellbaum, C., Gross, D., & Miller, G. A.: WordNet: A lexical database organized on psycholinguistic principles. In Zernik, U. (Ed.), Using on-line resources to build a lexicon. Hillsdale, NJ: Erlbaum in press
3. Birdsong, D., & Kassen, M. A.: Teacher's and students evaluations of foreign language errors: A meeting of minds? Modern Language Journal, 72, 1-12 (1988)
4. Caramazza, A., & Brones, I.: Semantic classification by bilinguals. Canadian Journal of Psychology, 34, 77-81 (1980)
5. Carter, R.: Vocabulary and second/foreign language teaching. Language Teaching, 2, 3-16 (1987)
6. Comu, A-M.: The first step in vocabulary teaching. Modern Language Journal, 63, 262-272 (1979)
7. Fellbaum, C.: English verbs as a semantic net. International Journal of Lexicography, 3/4, 278-301 (1990)
8. Fellbaum, C., and Miller, G. A.: Folk psychology or semantic entailment: A reply to Rips and Conrad. Psychological Review, 97, 565-570 (1990)
9. Green, D.: Control, activation and resource: A framework and a model for the control of speech in bilinguals. Brain and Language, 27, 210-23 (1986)
10. Gross, D., Fischer, U. & Miller, G. A.: The organization of adjectival meanings. Journal of Language and Memory, 28, 92-106 (1989)
11. Heltai, P.: Hierarchical lexical relations in English and Hungarian. In Proceedings of BudaLEX '88 (T. Magay and J Zigany, eds.). Budapest: Akademiai Kiado in press
12. Holisky, D. A., Tretcher, K., and Trump, S.: Walk, amble, stroll: Teaching vocabulary in semantic fields. Paper presented at the 24th Annual TESOL Convention, San Francisco, March 1990
13. Holisky, D. A., Tretcher, K., and Trump, S.: Vocabulary in domains. Boston, Mass.: Heinle and Heinle in press
14. Kirsner, K., Smith, M. C., Lockhart, R. S., King, M. L., & Jain, M.: The bilingual lexicon: Language specific units in an integrated network. Journal of Verbal Learning and Verbal Behavior, 23, 519-39 (1984)
15. Kolers, P. A.: Interlingual word associations. Journal of Verbal Learning and Verbal Behavior, 2, 291-300 (1964)
16. Levin, B., & Rapoport, T.: Lexical subordination. In Papers from the 24th Annual Regional Meeting of the Chicago Linguistic Society (L. MacLeod, G. Larson, & D. Brentani, eds.), pp. 275-289. Chicago: Chicago Linguistic Society 1988
17. MacWhinney, B.: The competition model and foreign language acquisition. (This volume)
18. McCormack, P. D.: Language as an attribute of memory. Canadian Journal of Psychology, 30, 238-248 (1976)
19. Miller, G. A.: Dictionaries in the mind. Language and Cognitive Processes, 1, 171-185 (1986)
20. Miller, G. A., Beckwith, R., Fellbaum, C., Gross, D., & Miller, K. J.: Introduction to WordNet: An on-line lexical database. International Journal of Lexicography, 314, 235-244 (1990)
21. Miller, G. A., & Fellbaum, C.: Semantic networks of English. Cognition (to appear)
22. Nagy, W. E., & Herman, P. A.: Breadth and depth of vocabulary knowledge: Implications for acquisition and instruction. In The Nature of Vocabulary Acquisition (M. G. McKeown & M. E. Curtis, eds.). Hillsdale, NJ: Lawrence Erlbaum Associates 1987
23. Potter, M., So, K-F., Von Eckhardt, B., & Feldman, L.: Lexical and conceptual representations in beginning and proficient bilinguals. Journal of Verbal Learning and Verbal Behavior, 23, 23-38 (1984)
24. Pullum, J.: The great Eskimo vocabulary hoax. Natural Language and Linguistic Theory, 7, 275-281 (1989)
25. de Saussure, F.: Course in general linguisncs. New York: Philosophical Library 1926/1959
26. Shanon, B.: Identification and classification of words and drawings in two languages. Quarterly Journal of Experimental Psychology, 34, 135-152 (1982)

27. Smith, M. C.: Accessing the bilingual dictionary. In Resolving semantic ambiguity (D. Gorfein, ed.), pp. 109-125. New York: Springer 1989
28. Swartz, M. L.: Issues for representing tutoring knowledge in foreign language intelligent tutoring systems. (This volume)
29. Talmy, L.: Lexicalization patterns: Semantic structure in lexical forms. In Language Typology and Syntactic Description, vol. 3, Grammatical Categories and the Lexicon (T. Shopen, ed.), pp.57-149. New York: Cambridge University Press 1985
30. Taylor, I.: Similarity between French and English words—A factor to be considered in bilingual language behavior? Journal of Psycholinguistic Research, 5, 85-94 (1976)

Semantic Discourse Processing and Tutoring Systems for Second Language Learning

Carl H. Frederiksen[1], Janet Donin[1], Michel Décary[2] and Michael Hoover[1]

[1]Laboratory of Applied Cognitive Science, McGill University, 3700 McTavish St., Montréal, Canada H3A 1Y2
[2]Recherches Neurox Inc., 1405 rue Bishop, Suite 100, Montréal, Canada H3G 2E4

Abstract: A stratified model of discourse comprehension and production is presented and its implications for second language learning are discussed. A distinction is made between language-specific syntactic and semantic processing at the sentence level, and nonanguage-specific conceptual and semantic processing at the discourse level. Results from studies of discourse comprehension in bilinguals that support this distinction are described. A computer model of semantic processing of sentences and its application to intelligent tutoring systems for developing syntactic and semantic processing skills in a second language are discussed. The problem of developing proficiency in applying discourse level conceptual and semantic processing to texts in the second language is considered.

Keywords: Discourse processing, semantic representation, second language comprehension, cognitive models, computer models, intelligent tutoring systems

1. Semantics and Second Language Learning

Second language learning, when viewed as a cognitive process, is similar to other situations of complex knowledge and skill acquisition in which what is acquired is proficiency in performing a class of complex information processing tasks. The objective of second language learning is discourse communication skill, that is, proficiency in the comprehension and production of connected discourse in a second language. Discourse comprehension is a complex multilevel semantic process in which discourse is understood in terms of its sentence meanings (i.e., propositions), and in terms of the underlying conceptual knowledge that is communicated through these sentence meanings. The global coherence and structure of the discourse are understood in terms of this underlying conceptual knowledge. In discourse production, conceptual knowledge is communicated to a reader or listener through the generation of coherent sequences of propositions and sentence structures. Sentence structures both encode propositional meanings and provide a thematic or topical organization for the underlying conceptual content of the discourse.

From a cognitive perspective, there is no reason *a priori* to regard the acquisition of these particular kinds of knowledge and skill as involving learning processes that are inherently different from those involved in acquiring other complex rules and skills. The acquisition of discourse processing competence in a second language entails the acquisition of knowledge of specific rules, e.g., for generating or modifying internal morpho-syntactic representations of language structures, representations of sentence meanings, and conceptual meaning representations for connected discourse, and the development of skill in the component processes that operate on internal representations at different levels to enable the comprehension and production of discourse to occur.

In learning a second language, some of the processes and representations that must be mastered are specific to the second language, and some are shared with discourse competence in one's first language. Second language learning requires that one acquire lexical knowledge and skill in the syntactic and semantic processing of sentences that are specific to the second

NATO ASI Series, Vol. F 80
Intelligent Tutoring Systems for Foreign Language Learning
Edited by M. L. Swartz and M. Yazdani

language. However, discourse competence in a second language also entails representations and processes that are shared with comprehension and production in one's first language, particularly conceptual and semantic representations of meaning structures and inferential processes that operate on meanings at the discourse level. Learning a second language, then, involves learning language-specific rules and processes, and learning to apply general, nonspecific semantic and conceptual processes to discourse comprehension and production tasks in the second language. Computer-based tutoring or performance environments for second language learning will require a precise specification of both language-specific knowledge and skills that must be acquired and general discourse comprehension and production processes that must be applied to understand or produce connected discourse in a second language.

Current cognitive models of discourse comprehension and production identify multiple levels of syntactic, semantic and conceptual representation of discourse, and provide a means of identifying language-specific and general processes that must be mastered in becoming proficient in discourse comprehension and production in a second language. Research on the nature of the semantic representations and component processes involved in discourse comprehension and production, and recent extensions of this research to second language and bilingual discourse processing, are beginning to provide a specification of the nature of the component knowledge and skills that must be learned in acquiring expertise in a second language. Formal models of semantic representation and processing have been developed and are now being implemented as computer models.

We will explore these models, their application to research on discourse comprehension in bilinguals, and their implications for the design of intelligent tutoring systems to assist second language learning. A computer model of syntactic analysis and semantic interpretation of sentences will be described and its potential use as an expert knowledge base in intelligent tutoring systems for acquiring syntactic and semantic processing skill in a second language will be discussed. The problem of designing performance environments that can build proficiency in applying general conceptual and inferential processes to the comprehension of connected discourse in a second language will be addressed as well.

2. The Stratified Model of Discourse Processing

Expertise in discourse processing includes expertise in the comprehension and production of connected discourse, both of which involve semantic processing. Discourse comprehension involves semantic processing at two levels. First, it involves the interpretation of local propositional meanings that are encoded lexically and syntactically in natural language expressions and inferences based on these propositional meanings. Second, it involves the construction of connected conceptual network representations that constitute "mental models" of the knowledge or situations that are described in a discourse. These conceptual meaning representations are constructed from the set of interrelated propositional meanings that make up a discourse and from prior situational and subject matter knowledge.

Efforts to model the cognitive processes and representations involved in discourse comprehension have resulted in a <u>stratified model</u> of discourse processing in which representations are generated for discourse at multiple levels. The levels of representation identified by this model include: (a) representations of the morpho-lexical and syntactic structures of natural language expressions, (b) semantic representations of the propositional meanings expressed in linguistic structures, and (c) frame-level conceptual representations of declarative knowledge or situations represented in connected discourse.

The stratified model provides a framework for identifying quasi-independent component processes in text comprehension and production, and for modelling their interactions in terms of a modular multilevel system. In this system, processing at one level is viewed as operating on the outcomes of processing at other levels. However, processing is not necessarily sequential. Processes may be operating in parallel with individual processes operating whenever they have data. For example, in comprehending a discourse in a particular situation, a reader or listener constructs a global knowledge representation from propositions derived from lexical and syntactic information. At the same time, knowledge representations that the reader or listener already possesses may be used both in the construction of a text representation and in processing at lower levels. The extent to which component processes are modular and the manner in which they interact with or influence one another are important areas of current research on discourse processing.

2.1 Comprehension Processes

Current theory has recognized that several types of representations and operations are involved in comprehending discourse. In Table 1, the component processes (listed at the left of each line) generate the specified representations (listed to the right) as output; each component process is assumed to receive as input the result of the previous process (listed above it). Thus, we may describe approximately the sequence of operations in comprehending discourse as follows.

First, natural language (NL) representations are generated from phonological or orthographic inputs by components of the natural language processing subsystem. These include the generation of: (1) lexical/morphological strings and (2) syntactic structures.

Second, local propositional meanings consisting of truth-valued expressions in a meaning representation language are generated for syntactically analyzed, natural language expressions: (1) by a semantic interpretation component, and (2) by means of inferences. Inferential processes include: (a) microproposition inferences that complete propositions by filling empty slots, resolving coreference within the sentence, modifying slot filling concepts, etc.; and (b) contextual inferences that generate propositions to connect or bridge sentence meanings, make logical deductions, resolve ambiguity, summarize or expand the pragmatic meaning of sentences, make predictions, resolve contextual anaphora, etc. [20].

Finally, conceptual representations are generated by: (1) integrative processes that link propositions into connected semantic network structures [23], and (2) frame processes that build specialized semantic network representations (i.e., conceptual frames) as mental models of declarative or situational knowledge of particular kinds [12, 27, 37, 40, 41]. Processes involving conceptual frames include: (a) general network operations that instantiate, generalize, elaborate, transform, or join semantic networks [40]; (b) operations to construct specialized conceptual frame structures (variously described as schemata, scripts, frames, "memory organization packets", etc.); (c) frame inferences that elaborate or transform conceptual frames of particular types; and (d) operations to integrate conceptual frame representations into prior knowledge structures in long term memory.

2.2 Production Processes

In discourse production this process is assumed to operate approximately "in reverse," consisting of a series of cognitive operations in which decisions are successively made which eventually result in the production of sequences of natural language expressions that form a connected coherent discourse. The principal problem for a theory of the generation of discourse is to specify the component processes a speaker or writer uses to: (1) construct and elaborate the conceptual content of his or her discourse; (2) decide what information to communicate explicitly to the listener or reader, in what sequence, and in relation to what themes or topics; (3) generate propositions (i.e., truth-valued statements about conceptual content) to be encoded in natural language; and (4) generate syntactic and morpho-lexical structures to encode these propositional meanings. This decision making process must produce discourse which is both locally coherent and globally constrained by the conceptual frame structures that are to be com

Table 1

Stratified model of component processes and representations in discourse comprehension

Component Processes	Resulting Representations
Processing Natural Language Structures	
Morpho-lexical processing	Lexical/morphological strings
Syntactic analysis (parsing)	Syntactic structures
Processing Propositional Meanings	
Semantic interpretation	Base propositions
Microproposition inferences	Complete base propositions
Contextual inferences	Augmented propositions
Conceptual Processing	
Integration of propositions into connected semantic networks	Propositional networks (conceptual graphs)
Network elaboration operations	Augmented propositional networks
Frame generation	Conceptual frame structures
Frame inference	Elaborated or generalized frames
Integration of frames into knowledge structure	Modifications to stored knowledge

municated. Considerations such as what prior knowledge readers or listeners are likely to already share with the writer or speaker and what inferences they are likely to make also guide the discourse production process. These levels of processing may be described approximately as follows (see Table 2).

First, the discourse production process begins with the retrieval and elaboration of a conceptual knowledge structure (i.e., conceptual frames) to be communicated to a listener or reader. This involves: (1) the retrieval of frame knowledge from one's prior knowledge structure; (2) inferences to generate, integrate or elaborate these representations (when retrieved frames are incomplete); (3) inferences to instantiate general frames (making them more specific to the situations being communicated); and (4) generation of propositional networks to specify fully these frame structures using the concepts and relations of propositional semantics. Before this semantic information can be communicated in discourse, a sequence must be established for the introduction of conceptual and propositional network information within discourse, decisions must be made as to what information to select for explicit communication, and a topical (or thematic) priority structure must be established to organize the information for communication to the intended reader or listener.

Second, the generation of sequences of interrelated propositions occurs. A sequence of propositions is subject to two types of constraints. First, it must reflect a consistent topical or thematic perspective on the conceptual knowledge structure that is to be communicated. Second, it must be contextually coherent, that is, propositions must be inferentially related to one another so as to form a linearly coherent sequence and they must be selected pragmatically so as to reflect characteristics of the communicative situation. The result of this processing of propositional meanings is a sequence of base propositions which are to be encoded in natural language expressions.

Finally, syntactic and morpho-lexical linguistic structures are produced to encode these propositional meanings as well-formed natural language expressions. The linguistic structures that are generated may be monitored and errors corrected. The selection among alternative syntactic and morpho-lexical encodings of propositions reflects previous decisions concerning the selection, sequencing and topicalization of information for communication to the reader or listener.

Like discourse comprehension, expertise in discourse production involves competence in all of these identified processing components which also must be integrated into a smoothly coordinated processing system. However, while the comprehension process is usually guided by the organization and conceptual content of the discourse being read (or heard) and the situation in which it is being used, discourse production frequently involves decision making and structure generation in the absence of strong structural constraints directly imposed by the communicative task. Discourse production competence, therefore, also may involve planning, use of scripts or topical outlines as templates for production, or use of other weak methods or strategies to help constrain the generation process.

2.3 Implications for Second Language Learning

The stratified model of discourse processing has important consequences for second language learning. First, it recognizes that second language learners must acquire automatized component processes for morpho-lexical and syntactic processing at the sentence level that are specific to the language being learned. However, it also makes explicit that the learning of rules that map between semantic representations at the propositional level and morpho-syntactic structures is a major aspect of second language acquisition. In addition, other semantic processes that depend on language-specific knowledge may have to be learned, for example, the production and comprehension of anaphoric expressions.

Second, the stratified model recognizes that these new language-specific component processes must be integrated into the complete meaning-oriented discourse comprehension (or production) system. Another important implication for second language tutoring systems, therefore, is that a tutor should develop expertise in the component processes specific to a second language in such a way as to facilitate their integration into a learner's full discourse processing system. In our view, a key to accomplishing this is to emphasize in instruction the semantic functions of morpho-lexical and syntactic structures in communicating propositional meanings.

Adult second language learners already know implicitly how to generate a variety of well-formed expressions to express a given propositional meaning in their first language, and when to select a particular linguistic structure. They also know how to interpret these semantically equivalent expressions in terms of a common meaning representation. What they must learn is how to routinely and automatically generate the set of alternative well-formed expressions that may be used to express a given propositional meaning in a second language, and how to routinely interpret the propositional meaning of such expressions. Once students learn syntactic

Table 2

Stratified model of component processes and representations in discourse production

Component Processes	Resulting Representations
Conceptual Processing	
Retrieval of frame representations	Conceptual frame structures
Frame generation, inference and integration	Elaborated frames
Frame instantiation and specification	Instantiated frames
Generation of propositional networks to specify frames	Propositional networks
Selection, sequencing and topicalization of information for communication	Modified propositional networks
Processing of Propositional Meanings	
Generation of propositions for communication	Propositions
Selection and generation of propositions for local discourse context	Propositions
Specification of propositions for encoding	Base propositions
Processing of Natural Language Structures	
Syntactic encoding of propositions	Syntactic structures
Morphological processing	Morpho-lexical strings
Monitoring and error correction	Syntactic and morpho-lexical structures

encoding and semantic interpretation rules and acquire skill in applying them in sentence generation and comprehension tasks in a second language, these skills must become integrated into a well-functioning discourse comprehension and production system extended to their second language.

The design of an intelligent tutoring system to build these skills will require not only a specification of morphological and syntactic rules for the second language; it also will require a well-defined semantic representation for propositions and an explicit specification of rules relating propositions to morpho-lexical and syntactic structures that express them in the second language. Finally, a secondlanguage learning system should be a part of a performance environment in which learners can gain experience in extending their already developed comprehension and production processes to the second language.

3. Discourse Processing in a Second Language

Comprehension of connected discourse has been studied most frequently using post-input tasks such as free verbal recall and question answering. This research has focused on the cognitive representations that are generated or manipulated and the relationship of these to properties of the text being understood. The research has demonstrated that local propositional representations are generated that involve both propositional interpretation of text sentences and inferences of various types. Propositions and inferences provide information for the construction of a conceptual network to represent the situations or knowledge that are described in a discourse [13, 16, 41]. Theoretical effort in this field has been directed towards these two major levels of processing: the local semantic processing of propositions in discourse context, and the construction of conceptual network or frame-level representations of a discourse. A major problem has been to explain precisely how processes at these two levels function online during reading or listening, and how they interact smoothly in real time to build an integrated conceptual representation for a text.

One popular theory of semantic processing has emphasized frame-based processes in which static network representations called "schemata" or "canonical frames" [e.g., 40] are retrieved from long term memory and modified to represent text information. However frame theory has difficulty explaining how unfamiliar, complex or novel semantic structures can be understood [11, 28, 37]. Schank [37] offered as a solution more abstract and flexible units called Memory Organization Packets ("MOPS") which are organized around themes, and Kintsch [28] has proposed unconstrained bottom up processing followed by an integration of activated patterns into a coherent structure. Both of these theories have difficulty explaining processes required to construct novel or complex representations in the absence of relevant prior knowledge.

An alternative to frame theory is a constructive rule-based theory of semantic processing in which competent readers or listeners are assumed to possess knowledge of rules for forming propositions and conceptual frames that they apply to actively build propositions and conceptual network structures [4, 12, 13]. Propositional meanings and conceptual knowledge structures are assumed to be represented in terms of abstract semantic representation languages described by means of <u>semantic grammars</u> [43]. Comprehension is regarded as a constructive process in which readers or listeners apply their knowledge of rules for forming representations at particular levels to generate and augment a conceptual model of the text. For example, propositions are generated by applying rules in a proposition grammar to parse input sentences that have been previously analyzed syntactically. Conceptual representations are constructed in stages; as new propositional information becomes available it is used to augment and modify a conceptual model that is constructed through inference and frame building activities that are guided by knowledge of frame building rules.

Recent research has employed online techniques to study component processes in discourse comprehension at the time at which they actually occur during reading or listening. These studies provide information about what component processes are involved in comprehension and how they are temporally organized. Among the measures used are eye movements, segment reading times for various text units, assessment of inferences (using interspersed questions or by testing activation of concepts that may have been primed by inferences), concurrent verbal reports (such as think aloud protocols), and online interpretation protocols (which assess the reader's developing interpretation of the text). Typically, these measures are analyzed in terms of linguistic and semantic units that reflect different syntactic and semantic structures identified by a formal analysis of the text being read. Recent studies employing the online interpretation method in combination with measures of sentence reading times and post-input recall have provided evidence for concurrent construction of semantic representations at the propositional and conceptual frame levels during input processing of sentences [14, 15,]. Since the methods used in these studies are based on formal models of semantic representation that are language independent, they may be used to study discourse comprehension processes comparatively across languages.

3.1 Bilingual Discourse Comprehension

Until quite recently, the focus within second language research has been almost entirely on the acquisition of syntactic knowledge by second language learners [30]. Following the shift in emphasis from sentence to discourse within language research in general, second language research has begun to employ discourse-level analyses but mainly within conversational settings [22]. Although an information processing or cognitive approach to second language reading has been advocated [2, 32], very little research within this framework has actually been reported. What research there is on second language text comprehension from a discourse analysis perspective tends to use a frame theory framework. This research has compared second language learners, who are usually not of the dominant culture, to native speakers of a particular language, and has demonstrated that second language readers' lack of familiarity with both culturally-specific conceptual content and context led to difficulty in understanding texts in the second language [2, 6]. However, the same socio-cultural factors that caused difficulty for these non-native speakers in their second language would also be expected to affect their comprehension of similar material even if it appeared in their first language. Therefore, while this research does implicate conceptual-level processing as a source of second language comprehension difficulties, it has been studying text comprehension processes at the conceptual frame level that are not language specific.

Although there has been much theorizing about transfer from the first to the second language and about the level of competence necessary in one to benefit the other [8, 29], there is a paucity of research that actually evaluates individuals' language facility in their first language when studying their facility in their second [1, 35]. It has been suggested, for example, that a lack of automaticity in the second language would affect reading in that language [32]. This could account for the hypothesis that when reading within a second language, readers "short circuit" their normal conceptual processing and become strictly "bottom up" processors [6, 7, 9]. Again, however, much of the research in this area has suffered from the fact that it is between subject research; one does not really know how second language learners operate in their first language. The research techniques and semantic representation models referred to previously could be applied to compare an individual's processing at different levels in discourse comprehension tasks across languages

Another weakness with much second language research is that it confounds comprehension and production. Virtually all of the research that suggests that there are major differences between comprehension processes in the first and second language has used second language production to assess comprehension. When first language production is used, the results are quite different, suggesting both that the earlier research tended to underestimate comprehension [31] and that adults reading text in their second language use higher-level conceptual processing to compensate for code-related difficulties [42].

A recent study of Silva and Donin [38] employed online interpretation and sentence reading time methods to compare anglophone nursing students' comprehension of medical case files in their first language (English) to their comprehension of matched case files in their second language (French). They found no differences in total amount of semantic information included in their interpretations of the passage, or in patterns of inferences in their interpretations when material was presented in English and interpreted in English, as compared to when material was presented in French and interpreted in English. They did, however, find differences between this second condition and a third condition in which material was presented in French and interpreted in French. In addition, longer sentence reading times for the third condition indicate that input processing was affected by the requirement of production of an interpretation in the second language. These results imply that when production was in the first language, processing at input was not as different for the two languages as has been suggested in the literature. Nevertheless, they do not imply that processing in the two languages was the same for these intermediate-level second language students. When the interpretation results were analyzed separately for different parts of the text, differences were found across English and French for that part of the text that may be considered to be the most complex (i.e., the patient's "presenting symptoms"). The form and content of this part was the least predictable and thus would be the least likely part of the text to allow for frame-based processing, that is, fitting of propositional information into slots in a frame structure retrieved from prior knowledge.

These comprehension results have been replicated in a study of francophone nurses at an intermediate level of English who were asked to interpret a text after reading each paragraph [19]. In this study, in addition to reading case files, the nursing students also read matched descriptive travelogue passages in English and French. While very few differences were found across languages, major differences were found for text types (travelogues vs. case files) for both languages. As in the earlier study, sentence reading times were longer for texts read in the second language than for those read in the first. In the previous study this result could have been accounted for by the fact that the French sentences were longer; in this study, the second language was English and the average sentence length was shorter. Therefore there was evidence for real differences in first and second language input processing, even when output differences (i.e., in interpretation) were not found. In general, these studies establish that with individuals at an intermediate level of second language proficiency, high-level conceptual processing is used to overcome limitations imposed by lack of automaticity in sentence-level syntactic and semantic processing. Preliminary results from a study in progress [10] with subjects at a lower level of second language proficiency suggest that there is a minimum required level of lexical and syntactic knowledge, without which processing at a conceptual level cannot occur. This level, however, appears to be much lower than has been suggested in the previous literature.

Similar results have been found in a recent study of Spanish-English bilinguals' sentence comprehension. Hoover and Berdugo [24] compared sentence-level processing in Spanish-English bilinguals to that of Spanish and English unilinguals. Analysis of word-by-word reading times indicated that the bilinguals ignored syntactic information which the unilinguals used; the bilinguals relied instead on semantic information to process the sentences. However, post-input sentence comprehension measures in the bilingual and unilingual groups were the same, indicating that the second language comprehenders were able to use semantic information efficiently to overcome a lack of automaticity in syntactic processing in their second language. The results of these studies suggest that if a tutoring system were used to develop efficient sentence-level processing skills in the second language, this would benefit the development of discourse comprehension competence in the second language.

4. Semantic Analysis System for Natural Language

Research in such areas as semantic interpretation of natural language, text generation, and machine translation has resulted in formalisms for representation and computational techniques that are increasingly compatible with psychological models of discourse processing [33]. These can be used to develop precise models of human discourse representation and processing. Such models can provide an expert knowledge base for tutoring systems to build syntactic and semantic processing skills in a second language.

An important development in research on semantic representation and processing of natural language has been the realization that precise models of semantic representation can be defined in terms of semantic representation languages [5, 43]. This view recognizes that, like natural languages, semantic representation languages can be defined in terms of semantic well-formedness rules that provide them with strong generative capacity with respect to their expressions

[25]. Thus, propositions may be generated by rules in a semantic grammar specifying a propositional meaning representation language (MRL) [12], and frame representations for discourse may be viewed as conceptual network structures formed by application of rules in knowledge representation languages (KRL) [4, 12]. Discourse comprehension, therefore, may be viewed as an activity of translation from natural language (NL) expressions to conceptual representations in a knowledge representation language mediated by the generation of propositions in the meaning representation language; and discourse production may be viewed as translation from conceptual knowledge representations to natural language discourse mediated by the generation of propositional meanings which are encoded in sentences [13].

From the standpoint of formal representation languages, discourse processing therefore may be viewed in terms of the following mapping relations:

NL expressions	**<-->**	**MRL expressions**	**<-->**	**KRL structures**
(sentences)		(propositions)		(conceptual networks)

The propositional meaning representation language is independent of any particular natural language and consequently, in the terminology of machine translation, it serves as an "interlingua" [34]. However, the mapping from a particular natural language to the meaning representation language is not language independent since it depends on rules that specify the set of linguistic structures in a particular language that correspond to (i.e., that can encode) a particular propositional meaning:

L1 expressions	**<-->**	**MRL expressions**	**<-->**	**L2 expressions**
(sentences in L1)		(propositions)		(sentences in L2)

Acquiring discourse processing competence in a second language therefore involves not only the acquisition of morpho-lexical and syntactic knowledge necessary to parse or generate syntactically well-formed expressions in a second language; it also involves competence in semantic interpretation of natural language expressions, that is, ability to generate well-formed representations in the meaning representation language (i.e., "propositions" or "logical forms") from natural language expressions, and competence in sentence generation, that is, ability to generate well-formed natural language expressions to represent propositional meanings. An expert knowledge base for a second language learning system will have to specify these mappings in order to develop semantic processing skills at the sentence level.

4.1 CODA-X: A System for Semantic Interpretation of Sentences

We have been developing a computer system for the semantic interpretation of English called CODA-X that generates well-formed representations in a propositional meaning representation language from syntactically analyzed natural language inputs [17, 18]. The operation of CODA-X may be illustrated by viewing the results of a semantic analysis of a sentence input to the system as it is displayed to the user by means of the program's graphic interface [17]. When CODA-X is used for analysis (as opposed to rule programming), the user begins an analysis by typing a sentence into an input window and selecting the option "parse" (we will illustrate an analysis of the sentence *it is possible that he has to go)*. Then a parse window appears which graphically displays the syntactic tree which is the result of the parse and provides editing functions (see Figure 1). Selecting "Generate Proposition" from a menu starts the semantic interpreter which displays the results of the semantic analysis as one or more propositional parse trees together with functions for editing the trees (see Figure 2).

In CODA-X, propositions are expressions in a meaning representation language that is defined by rules in a recursive context-free semantic grammar. Attached to all semantic production rules in the grammar are specifications of sets of syntactic patterns that can be used to express them in a specific language. Sentences are analyzed by a semantic parser that applies rules in the semantic grammar in a top down analysis (with backtracking) of syntactic parse trees

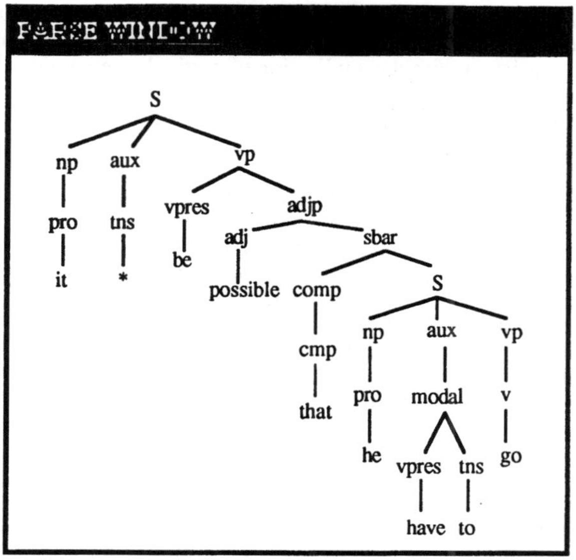

Figure 1. Syntactic parse tree for the sentence ***it is possible that he has to go.***

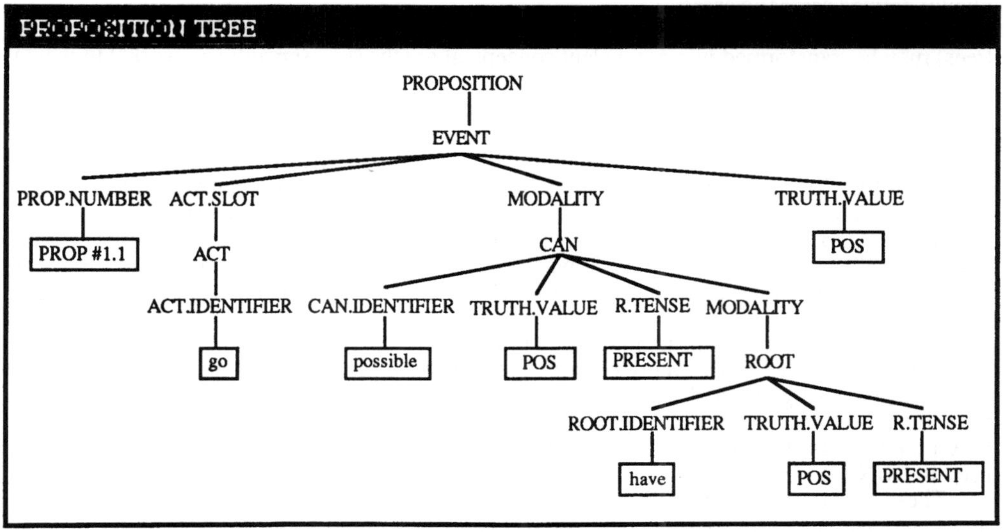

Figure 2. Proposition tree for the sentence ***it is possible that he has to go.***

generated previously by a syntactic parser. Semantic parse trees (i.e, propositions) are generated as syntactic patterns and lexical information are found (in the syntactic parse tree for the input sentence) that are consistent with the application of particular semantic rules.

Before discussing the applicability of CODA-X as an expert domain knowledge model for a second language tutoring system, let us briefly review the approach taken to semantic analysis and its pertinence as a computational model of the semantic interpretation component of a discourse comprehension system.

First, there is an explicit semantic grammar defining well-formed expressions (propositions) in the meaning representation language (MRL). The necessity of a well-defined MRL has been recognized by many studies concerned with the semantics of natural languages [21, 25, 27]. The explicit definition of the MRL in the form of a recursive grammar is essential in order to determine the well-formedness of MRL expressions.

Second, sentence meanings are represented in terms of semantic parse trees. Propositions are assigned a structure by application of rules in a context-free semantic grammar. What distinguishes parsers from recognizers is the generative capacity of the former, i.e., their capability to display the underlying syntactic structure of a sentence and not simply accept it as a sentence of a language. This property of syntactic parsers is rarely met in systems for semantic interpretation. Usually the output of the semantic interpretation is limited to the terminal nodes and some non-terminal nodes such that the result of the semantic parse does not give the underlying semantic structure from the root. The approach taken with CODA-X is to output, as the result of the semantic interpretation, a semantic parse tree that contains the terminal nodes as well as all the intermediary nodes linking them to the root node. Burton and Brown have taken a similar approach with SOPHIE [5].

Third, representations in the MRL employ explicitly defined relational categories identified in research on natural language semantics. The semantic grammar used by CODA-X is based on relational semantic categories. Relational semantic cases have been recognized as important for both semantic description of languages and characterization of conceptual structures [25]. Many semantic interpretation systems such as SOPHIE ([5], GUS [3] and ANDI [36] use explicitly defined semantic cases.

Fourth, meaning representations generated during semantic interpretation (semantic parse trees) may be transformed into equivalent conceptual graphs (i.e., semantic networks) in which all relations are specified by the grammar (as relational categories) and have a well-defined meaning [13]. Consequently all relations assert properties which may be verified against a representation of situations or knowledge. Since conceptual graphs are equivalent to expressions in a first (or higher-order) predicate calculus, they may be objects of deductive reasoning operations [40]. Conceptual graphs also may be regarded as frame representations and operated on by frame and generalization operations [40]. That is, the semantic cases that correspond to semantic categories in the meaning representation language correspond to links in semantic networks [39]. The specification by Sowa [40] of formation rules and logical operations for conceptual graphs allows the output of CODA-X to be treated by a module for generating inferences.

Finally, input to the semantic interpreter is a syntactic parse tree for which a meaning representation is generated [43]. Many cognitive studies have provided evidence of a module for syntactic processing of which the output is subject to semantic processing. CODA-X assumes the same modularity in natural language comprehension and the process of semantic interpretation takes as an input the result of a syntactic analysis. The approach is similar to the one used in LUNAR [43].

These characteristics of CODA-X are consistent with modular and stratified models of human discourse processing and are the main mechanism for relating semantic representations to linguistic structures. CODA-X combines these characteristics into a coherent system for semantic interpretation. The implementation of this approach to semantic analysis led to a distinction between "static" and "dynamic" rules. The "static" and "dynamic" rules represent respectively: (a) the recursive context-free grammar for propositions, and (b) the set of parameters, conditions and actions associated with each "static" production rule in the grammar that identify linguistic structures associated with the rule. This distinction means that the user has access to both a context-free formulation of the semantic grammar (the static rules) as well as the specific conditions of application of static production rules (the dynamic rules). The distinction between "static" and "dynamic" rules also supports the generality of the system because it allows the user to have access to: (a) the grammar determining the well-formedness of expressions of the meaning representation language (independently of its application to any particular natural language), and (b) the specific conditions required to apply this grammar to a specific natural language. The static rules of the grammar define the propositional representations of sentence meanings, and the dynamic rules define the mapping from natural language expressions to propositions.

In CODA-X, static and dynamic rules are essentially declarative information. However, the dynamic rules have a procedural interpretation according to a well-defined inference engine that works on those rules. Although the CODA-X knowledge base was developed to implement a semantic interpreter for natural language, its declarative representation of rules relating semantic representations to syntactic patterns (as packets of dynamic rules associated with static production rules in the proposition grammar) makes it potentially suitable as an expert knowledge base for tutoring systems for learning the linguistic structures that express propositional meanings. The specific nature of static and dynamic rules will be further described in discussing the use of the CODA-X grammar as an expert knowledge base for second language tutoring systems. For a more complete description of the CODA-X grammar, dynamic rules and inference engine, see Frederiksen & Décary [17].

5. CODA-X and Intelligent Tutoring Systems for Second Language Learning

The purpose of an intelligent tutoring system for second language learning should be to develop expertise in discourse processing in a second language in a manner that is consistent with current stratified models. The system that will be described here is centered around two requirements that are dictated by the stratified model as it has been applied to second language learning and discourse processing across languages. First, a learner must acquire knowledge and procedures for mapping between expressions in the meaning representation language (propositions) and the set of well-formed expressions in the second language. Second, a learner must successfully embed these procedures in his or her general discourse processing system, thus enabling text understanding and production in the second language to be at a level consistent with expertise in one's first language. We will examine first the CODA-X rule base as an expert knowledge base for a tutoring system to develop skills in mapping between propositional sentence meanings and their encodings as well-formed expressions in the second language. Then we will discuss the type of learning environment that is required to develop proficiency in discourse comprehension in the second language.

5. 1 The Expert Knowledge Base: Mapping between Syntactic and Semantic Representations

A tutoring system for learning to understand and produce well-formed sentences to express propositional meanings in a second language will require an expert knowledge base consisting of (a) an explicit representation of semantic information expressed in sentences (i.e., propositions), and (b) explicit rules linking propositions to their possible expressions in natural language. Such a specification would provide a knowledge base for constructing semantically-driven tutoring environments to teach the syntax-semantics mappings of a particular language. The static and dynamic rules of CODA-X grammars provide this specification and therefore can provide the expert domain knowledge needed for a second language tutoring system.

This may be illustrated by the dynamic rules for representing modality categories in English. In the semantic grammar, each proposition calls rules specifying tense, aspect, modality and truth value as well as rules specifying the type of proposition (e.g., **EVENT**, **STATE**, etc.). For example, the static grammar rule **EVENT** includes an optional call to the rule **MODALITY**.

EVENT ::= PROP.NUMBER ACT.SLOT {RESULTIVE.FRAME} {ACT.IDENTIFYING.RELATION}* {R.TENSE} {R.ASPECT} {MODALITY} TRUTH.VALUE*

The rule **MODALITY** is specified by a packet of four static rules, one of which may be selected to specify a type of modality:

MODALITY ::= QUAL	(qualifier modal)
MODALITY ::= COND	(conditional modal)
MODALITY ::= CAN	(ability modal)
MODALITY ::= ROOT	(necessity or social obligation modal)

Each type of modality, e.g., **ROOT**, corresponds to a rule calling other rules that specify the structure of the modal information, including a (lexical) identifier for the modal category and other optional rules, such as degree (*it is very necessary*), truth value (*it is not necessary*), tense (*it was necessary*), aspect (*it had been necessary*), or a recursive call to **MODALITY** for complex modal expressions (*it may be necessary*):

ROOT ::= ROOT.IDENTIFIER {DEGREE}* {TRUTH.VALUE} {R.TENSE} {R.ASPECT} {MODALITY}

The static rule **ROOT** has nine dynamic rules associated with it (each of which corresponds to a different syntactic pattern expressing the necessity modal):

Dynamic rule name	Example containing syntactic pattern
modal.root	"he must go"
modal.adv.root	"he necessarily will go"
modal.adj.root	"he is required to go"
modal.adj.root.intens	"he is absolutely required to go"
modal.plus.to	"he has to go"
matrix.modal	"it is necessary that he go"
matrix.modal.intens	"it is absolutely necessary that he go"
vpprt.root	"his going is required"
be.plus.to	"he is to go"

Each dynamic rule specifies a syntactic pattern to be matched as well as tests on elements of these patterns, actions to be carried out, and calls to other rules. For example, the dynamic rule "matrix.modal" associated with the **ROOT** (i.e., necessity or obligation) modal matches the following pattern to the syntactic tree passed to it (@ is a "wildcard" symbol):

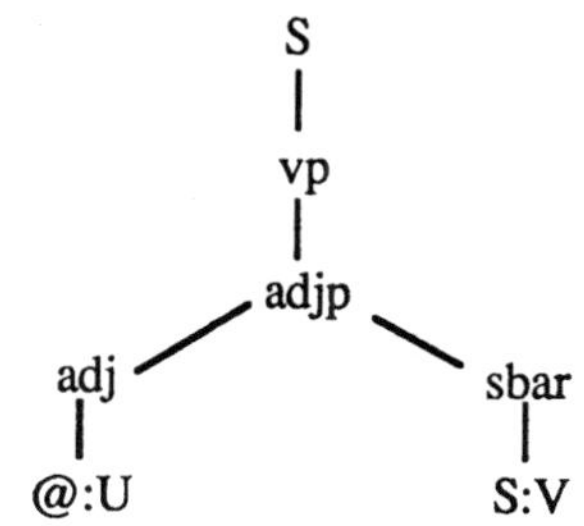

Figure 3. Pattern for "matrix.modal" dynamic rule.

If this pattern matches the input tree, the variable U is tested to see if it is in a set called "modroots." If this test succeeds, U is deleted from the tree, and the "pruned" tree is passed as a parameter to other rules which are called by **ROOT**. An example of a parse tree matched by this pattern was given previously in Figure 1. The proposition tree generated by CODA-X for this example was given in Figure 2. Note that the modal expression in this example contains two modals: the **CAN** modal ("possibility") is applied to a **ROOT** modal ("has to"). Complex modal expressions such as this require a recursive grammar for their analysis.

Packets of dynamic rules associated with semantic categories thus provide an explicit representation of the set of expressions in a second language that can be used to express a given component of meaning. The objective of a tutoring system is to teach these rules for expressing the range of propositional structures that can be generated by the semantic grammar. In such a system, the learning of linguistic rules (morphology, syntax) is subordinated to and motivated by the use of these rules to express particular propositional meanings.

5.2 Tutoring Systems for Acquiring Linguistic Knowledge

How can the CODA-X rule base can be used to organize an environment for learning the syntax-semantics mappings of English? Some of the possibilities may be seen by considering the example of the modal system. Suppose that we are considering a component of a tutoring system that is teaching a user how to understand and produce expressions in a second language that express modal information. A typical sequence of events that might take place in a tutorial environment in which a person was learning the modal system of English might be as follows.

First, one would begin by learning the semantics of modality with reference to examples in the learner's first language. Users would be given examples that illustrate different types of situations of use of different types of simple modal and complex modal expressions. These could be given by sentences or discourse in the users' first language. The series of examples and their explanations would be generated from the static rules for modality. For example, an event could be repeatedly presented with type of modality varied. The explanations would highlight the semantics of modality. A pedagogically appropriate representation based on the semantic parse tree for the examples would be presented and used as a basis for explaining the semantic rules. The proposition tree could be displayed as a parse tree, a simplified network, as a predicate argument structure, or lists of properties. A student would learn to answer questions about the meaning of modal expressions (e.g., type of modal), and explanations would be given to explain categories, structures of complex modals, or answers to questions.

Once users had learned a particular semantic structure, they could request paraphrases of the original sentence. The system would generate alternative expressions that could be used to represent the proposition (e.g., the particular type of modal) as specified by the dynamic rules. For each alternative expression, an explanation of the particular syntactic structure would be given. Then the user would begin to explore the expressive possibilities of the second language. For example, the user could begin by identifying lexical equivalents for words in the semantic representation (with the help of a dictionary if necessary). Then the system would generate sentence alternatives expressing the proposition in the second language. Explanations of applicable grammatical rules of the second language would be available to the user. The user would practice comprehending examples of expressions of modality in the second language, with appropriate tests of comprehension. At a later stage, the user would be given sentences in the second language and asked to generate sentences in the second language to express variations in modality. The system would carry out syntactic and semantic analysis of the user's responses, and identify the user's errors keeping track of what rules the student had mastered. By this means, the student would acquire skill in comprehending and producing modal expressions in the second language. The motivation for the instruction would always be to learn how meanings are expressed in the second language. The training would capitalize on learners' knowledge and expertise in their first language to facilitate and motivate learning.

5.3 Performance Environments for Developing Proficiency in Discourse Processing

As learners acquire facility in comprehending and expressing propositional meanings in their second language, they must successfully embed these procedures in their general discourse processing system. Computer environments for second language learning must facilitate the development of proficiency in discourse comprehension and production in the second language and maintain a focus on the main purpose of second language learning which is to acquire communicative competence in the second language. Therefore, it is our view that a second language learning system must be built around an authentic performance environment in which learners use and produce discourse in the second language in realistic situations that reflect their natural situations of discourse communication. For example, nurses should be able to obtain practice in the use of discourse in the second language that is typical of the discourse and communicative situations that they encounter in their normal work settings. It will be important to design discourse and communicative situations that are both authentic and that permit practice with discourse that incorporates linguistic structures that have been studied in the tutorial environment.

For example, exercises involving comprehension of texts in the second language can incorporate sentence structures and semantic structures that have been studied. By interspersing these structures throughout texts, users can learn to integrate newly acquired semantic and syntactic processing skills in the second language into their conceptual discourse processing system. By this means, users would learn to apply their knowledge of semantic and syntactic rules, of alternative syntactic structures that can be used to express propositional meanings (i.e., the dynamic rules), skill in producing alternative sentence structures to express meaning, and proficiency in comprehending a variety of sentence forms.

The kind of performance environment we envisage centers around connected discourse and its situations of use. A discourse should not be regarded as a static entity; rather it should be used to provide dynamic access to a variety of information, exercises and forms of expression. For example, a sentence can provide access to a tutor, paraphrases, exercises requiring paraphrasing or modifying its meaning, or comprehension questions. Students can be evaluated in terms of their performance on a variety of tasks reflecting different component skills in comprehension and production of discourse in the second language, and a variety of pedagogical strategies can be used to build discourse processing expertise in the second language. The tutorial system for building syntactic and semantic processing competence at the sentence level can be made available as a help system in this performance environment, and the extent of system support for comprehension or production processes can be gradually reduced as the student becomes more proficient. We might think about this second language performance environment as simulating an instructional situation in which students comprehend or produce discourse with an expert language teacher always available to assist them by explaining different points of grammar, comprehension and production. In this way, systematic instruction can be embedded in natural performance situations and made pertinent to everyday problems of discourse communication in the second language.

6. Conclusions

We have examined current cognitive theory and research on discourse representation and processing, particularly as it has been applied to the study of discourse comprehension in bilinguals. This research has demonstrated that second language learners must acquire knowledge and skill in morpho-syntactic and semantic processing at the sentence level, that is, skill in the semantic interpretation of linguistic structures in the second language and in the generation of linguistic forms to express propositional meanings in the second language. Second, it has demonstrated that in order for them to develop communicative competence in the second language, they must learn to apply discourse-level conceptual and inferential processes already developed in the first language to the comprehension and production of connected discourse in the second language. The goals of second language instruction, therefore, ought to reflect the development of both sentence-level linguistic and semantic processes and discourse-level conceptual processing abilities.

Computer-based systems for second language learning, therefore, require a precise specification of (a) the linguistic and semantic knowledge and processes that are involved in the comprehension and generation of sentences, and (b) the conceptual representations and inferential processes that underlie expertise in comprehension, production, and use of connected discourse in communicative situations. Current stratified models of discourse comprehension and production provide a theoretical framework for the design of tutorial systems and performance environments to support the acquisition of linguistic knowledge and discourse competence in a second language. We described one recent computational model of the representation of sentence meanings and of sentence interpretation processes, and discussed how it can provide a well-defined expert knowledge base for a tutorial system to teach the syntax-semantics mappings of a second language. By basing instruction on how linguistic forms in a second language are used to express particular meanings, instruction in the morpho-syntactic rules of the language can be semantically motivated and made systematic.

Despite the importance of developing facility in morpho-syntactic and semantic processing in the second language at the sentence level, morpho-syntactic and semantic processing are only one component in the full discourse processing system. For this reason, we advocate an approach to second language learning that is based on practice using discourse in the second language to communicate meaning in authentic situations. A computer-based second language learning system should include a performance environment that simulates situations in which discourse is understood or produced to achieve clearly specified goals. These should be typical of natural discourse communication relevant to the experience of the learner. We discussed briefly some of our ideas concerning the characteristics of such a performance environment and the means by which a tutorial system could be embedded within it. We believe current models are now sufficiently well-defined to provide a foundation for the development and testing of such semantically-based tutoring systems and performance environments for second language learning.

References

1. Alderson, J. C. : Reading in a foreign language: A reading problem or a language problem? In: Reading in a foreign language. (J. C. Alderson & A. H. Urquhart,Eds.). New York, Longman 1984
2. Bernhardt, E.: Toward an information processing perspective in foreign language reading. Modern Language Journal, 68, 322-331 (1984)
3. Bobrow, D., Kaplan, J., Norman, D., Thompson, H., & Winograd, T.: GUS: A frame-driven dialog system. Artificial Intelligence, 8, 155-173 (1977)
4. Bobrow, D.G., & Winograd, T.: An overview of KRL, a knowledge representation language. Cognitive Science, 1, 3-46 (1977)
5. Burton, R.R., & Brown, J.S.: Towards a natural-language capability for computer-assisted instruction. In: Procedure for instructional systems development. (H. O'Niell, Ed.). New York: Academic Press 1979
6. Carrell, P. L.: Three components of background knowledge in reading comprehension. Language Learning, 33, 183-207 (1983)
7. Clarke, M. A.: The short circuit hypothesis of ESL reading: Or when language competence interferes with reading performance. Modern Language Journal, 64, 203-209 (1980
8. Cummins, J.: Linguistic interdependence and the educational development of bilingual children. Review of Educational Research, 49, 221-251 (1979)
9. Cziko, G. A.: Language competence and reading strategies: A comparison of first- and second- language oral reading errors. Language Learning, 30, 101-116 (1980)
10. Donin, J.: Reading comprehension in a second language. Manuscript in preparation 1991
11. Frederiksen, C. H.: Text comprehension in functional task domains. In: Learning to use literacy in educational settings. (D. Bloom, Ed.). Norwood, NJ: Ablex 1989
12. Frederiksen, C. H.: Cognitive models and discourse analysis. In: Written communication annual: An international survey of research and theory, vol. 1: Studying writing: Linguistic approaches. (C. R. Cooper & S. Greenbaum, Eds.). Beverly Hills, CA: Sage 1986
13. Frederiksen, C.H., & Donin, J.: Constructing multiple semantic representations in comprehending and producing discourse. In: Texts and text processing. (G. Denhière & J.-P. Rossi, Eds.). Amsterdam: North Holland 1990
14. Frederiksen, C.H., & Renaud, A.: Real time processing in comprehension of a procedural text. Manuscript submitted for publication 1991
15. Frederiksen, C.H., & Roy, M.: Effects of prior knowledge and linear vs. hierarchical topicalization structure on comprehension of procedural text. Paper presented at annual meeting of the Canadian Psychological Association, Ottawa, May 31 1990
16. Frederiksen, C.H., Bracewell, R.J., Breuleux, A., & Renaud, A.: The cognitive representation and processing of discourse: Function and dysfunction. In: Discourse ability and brain damage: Theoretical and empirical perspectives. (Y. Joanette & H. Brownell, Eds.). New York: Springer-Verlag 1989
17. Frederiksen, C.H., & Décary, M.: Cognitive discourse analysis Xerox 1186, Version 1.0. Technical Manual, Laboratory of Applied Cognitive Science, McGill University, Montréal, Canada 1990
18. Frederiksen, C.H., Décary, M., & Emond, B.: CODA-X: A semantic parsing approach to natural language interpretation. Technical Report, Laboratory of Applied Cognitive Science, McGill University, Montréal, Canada 1990
19. Goyette, E.: Second-language text comprehension: Knowledge and text types. Unpublished master's thesis, McGill University, Montréal 1991
20. Graesser, A.C., & Bower, G.H.: Inferences and text comprehension. New York: Academic Press 1990
21. Guenthner, F., Lehnmann, H., & Schönfeld, W.: A theory for the representation of knowledge. IBM Journal of Research and Development, 30(1), 39-56 (1986)
22. Hatch, E.: Discourse analysis and second language acquisition. In: Second language acquisition: A book of readings. (E. Hatch, Ed). Rowley,MA: Newbury House 1978
23. Hayes-Roth, B., & Thorndyke, B.W.: Integration of knowledge from text. Journal of Verbal Learning and Verbal Behavior, 18, 91-108 (1979)
24. Hoover, M.L., & Berdugo, G.: The processing of ambiguous sentences by bilinguals. Manuscript in preparation 1991
25. Jackendoff, R.: Semantics and cognition. Cambridge, MA: MIT Press 1983
26. Johnson-Laird, P.: Mental models. Cambridge, MA: Harvard University Press 1983
27. Kamp, H.: A theory of truth and semantic representation. In: Formal methods in the study of language. (J. A. G. Groenendijk, T. M. V. Janssen, & M. B. J. Stokhof, Ed.). Amsterdam: North Holland 1981
28. Kintsch, W.: The role of knowledge in discourse comprehension: A construction-integration model. Psychological Review, 95, 163-182 (1988)

29. Lambert, W.E. : Culture and language as factors in learning and education. In: Education of immigrant students. (A. Wolfgang, Ed.). Toronto: Ontario Institute for Studies in Education 1975
30. Larsen-Freeman, D.: Discourse analysis in second language research. Rowley, MA: Newbury House 1980
31. Lee, J. F.: On the use of recall task to measure L2 reading comprehension. Studies in Second Language Acquisition, 8, 201-212 (1986)
32. McLaughlin, B., Rossman, T., & McLeod, B.: Second-language learning: An information-processing perspective. Language Learning, 33, 135-158 (1983)
33. Nirenburg, S.: Machine translation: Theoretical and methodological issues. Cambridge, UK: Cambridge University Press 1987
34. Nirenburg, S., Raskin, V., & Tucker, A.B.: The structure of interlingua in TRANSLATOR. In: Machine translation: Theoretical and methodological issues. (S. Nirenburg, Ed.). Cambridge, UK: Cambridge University Press 1987
35. Rahming, J., & Frederiksen, C.H.: A discourse processing approach to bilingualism and second language learning. Paper presented at American Educational Research Association. Montréal, Canada 1983
36. Sabah, G., & Rady, M.: A deterministic syntactic-semantic parser applied to French. Actes °8 IJCAI, Karlsruhe: 707-710 1983
37. Schank, R. C. : Dynamic memory: A theory of learning in computers and people. London: Cambridge University Press 1982
38. Silva, M., & Donin, J.: Nursing students' comprehension of case files in their first and second language. Paper presented at American Educational Research Association, Boston 1990
39. Simmons, R. F., Burger, J. F., & Schwarcz, R. M.: A computational model of verbal understanding. AFIPS, 441-456 1968
40. Sowa, J.F.: Conceptual structures: Information processes in mind and machine. Reading, MA: Addison-Wesley 1984
41. van Dijk, T., & Kintsch, W.: Strategies of discourse comprehension. New York: Academic Press 1983
42. Wolff, D.: Some assumptions about second language text comprehension. Studies in Second language Acquisition, 9, 307-326 (1987)
43. Woods, W.A.: Semantics and quantification in natural language question answering. In: Advances in computers, vol. 17. (M. Yovits, Ed.). New York: Academic Press 1978

Section Three

Modeling the Language Learner: Computational Methods

The process whereby the computer system reasons about the learner in order to understand what is known and not known in the domain is called 'diagnosis'. AI techniques are used to make inferences about learner performance and construct a model of the learner. In traditional ITS domains, this has been the focus of much research [11, 12, 18]; however, recently some have suggested that formal, deep models are not always necessary [12]. In highly interactive learning environments, it may be possible to get sufficient information from the learner directly in order to build a simple, but useful learner model. This type of modeling may provide some economy over the labor intensive efforts required by more complex, inferential modeling methods. Nevertheless, work in formal modeling has resulted in many advances in AI methodology. Regardless of whether formal or informal modeling techniques are used, special challenges in diagnosing language errors exist.

We discussed the level of modeling needed for an FL ITS at our Workshop and the trade-offs we should consider. For example, the grain size of the learner model might be considered. Can we develop methods of diagnosis that are more course-grained (and thus require less effort to design and implement) but still provide adequate information for generating a learner model? This type of modeling can be called shallow modeling and promises to be a new area of learner modeling research. However, many of us are still examining methods of deeper modeling. While both approaches will contribute to ITS research in general, individual preference, system requirements, and cost of effort are to be considered when choosing a modeling methodology.

In Chapter 8 we are shown an error analysis technique that introduces the concept of learners' 'applicable rules'. This is a novel data structure for learner modeling which shows promise for FL ITS applications. These rules are usually predictable perturbations representative of a kind of interlingua that develops during L2 acquisition. The authors use a protocol method to extract learners' reasoning about linguistic phenomena and then build data structures for these rules that are used by the system to perform diagnosis in the modeling process.

Chapter 9 presents an approach to the model acquisition process based on knowledge acquisition methodology. The authors assume that the FL ITS will use a tutorial-style interaction rather than a discovery learning environment. The methodology they propose follows a multi-step process to define the representation for the formal knowledge base and construct an initial set of learner models through a knowledge engineering effort with a domain specialist (the foreign language teacher). Next we are shown how diagnosis is performed using these types of learner models in a language tutoring prototype that uses a dialogue as the method of interacting with the system and an overlay modeling technique with bug catalogues for diagnostic processing.

The next paper describes a very formal approach to modeling that creates deep learner models. Chapter 10 combines a standard bug catalogue method for representing learners' mal-rules in the L2, but introduces an innovative machine learning technique to reason about verb tense errors that are encountered during the modeling process. The modeling environment then uses the behavioral information from the learner to run a simulation of the chain of reasoning the learner may have used when generating the error.

From these formal modeling processes, we can see that much effort is needed in order to implement just this one component in the FL ITS. Although we did not reconcile the

NATO ASI Series, Vol. F 80
Intelligent Tutoring Systems for Foreign Language Learning
Edited by M. L. Swartz and M. Yazdani

deep-shallow modeling problem at our Workshop, Chapter 11 in this section reminds us that other methods are possible for modeling the learner. The author reviews modeling techniques used in three different CALL systems for diagnosing word-level errors. Both deep and shallow modeling techniques are compared. We are shown a search technique for diagnosing inflectional errors, a parsing algorithm for detecting agreement errors, and a spell-checker for detecting sound-based errors. The author closes this paper with suggestions for alternative modeling techniques which promise to identify sufficient error diagnostic information without the labor intensive effort of deeper modeling strategies.

Conceptual Modelling in Error Analysis in Computer-Assisted Language Learning Systems

Thierry Chanier[1], Michael Pengelly[2], Michael Twidale[2], and John Self[2]

[1] ICF (Research Assoc.: Ingénierie Cognitive et Formation), 49 av Jean Jaurès, 63400 Chamalières, France.
[2] Computing Department, Lancaster University, Lancaster, LA1 4YR, UK

Abstract: Many computer-assisted language learning systems specifically designed to be used in the curriculum and which exploit AI techniques have neither a learner model nor consequently any deep error analysis. Evidence from applied linguistics shows that learners have their own system of rules for the production of a foreign language. We believe the central issue is to determine the appropriate level of description of these rules and uncover the strategies used by the learners in particular situations. This information represents the major part of the learner model. We review error analysis in second language learning and tutoring systems related to this perspective. We introduce a new structure, called an "applicable rule", that can be used to help diagnose and to represent a learner's performance. We propose a design for the architecture of a system for computer diagnoses of learners' grammatical performances in a communicative environment. Examples of diagnosis using applicable rules illustrate the functioning of this architecture.

Keywords: Learner modelling, Error Diagnosis, Intelligent Tutoring System.

1. Introduction

Evidence in the literature of applied linguistics indicates that learners have their own systems of rules for the production of the foreign language that they practise. It suggests that they use various heuristics and strategies both to *acquire* these rules and to *use* them in communicative processes. We would like to find an appropriate description of these rules and determine what strategies are being used in a given situation to diagnose better a learner's performance as a major contribution towards the learner model, a primary element of an intelligent tutoring system (ITS).

Work in the field of applied linguistics suggests potential methods of modelling learners' behaviours in terms of their strategies of language acquisition. These methods have found little application in building computer-assisted language learning (CALL) systems, which when employing learner modelling techniques still view errors as undesirable elements of performance and something to be prevented and have tended only to diagnose the learner's behaviour at a superficial level, thus following the traditional mal-rule/bug catalogue approach of ITS. Many explanations account for this situation: there is a lack of formalised human expertise on the subject; the management of non-strictly predefined divergences is a hard computational problem which lies on the edge of the main stream of computational linguistics; and the harmonisation of a number of knowledge sources, computational linguistics, pedagogical knowledge of grammar, learning and teaching strategies, in a collaborative manner is not an easy task.

In our approach to learner modelling we follow the direction of the applied linguistics community in viewing second language learning (SLL) as a process of building and updating rules for language production through the use of heuristics and strategies brought about by the circumstances in which a learner finds herself. This positive view of the rules a learner is currently employing de-emphasises the learners failures. The process of learner modelling is to identify the

NATO ASI Series, Vol. F 80
Intelligent Tutoring Systems for Foreign Language Learning
Edited by M. L. Swartz and M. Yazdani

set of rules and their causal mechanisms that are currently active. Because this diagnosis requires interacting with the learner and reasoning about competing explanations of performance, an appropriate representation for both activities must be found.

We introduce here the concept of "applicable rules" (AR) as a basis for this representation and illustrate their use in dialogues between a learner and a system, we call BELLOC, that we are developing in order to automatically build a learner model through the diagnosis of her applicable rules. Although the use of the applicable rules is immersed within a learner-system dialogue environment, semantic problems associated with following the dialogue, such as modelling the learner's actions and intentions related to the problem she has to solve [22], are not considered. But the communicative environment within which they are used provides the context for their diagnosis.

The specification of the BELLOC system has been through a three phase approach. Using the available evidence we proposed a tentative structure for an applicable rule that incorporated the knowledge needed for use in automated learner modelling. We then set up two experiments: the first to acquire the knowledge to partially validate this structure; the second to use the rules in a dialogue game with learners to further validate and refine the learner modelling process. An interface for the the first experiment has been developed and has been used to acquire applicable rules from experts [30,11]. The third phase was to propose an architecture for BELLOC and illustrate its functioning, and that is our focus here.

Section 2 introduces the notion of conceptual diagnosis of a learner's rules through a sample dialogue between the learner and the system. In section 3 the procedure of Error Analysis in applied linguistics and its influence on the perception of language acquisition are described. The learner's main strategies for the acquisition of a second language are sketched. Section 4 gives a snapshot of the mal-rule and bug catalogue modelling techniques frequently encountered in ITSs and briefly indicates their shortcomings. Section 5 surveys ITSs for second language learning, pointing out their treatment of errors and their modelling techniques. Section 6 is devoted to the BELLOC system. It presents an architecture, which has not yet been implemented, for use in the diagnosis of learners' applicable rules, defines refined versions of applicable rules, and illustrates their use though examples. Lastly section 7 gives the conclusions and a perspective on future research.

2. Conceptual Diagnosis in a Communicative Environment

In order to give a flavour of what we mean by a conceptual diagnosis of a learner's errors, we first present an imaginary dialogue between a learner and the system in the context of our BELLOC application.

Much SLL ITS work has been restricted to relatively narrow, artificial exercises. To avoid this situation and to have an opportunity of moving towards a more open learning environment we have tried to place the learner in a problem-solving situation where the second language is being used for a purpose, but where the domain of discourse is sufficiently restricted so that a system could be developed to understand the meaning of inputs well enough to sustain a dialogue. The problem solving situation we propose is for learners to try to determine what inheritance is due to them, given the conditions of a will, by finding out details of past and present family relations.

At the present stage, the dialogue is sustained off-line with English native learners asking their questions in French. Here, for the sake of the presentation we have extracted some pieces of the dialogue just before the occurrence of an error and have imagined how the system would diagnose the learner's rules and maintain a learner model.

In the dialogue[0] of Figure 2.1 the learner has uttered a sentence that includes two errors. When trying to find out the address of Jean's sister, she said: "Que est sa adresse ?" instead of "Quelle est

[0] In the kind of dialogue presented here and in the other examples the interactions with the user are very limited. We give them only to illustrate our concern, not as an example of typical dialogue to hold in an ITS.

son adresse ?". Leaving aside the problem of tackling two errors at the same time, the system focuses on the diagnosis of the learner's behaviour relating to the mismatch between "sa" and "adresse".

```
Dialogue1    ("L" stands for "learner" and "S" for "system")

L: Jean a-t-il une soeur?                                 (Has Jean a sister ?)
S: Oui.
L: Est-elle vivante ?                                     (Is she alive ?)
S: Oui.
L: Que est sa adresse ?                                   (What is her address ?)
S: There is a problem in your last sentence.
   Would you accept this utterance (yes/no) ? :
  (Cecile lives with her brother)  Cécile vit avec son frère.        (i)
L: yes
S: OK.  Would you accept this utterance (yes/no) ?:
   ta autre soeur                                                    (ii)
L: yes
S: I think the problem is the following:
  You cannot say: ta autre soeur                                     (iii)
  But you can say: ta soeur, ton autre soeur
  Explanation (yes/no) ?
L: yes
S: You can also say: ma belle héritière, mon héritière
   Because : the masculine forms "mon", "ton", "son" are found
   qualifying a feminine singular noun, when they are followed by a
   word beginning with a vowel or h-mute.
   Do you want a complete presentation of the rule
    <Possessive Adjective Agreement> (yes/no) ?                      (iv)
```

Figure 2.1. Discrimination between two possible explanations of the learner's behaviour relating to a morphological agreement error between "sa" and "adresse".

The system has two possible explanations of this error relating to two different *applicable rules* (definition of an AR is given in section 6). It is going to discriminate between them in order to know which one may be applicable to the learner. First the system tries to discover if this is a transfer problem, i.e. an application of an English grammar rule (gender agreement with the possessor when, in French, the possessive adjective agrees in gender with the possessed object). The system uses a discriminative example associated with the first applicable rule: it asks the learner her opinion about sentence (i). Since she accepts this sentence, it means that the English rule is not applicable, provided she shows this behaviour consistently[1].

Then the system tries the other explanation: the learner ignored or forgot the morphological agreement between the possessive adjective "sa" and the following noun. The teacher's applicable rule describing this agreement has the discriminative example (ii). Since the learner accepts it, the system interprets the answer as a rejection of this rule, which is a special case of the general rule of the possessive adjective agreement. It deduces that the learner has used a strategy of simplification when learning and thus "forgot" this special case. Having found the explanation of the learner's behaviour, the system can now present the teacher's applicable rule using the examples (iii) and a pedagogical explanation. It can also propose presenting to the user the general rule (iv). After this dialogue the learner's model is updated and contains (among others) the following learner's applicable rule :

[1] This may be considered as a strong hypothesis because we often are inconsistent when learning. But in this paper we will restrict ourselves to the diagnosis of some learner's rules consistently applied.

```
Learner model:
AR3.1, Learner's rule
Divergent sentence: Que est sa adresse ?
Name: Incomplete application of rule
     <AR2,Possessive Adjective Morphological Agreement>
Causal explanation:
  Learning strategy, simplification
...
```

In order to perform this diagnosis, different kinds of knowledge and techniques need to be used. We will present them later on and detail the applicable rules which have been referred to in this example. Before we explain our system in detail, we first review Error Analysis and traditional methods of learner modelling in ITS. Then we review other approaches to modelling SLL as background.

3. Error Analysis in Applied Linguistics

First we have to make a clear distinction between what are errors on the one hand and lapses and slips on the other hand. In the Applied Linguistics field, the term "error" is taken to mean some idiosyncratic or 'un-nativelike' piece of language produced regularly and systematically by a foreign language learner. Lapses and slips refer to occasional actions which are not systematic and which the learner herself can correct. They are often called mistakes. They are of no interest to the Error Analysis since they say nothing about the true state of the learner's knowledge.

Error Analysis has a long tradition. Until the late 1960s, it consisted mainly in building large collections of "common" errors and their linguistic classification [16]. The goals were pedagogic: errors provided information for teaching and for designing remedial lessons. No theoretical framework existed for explaining the role played by the errors. In accordance with Behaviourist learning theory, the prevention of errors was more important than the identification of errors. Most people considered errors as a faulty version of the foreign language. The Contrastive Analysis Hypothesis[2] reinforced this view with the notion of "interference": existing habits prevent correct utterances from becoming established; errors are signs of learning failure and thus are not tolerable.

At the beginning of the 1970s new studies [34] changed the approach to the Error Analysis problem. Following the new Mentalist theory of language learning, these theorists asserted that the second language learners could be viewed as actively constructing rules from the data they encounter and gradually adapting these rules in the direction of the target-language system. This means that learners' errors need not be seen as signs of failure. On the contrary, they give some evidence for the learner's development systems [24]. Today theories of language learning are increasingly learner-oriented. Error Analysis is still of interest since errors which represent the product of learning, can be used to get hints about the underlying process of learning and particularly the learner's strategies.

Next we will briefly introduce the general procedure of Error Analysis and examine more closely the step concerned with the explanations. Some learner's strategies will be illustrated before drawing conclusions on the interest of Errors Analysis to ITSs in second language learning.

3.1 What is Error Analysis ?

We will describe the procedure for Error Analysis following the six-steps method set by van Els & al [44]. (1) A corpus of language is selected. This involves deciding on the size of the sample, the medium to be sampled and the homogeneity of the sample (by taking into account the learner's characteristics: age, stage of development, motivation, etc.). (2) The errors in the corpus are

[2] According to the Contrastive Analysis, L2 errors are the result of differences between the learner's first language and the foreign language.

identified. Here one needs to distinguish between true errors and slips. Errors can be "overtly idiosyncratic" (ill-formed in terms of target language rules) or "covertly idiosyncratic" (sentences superficially well-formed but when taking the context into account they are clearly ungrammatical). (3) The errors are classified. This involves assigning a linguistic description to each error. (4) The errors are explained. In this stage of the procedure, an attempt is made to identify the psycholinguistic cause of the errors. (5) The errors are evaluated. This stage involves assessing the seriousness of each error in order to make principled teaching decisions which are to be processed in step (6), prevention/correction of errors.

In this paper we are mainly interested by the first four steps. Step one is determined by the choice of the application: in BELLOC the coverage of the corpus is essentially centred around interrogatives in French. The identification of the errors and their location within the linguistic knowledge described in the ITS is a hard problem which will be referred to later on. The classification of an error (step three) in the procedure for Error Analysis consists of characterising the linguistic knowledge concerned by the error.

Some language books present a wide range of typical errors classified by knowledge sources which can give useful hints when developing a system. Swan and Smith [39], for example, presents a good overview of the different sources relating to interference problems between French native speakers speaking English: grammar, phonology, morphology, punctuation, vocabulary. But these criteria are insufficient for classifying an error in an ITS: firstly, because the way the linguistic knowledge is described does not allow a clear distinction between these sources and, secondly, because several different levels of such knowledge are often involved in an error. One needs to distinguish, as we will see, the level of generality of the rules describing the error and the kinds of techniques needed to tackle them. Step four, the explanations of errors, is our main concern here. We will now detail the related applied linguistics approach.

3.2. Learner's processes and explanations of interlanguage errors

One of the most significant contributions of Error Analysis lies in its success in elevating the status of errors from undesirability to that of a guide to the learner's internal processing used for *acquiring* L2 knowledge and *using* it for creating speech. These processes/strategies are often classified into three different types [16]: strategies of learning (how to internalise and automatise L2 knowledge), of production (how to use existing resources automatically), and of communication (how to compensate for inadequate resources). The first type of process relates to the learning language aspect, the others two types to the use of it, the whole set of cognitive processes provide us with a general explanation of the second language acquisition (or the interlanguage[3]) problem. Whilst presenting these strategies, we associate the respective explanations of errors. Figure 3.1 sums up the links between processes/strategies and errors.

Learner's Strategies of Learning

When the learner tries to create new knowledge about the target language, she first tries to make some hypothesis by using prior knowledge (of L1, L2 or another foreign language) or by inferring new rules from the input data on which she has to work. When relying on prior knowledge, she mainly uses two strategies: transfer of rules from the first language and generalisation (and overgeneralisation) of second language rules. Transfer and generalisation can be seen as a form of simplification. Simplification strategies consist of attempts by the learner to ease the burden of learning, to restrict hypothesis formation to those hypotheses which are relatively easy to form and will facilitate the communication. Once the learner has developed a hypothesis, she can test it out in a variety of ways such as: receptively (the learner attends to inputs expressed in the second

[3] Interlanguage is the term coined by Selinker [37] to refer to the systematic knowledge of a second language which is independent of both the learner's first language and the foreign language.

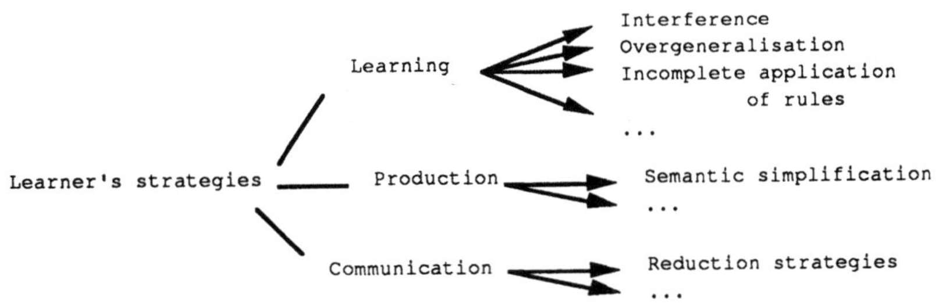

Figure 3.1. Simplified classification of the learner's strategies and the associated causes of errors.

language and compares her hypotheses with the data provided), productively (the learner produces L2 utterances containing rules representing the hypotheses she has formed and assesses their correctness in terms of the feedback received), meta-lingually (the learner consults a native speaker, teacher, grammar, or dictionary to establish the validity of the feedback received), or interactionally (the learner elicits a repair from her interlocutor). After having tested some hypotheses, part of the learning process involves consolidating them by accumulating confirmatory evidence, i.e. to practise L2 language either on formal aspects or on functional aspects. This is the automatisation process.

Some strategies used by the learner in order to simplify the task of learning L2 may have the side-effect of generating errors. Here is a description from [33]:

Language Transfer or Interference

The learner uses her previous mother-tongue (or possibly some other foreign language distinct from the target language) experience as a means of organising the second language. Here is an example of a transfer error from an English speaker in French:

> `Je suis fait mon devoir` *(Attempt to form a present continuous tense based on the pattern in English)*

It should be noted than the cause of this error is one with which every teacher is familiar, but is by no means the only one or even the most important (Contrastive Analysis asserted that this cause was the most important if not the only one, but studies done since the 1970s have indicated the contrary).

Overgeneralisation of the target language rules

The learner has acquired a particular piece of linguistic knowledge and some strategies which she had found helpful in organising the facts about the target language, but applies them too widely. This is a phenomenon frequently encountered.

> `Who did write this book ?` *(If this kind of sentence is uttered without any emphatic purpose, this means we have an overgeneralisation of the rule for inserting "do" into interrogatives.)*

Ignorance of rule restrictions

The previous example can also be explained as an ignorance of the restriction of the usage of "do" into interrogatives.

Incomplete application of rules

Incomplete application of rules involves a failure to learn more complex types of structure because the learner finds she can achieve effective communication by using relatively simple rules.

```
Teacher: Ask her how long it takes.
Student: How long it takes ?
```

False concepts hypothesized

False concepts hypothesized may derive from faulty comprehension of a distinction in the target language.

he is speaks French *("is" may be understood to be the marker of present tense, as "was" is a marker of the past tense).*

Transfer on training

Errors may also come from the influence of a teacher and/or a textbook writer who, inevitably, emphasises some aspect of the target language and neglects others, according to his own beliefs and experiences. For example, teachers and materials place special emphasis on the present continuous form in English because they know that the learner generally does not have an equivalent form in her native language and may thus be inclined to ignore it. This presentation may have the undesired effect of making the learner overuse this form as in:

In French we are not having a present continuous tense and we are not knowing when to use it.

Learner's Strategies of Production

Strategies of production relates to the unproblematic use of L2 knowledge, i.e. the learner relies on acquired knowledge to communicate. Starting from her communicative goal she will use planning strategies to create new utterances. Here again, she tries to simplify the task and thus errors may be generated, even if she has a correct knowledge. Two basic planning strategies can be identified: semantic simplification and linguistic simplification. For example, the learner can simplify a sentence by reducing the number of semantic cases and presupposing that the listener will infer the gaps, as in:

Hitting me *(Action + Patient)*
instead of :
He is hitting me *(Agent + Action + Patient).*

Learner's Strategies of Communication

Strategies of communication occur when the learner has a gap in her knowledge and has to fill it or by-pass it in order to achieve the communication. In the second case, she can use *reduction strategies*, i.e. gives up part of his original communicative goal:

He plays ... *(the learner cannot find the name of the sport, thus does away with the problem and reformulate her sentence)*
He does sport.

In the first case, when she wants to compensate for insufficient means, she uses *achievement strategies* , such as the replacement of an L2 item with an item made up from L2 forms, e.g. utters "picture place" instead of "gallery".

3.3 Application of Error Analysis in ITS for SLL

The recommended incorporation of an Error Analysis approach into the teaching process is important for two reasons: firstly, it provides insights into the process of language acquisition;

and, secondly, it de-emphasises the idea of errors as failure. Its disadvantage is that it is time consuming and suitable only for one-on-one tutoring and thus is an obvious candidate for computer-based teaching. The Error Analysis approach is also beneficial in determining remediation strategies since it identifies errors and gaps in the acquisition process itself as well as the acquired knowledge. However, this knowledge is not described in a formalized way that we could translate directly into rules. We need systems which could collect the expertise of expert teachers for that purpose (see section 5.4).

4. Overview of Learner Modelling

The aim of learner modelling is to provide a more responsive and individualised form of tutoring. Most of the modelling has been related to domain knowledge at the level of the observed performance. Generally speaking, a multi-level approach, incorporating information for the generation of the rules that directly produce the behaviour, has seldom been used. The use of information about a learner's meta-level rules we believe to be necessary for a cognitive diagnosis that can lead to more effective remediation and instructional methods. A general framework for the describing cognitive diagnosis with this level of detail can be found in Dillenbourg and Self [15]. Here, we consider previous attempts to implement learner models and highlight some of the problems that have been encountered.

Modelling techniques

The two most common techniques for representing a learner in an ITS are *overlay* and *bug* modelling. The overlay model is applicable where the expertise can be expressed as a set of rules. The learner's state of knowledge is viewed as a subset of this expert rule set. Each rule is evaluated for the likelihood of the learner possessing it. A number of sources of evidence are used to assign a probability to the learner's possession of a rule; such as implicit sources by comparing the learner's behaviour with an expert's, or explicit sources by directly querying the learner about her beliefs. Even though overlay models have been a common structure for learner models they do have significant limitations; they assume that all errors are gaps in the learner's knowledge, as compared with the expert's, whilst it is clear that errors are produced by the use of distorted and replacement correct rules.The "buggy" approach to learner modelling tackles this problem by substituting variants of the correct rule or rules into the problem solving procedures. Generally speaking, in both these techniques the learner is represented as a set of production rules that, if applied to a problem, duplicate the learner's performance or behaviour. In the buggy models the rules that account for the learner's non-standard performance are usually drawn from a set of known possible rules, usually called a bug catalogue. This approach has been used in subject areas such as subtraction [6], fractions [29], and Lisp programming [2]. The development of the bug catalogues - which can run into several hundred rules - has been very labour-intensive. The implication is that it requires a great deal of time and expertise (through experimental studies and laborious analyses of learners' problem solving) to develop a bug catalogue which is adequate to support intelligent tutoring. Additionally, bug catalogues are concerned with relatively superficial differences in the behavioural models and not directly with the underlying misconceptions which gave rise to the bugs. The use of bug catalogues model the learner's problem solving as a set of uninterpreted syntactic rules; whereas it is likely that the syntactic manifestations are produced by the learner reasoning about the semantics of the problem. This lack of deeper representations limits the ITS 's ability to remediate successfully.

Generation techniques

The generation of bugs has been explained in a number of ways, for instance by Repair Theory [7] and by extrapolation techniques [25]. Repair Theory is intended to be domain independent, with new rules being produced by skipping steps and replacing steps by analogous ones in existing rules. Unrestricted use of repairs leads to some very peculiar errors that have not been observed in real learners. But again these operations are carried out at a syntactic level and an ITS is still unable to capitalise on the fact that the learner has actually attempted a repair at all. Laurillard [23] also points out that the method still fails to capture the necessary nature of the learner's misconceptions that can be used in selecting an appropriate teaching action. Matz [25] also has proposed a mechanism for the generation of bugs. The cause of errors in her theory (which has never been implemented) is the application of general extrapolation techniques to example problems in one domain from domains with which the learner is already familiar, and which under different circumstances would lead to correct actions. Matz cites the case of novices' attempts to transfer techniques from arithmetic to algebra. This requires knowledge of comparable domains to be encoded in the system with the concomitant effort. Although both these techniques would be applicable to mal-rule generation for SLL neither on their own has the power to produce the variety of rules that are known to exist in SLL; although the extrapolation technique does appear to be the analogue of 'language transfer', described in the previous section. Hence it will be necessary to augment these techniques by more varied generation techniques and by the acquisition of expert rules that are a direct result of teaching experience.

5. Treatment of Errors in SLL ITSs

5.1. Different Approaches in SLL ITSs

The primary components of the construction of language competence and skills in communication are, among others, formal linguistic competence (knowledge of morphology, syntax, etc.) and functional competence (the ability to use the language to express meaning). Because of the difficulties encountered in natural language processing, currently functional and formal competences cannot be simultaneously cultivated with the same degree of accuracy in ITSs for second language learning. This implies, at least, two different approaches to modelling which are not related in the same way to the Error Analysis problem.

Functional Approach

Since the focus is to facilitate the expression of meaning, ITSs based on the functional aspect of natural language [27, 20, 28] are not directly concerned with the formal correction of the learner's production. When a sentence cannot be parsed as correct, computational linguistics techniques may still be used but only to handle the ill-formed input and to manage the dialogue in order to try to understand the meaning of the utterance. The strategies of communication described in applied linguistics may supplement part of the learner model and make a link between this model and the computational linguistics techniques. Within these problem areas user modelling techniques used in computational linguistics [22] and learner modelling techniques in ITS seem to converge. This is an area of research which has not been much explored, since most of the systems dealing with the functional approach have, at the present stage, no learner model. But we will not pursue this learner modelling problem here since we are focusing on the formal approach.

Formal approach

With regards to SLL ITSs concerned with formal aspects of natural language, we will distinguish, for the sake of this presentation, two types of systems: *computational-errors systems* and *early deeper Error Analysis systems*. Broadly speaking, until recently, two competing factors seem to differentiate existing systems: the linguistic coverage versus the depth of the Error Analysis. Computational-Errors systems have, relatively speaking, a large linguistic coverage but depth limited Error Analysis procedures. We are mainly referring here to the variety of errors handled and, especially, the limited diagnosis of their causes. Early systems with a deeper Error Analysis had, on one hand, a narrow linguistic coverage but, on the other hand, a quite exhaustive description of the possible errors which may have occurred in their domains.

We present these two kinds of approaches, with their advantages and drawbacks, trying to differentiate the computational linguistics problems from the tutoring ones[4]. After this, ongoing research on capturing and modelling learner's processes will be introduced. This aims at filling the gaps highlighted in the two previous approaches and at moving towards a better error diagnosis.

5.2 Computational-Errors systems

A Computational-Errors system consists mainly of a computational grammar and a *computational-errors-parser*. A computational-errors parser is a parser which uses some computational strategies to recognise an utterance as erroneous, to locate this error with respect to the computational grammar and is, sometimes, able to help to remediate. The underlying teaching strategy in these systems is to show the learner her errors (with respect to the computational grammar) and possibly initiate a dialogue with her to help correct this particular utterance. Below we present some Computational Errors systems in terms of their skill in the computational diagnosis process.

The French Grammar Analyser

The French Grammar Analyser (FGA) [3] is one of the early system of grammatical error analysis. Here, every error has to be predicted and described explicitly by hand in the grammar. For example, if one is concerned with agreement problems between two categories, one has to foresee all the different situations in which such a problem may occur. The system cannot access the existing linguistic knowledge to diagnose problems. Some strategic choices appear to have been made without much concern for linguistic or pedagogic relevance (cf. procedures about unknown words). This may explain why the system proposes some wrong corrections and eventually accepts incorrect sentences.

The XTRA-TE system

The XTRA-TE system [12] is an ITS built on the top of XTRA, a translation Chinese-English grammar, which has a large coverage: 7000 English words, 10000 Chinese words, 500 grammar rules. Error diagnosis is handled by a multi-pass parser. Syntactic and semantic knowledge are separated in the grammar so that it is possible to distinctly relax some of the corresponding constraints. Instead of adding a new grammar rule for each possible error, definitions of grammatical categories are expanded in a traditional way (with respect to computational linguistics techniques). Figure 5.1 presents a simplified example of the definition of a verb phrase category

---

[4] A different presentation of ITSs on SLL can be found in [40].

which allows the identification of a non-agreement in number between the subject and the verb. It is given in the Definite Clause Grammar format.

```
sentence(Np, Vp) -->
        noun_phrase(Np,Num),
        verb_phrase(VP,Num).

verb_phrase(vp(v(V),np(Np)), Num) -->
        trans_verb(V,Num,Relax_flag),
        noun_phrase(Np).

trans_verb(V,Num, _) -->
        t_verb(V,Num).                                              (i)
trans_verb(V,Num, Relax_flag) -->                                   (ii)
       Relax_flag == true,
       t_verb(V, WrongNum),
       WrongNum \= Num,
       error_flaggin(X,subject_verb_agreement,[Num, WrongNum]).

t_verb(likes,single).
```

In a correct sentence the verb is analysed by the clause (i). If there is a problem of number agreement between the subject and the verb ("The old men likes golf"), clause (i) will fail. After the detection of this failure the program sets the error flag, *Relax-flag* to *true* and calls for another parse. The clause (ii) notes a difference of number and stores the corresponding error.

Figure 5.1 . Relaxation constraints in XTRA-TE

The authors argue that this strategy avoids duplication of grammar rules, but some duplication still exists in the definition of grammatical categories. In this example all the definitions of verb phrases in the complete grammar have to be extended in order to tackle all the different cases of subject-verb disagreement. The extension of the whole grammar may be limited because they only have a full cover of subject-verb agreement and of pronominal errors. XTRA-TE is able to diagnose others types of errors but leaves aside the problem of incorrect word order which may imply an expansion of the grammar.

A learner model is built on the evaluation of the learner's errors which reflect her lack of certain concepts. A score is attributed to each learner. XTRA-TE uses this score to differentiate its strategies of correction during the session (indirect correction, direct correction, etc.).

Menzel's approach

Menzel presents an error diagnosis procedure [26] which tries to concentrate on an exact localization of rule violations and is able to infer information about factual faults as well. His approach is based on the following basic principles: (1) supply the system with only knowledge about correctness; (2) devise a diagnosis procedure which is independent of the content of the knowledge base. In order to achieve his aim he chose the restricted domain of the morpho-syntactic agreement in German.

When an error is encountered, his idea is to select a set of relevant constraints C, build a resolution proof on them which finds the minimum set of constraints which have been violated, and negate them in order to let C accept the divergent sentence. From this subset of negated constraints the system is then able to explain the failure in the parse and to propose a remediation.

This strategy avoids the duplication of rules in the grammar due to a change in the unification algorithm. It is an interesting approach but one which needs much more work in order to be incorporated in a large grammar. As a matter of fact, when the parser has to manage a great number of rules, the selection of the relevant subset of constraints without any hint seems to be an intractable problem.

The ILTS for German system

The ILTS for German [36] handles a variety of errors and corresponding strategies in a way close to the XTRA-TE system, plus a treatment of certain word-order problems. A menu-based interface offers the learner the possibility of accessing part of the system's knowledge and of self-correcting some errors. The agreement errors procedure is quite original. Let us present it through the analysis of the divergent sentence:

```
Der Götter zümen (the gods are angry).
```

Within the unification grammar formalism of ILTS each word may be defined as a set of couples (feature, value). Hence the definitions of *der* and *Götter*:

```
der: {[Art-cat(def),Gender(masc),Case(nominative),Number(singular)],
      [Art-cat(def),Gender(fem),Case(or(genitive,dative)),Number(singular)],
      [Art-cat(def),Gender(_),Case(genitive),Number(plural)]}.

Götter: {[Gender(masc), Case(neg(dative)), Number(plural)]}.

der Götter: {[Art-cat(def),Gender(masc),Case(genitive),Number(plural)]}.
```

There are two possible diagnoses of the error: (1) *Der Götter* is genitive plural (unification of *der* and *Götter*), but since it is the subject of the sentence, the right case should have been nominative. This is a disagreement on the case. (2) *der* is singular and *Götter* is plural ; this a disagreement on the number (the system can find this error since the unification process keeps the trace of all the pairs of value sets which have not been unified).

Schwind argues that the first case is improbable since it is harder, for the learner, to build a genitive case, which is a "difficult case", when the nominative is required, which is the "easiest" case. She explains this choice by the fact that "people make errors in order to make their life easier". But this relevant argument is not declared explicitly in the system as a learner strategy. The choice of (2) is made by a procedure which filters cases and may have no such concern.

Error diagnosis in Computational-Errors systems

In the Computational-Errors systems the ITS paradigm is encompassed by the juxtaposition of a computational grammar and a computational-errors procedure. Such procedures which try to locate the error within the computational grammar and find a way to repair the failure that occurred during the parse have been presented. This is a difficult computational problem which has not been fully achieved.

However, we think that, even if those techniques are necessary in a SLL system, they should not represent the final aim of an ITS. The computational grammar is not the grammar that the learner uses to learn (or the teacher to teach) a language (see section 6). Thus the diagnosis of an error and the corresponding explanations given by a Computational-Errors system reflect the system/parser behaviour but account very badly for the learner's use of her own grammar rules. Since the processing of an incorrect sentence may make the parser fail, the learner's errors are still considered as a failure in the learner's process of learning, reflecting a gap in her knowledge with respect to the "complete" knowledge of the system. Thus the learner is never considered as an agent who creates new knowledge and the acquisition of a second language is never understood as an elaborative process[5].

5.3 Early systems with a deeper Error Analysis

Some SLL systems tried to achieve a deeper Error Analysis of the learner. In restricted domains errors have been analysed and explained with respect to criteria used in applied linguistics which may better reflect the learner's own process of acquisition. Two representative systems are presented.

The VP2 system

VP2 [35], an ITS dedicated to teaching English to a native Spanish speaker, uses, like the previous systems, a computational grammar. But here the emphasis is put on the explanation of some learner's errors. Arguing that computer-assisted instruction systems should include a model of relevant aspects of users' prior knowledge to predict and prevent errors or detect and correct them easily, the author decided to focus on interference problems. More precisely, she chose to work on the acquisition by non-English speakers of English verbal constructions formed from a verb plus particle or verb plus prepositional phrase. In this domain there is a large variation between English and Spanish languages.

The system is provided with grammars of both languages. The Spanish grammar models the learner behaviour. From this modelling the system is able to give some explanations to the learner, both whether a sentence is correct or incorrect. In this example of a correct answer, VP2 provides the learner with some further explanation and draws her attention to some underlying problems.

```
Tutor: Translate the following sentence:
       yo soñé con los 'angeles.
Student: I dreamed of the angels.
Tutor: Correct! Note that the direct translation of <soñar con>-<dream with>
       does not exist in English. In English you can also use <dream about>
       in this sentence.
```

When a divergent sentence makes the parser fail, the system, after having used the English grammar, tries to parse it with the Spanish grammar. It then compares the two parse trees (English parse of the correct sentence, Spanish parse of the learner answer), identifies the wrong prepositions or missing particles and accesses the Spanish dictionary to explain the differences. An open question with this approach is whether it is possible to extend it to take into account other linguistic phenomena where there are deep differences between the source and the target languages. Another problem is how this treatment of interferences could be integrated within a more general model of the learner's interlanguage, the transfer strategies being only a subset of the learner's ones.

---

[5] Improvement of parsing techniques does not necessarily entail equivalent enhancement of the diagnosis of the learner's processes. eL [46], for example, is a much cleverer system than its predecessor, FGA: a declarative computational grammar, new parsing strategies enable the system propose corrections relating to word-order, agreements,... problems. But the learner's linguistic knowledge and its strategies have not yet been taken into account.

The ALICE system

ALICE [8] is a system which concentrates on the translation of temporal and causal conjunctions from Italian to English or French. This restricted domain has been chosen to investigate how a deep linguistic description could be associated with the understanding of conceptual difficulties by the learner.

The knowledge about the conjunctions is described quite exhaustively in a network of concepts. All the possible errors are tackled as well. They are divided in two categories: the ones which can be easily identified and linked with a predefined message of explanation (i.e. literal translation, confusion with adverbs, etc.), and those which need a deeper diagnosis process which will be achieved through a dialogue with the learner (i.e. interference, errors due to similarity, errors involving discrimination between concepts). In ITS terms, the diagnosis and correction of the errors in the first category rely on the use of a simple bug catalogue; those corresponding to the second category rely on a pattern matching process to find the closest learner model in a predefined set.

The answers given by the system to the learner, the characterisation of her errors are very precise and accurate at a linguistic level, but from a pedagogical aspect the learner's role seems to be passive during the whole session. In effect, it seems that after the learner has chosen a set of conjunctions to work on, the system will follow its own predefined sequence of exercises and will never take into account the learner's answers, or the set of learner's models which it has diagnosed as being close to the learner behaviour. The learner modelling does not seem to be reflected in the system's behaviour. Despite all the learner's answers being stored in the system for the teacher, the system cannot exploit them.

If the aim of ALICE were the validation, through a sequence of tests with learners, of the linguistic description of the chosen domain, this aim is accurately achieved. From an ITS standpoint, the current learner is not modelled specifically. The extension of the tools defined to associate a particular learner with a set of models to another domain may be problematic. Also, the extension of the linguistic knowledge may be difficult to achieve since no computational linguistics techniques are used.

5.4 Capturing and modelling the learner's processes

The systems mentioned above have addressed subspaces of the error diagnosis problem, but they lack generality and are thus hardly extendable to the whole space. Obviously, both a better understanding and a better formalisation of the learner's processes are required to extend the diagnosis space. During the last two or three years the research community in ITS for SLL has made inroads into these problems from a number of different perspectives.

Firstly, systems are being developed to support the acquisition of fundamental knowledge for the learner model from the various agents involved in language apprenticeship. The NOBILE system [9] allows experts, i.e. teachers, to design learner models through different kinds of interactions with the system, such as the "inverted dialogue" where the computer plays the role of the learner and produces divergent sentences and the user/teacher acts as the expert. The prototype IFAAR [30] offers an interface for knowledge acquisition from experts about learners' divergent sentences in order to capture the experts' diagnoses and the procedures they use. From the experiments undertaken with both experienced and trainee teachers, it transpires that these "experts" were not used to carrying out such deep and individual diagnoses, and that current knowledge acquisition techniques used in expert systems were hardly applicable [43]. There is an urgent need in the ITS field for appropriate techniques to capture experts' diagnoses.

Secondly, prototypes that aim at effectively computing a deep diagnosis of the learner's processes are under development. The ET system [19] proposes a methodology to integrate bug catalogue and bug generation techniques, partly based on the use of explanation-based learning techniques, in order to get a deep modelling of the learner's performances in the apprenticeship of tense aspects of English. In the BELLOC system we propose a structure to represent the learner's rules and an architecture to manage a conceptual modelling of a learner's strategies (see next section).

Lastly, another perspective is the explanatory approach adopted in Zock's system [47] which allows the learner to explicitly build hypotheses about the interlanguage, to test them, and subsequently update her own rules. Even if no learner modelling is explicitly at stake in this system it provides insights on how language structures are learned. Interestingly, within this perspective, errors are not only considered as unavoidable parts of the learning process, but also as an indispensable source of information.

6. The BELLOC System

We now present the architecture of the part of BELLOC for building and updating the learner model through the conceptual diagnosis of her errors. We introduce the different components necessary to achieve this task and their inter-relations. The main component is the set of applicable rules which describes the teacher's as well as the learner's linguistic knowledge. Several kinds of ARs are necessary. We explain why and how each AR should be structured. Several examples indicate how they could be used in the diagnosis of the learner's behaviour.

6.1. General Architecture

Figure 6.1 presents the general architecture which supports the handling of the conceptual diagnosis of the learner's rules with respect to the formal aspect of natural language. In order to introduce its main components we will sketch what happens from the time a sentence, which makes the parser fail, is entered until the diagnosis of the applicable rule which describes the problem and is relevant to the current user occurs.

When a sentence provokes a failure in the parser it means that some constraints in the computational grammar have been violated. A sequence of computational diagnostic procedures tries to give a partial diagnosis by identifying the relevant constraints. This corresponds to Part I in the Figure 6.1 of the architecture.

Starting from this partial diagnosis a theorem prover identifies *candidate* applicable rules which could give a description of the learner's rule and strategies. The theorem prover searches among the set of applicable rules, some of them describing rules common to teachers and learners, others typical learners' rules, or general learners' meta-rules. During the deductive process, information coming from the previous state of the learner model can be used to prune the search space and make some preferences.

This process of identification of an applicable rule can be straightforward. In parallel with the call to computational diagnosis procedures, a second parse can be attempted with the computational linguistic grammar augmented by predefined learner's rules described in the same formalism. If one of these rules accepts the sentence, then an applicable rule is automatically found because of the one to one correspondence between these extra rules and a subset of the applicable rules. This corresponds to Part II in the Figure 6.1 of the architecture.

The candidate applicable rules are passed to the *pedagogical module* (see Part III of the picture of the architecture). It holds a dialogue (like the one in Figure 2.1) with the learner to check which ones apply effectively to him. This stage is what we call the *conceptual diagnosis*. During this process, information contained in the slots of the candidate ARs is used. Once it has diagnosed the AR(s) applicable to the current learner, the pedagogical module can update the *learner model* and decide to react (or not) in order to remediate or encourage, taking into account the aim of the working session (stress on communication, or formal aspects), the degree of seriousness of learner's divergence, previously related problems, teaching principles (see [42] on that point), etc.

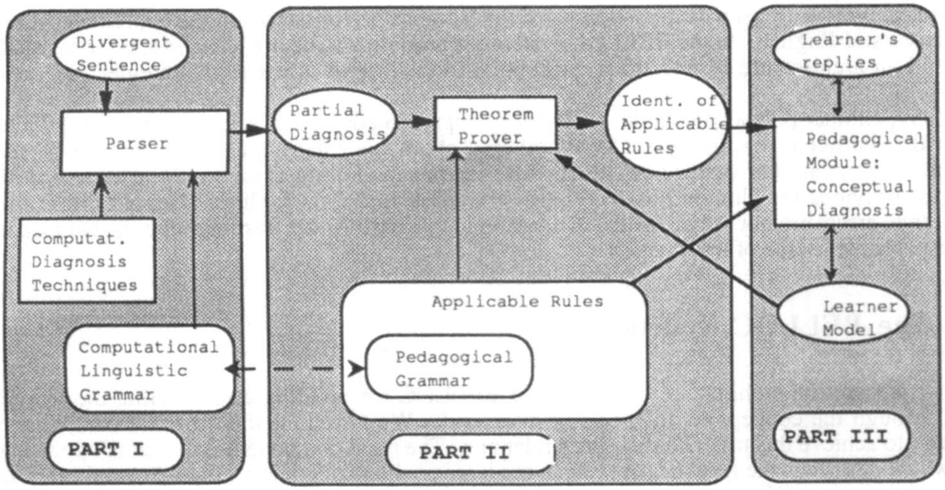

Figure 6.1 . Overview of the architecture for the treatment of errors in BELLOC. Ellipses represent dynamic information, Square rectangles procedures, and rounded rectangles static information. Dash arrows represent the relationships between static data.

As a first approximation, the kinds of information relating to formal aspects of the target language that the pedagogical module would need to find in the learner model include at least: a set of ARs describing her linguistic knowledge and her strategies, possible fossilizations on some ARs, her level of knowledge of the meta-language necessary to talk about grammatical problems, history of previous identified ARs and of the dialogue. From now on, when detailing Part III of the architecture, we will restrict ourselves to the problem of diagnosing the relevant applicable rules, given an empty learner model. The history of the learner and the pedagogical reactions will be left aside.

Divergent sentences

We call it a "divergent" sentence and not an "incorrect" one, because the appreciation of its level of correctness may vary from one learner to another. The sentence is divergent with respect to a *standard grammar*[6]. When a computational linguist develops a grammar, he tends to give a *correct exhaustive description* of a subset of a language. We refer to that knowledge of the language as the "standard" grammar. This standard grammar represents a viewpoint on a correct subset of a language, but by no means the definitive one, since one may have different views on what is correct or not in a given situation or the grammar may have some gaps.

[6] We leave aside here divergences coming from slips, spelling errors and keyboard typing errors. For the treatment of these problems see [17].

Computational linguistic grammar and diagnosis techniques

The role of the computational linguistic grammar is controversial. Obviously we need such a grammar to parse the learner's inputs, to give her answers about the family database. In the IFAAR prototype, we have used a unification-based formalism, LUGA [21], to develop the syntactical grammar of a subset of French to cover the interrogative sentences of the learners. This formalism was chosen since unification grammars are a well tried and frequently used method of language representation (mainly syntactic) in the computational linguistics community (see [5,1,10] for example). But then two pointed questions arise: is the computational grammar formalism well suited to represent the linguistic knowledge of the learner, and how can we have a relevant diagnosis on the failure of the parse ? Let us try first to tackle the second question, i.e. the computational diagnosis techniques.

As pointed out in section 5, the description in the grammar of all the possible violations of constraints is unrealistic. The approach consisting of *modifying the unification process* in order to deduce what are the relevant violated constraints is certainly a promising area of research. But one needs some mechanisms to reduce the search space and help the unification solver to focus on preferable paths. Indeed even with a grammar which has a limited coverage several thousands of failures in the unification process occur in a successful parse! The second kind of diagnosis techniques which we can apply are the ones used in computational linguistics for the treatment of *ill-formed inputs* [13,45]. As illustrated in the example of diagnosis in Figure 6.4, an ordinary grammar cannot handle the semantic simplifications of the learner, which are quite frequent. Semantically-based techniques need to be used after the first parse, even on problems relating to formal aspects of natural language.

If we quote Shieber [38], one of the criteria against which to judge linguistic formalisms is linguistic felicity, i.e. the degree to which descriptions of linguistic phenomena can be stated directly (or indirectly) as linguists would wish to state them. This may be interpreted in two very different ways by computational (or theoretical) linguists and applied linguists. The former tend to describe and explain as fully as possible the phenomenon of language. The grammars they produce are by their very nature descriptive. Grammars used in applied linguistics are prescriptive. One lesson learned from the experiments with the IFAAR prototype is that a grammar developed on the traditional computational linguistics criteria is unreadable by expert teachers, even if explanations are provided. Secondly, one needs to incorporate in the ITS knowledge about linguistic problems usually encountered by learners of a given source language during their apprenticeship in the target language. It is encoded in what we call *predefined rules* (which represent one kind of applicable rule) and is not usually part of the background knowledge needed to develop a "traditional" computational grammar.

One way to bypass these drawbacks could be to rewrite the computational grammar with other criteria in mind, using a more restricted and accessible meta-language. We want to experiment with this option. But we think a more probable solution would be to also set out a pedagogical grammar.

Pedagogical grammar

We call "pedagogical grammar" the grammar created for instructional purposes in an ITS. It is supposed to be close to the one used by teachers during instruction. Obviously there exists no unique form upon which all teachers would agree. The question of teaching grammar explicitly or implicitly is still very controversial and answers vary much from one country to another. Some school text books offer a good picture of what a pedagogical grammar is: the words in which the linguistic knowledge is explained are carefully chosen and pedagogically presented (see

Bescherelle[7] for a reference in French [4]). The rules are explained in plain natural language and significant examples and warnings about potential difficulties are explained

Swartz [41] has shown the central role that the design of the pedagogical grammar in a CALL system occupies, and the help that a hypertext tool can provide to support the structuring of this conceptual design in order to develop foreign language instruction. Unfortunately, as mentioned in her paper, the question of implementing this pedagogical grammar has been left aside at this stage. In fact this is a critical point. When one tries to formalise the knowledge presented in text books its incompleteness and even inconsistencies in the terminology are striking. On that aspect, research undertaken in Nijmegen provides elements of the answer. They have developed a pedagogical grammar, IPG, which can parse sentences and is used for Dutch grammar instruction [31,32]. They have adopted a consistent terminology to develop the grammar. Meaningful tree structures can be displayed to the learner with a level of detail depending on her mastering of the meta-language. For the purpose of learning a foreign language in a communicative environment, as we made the choice for BELLOC, it could be of interest to know if the IPG formalism can support the semantic features necessary to process the dialogue with our family database.

For the present, we have started to formalise a pedagogical grammar extracted from text books in order to describe it as a set of production rules. We want to investigate the links between this grammar and the computational linguistic one[8]. As we will see in the next paragraphs the pedagogical grammar is a subset of the set of applicable rules on which the theorem prover could operate in order to diagnose the learner's rules. Hence all pedagogical grammar rules will have a common structure in which their computational code (the production rule) will be contained in the "computational code" slot.

6.2 What is an applicable rule ?

The concept of an applicable rule is based on a number of ideas. Firstly, we want to separate the grammatical explanation which characterises the divergence of a sentence from the explanation that identifies the strategies the learner used to generate it. Next, we wish to move away from the concept of a mal-rule, which tends to emphasise the idea of failure, and move towards a concept that recognises the generation and updating of the language production rules as signs of learning. The de-emphasis of absolute correctness is important for other reasons. It is important to recognise that teachers also use applicable rules as approximations to the desirable performance as pedagogic devices to simplify the problems of learning. A common frame to describe the learner's and the teacher's rules would give a fairer reflection of this situation. Lastly, the domain of language is less clear cut than parts of mathematics and physics, traditionally used in ITSs. In consequence absolute correctness does not have any meaning. For example, the sentence "Combien de frères est-ce qu'il a?" would be considered incorrect in written French but is acceptable as spoken French.

The definition for the structure of an applicable rule, as described here, arose from these ideas refined by experimentation with the IFAAR prototype. During the elaborative process we tried to find answers to the following questions: how can we represent better the learner's state of understanding in the domain? what sort of linguistic and pedagogical knowledge does an expert

---

[7] We hope the reader will understand that we are not committed to the definitions used in that book. We give it as an example of how a given linguistic terminology may be introduced for instructional purposes. Very different proposals have been made in CALL for the specification of this terminology: they range from a fixed vocabulary defined by psycholinguists in accordance with a theory [32] to an adaptation of the words effectively used by learners [14].

[8] In ET [18] the authors come to the same conclusion but from a different starting point. The first version of ET partly relied on a pedagogical grammar directly extracted from the literature ("naive grammar"); the second version will benefit from the coupling of this naive grammar with the formal systemic one in order to obtain a tractable and neat pedagogical grammar.

bring to bear on the problem of diagnosing a learner's performance? in what terms would the expert prefer to express himself? what formalisms and implementations are suitable for encapsulating this knowledge? and what information is needed to discriminate between competing applicable rules that explain a particular behaviour. This gave rise to a six-slot structure for an AR (Figure 6.2), that we now detail.

Applicability slot: an AR is either applicable to the learner (a learner's rule), or to the teacher (a teacher's rule) or to both at the same time. In the first case it characterises the learner's performance, and, in the second, what the performance should have been. The third case will be illustrated in the last example of section 6.3.

Explanation slot: in a learner's rule the explanation slot contains a causal explanation of the learner's behaviour and optionally an explanation of grammar rules that could be used in the production of a sentence. In a teacher's rule, this slot contains a pedagogical explanation of the grammar rule expressed in meta-linguistic terms selected from a set generally used by the teacher and understandable by the learner.

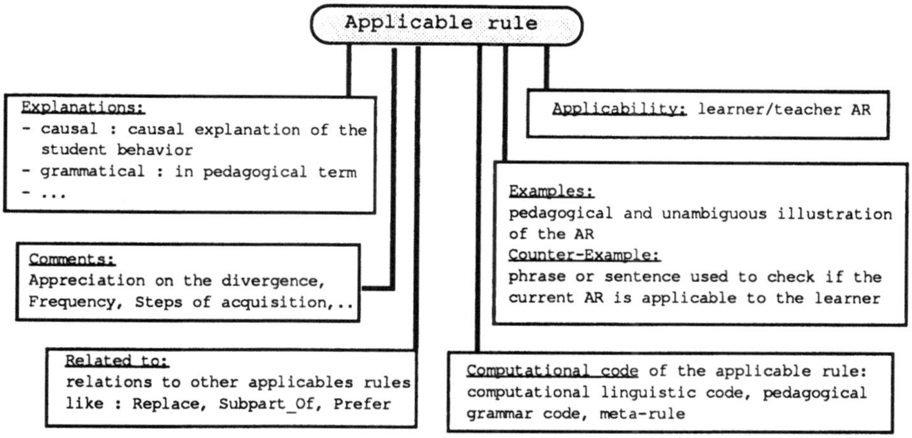

Figure 6.2. Structure of an applicable rule. Each box explains the type of information placed in the slot. Slot types are underlined.

Example slot: because a number of applicable rules may be capable of explaining a particular behaviour, it will be necessary to disambiguate them if effective remediation is to be carried out. Typically, a teacher does this by the use of examples and counter examples in a dialogue with the learner. Thus the AR structure should allow for the inclusion of sentences and phrases that both correspond to the current rule and to other rules that produce similar but not necessarily identical behaviour. These examples may also be used to illustrate points of grammar in later remediation or instruction. For the present time we have a restricted use of the corresponding slot. Examples convey information to the learner after the conceptual diagnosis and to the developer of the computational grammars (linguistic and pedagogical). The examples should be pedagogically and unambiguously selected with respect to those presented in related ARs. The counter-example is a discriminatory one, it allows the test of the applicability of the current AR to the learner.

Related-to slot: although a general network of explanations may not be established there are a number of obvious links between explanations. The most obvious is the relationship between rules that explain the same learner behaviour. Another potential link is between rules that have some superficial resemblance, such as rules that require agreements between various parts of speech in the foreign language that are not required in the native language. There are also obvious links between rules that have specialisations and exceptions and naturally form themselves into a hierarchy. Therefore part of the structure of the applicable rule must represent the relationships with other applicable rules. The main kinds of relations, which will be illustrated in the following examples, are those linking teacher's rules and those linking learner's rules to teacher's ones.

Computational-code slot: how an applicable rule relates to a particular divergent sentence and how it can be automatically selected as a possible candidate to explain the divergence is described in the computational-code slot. Since ARs can be of very different sorts, procedures can be expressed in the computational linguistic formalism, or in the pedagogical grammar formalism or as meta-rules. The coupling of a divergent sentence to an applicable rule is either straightforward (the linguistic computational code successfully parses the sentence) or is the result of a deductive process.

Comments slot: lastly the structure of the applicable rule should be able to represent ad hoc information that teachers commonly have about certain errors, such as at what stage of learning they are mostly likely to occur, possible remediation techniques, and the seriousness of the error. This informal information fills the comments slot.

6.3 Examples of AR diagnosis

Through different examples we introduce three kinds of applicable rules and how they are used for conceptual diagnosis. Figure 6.3 presents the three applicable rules used in dialogue1.

AR1 is a learner's rule describing an interference/transfer problem (special case of learning strategy, see Figure 3.2). The learner tries to apply the English rule about possessor gender agreement to French sentences including possessive adjectives, as in the example: "Jean vit avec son soeur " (*Jean lives with his sister*) [9]. The computational code is written in LUGA. This code is included in the computational grammar, but can be fired only after a first failure in the parser and then will accept the divergent sentence. The use of the counter-example is twofold: firstly, the LUGA code should fail on this sentence; secondly, it serves as a discriminatory example during the dialogue with the learner. If she accepts "Cecile vit avec son frère", the system will conclude that she does not have this rule in mind. AR1 is what we call a *predefined rule*. This rule is part of the knowledge of teachers in foreign language. It has to be described explicitly in advance by hand. Any automation of their production is hard to foresee. It is the aim of the IFAAR prototype to capture them.

AR2 is a teacher's rule and it is a *pedagogical grammar rule*. It describes the morphological agreement with possessive adjectives which is a special case of the possessive adjective agreement (rule AR4). Its computational code is a production rule because AR2 is a subpart of the pedagogical grammar. The direct relation with the LUGA code is not obvious because the agreement constraints may be expressed through several LUGA rules[10]; except that the standard LUGA grammar (i.e. the one which does not contain any predefined learner's rules) should accept the examples and reject the counter-example. "ta autre soeur" is also a discriminatory example. Its acceptance by the learner implies a rejection of AR2.

---

[9] Standard French version should be:"Jean vit avec sa soeur " because "soeur" is feminine.

[10] On such a simple example it is obvious that we could have a one to one correspondence between the computational rule and the pedagogical one. But if such a correspondence could be guaranteed at the level of the whole grammar there are few reasons to distinguish them. As we said, this is a point we want to investigate and so far, our experiments on more complex examples have found that strict correspondence was hard to maintain.

```
AR1. Learner's rule
Name: Possessor Gender Agreement
Examples:
  Jean vit avec son soeur.
  Mary vit avec sa frère.
Counter-example:
  (Cecile lives with her brother.)
  Cecile vit avec son frère.
Causal explanation:
  Learning strategy, Transfer problem:
  In English gender agreement with the
  possessor. In French gender and number
  agreement with the possessed object,
  person and number agreement with the
  possessor.
Computational code:
  #define relations
  Possessor_Gender_Agreement
      < syncat> = [Possessor, Possessed]
      < Possessor head agree gender> =
          < Possessed head agree gender>
Related rule: Replace by: AR4, Possessive
  Adjective Agreement.
```

```
AR2. Teacher's rule
Name: Possessive Adjective Morphological
  Agreement
Examples:
  ta soeur, ton autre soeur
  ma belle héritière, mon héritière
Counter-example:
  ta autre soeur
Pedagogical explanation:
  the masculine forms "mon", "ton", "son"
   are found qualifying a feminine
  singular noun, when they are followed
  by a word beginning with a vowel
  or h-mute.
Computational code: production rule
Related rule: Subpart of : AR4,
  Possessive Adjective Agreement.

AR3. Learner's rule
Name: Incomplete application
  of rule <RULE>
Causal explanation:
  Learning strategy, simplification
Computational code: ...
```

Figure 6.3. Applicable rules related to dialogue1 (see Figure 2.1) including a predefined rule (AR1), a meta-rule (AR3), and a pedagogical grammar rule (AR2).

AR3 is a *meta-rule* describing a particular general learner strategy consisting of the incomplete application of rules in order to simplify the learning process. This rule is fired if a pedagogical rule ARn which is a special case of another one has been rejected. Then the variable <RULE> is instantiated with the name of ARn. This strategy may be a consequence of the teaching process. When introducing a grammatical problem the teacher can decide, as a first step, to leave aside special cases such as morphological agreement. This simplification can therefore induce the situation encountered here.

How does the system use these rules to arrive the diagnosis of figure 2.1? The analysis of the sentence "Que est sa adresse?" provokes a failure in the parser. A second parse is accomplished successfully with inclusion of predefined rules. AR1 accepts the phrase "sa adresse". The computational diagnosis procedures give partial information about the failure in the first parse to the theorem prover; from this information the theorem prover is able to select AR2 as the rule that has not been applied. It is also able to show that the application of the meta-rule, AR3, to the higher level rule AR4, of which AR2 is a subpart, produces the same effect. By the use of the counter examples in AR1 and AR2 the system deduces that AR3 is the appropriate learner's applicable rule and is able to offer the teacher's applicable rules AR2 and through the relationship slot the higher level rule AR4 that fully describes possessive adjective agreements.

Through this example we have presented the three types of applicable rules: predefined rules, pedagogical grammar rules, and meta-rules. Meta-rules, such as AR3, are very important. They allow the generation of specific learner's ARs from the pedagogical grammar. This approach may give the answer to one of the drawbacks of the mal-rule approach described in section 4, that of having to describe by hand each individual learner's rule.

```
Dialogue2

L: Qui sont les frères de Jean ?
S: Robert et Tom.
L: Qui est marié à Tom ?
S: Anne.
L: Est-ce que je le fils de Tom ?                                    (i)
S: There is a problem in your last sentence.
   Would you accept this utterance (yes/no) ? :
   Est-ce qu'il est vivant ?.
L: yes
S: OK.I think the problem is the following:
  Even if your utterance is comprehensible, there is a missing
  constituent of <the verb etre>
```

Figure 6.4 . In the divergent sentence (i), the verb "to be" has been omitted.

A semantic simplification

In dialogue2 the learner has omitted the verb "to be" (Figure 6.4, sentence (i)). The standard form should have been "Est-ce que je suis le fils de Tom ?". Two applicable rules are candidates (Figure 6.5). AR5, which is a predefined rule, states that the learner may have confused the interrogative phrase "est-ce que" with the verb "to be" (compare the word order in sentence (i) with the English one in the translation "Am I Tom's son"). AR5 is encoded as a LUGA rule.

```
AR5. Learner's rule
Name: Omission of "etre" with "Est-ce que"
Example:
  Est-ce que Richard le fils de Cécile ?
Counter-example: Est-ce qu'il est vivant ?
Causal explanation: Learning strategy,
false concept hypothesized
  "Est-ce que" performs the function of
the verb to be
Computational code:...
```

```
AR6. Learner's rule
Name: semantic simplification of
   <CONSTITUENT>
Causal explanation:
  production strategy
  omission in a sentence of <CONSTITUENT> =
   (verb, auxiliary, subject, DOC ,SOC)
Pedagogical explanation:
  Even if your utterance is comprehensible,
  there is a missing constituent of
   <CONSTITUENT>
Computational code: ....
```

Figure 6.5 . Applicable rules relating to dialogue2.

AR6 is a meta-rule describing the semantic simplification of a constituent in a sentence like the verb, subject, direct object complement. The constituent(s) deleted are not syntactic but semantic. They consist of cases such as agent, object, patient, etc... The detection of the missing element is undertaken by special kinds of computational diagnosis procedures, fired after the first parse, which we referred to as treatments for ill-formed input.

Again the diagnosis between the two candidates rules begins with the most specific one, AR5. This is rejected after the acceptance of its counter-example. Since AR6 has no example/counter-example, nor is it related to any other rule, it is always an acceptable candidate. After the diagnosis the following rule will be added to the learner model:

```
AR6.1, Learner's rule
Divergent sentence: Est-ce que je le fils de Tom ?
Name: semantic simplification of <the verb être>
Causal explanation:
  production strategy
  omission in a sentence of <CONSTITUENT> = verb
...
```

A Learner's/Teacher's Applicable Rule

The diagnosis in Dialogue 3, shown in Figure 6.6, is accomplished by a rule that is both applicable to the learner and the teacher. Although sentence (i) is, on the one hand, a cumbersome construction, because it includes a double interrogative phrase, and is therefore not recommended in writing, it is, on the other hand, very frequently used by the French in speech because it avoids the difficult subject-verb inversion.

```
Dialogue3

L: Qui est mon père ?
S: Richard
L: Combien de frères est-ce qu'il a?                              (i)
S: There is a problem in your last sentence.
   I think the problem is the following:
    you can say :  Pourquoi est-ce que Robert a hérité ?          (ii)
    but it is better to say :   Pourquoi Robert a-t-il hérité ?   (iii)
   Explanation (yes/no) ?
L: yes
    Good, you seem to know a construction frequently used in speech,
    but be careful not to use it in formal writing,...
```

Figure 6.6 : The correctness of a sentence is a relative notion as illustrated in this dialogue.

Thus this double interrogative phrase construction is part of the the teacher's grammar, and therefore should be expressible within the pedagogical grammar, but it is also one of the learner's rules, in that it describes a particular type of simplification, and hence could be encoded as predefined rule in the computational linguistic grammar. This rule would be related to the pedagogical rule that calls for a "repeated subject in version in a constituent question" through a "preference" link. The necessity of updating the learner model with this rule would be a decision for the pedagogical module to take, probably based on past observations.

7. Conclusion and Future Work

One important challenge for CALL systems which tackle the formal aspects of second language learning is the modelling of the ways the learner handles heuristics and strategies to acquire and use the rules of the target language. Research in applied linguistics has shown that Error Analysis provides the basic elements on which to build relevant systems.

The recent developments in ITSs in second language learning have begun to demonstrate how it is possible to bypass the limitations of the traditional CALL systems and have pointed out how crucial the modelling of the learner is. However, the modelling of the learner's errors still remains superficial in systems which do not restrict themselves to a narrow linguistic corpus, i.e. systems which immerse the apprenticeship within a fruitful communicative environment. The extension of the linguistic coverage of a CALL system requires the use of computational linguistic techniques. The current state of the art in computational linguistics does not offer satisfactory answers to the modelling of the learner through the treatment of her errors. It is hard to develop a meta-level on top of the computational linguistic grammar which can at the same time handle divergent sentences and be relevant to the learner's processes.

In order to conceptually model the learner's errors it is indispensable to find out what is the right level of description of her rules and what are her strategies. Through the presentation of the architecture of the BELLOC system we have discussed a set of requirements which can help to fulfil these aims. We emphasised the need of a pedagogical grammar, beside the computational linguistic one, which plays a central role in the diagnosis.

We introduced the notion of an applicable rule, a structure which aims at representing learner's rules, as well as teacher's ones. This degree of equivalence between the learner and the teacher de-emphasises the learner's failures and draws closer links between the learner's process of production and refinement of her rules, and the teacher's process of simplification of his knowledge for pedagogical purposes. By examples, we illustrated how an ITS can lead to a deeper conceptual diagnosis of the learner's behaviour. The information that applicable rules encapsulate outlines the strategies a learner uses and thus provides the learner model with a fundamental source of knowledge.

In applicable rules the implementation level is clearly separated from the conceptual one. Despite the very different ways they can be implemented, and the different strategies they use for recognising a divergent sentence, they all have the same general structure. We distinguished three kinds of applicable rules. Firstly, predefined rules recognise divergent sentences relating to specific linguistic difficulties that only an expert teacher can predict. When considering the computational code of a predefined rule, expressed in a computational linguistic format, one can compare it with the mal-rule approach used in other ITSs on SLL. Secondly, pedagogical grammar rules correspond to the teacher's rules. Being part of the objective of the apprenticeship, they are expressed in a formalism close to the one used by teachers during instruction. Thirdly, the meta-rules describe general learner's strategies. They allow automatic generation of particular applicable rules specific to the current learner in close relation (for part of them) with the pedagogical grammar.

We have presented here what we believe is a novel approach to the problem of cognitive diagnosis in ITSs for SLL. It is based on established techniques in applied linguistics and on observations of expert teachers analysing the performance of learners. We should emphasise that the framework presented is a conceptual model only. The detail, we hope, is sufficient to provoke discussion on both representational issues of learner modelling and on architectural aspects of encapsulating the diagnosis process.

In the short term, we intend to implement a pedagogical grammar and use it to build learners' applicable rules from the partial diagnoses coming from the computational linguistic part of the BELLOC system. Also, experiments with learners will be set up in order to validate and refine the user modelling process by building applicable rules within a dialogue game interaction.

Acknowledgements

This research was partially funded by the CEC NAT*LAB project within the exploratory action of the DELTA programme and by the *Institut National de Recherche en Informatique et Automatique* (INRIA, France). The views and conclusions contained in this document are those of the authors and should not be interpreted as representing the official policies of DELTA or INRIA.

References

1. Abeillé A.: A Lexicalized Tree Adjoining Grammar for French and Its relevance to language teaching (this volume)
2. Anderson J.R. and Reiser B.: The Lisp tutor. Byte, 10,159-175 (1985)

3. Barchan J., Woodmansee B.J., and Yazdani M.: A PROLOG-based tool for French grammar analysis. Instructional Science, 14, 21-48 (1986)
4. Bescherelle, D.: Le nouveau Bescherelle, 3. La grammaire pour tous. Paris: Hatier 1984
5. Boguraev B., Carrol J., Briscoe T., and Grover C.: Software support for practical grammar development. COLING 88, Budapest 1988
6. Brown J.S. and Burton R.R.: Diagnostic models for procedural bugs in basic mathematical skills. Cognitive Science, 2, 155-192 (1978)
7. Brown J. S. and van Lehn K.: Repair theory: a generative theory of bugs in procedural skills. Cognitive Science, 4, 379-462 (1980)
8. Cerri S.A.: ALICE: Acquisition of Linguistic Items in the Context of Examples. Instructional Science, 18, 63-92 (1989)
9. Cerri S., Cheli E., and McIntyre A.: Nobile: Object-based user model acquisition for second language learning (this volume)
10. Chanier T.: Compréhension de textes dans un domaine technique : le système ACTES. Application des grammaires d'unification et de la théorie du discours. PhD Dissertation, Université Paris-Nord, Villetaneuse, June 1989
11. Chanier T., Dillenbourg P., Hartley R., Hinzte D., Nichols D., Pengelly M., Self J., and Twidale M.: A Prototype for the acquisition of rule-based student models. AI-Report n° 40, Computing Department, University of Lancaster, January 1990
12. Chen Li and Barry L.K.: XTRA-TE: Using natural language processing software to develop an ITS for language learning. 4th International Conference on Artificial Intelligence and Education; Amsterdam, May, pp. 54-63 1989
13. Computational Linguistics: Special issue on ill-formed input. American Journal of Computational Linguistics, 9, 3-4 (1983)
14. Demaizière F., Blanvillain O.: Learners' intuitions, misconceptions and errors (this volume)
15. Dillenbourg P. and Self J.: A framework for cognitive diagnosis. AI-Report n° 48, Computing Department, University of Lancaster 1990
16. Ellis R.: Understanding second language acquisition.. Oxford: Oxford University Press 1985
17. Fouqueré, C.: Systèmes d'analyse tolérante du langage naturel. PhD Dissertation, Université Paris-Nord, Villetaneuse, January 1988
18. Fum D. Pani, B. and Tasso C.: Naive vs. formal grammars: A case for integration in the design of a foreign language tutor (this volume)
19. Tasso C., Fum D., and Giangrandi P.: The use of explanation-based learning for modelling student behavior in foreign language tutoring (this volume)
20. Hamburger H. and Hashim R.: Foreign language tutoring and learning environment (this volume)
21. Johnson R. and Rosner M.: A rich environment for experimentation with unification grammars. Proceedings of the European Association for Computational Linguistics, Manchester 1989
22. Kobsa A. and Wahlster W.: User models in dialog systems. New York, NY: Springer-Verlag 1989
23. Laurillard D.: The pedagogical limitations of generative student models. Instructional Science 17, 29-55 (1988)
24. Littlewood, W.T.: Foreign and second language learning. Language acquisition research and its implications for the classroom. New York, NY: Cambridge University Press 1984
25. Matz M.: Towards a process model for high school algebra errors. In D.H. Sleeman and J.S. Brown (eds.), Intelligent tutoring systems, New York, NY: Academic Press 1982
26. Menzel W.: Error diagnosis and selection in a training system for second language learning. COLING 88, Budapest, August 1988
27. Mulford G.W.: Semantic processing for communicative exercises in foreign-language learning. Computers and the Humanities, Special Issue on the Intelligent Computer-Assisted Language Instruction. Vol. 23, 1, January 1989
28. Murray J., Morgensten D., and Furstenberg G.: The Athena language learning project: Design issues for the next generation of computer-based language learning tools. In Smith W.S. (ed.), Modern technology in foreign language education: Applications and projects. American Council on the Teaching of Foreign Languages 1987
29. Nwana H.S. and Coxhead P.: Fraction bugs: explanations, theories and implications for intelligent tutoring systems. Proceedings of 6th Workshop of European Soc. for the Study of Cognitive Systems, Varena 1988
30. Pengelly M., Chanier T.: Knowledge acquisition for learner modelling in second language learning. Paper presented at the NATO advanced educational technology workshop 'Cognitive Modelling & Interactive Environments'. Eindhoven, The Netherlands 1990
31. Pijls F., Daelemans W., and Kempen G.: Artificial intelligence tools for grammar and spelling instruction. Instructional Science. 16, 319-336 (1987)

32. Pijls F., Kempen G., and Janner E.: Intelligent modules for Dutch grammar instruction. Report of the Experimental Psychology Department. University of Nijmegen. The Netherlands 1989
33. Richards J.C.: A non-contrastive approach to error analysis. In Richards J.C (ed.) Error analysis: Perspectives on second language acquisition. Longman 1984
34. Richards J.C.: Error analysis: Perspectives on second language acquisition.. Longman 1984
35. Schuster E.: The role of native grammars in correcting errors in second language learning. Computational Intelligence, 2, 93-98 (1986)
36. Schwind, C.: An intelligent language tutoring system. International Journal of Man-Machine Studies, 33, 557-579 (1990)
37. Selinker L.: Interlanguage. In Richards J.C (ed.) Error analysis: Perspectives on second language acquisition. Longman 1984
38. Shieber S.M.: An introduction to unification-based approaches to grammar. CSLI Lecture Notes. University of Chicago Press 1986
39. Swan M. and Smith B.: Learner English. A teacher's guide to interference and other problems. London, UK: Cambridge University Press 1987
40. Swan P.: Theory and practice of computer-assisted language learning. PhD dissertation, Open University, Milton Keynes, UK, August 1990
41. Swartz M.L. and Russell D.M.: FL-IDE: hypertext for structuring a conceptual design for computer-assisted language learning. Instructional Science, 18, 5-26 (1989)
42. Swartz M.L.: Issues for tutoring knowledge in foreign language intelligent tutoring systems (this volume)
43. Twidale M.B.: Knowledge acquisition for intelligent tutoring systems. Paper presented at the NATO advanced educational technology workshop 'Cognitive Modelling & Interactive Environments'. Eindhoven, The Netherlands 1990
44. van Els T., Bongaerts T., Extra G., van Os C., and Janssen-van Dieten A.M.: Applied linguistics and the learning and teaching of foreign languages. London: Edward Arnold 1984
45. Wilks Y. and Farwell D.: Building an intelligent second language tutor from whatever bits and pieces you have lying around (this volume)
46. Yazdani M., O'Brien P., Byron G.: An English tutor: Project Report (1987-1989). Report of the Computing Department, University of Exeter, UK 1989
47. Zock, M.: SWIM or sink : The problem of communicating thought (this volume)

The Use of Explanation-Based Learning for Modelling Student Behavior in Foreign Language Tutoring

Carlo Tasso [1], Danilo Fum [2], and Paolo Giangrandi [1]

[1] Laboratorio di Intelligenza Artificiale - Dipartimento di Matematica e Informatica - Università di Udine, via Zanon 6, I-33100 Udine (Italy) - tasso@uduniv.infn.it.bitnet

[2] Dipartimento di Psicologia - Università di Trieste, via dell'Università 7, I-34123 Trieste (Italy) - fum@uts882.units.infn.it.bitnet

Abstract: An original methodology to model student performance which features a profitable integration of the bug collection and bug construction techniques is presented. This methodology has been used for building the modelling module of a new version of ET *(English Tutor)*, an ITS aimed at supporting the learning of the English verb system. The proposed approach is based on the idea of analyzing the reasoning process of the student by reconstructing, step by step and in reverse order, the chain of reasoning (s)he has followed in giving his/her answer. Two kinds of errors, i.e., commission and omission errors, are considered by the the modeler and the student modelling process is supported by correct domain specific knowledge and by a catalogue of stereotyped errors (mal-rules). When the system is unable to explain the student behavior by exploiting its previous knowledge, new mal-rules are generated dynamically by utilizing explanation-based learning techniques. The overall process is based on a deep modelling of the student problem solving and the discrimination among possible explicative hypotheses about the student behavior is carried on non-monotonically through a truth maintenance system. The proposed approach has been fully implemented in a student modelling module developed in PROLOG.

Keywords: intelligent tutoring systems, foreign language teaching, student modelling, explanation-based learning.

1. Introduction

One of the most important features an intelligent tutoring system (ITS) should provide is the capability to adapt instruction to the specific traits of the student. To this end, a fundamental contribution is given by the ITS component aimed at building and maintaining the student model. The student model describes the knowledge and beliefs of the student in the specific subject domain and is used for designing and taking appropriate tutorial and remedial actions tailored to the peculiarities of the student.

Building an ITS with a student modelling component is hindered by several problems concerning both theoretical and practical issues. There is a sufficiently general agreement for the fact that the modelling activity cannot be based only on the knowledge provided by an expert in the domain but it is better performed by relying on an explicit description of possible student (mis)behaviors [5]. Unfortunately, no definite solution exists for this issue and the three main approaches adopted for building student modelers (i.e., overlay, bug collection and bug construction [17]) directly reflect this situation. In fact, each technique has been generally used alone and no clear methods have been proposed to combine these techniques in order to exploit their respective advantages. Considered individually, each technique has known drawbacks and

NATO ASI Series, Vol. F 80
Intelligent Tutoring Systems for Foreign Language Learning
Edited by M. L. Swartz and M. Yazdani

falls short of constituting an ideal tool for building cognitively adequate and computationally sufficient student models. Overlay is generally considered as not sufficiently powerful to perform sophisticated modelling, collecting catalogues of bugs is notoriously a dull and labor-intensive endeavor, while bug construction has not yet proven to be a reliable and sufficiently comprehensive approach.

In this paper we present an original methodology, called *backward model tracing*, to model student performance which features a profitable integration of the bug collection and bug construction techniques. The work has been carried on in the framework of a research project devoted to the development of ET *(English Tutor)* [10], an ITS aimed at supporting the learning of the English verb system. The new methodology has been used for building a new version of the modelling module [12]. Backward model tracing is based on the idea of analyzing the reasoning process of the student by reconstructing, step by step and in reverse order, the chain of reasoning (s)he has followed in giving his/her answer. In order to do this, both correct domain specific knowledge and a catalogue of stereotyped errors *(mal-rules)* is utilized. When the system is unable to explain the student behavior by exploiting its previous knowledge, new mal-rules are generated dynamically by utilizing explanation-based learning techniques. The overall process is based on a deep modelling of student problem solving and the discrimination among possible explicative hypotheses about the reasons underlying the student behavior is carried on non-monotonically through a truth maintenance system.

Backward model tracing seems a promising approach to tackle the hard problem of student modelling [15] for the following reasons:

- it shares the benefits of the model tracing methodology [1];
- it exploits the respective advantages of bug collection and bug construction without the limitation of the exclusive usage of a single technique;
- it exploits a sophisticated technique, i.e., explanation-based learning, to push the limits of the bug construction methodology.

The paper is organized as follows: The following section briefly presents the ET system where backward model tracing has been applied. Section 3 illustrates the general criteria upon which the methodology is grounded. Section 4 and 5 describe the modelling process focusing on its basic features, the architecture of the Modeler, and its overall operation. Section 6 presents a fully worked out example and section 7 concludes the paper. An Appendix illustrates the different kinds of knowledge utilized in the example.

2. Second Language Tutoring in ET

The backward model tracing methodology has been utilized in the new version of the ET system, an ITS aimed at supporting Italian students in the learning of the English verb tenses. ET comprises a *Verb Generation Expert,* an articulated knowledge-based domain expert [11] devoted to tense generation and capable of solving fill-in exercises constituted by one or more sentences in which some verbs have to be conjugated into the appropriate tenses. The operation of the domain expert is organized around a sequence of five phases each devoted to a specific subtask, namely:

- parsing the exercise sentence(s);
- recognizing the temporal relations among the events described in the sentence(s);
- identifying the reference time for every clause in the sentence(s);
- selecting the correct tense to be used for each verb;
- conjugating the verb(s) into the appropriate tense.

Each process is carried out by a dedicated processor, which is supported by a knowledge base representing the knowledge usually exploited by humans for that subtask. The main representation paradigm utilized in the knowledge bases is constituted by production rules. The Verb Generation Expert also produces a precise trace of the reasoning performed and of the knowledge utilized for solving the exercises.

The second fundamental module of ET is the *Tutor* which is devoted to defining the modalities of the teaching activity. More particularly, the Tutor assigns the exercises according to a given syllabus, manages the dialogue with the student, and cooperates with the Modeler in order to discriminate among alternative hypotheses about the student behavior (see the section on Tutoring Strategies and Learner Control, this volume, for more detailed information on this aspect of ITSs).

The *Student Modeler* (or simply the Modeler) is the module which implements the backward model tracing methodology. The general goal of this module is to discover the domain specific knowledge the student has utilized in order to derive her/his answer(s). The modelling process aims at constructing a model of the student's beliefs in which both correct knowledge and misconceptions are explicitly represented. The student model, which is partitioned into different parts, one for each computational phase, contains, therefore, a collection of facts and rules that have been utilized in order to interpret the student behavior and that are supposed to mirror what the student knows/believes about the subject domain. The student model supplies the basis for remedial activity which is aimed at correcting the student misconceptions.

The structure and the functioning of the Student Modeler constitutes the subject of this paper. More precisely, we will introduce in section 3 the general methodology of backward model tracing and then, in the following sections, we will focus on the mechanisms utilized in the modelling process devoted to reconstructing the student reasoning within a single phase (subtask) of the tense generation process.

3. Backward Model Tracing: A General Strategy for Modelling Student Performance

Backward model tracing relies on two basic assumptions:

(i) in achieving the solution, the student follows a process akin to that used by the Verb Generation Expert module i.e., it goes through the same phases and performs essentially the same kind of computations, and

(ii) the student mistakes can be modelled by appropriately perturbing the knowledge utilized by the Verb Generation Expert module.

Some words are needed in order to justify these assumptions. It could be claimed that assumption (i) is unrealistic. In fact, it is easy to find evidence that novices solve problems by using strategies that are different from those utilized by experts (see for example [8, 14]). While this cannot be denied, it is also true that, in order to be able to model possible student misbehaviors, a model of the correct performance is required. The student behavior needs thus to be compared with that of an 'expert', be this a real domain expert, a teacher or an 'ideal student' [1]. The general philosophy followed in ITS development is to locate the relevant domain knowledge in the Domain Expert module which plays therefore a twofold role: it acts as the *source* for the knowledge to be presented and, at the same time, it serves as the *standard* for evaluating the student's performance [17]. In our context we assume that a student, trying to figure out the correct answer for an exercise, follows the same reasoning steps of the expert module, i.e., after interpreting the meaning of the exercise sentences (s)he computes the temporal relations between the states/events described in the sentence, calculates the reference times for every clause of the sentence, chooses the tense for the verb and, finally, conjugates the verb in that tense. Assumption (i) implies that the errors the student makes could derive only from the fact that some of the rules (s)he applies are 'bugged', not from the fact that (s)he can follow computational paths different from those of the expert. Assumption (ii), (shared by other authors [3, 4, 16]) states that it is possible to model these bugs by assuming more or less severe deviations from the knowledge base actually represented in the expert module.

Backward model tracing is grounded on the idea of trying to reconstruct, step by step and in reverse order, the chain of reasoning the student has followed in building the answer. Backward model tracing is triggered by the discovery of a mismatch between the answer given by the student and that provided by the expert module. The goal of the modelling process is to identify the phase(s) where the reasoning process of the student and of the expert differ, and the specific erroneous rules *(mal-rules)* applied by the student (see [5] for a method of describing learners' mal-rules). Backward model tracing analyzes the reasoning process performed by the student starting from the last phase and going back toward the first ones. For each phase, the Modeler tries to determine the input to the phase and the knowledge the student has utilized in order to produce the corresponding output. If a mismatch between the student and the expert output is discovered, it could mean that:

(a) some of the rules contained in the knowledge base utilized by the student in that phase, or
(b) some of the data utilized as input for that phase or,
(c) both some of the rules and the data

differ from those utilized by the expert.

The goal of the diagnostic process performed by the Modeler is to realize which of the above alternatives holds. Case (a) is true when both the expert and the student work with the same input data but their output is different because some of the rules contained in the student knowledge base are actually bugged. In this case a remedial activity could be planned in order to clarify the student misconceptions. As an example of case (a) let us consider the case when both the student and the expert have to form the present perfect of *to study* and the student produces as an answer *has studied.* If (b) is true, then at least one of the previous phases should be blamed for producing the erroneous data and the diagnostic process is repeated focusing on the phase immediately preceding the current one. As an example of (b) let us consider the case of the student answering *has studied* when in fact the correct verb tense is the past perfect. If (c) is true, then both the above mentioned activities should occur, i.e., the mal-rules responsible for the mistake made in that phase have to be identified and the diagnostic process will continue with the preceding phases. An example of case (c) is the wrong answer *has studyed* when the past perfect is required.

Backward model tracing shares all the features of the model tracing methodology [1], i.e., it tries to simulate dynamically a student's problem solving and uses that simulation to interpret the student behavior. Differently from Anderson's approach [1]:

- it does not rely only on an *a priori* established catalogue of correct and incorrect productions but is able to dynamically generate the mal-rules necessary to explain the student performance;
- the tracing occurs *after* the student has produced his/her performance and it is not used to monitor the student during the solution process just to assure that the correct path will be followed.

As a result, backward model tracing possibly represents a less intrusive modelling methodology and a more general diagnostic procedure.

Having established the general features of our approach to student modelling, we concentrate now on the technical details of the diagnostic process as it is performed within a single phase.

4. Reconstructing the Student Reasoning within a Single Phase of the Tense Generation Task

The process of modelling the student reasoning within a single phase is aimed at discovering the status of the student knowledge utilized in that specific phase of the tense generation task. The approach utilized is the same for each phase, so we will concentrate on a single, generic one. During the diagnostic process, the Modeler interacts with the student and collects information which is utilized to analyze his/her behavior. The status of student knowledge is represented in the Student Model[1], a dynamically updated information structure which stores the knowledge which can be reasonably considered as present in the student mind, given the results obtained from the analysis of the observed behavior.

An important feature of our approach concerns the method adopted for evaluating the student performance. At each step of the interaction, the observed student behavior is not compared simply with an 'ideal' behavior (like that which could be obtained by utilizing only the correct expert knowledge), but with an 'expected' behavior. By this we mean the behavior which the student should manifest provided (s)he would reason according to the knowledge present in the Student Model. The expected behavior is computed by means of a simulation of the reasoning processes carried out by the student, and this is accomplished by taking into account the knowledge contained in the Student Model. From this perspective, therefore, the Student Model not only serves as a repository of the current representation of the student knowledge, but it also plays a fundamental role in the simulation of the student.

The main task performed by the Modeler is error analysis. When the student behavior differs from the expected behavior a twofold problem arises. On one hand, the student has made some mistake and this fact means (s)he has applied some kind of incorrect knowledge (this error is called *commission error)*. On the other hand, the student has not performed in the expected way because (s)he has ignored some knowledge and possibly replaced it with some other knowledge (this error is called *omission error)*. The operation of the Modeler reflects this twofold problem. In fact, the Modeler proceeds during its analysis in two different directions. First, it analyzes the student behavior and tries to reconstruct the student reasoning (the so-called *commission error analysis)*. Second, it analyzes the expected answer and tries to identify which knowledge has been ignored by the student (the so-called *omission error analysis)*. Due to this twofold nature of errors, the knowledge contained in the Student Model appears in two different modalities. The first modality is suitable for encoding the fact that the student believes (correctly or incorrectly) something, i.e., there is evidence that (s)he has utilized it during an interaction. This knowledge is labelled as *applied*. The second modality is used for keeping an account of the pieces of information which are not known by the student. This knowledge is labelled as *missing*.

After each interaction with the student, the Modeler produces two kinds of results. The first concerns new information (applied and/or missing) that has to be inserted into the Student Model. This situation arises whenever the new information adequately justifies and explains the current interaction, and it is also consistent with conclusions drawn from the previously observed behavior. A second possible outcome is constituted only by hypothetical results, which are not inserted into the Student Model and which need further observations in order to be accepted or rejected. This second case arises when the Modeler produces multiple mutually exclusive hypotheses, or hypotheses which contradict previous conclusions.

It might happen that the Student Model, being incomplete, could not give a precise account of the observed behavior since on some specific aspects only preliminary hypotheses have been made which have yet to be validated. Due to this incompleteness, during the analysis of the student behavior or during the simulation of the expected behavior, whenever the need arises to consider aspects of domain knowledge not present in the Student Model, the Modeler has to find this knowledge somewhere else. The precise strategy utilized is the following: First the Modeler tries to refer to the correct expert knowledge. If this fails, it looks in a bug library of stereotyped mal-rules, and if this also fails, it generates at run time new mal-rules that adequately explain the behavior. This means that the Modeler first assumes that the student knows what (s)he should know, and only later hypothesizes some misconception. A consequence of this approach is that, at the beginning of the interaction when the Student Model is still empty, the first assumption made by the Modeler is that the student behaves correctly as

[1] As it has been already stated , the Student Model contains several partitions, one for each phase of the overall tense generation task. In this section, however, we will use for brevity only the term 'Student Model' instead of the term 'a partition of the Student Model'.

an 'ideal' student. Only later, when the Modeler detects some misconceptions in the student knowledge, the expected behavior is found to differ from the ideal behavior by taking into account the specific individualities of the student.

The mal-rule generation (or bug construction) process is based on machine learning techniques and on general diagnostic knowledge about possible perturbations of correct knowledge which may occur in the learning process of a student. Among the possible machine learning techniques usable for generating new mal-rules, we have adopted an explanation-based approach [7, 13]. This approach, which has been already exploited in the field of ITSs [2], seems particularly promising to be utilized for student modelling for the following reasons:

- in contrast to other machine learning techniques, this approach requires a few training instances (possibly only one) and seems therefore particularly suitable for modelling when only a few student answers are available;
- it is an intensive knowledge-based technique and seems suitable in a field where a lot of domain-dependent knowledge is available in terms of both the expert knowledge base and of diagnostic knowledge (i.e., knowledge about possible student errors).

Bug construction thus constitutes the major tool in the Modeler when no *a priori* information about a specific student (mis)behavior is available, i.e., when a student makes an error not contained in the bug library.

Another major characteristic of the Modeler is its ability to deal non-monotonically with the incremental development and refinement of the Student Model. Since at each step of the interaction a better understanding of the status of student knowledge is reached and new hypotheses are made in order to further refine it, continuous updates (both insertions and deletions) are performed on the Student Model. A truth maintenance system [9] is specifically devoted to manage this process.

Before describing the architecture and the overall operation of the Modeler we point out that the kind of interactions considered in the current versions of the ET system is restricted only to exercises proposed by the system to the student. We are planning to extend this capability to other kinds of interaction modes such as direct questioning from the system about specific aspects of the student's reasoning process or the provision of interactive graphical ways to represent and manipulate information related to the student's reasoning process.

5. Modeler Architecture and Overall Operation

In this section we illustrate the main modules of the Modeler and we describe its overall operation. The Modeler, whose overall architecture is illustrated in Figure 1, is made up of three main modules:

- the *Commission Error Analyzer*, devoted to analyzing the answer produced by the student and to producing hypothetical explanations of his/her reasoning. These explanations are represented in the form of derivation trees which contain reference to knowledge present in the Student Model or to correct domain knowledge or to diagnostic knowledge (i.e. stereotyped mal-rules or newly generated mal-rules).
- the *Omission Error Analyzer*, devoted to identifying possible hypotheses of omission errors in the student reasoning by considering the expected behavior of the student. The expected behavior, in the current version of the system, constitutes only an expected answer to the current exercise. The process devoted to simulating the student reasoning and to identifying the expected answer is performed by utilizing the same inference engine of the Verb Generation Expert and the current Student Model as the knowledge base;
- the *Hypotheses Discriminator,* devoted to evaluating all the hypotheses produced by the above two modules and to identifying the specific update operations to be performed on the Student Model. This module operates only on the so called *active hypotheses*, i.e., hypotheses which have not yet been either confirmed or disproved. In general, after its activity is completed, some hypotheses may possibly remain active, since the Hypotheses Discriminator may not

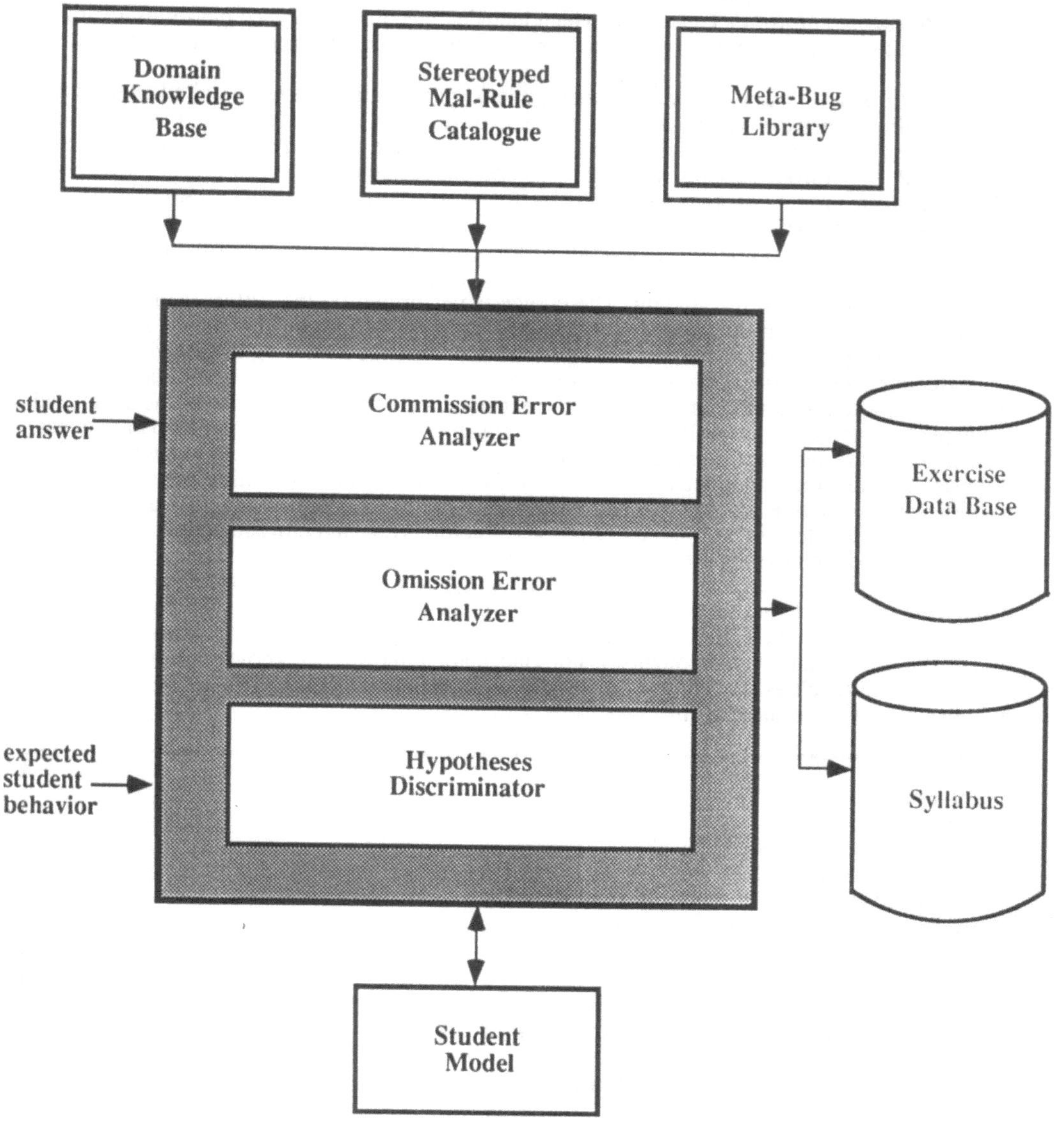

Figure 1. Overall Architecture of the Modeler

have been capable of confirming or disproving them. Therefore, other interactions with the student will be needed in order to gather new observations related to these hypotheses.

The above mentioned modules are supported by the following three knowledge bases:

- the *Domain Knowledge Base,* which contains the correct knowledge necessary for solving the task corresponding to the specific phase at hand;

- the *Stereotyped Mal-Rule Catalogue,* which includes specific stereotyped mal-rules identified *a priori* through the analysis of protocols taken from students working in the domain of interest;
- the *Meta-Bug Library,* which includes generic perturbation patterns called *meta-bugs* describing generic ways of altering correct knowledge, and producing in such a way possible student misconceptions. Meta-bugs are identified *a priori* through the analysis of protocols taken from students working in the domain of interest.

The modelling process is also supported by the *Exercise Data Base,* i.e., a collection of exercises in the domain at hand, and the *Syllabus,* i.e., an organized collection of the specific topics included in the domain. The overall operation of the Modeler conforms to the general iterative procedure shown in figure 2. At the beginning of each cycle an exercise is selected in order to be presented to the student. The choice is performed by the Tutor. If there are still active hypotheses from the preceding cycle, the exercise is chosen in order to support the Modeler in its operation. Otherwise the Tutor selects an exercise according to the Syllabus.

After the student answer has been acquired, the Modeler carries out a simulation of the student's expected reasoning and identifies the expected answer. A comparison of the actual and the expected answer allows an evaluation of the student behavior. If the two answers are equal, the Modeler assumes that the student has applied the same knowledge utilized in the simulation process and this constitutes a useful piece of information for discriminating among possible hypotheses still active from preceding cycles. On the other hand, if the two answers are different, the Modeler executes the two analyses of commission and omission errors, which will eventually produce new hypotheses about the student knowledge. In both cases, the Modeler will then discriminate among the different active hypotheses with the aim of confirming or disproving them, and then execute the corresponding update operations on the Student Model.

At the end of the cycle, if no more hypotheses are active, the Modeler terminates the specific diagnostic activity and all the conclusions produced about the student knowledge are usable by other modules (such as the Tutor) for specific remediation activities. If there are still active hypotheses, the cycle starts again.

```
Start-cycle
Select exercise
Assign exercise to the student
Get student answer
Simulate student expected reasoning and Identify expected answer
IF student answer = expected answer
      THEN assume student has applied the same knowledge of the simulation process
      ELSE begin
                  activate Analysis of Commission Errors
                  activate Analysis of Omission Errors
               end
activate Hypotheses Discriminator and update Student Model
IF no more active hypotheses
      THEN terminate diagnosis session
End-cycle
```

Figure 2. Overall Operation of the Modeler

In the next section we will further clarify our approach by means of an example which will also allow us to point out more specific details of the modelling process.

6. An Example

In this section we present an example of interaction with the ET system. We will consider only the last phase of the tense generation process, i.e., verb conjugation. More precisely, we will utilize the conjugation exercises and show how the Modeler is able to diagnose the status of student knowledge with reference to this task. The domain knowledge includes conjugation rules (represented as productions) and a dictionary of English verbs. Diagnostic knowledge is comprised of both stereotyped mal-rules and meta-bugs which have been collected from an analysis of protocols taken from Italian students.

At the beginning of the interaction the Tutor selects an exercise according to the Syllabus and assigns it to the student:

ex1: Please conjugate the present perfect, third person singular, of the verb to go.

Let us assume that the student gives the incorrect answer *is gone*. Since we are at the beginning of the interaction, the Student Model is still empty and the simulation process is performed taking into account the correct conjugation rules. The expected answer therefore coincides with the correct answer, i.e., *has gone*. Since the expected and actual behavior are different, the Modeler carries out an analysis of the exercise following the three standard steps: commission error analysis, omission error analysis, and discrimination of the hypotheses.

As the system is implemented in PROLOG, we will utilize a PROLOG-like notation for describing the knowledge and the data utilized in this example (the minus sign meaning difference list). All the knowledge utilized in the example is reported in the Appendix.

6.1 Commission error analysis

In order to analyze the student answer, the Modeler transforms it into the PROLOG goal

conjugate(go, present_perfect, 3, singular, [is, gone]-[]).

This goal embodies information concerning the kind of task to be performed (verb conjugation), the input data (verb root, tense, person, and number) and, finally, the answer given by the student (*is gone* in our example). The Modeler starts to build the derivation tree(s) for the above goal. To this end, the system searches in the Student Model for those rules whose right hand side matches the current goal (if various rules match the goal, the Modeler constructs several derivation trees in parallel). Since the Student Model is still empty, the Modeler looks for appropriate rules in the knowledge base of correct conjugation rules. When a rule is found, the process continues by proving each antecedent clause in the left hand side of the rule. If a clause constitutes a *primitive goal* (i.e., a fact contained in the Dictionary or an elementary operation, e.g., string concatenation) it is directly solved by looking in the Dictionary or by executing the elementary operation; otherwise the Modeler proceeds recursively by trying to build a derivation (sub)tree for that clause. When a clause has been solved, the Modeler goes on with a new one until all the clauses have been analyzed.

The main improvement of our algorithm in comparison with similar approaches (e.g., classic backward chaining, the resolution plus oracle method reported in [6], and the technique utilized in [16]) concerns the treatment of failing situations. When the Modeler finds a subgoal which is unprovable (i.e., which is neither a primitive goal nor can be solved by utilizing the rules contained in the Student Model or in the base of correct knowledge) it tries to recover from this situation by exploiting two different modelling strategies. First, it can rely on the bug collection by selecting an appropriate mal-rule in the Stereotyped Mal-rules Catalogue which could be used to prove the current goal. If none of the available mal-rules is suitable to prove the goal, the Modeler follows a bug construction strategy and tries to generate a new mal-rule by perturbing an expert rule in accordance to some generic perturbation pattern specified in a meta-bug. While the first strategy simply utilizes the classic bug collection approach, the second strategy exploits explanation-based learning in order to generate new mal-rules. Meta-bugs are represented by productions whose condition specifies a failing situation (a general pattern for a clause which cannot be otherwise proven) and whose conclusion specifies an action to perturb the given clause.

Coming back to the example, when the Modeler tries to account for the incorrect use of the auxiliary verb *is*, it fails to explain it and thus attempts to recover from this situation by exploiting the Meta-Bug Library. In fact, trying to prove the original goal

conjugate(go, present_perfect, 3, singular, [is,gone]-[]).

the Modeler finds a match with the right hand side of the following correct conjugation rule:

%% r2:
%% The present perfect of a verb is formed with the simple present of 'to have'
%% followed by the past participle of the verb.
IF conjugate(have, simple_present, Person, Number, V1-V2),
conjugate(Verb, past_participle, V2-V3)
THEN conjugate(Verb, present_perfect, Person, Number, V1-V3).

The substitution needed for the unification, i.e., *{Verb/go, Person/3, Number/singular, V1/[is, gone], V3/[]}* is then applied to the antecedent clauses which must be proven in order to prove the original goal. The second clause is transformed into the goal

conjugate(go, past_participle, [gone]-[]).

which is proven by means of rule *r4*

%% r4:
%% The past participle of an irregular verb is given in the dictionary
IF word(Verb, irregular_form(past_participle, V1-V2))
THEN conjugate(Verb, past_participle, V1-V2).

and by looking up in the Dictionary, while the first clause is transformed into the goal

conjugate(have, simple_present, Person, Number, [is]-[])

(i.e., the simple present of *to have* is *is*) which is obviously unprovable. The Modeler can proceed to the construction of the derivation tree by exploiting the following meta-bug

%% mb2:
%% It is possible for a student to utilize 'to be' instead of 'to have'
IF LHS CLAUSE: conjugate(have, Tense, Person, Number,V1-V2),
THEN REPLACE WITH: conjugate(be, Tense, Person, Number, V1-V2).

This meta-bug takes care of the case in which a student could use the auxiliary *to be* instead of *to have* (auxiliary inversion with intransitive verbs represents a typical error made by Italian students) by specifying that, in order to prove a failing clause containing the auxiliary *to have*, it is possible to replace it with a clause containing the verb *to be*. By applying *mb2* we obtain the clause:

conjugate(be, simple_present, Person, Number, [is]-[]).

which is proven by means of rule *r1* and by looking up in the Dictionary. By means of this new clause it is possible to positively conclude the construction of the derivation tree (labelled for reference *dtree1*) which is illustrated in Figure 3 shown on the next page. Each node of the derivation tree (with the exception of the root) specifies a (partial) conclusion produced during the hypothesized reasoning process of the student, while the root contains the student answer.

Since a derivation tree describes a possible reasoning path followed by the student in a very specific situation, in order to model his/her misconceptions in a more general way it is necessary to generalize the derivation tree containing the mistake. To this end, the Modeler considers a more general structure, called *explanation structure*, which contains reference to the various rules utilized in the derivation tree and to the specific unifications performed. The explanation structure for the example is shown in Figure 4, where each thick horizontal line within a box indicates the pair of rule clauses unified during the construction of the derivation tree.

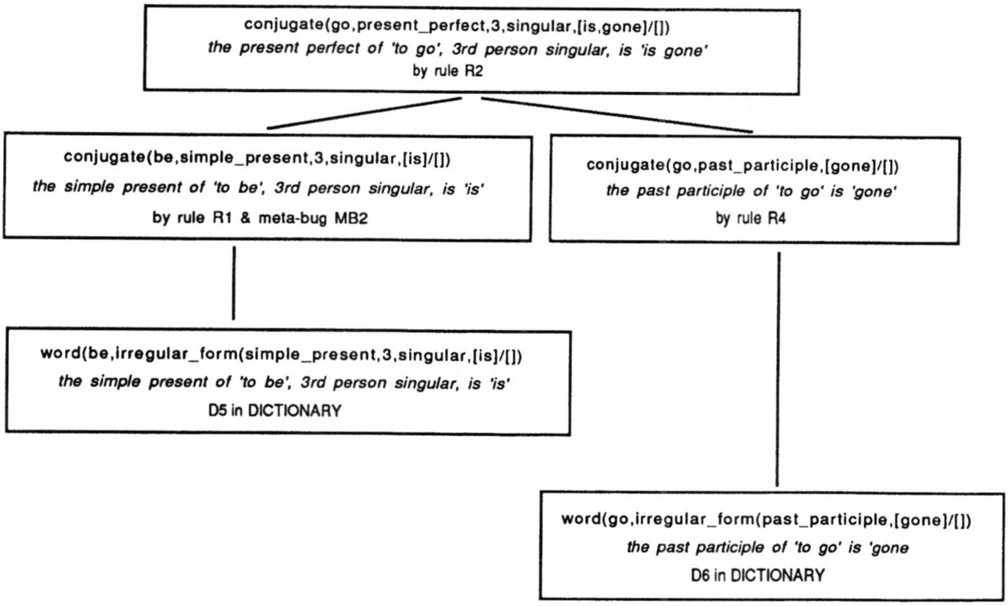

Figure 3. The Derivation Tree *dtree-1*

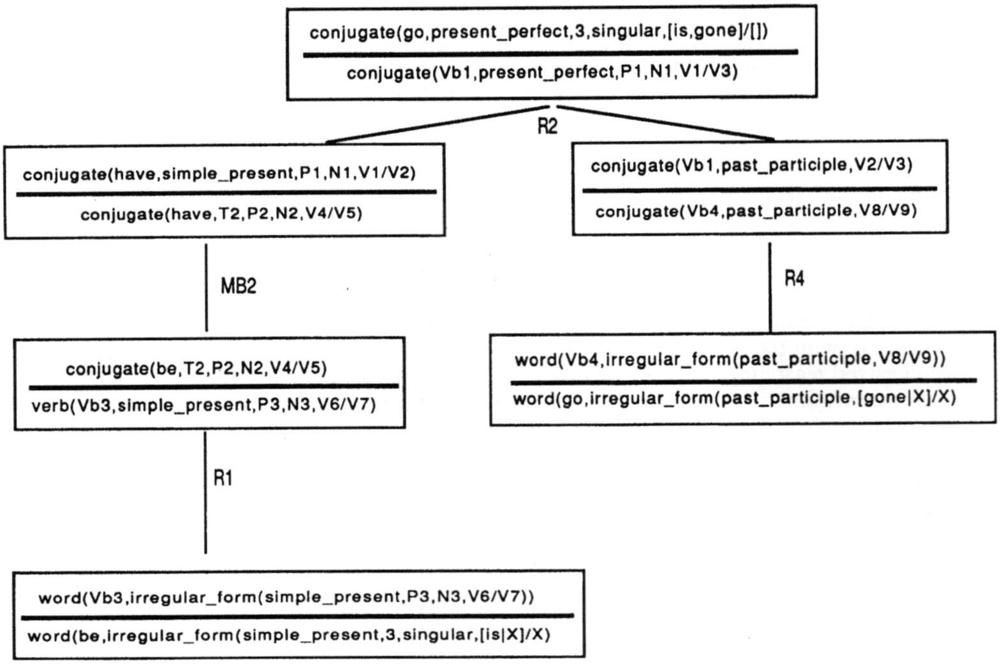

Figure 4. Explanation Structure for the Example

At this point, while the standard explanation-based learning technique works on the whole structure in order to extract a single general concept, our algorithm focuses only on the subtree(s) containing meta-bugs in order to induce general mal-rules representing the student misconceptions. In our example, the Modeler concentrates upon the subtree constituted by rule *r2* and the meta-bug *mb2*, it unifies the rule clauses to which a meta-bug has been applied with the left hand side of the meta-bug, and then it applies the substitution to the right hand side of the meta-bug. In our example, the antecedent clause of *r2*

conjugate(have, simple_present, Person, Number, V1-V2).

is unified with the left hand side of meta-bug *mb2* and, after the appropriate substitution has been applied to the right hand side of the meta-bug, the following clause results:

conjugate(be, simple_present, Person , Number , V1-V2).

The final step consists in substituting this clause to the antecedent of the rule *r2*, generating in such a way the following new mal-rule

%% bug1:
%% the present perfect of a verb is formed with the simple present of 'to be' and the %% past participle of the verb
IF conjugate(be, simple_present, Person, Number, V1-V2),
conjugate(Verb, past_participle, V2-V3)
THEN conjugate(Verb, present_perfect, Person, Number,V1-V3).

This concludes the commission error analysis. It must be noticed again that the results obtained at this stage of the modelling process, i.e., the derivation tree *dtree1* and the new mal-rule *bug1*, are considered only as hypotheses and they do not yet affect the content of the Student Model.

6.2 Omission Error Analysis

This phase is aimed at explaining why the student has not given the answer foreseen according to the simulated behavior. In fact, the expected answer is here *has gone* while the student has given the answer *is gone*. The Modeler tries to formulate possible causes, called *omission causes*, for the omission error. In general, an omission cause specifies a pair of rules (or facts): a rule/fact ignored by the student that will be deleted from the Student Model and an incorrect rule/fact, which the student believes should be applied to the situation at hand, that will be inserted into the Student Model. In some cases, when the student completely misses a rule/fact and is unable to replace it with something else, the omission cause specifies only what is ignored by the student.

In order to discover the omission causes, the Modeler starts its analysis by considering the expected answer and the derivation tree (labelled *exp_dt1*) generated by the simulation of the student reasoning which is illustrated in Figure 5. The expected answer, contained in the root

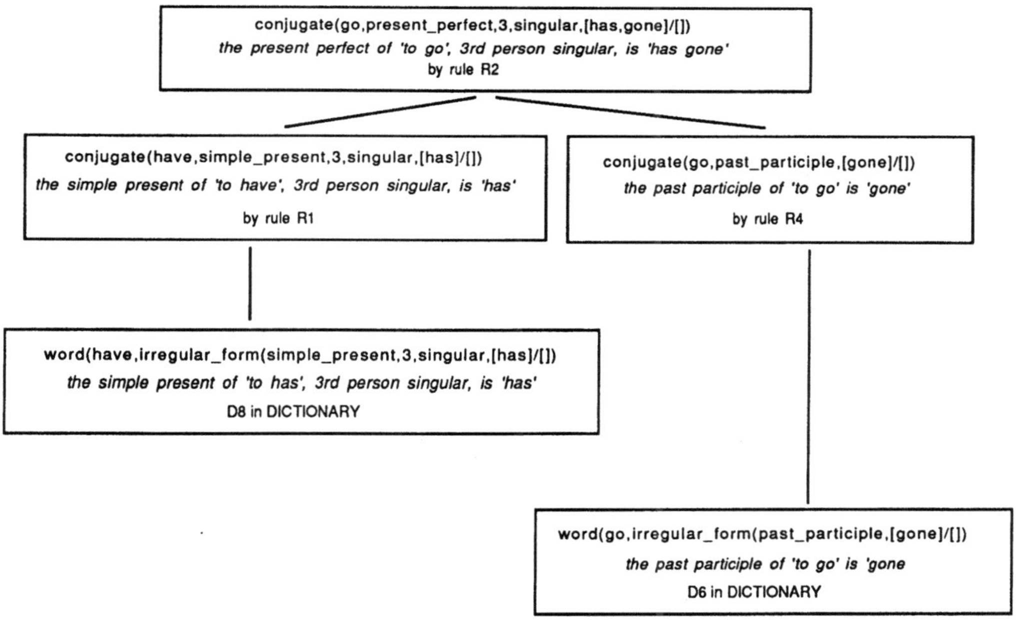

Figure 5. Derivation Tree *exp_dt1*

of *exp_dt1*, is not provable if some of the lower level goals contained in the tree become unprovable. In particular, a goal contained in the tree becomes unprovable if the rule (or fact) used to solve it is labelled as missing in the Student Model, or it is replaced with a mal-rule not applicable to the given goal. For example, the goal contained in the root of the derivation tree *exp_dt1* becomes unprovable if the student ignores the rule *r2*, or if he knows a perturbed form of the rule which is not applicable to the goal in the root.

For each node of the derivation tree two general types of hypotheses about the omission causes can be formulated by the Modeler:

i) *omission by ignorance:* the student totally ignores a rule/fact utilized to build the derivation tree (if this hypothesis of omission is later validated the corresponding rule/fact will be inserted into the Student Model with the label 'missing'); and

ii) *omission by perturbation:* the student knows a perturbed form of a rule utilized to build the derivation tree (if this hypothesis of omission is later validated the corresponding perturbed version of the rule will be inserted into the Student Model with the label 'applied').

According to the first type of omission cause, from the derivation tree *exp_dt1* the Modeler could hypothesize as missing the rules *r1, r2, r4,* and the facts *d6* and *d8*. However, there is some evidence that the student has used these facts and rules for solving the exercise *ex1*. The Modeler labels a fact or a rule as applied when it is contained in *all* the derivation trees concerning the student answer. In our case, since the only explanation tree is *dtree1*, all the knowledge utilized in it (i.e., *r1, r4, d5, d6* and *bug1)* can be considered as applied. For this reason, the only remaining concepts which can be hypothesized as missing are *r2* and *d8*. This conforms to a general heuristic followed by the Modeler: Hypotheses of omission cannot be made about rules and facts which have likely been applied by the student.

The identification of the second type of omission cause (omission by perturbation) follows a more complex process based on the exploitation of diagnostic knowledge (stereotyped mal-rules and meta-bugs). In this case, the Modeler tries to substitute a rule (or a fact) utilized in some node of the derivation tree *exp_dt1* with a perturbed version of it. More precisely, for each rule (or fact) applied in the derivation tree, the Modeler tries to find a perturbation which makes the goal solved by this rule (or fact) unprovable. In order to clarify how this procedure works, we illustrate the perturbation of rule *r2* (applied to the root of the derivation tree *exp_dt1)*.

The Modeler starts by considering all the meta-bugs applicable to the rule *r2*. In particular, a suitable meta-bug for *r2* is the meta-bug *b3*:

```
%% mb3:
%% The conjugation of the present perfect depends on the transitiveness of the verb (as
%% in Italian)
IF   RHS CLAUSE: conjugate(Verb, present_perfect, Person, Number, V1-V2),
THEN ADD IN LHS: word(Verb, transitive).
```

which is applicable to *r2* because its condition part is satisfied by the right hand side of *r2*.

The perturbation of *r2* is performed by unifying the condition part of the meta-bug *mb3* with the right hand side of *r2* , and by adding the clause specified in the right hand side of the meta-bug to the condition part of the rule *r2*. The following new mal-rule is thus obtained:

```
%% bug 2:
%% If a verb is transitive, its present perfect is formed with the simple present of the
%% verb 'to have' and the past participle of the verb
IF   conjugate(have, simple_present, Person, Number, V1-V2),
     conjugate(Verb, past_participle, V2-V3),
     word(Verb,transitive)
THEN conjugate(Verb, present_perfect, Person, Number,V1-V3).
```

Not all the possible perturbations resulting by applying meta-bugs to a rule are allowed as omission causes. In order to be accepted as an explanation for a student omission error, a mal-rule should not be applicable to a node of the derivation tree where the original (not perturbed) rule has already been applied. In our case, the goal solved by the original rule *r2* becomes unprovable if we use the new constructed mal-rule *bug2:* in fact, *bug2* requires a transitive verb while *to go* is classified as intransitive in the Dictionary. For this reason, a student who knows *bug2* instead of *r2* cannot give the answer *has gone*. Thus, a first hypothesis about a perturbation omission cause is that the student knows the mal-rule *bug2* instead of the correct rule *r2*.

Another meta-bug applicable to the rule *r2* is:

%% mb2:
%% It is possible for a student to utilize 'to be' instead of 'to have'
IF LHS CLAUSE: conjugate(have,Tense, Person, Number,V1-V2),
THEN REPLACE WITH: conjugate(be,Tense, Person, Number,V1-V2).

With a procedure similar to the previous one, the Modeler can generate the following mal-rule for explaining the student omission error:

%% bug1:
%% The present perfect of a verb is formed with the simple present of 'to be' and the %% past participle of the verb.
IF conjugate(be, simple_present, Person, Number, V1-V2),
conjugate(Verb, past_participle, V2-V3)
THEN conjugate(Verb, present_perfect, Person, Number ,V1-V3).

which is exactly the same mal-rule generated during the analysis of commission errors. Also in this case the root goal of the derivation tree *exp_dt1* becomes unprovable when we substitute the rule *r2* with the mal-rule *bug1*. Thus this bug represents another possible explanation for the omission error.

By utilizing the knowledge contained in the Meta-Bugs Library illustrated in the Appendix, the Modeler ends up this phase by formulating the following hypotheses for possible omission causes:

- *omiss1: the student does not know the rule r2;*
- *omiss2: the student does not know the fact d8;*
- *omiss3: the student believes bug2 instead of the correct rule r2;*
- *omiss4: the student believes bug1 instead of the correct rule r2.*

If some of these hypotheses are later confirmed, the missing rules or concepts will be inserted into the Student Model with the label *missing* and the replacing mal-rules will be inserted with the label *applied.*

6.3 Discriminating among the Hypotheses

This last phase aims at analyzing all the active hypotheses generated in the previous phases or in previous interactions. During this phase the Modeler tests the various hypotheses and tries to discriminate among them. The confirmed hypotheses are then taken into account for updating the Student Model and the discharged hypotheses are eliminated. The specific criteria utilized to discriminate among the different hypotheses and to update the Student Model are the following:

(a) If the student answer is explained by a single derivation tree, the mal-rules contained in that tree are inserted into the Student Model.

(b) If the student answer is explained by a single omission cause, the corresponding missing rules or facts are inserted into the Student Model with the label *missing* and the replacing mal-rules (if any) are inserted with the label *applied.*
(c) If a hypothesized mal-rule appears in all the alternative derivation trees explaining the student answer, it can be considered as *applied* and is inserted into the Student Model.
(d) If a hypothesized mal-rule, utilized to simulate the student reasoning in an exercise different from that in which it was originally derived, produces an answer different from that given by the student, then the mal-rule is discharged.
(e) If a hypothesized omission cause, applied to simulate the student reasoning in an exercise different from that in which it was originally derived, produces an answer different from that given by the student, then the hypothesis of omission is discharged.

Note that, for testing the alternative hypotheses according to the above criteria (d) and (e), the Hypotheses Discriminator utilizes the capability to simulate the student reasoning. In our example, according to the criterion (a) the Modeler validates the derivation tree *dtree1* (in fact, this tree is the only explanation for the incorrect student answer) and the mal-rule *bug1* (utilized in *dtree1)* is introduced in the Student Model. The other hypotheses *(omiss1, omiss2, omiss3* and *omiss4)* remain active.

6.4 Managing the Hypotheses with a Truth Maintenance System

All the hypotheses made by the Modeler about the student behavior are managed through the TMS included in the Modeler. In particular, the hypotheses are organized into a network (called *dependency network)* which describes the dependency relations among different hypotheses. We say that a derivation tree is *justified* by all the facts and rules (correct or incorrect) utilized for its construction. More precisely, this fact is represented with a *justification link* which specifies the supported tree and the supporting facts and rules. For example, the derivation tree *dtree1* is supported by the rules *r1* and *r4*, by the mal-rule *bug1* and by the facts *d5, d6*. This is represented by the assertion:

just(j1, dtree1, [bug1, r1,r 4, d5, d6]).

In general, an omission cause is justified by the missing fact or rule and by the new replacing fact or rule (not always present). The omission causes generated from the first exercise have therefore the following justifications:

just(j2, omiss1, [missing(r2)]).
just(j3, omiss2, [missing(d8)]).
just(j4, omiss3, [missing(r2), bug2]).
just(j5, omiss4, [missing(r2), bug1]).

If some node of the network is deleted during the modelling process, then all the nodes that are dependent on it are also deleted. This operation is achieved by following the justification links in the dependency network.

6.5 Selecting New Exercises

At the end of an analysis, several alternative hypotheses are usually active and therefore the system tries to collect new data from the student in order to better understand his/her misconceptions. In particular, the Tutor assigns a new exercise to the student with the purpose of supporting the Modeler in gathering new elements for discriminating among the alternative hypotheses. In order to select a new exercise the Tutor proceeds through three steps:

- it selects one or more alternative hypotheses to be further analyzed;

- it looks for an exercise related to these hypotheses in the database; and then
- it verifies whether the chosen exercise is discriminatory for the selected hypotheses.

An exercise is considered useful for discriminating among different hypotheses if the hypotheses produce different answers to it. In our example we have to discriminate among hypotheses of omission causes *(omiss1, omiss2, omiss3*, and *omiss4)*. Let us consider for example the two hypotheses *omiss1* and *omiss3*.

As the two hypotheses concern rules for the conjugation of the present perfect, the Tutor uses this element for identifying suitable exercises in the Exercise Database. A first possible exercise selected from the database is:

ex2: Please conjugate the present perfect, first person singular, of the verb to arrive.

In order to verify the discriminating degree of the exercise, the Tutor exploits the capability of simulating the student reasoning. The simulation concerns the reasoning process aimed at solving the exercise and it is performed assuming in turn each alternative hypothesis (*omiss1* and *omiss3)*. Then the results of the two simulations are compared. In our example, the simulation of the first omission cause (*omiss1*) produces the result:

am arrived.

The result of the simulation for the second hypothesis is again

am arrived.

As the two simulations produce the same answer, this exercise cannot be used to discriminate the two hypotheses and thus it is not considered by the Tutor. The next exercise selected from the database is:

ex3: Please conjugate the present perfect, first person singular, of the verb to ask.

In this case the two simulations give the following results:

am asked (omiss1)

have asked, am asked (omiss3).

Since this exercise gives two different sets of solutions for the two hypotheses it is considered useful for the discrimination and can thus be assigned to the student.

6.6 Concluding the diagnosis

Let us suppose now that the student gives *have asked* as a reply. The expected behavior of the student includes two different answers: *have asked* and *am asked.* The former answer is equal to that provided by the student and thus does not need a further analysis. The latter answer is different and therefore it is necessary to proceed with the omission error analysis. New possible omission causes are generated and all active hypotheses are again discriminated by means of the same procedure illustrated above: as a result, two omission causes (concerning respectively the fact that the student does not know that the irregular third person singular form of the verb *to have* is *has* and the fact that the correct conjugation rule *r2* is replaced by the mal-rule *bug2*) are still active for explaining the first exercise, and two other hypotheses are active for the second exercise (concerning respectively the fact that the student does not know that the irregular first person singular form of the verb *to be* is *am,* and a new mal-rule stating that the present perfect of intransitive verbs is formed by utilizing the auxiliary *to be*).

The control is again given to the Tutor which selects a new exercise (about the conjugation of the present perfect, first person singular, of the verb *to arrive*). Assuming that the student answer is *am arrived*, the Modeler is able to confirm two hypotheses: one about the incorrect use of the auxiliary *to be* with intransitive verbs and another hypothesis (produced by the omission error analysis of the answer just given) about the use of the auxiliary *to have* only with transitive verbs. All the other hypotheses still pending are discarded except one concerning the possible ignorance about the simple present of *to have*; the Tutor assigns therefore a specific exercise about this point.

The student answer is now *has*, which allows to discard the last hypothesis still active. At this point, the Modeler has completed the evaluation of all the hypotheses: the diagnosis has revealed that the student has incorrect knowledge about the use of auxiliary verbs in the present perfect. More specifically, he has replaced the correct rule *r2* with two different mal-rules: one rule for the case of transitive verbs (the present perfect is formed with the auxiliary *to have* and the past participle), and another rule for the case of intransitive verbs (the present perfect is formed with the auxiliary *to be* and the past participle).

6. Conclusions

A new methodology for modelling student performance has been presented which could be used in those systems that, like ET, are based on processes decomposable into a finite number of subtasks related to each other through producer-consumer dependencies. It is claimed that the deep modelling process illustrated in the paper has general significance beyond the domain of second language teaching. Our approach constitutes an attempt to deal with the problem of finding the reasons for, and giving a satisfactory explanation to, student performance. Some features of the proposed approach that we find particularly original are: (i) the integration of the bug collection and bug construction techniques, (ii) the use of diagnostic knowledge contained in a meta-bug library in order to help the process of bug construction, and (iii) the use of explanation based-learning techniques in the domain of modelling students' misconceptions. The proposed approach has been fully implemented in PROLOG on a Macintosh II.

References

1. Anderson, J.: Production systems, learning, and tutoring. In: Production system models of learning and development (D. Klahr, P. Langley, and R. Neches, eds.). Cambridge, MA: The MIT Press 1987
2. Bar-On, E. and Or-Bach, R.: Explanation-based learning in intelligent tutoring systems. In: Artificial intelligence tools in education (P. Ercoli and R. Lewis, eds.). Amsterdam, NL: Elsevier Science Publ. 1988
3. Bonar, J.G. and Soloway, E.M.: Pre-programming knowledge: A major source of misconceptions in novice programmers. Human-Computer Interaction 1(2), 133-161 (1985)
4. Brown, J. and Burton, R.: Diagnostic models for procedural bugs in mathematical skills. Cognitive Science 4, 379-426 (1980)
5. Chanier, T. and Pengelly, M.: Conceptual modelling in error analysis in computer-assisted language learning systems, this volume
6. Costa, E., Duchenoy, S., and Kodratoff, Y.: A resolution based method for discovering students' misconceptions. In artificial intelligence and human learning (J.A. Self ed.). London, UK: Chapman and Hall 1988
7. DeJong, G.F. and Mooney, R.J.: Explanation-based learning: An alternative view. Machine Learning 1, 145-176 (1986)
8. diSessa, A.A.: Unlearning Aristotelian physics: A study of knowledge-based learning. Cognitive Science 6, 37-75 (1982)
9. Doyle, J.: A truth maintenance system. Artificial Intelligence 12, 231-272 (1979)
10. Fum, D., Giangrandi, P., and Tasso, C.: ET: An intelligent tutor for foreign language teaching. Proceedings ITS-88, Montreal, pp. 462-468, 1988

11. Fum, D., Giangrandi, P., and Tasso, C.: Tense generation in an intelligent tutor for foreign language teaching: Some issues in the design of the verb expert. Proceedings 4th Conference of the European Chapter of the Association for Computational Linguistics, Manchester, pp. 124-129, Association for Computational Linguistics 1989
12. Fum, D., Giangrandi, P., and Tasso, C.: Backward model tracing: An explanation-based approach for reconstructing student reasoning. Proceedings AAAI-90, Boston, MA, pp. 426-433. Menlo Park, CA: AAAI Press 1990
13. Mitchell, T.M., Keller, R., and Kedar-Kabelli, S.: Explanation-based generalization: A unifying view. Machine Learning 1, 47-80 (1986)
14. Reif, F.: Interpretation of scientific or mathematical concepts: Cognitive issues and instructional Implications. Cognitive Science 11, 395-416 (1987)
15. Self, J.A.: Bypassing the intractable problem of student modelling. Proceedings ITS-88, Montreal, pp. 18-24, 1988
16. Sleeman, D.: Inferring (mal) rules from pupils' protocols. Proceedings Second International Machine Learning Workshop, Chicago, pp. 221-227, 1983
17. Wenger, E.: Artificial intelligence and tutoring systems. Los Altos, CA: Morgan Kaufmann 1987

Appendix

CONJUGATION RULES

```
%% r1:
%% The simple present of an irregular verb is given in the dictionary
IF   word(Verb, irregular_form(simple_present, Person, Number,V1-V2))
THEN conjugate(Verb, simple_present, Person, Number,V1-V2).

%% r2:
%% The present perfect of a verb is formed with the simple present of 'to have' followed by
%% the past participle of the verb.
IF   conjugate(have, simple_present, Person, Number, V1-V2),
     conjugate(Verb, past_participle, V2-V3)
THEN conjugate(Verb, present_perfect, Person, Number,V1-V3).

%% r3:
%% The past participle of a regular verb is formed with the ed-form.
IF   form_ed(Verb,V1-V2),
     word(Verb,regular(past_tense))
THEN conjugate(Verb,past_participle,V1-V2).

%% r4:
%% The past participle of an irregular verb is given in the dictionary
IF   word(Verb, irregular_form(past_participle, V1-V2))
THEN conjugate(Verb, past_participle, V1-V2).
```

DICTIONARY

```
%% The verb 'to arrive' is regular in the past tense
d1: word(arrive,regular(past_tense))
```

%% The verb 'to ask' is regular in the past tense
d2: word(ask,regular(past_tense))

%% The verb 'to ask' does not double the last letter when
%% some suffix is added to it
d3: word(ask,no_double_last_letter)

%% The simple present of the verb to be, first person singular,
%% is 'am'.
d4: word(be,irregular_form(simple_present,1,singular,[am|X]-X))

%% The simple present of the verb 'to be', third person singular,
%% is 'is'.
d5: word(be,irregular_form(simple_present,3,singular,[is|X]-X))

EXERCISE DATABASE

%% ex1:
%% Conjugate the present perfect, third person singular, of the verb 'to go'.
conjugate(go,present_perfect,3,singular,V-[])

%% ex2:
%% Conjugate the present perfect, first person singular of the verb 'to arrive'
conjugate(arrive,present_perfect,1,singular,V-[])

%% ex3:
%% Conjugate the present perfect, first person singular, of the verb 'to ask'.
conjugate(arrive,present_perfect,1,singular,V-[])

META-BUG LIBRARY

%% mb1:
%% It is possible for a student to utilize 'to have' instead of 'to be'
IF
LHS CLAUSE: conjugate(be,T,P,N,V1-V2),
THEN REPLACE WITH: conjugate(have,T,P,N,V1-V2).

%% mb2:
%% It is possible for a student to utilize 'to be' instead of 'to have'
IF LHS CLAUSE: conjugate(have, T, P, N,V1-V2),
THEN REPLACE WITH: conjugate(be, T, P, N, V1-V2).

%% mb3:
%% The conjugation of the present perfect depends on the transitiveness of the verb (as in
%% Italian)
IF RHS CLAUSE: conjugate(Verb, present_perfect, Person, Number, V1-V2),
THEN ADD IN LHS: word(Verb, transitive).

Nobile: Object-Based User Model Acquisition for Second Language Learning

Stefano A. Cerri, Elena Cheli & Angus McIntyre

DIDA*LAB , Research and Development Laboratory, DIDA*EL , Via Lamarmora, 3, 20122 Milano, Italy

Abstract: The development of intelligent tutoring systems based on models of the user requires that a practical and efficient method be found for designing and implementing such models. This paper describes the 'natural laboratory' methodology for user model acquisition, and "Nobile" prototype, one of the systems developed to serve as an experimental platform for the 'natural laboratory' methodology being developed within the European Community Delta project "Nat*Lab". The paper also includes a description of a re-implementation of the "ALICE" tutoring system, developed as a testbed for use with the Nobile shell. This system deals with the translation of temporal conjunctions in context and with associated concepts in the field of temporal reasoning and language learning.

Keywords: student models, intelligent tutoring, knowledge acquisition

1. Introduction

A substantial proportion of current intelligent tutoring systems (see [3, 17, 19]) make use of a model of the user in order to allow the system to adapt to the user's particular needs, and debates about the universal applicability of such an approach aside (see [18]), it seems clear that as more intelligent tutoring systems are developed, there will be a corresponding growth in the demand for effective models of the user. The development of such models is, however, both time-consuming and labour-intensive, like any other knowledge engineering activity, and represents a significant part of the cost and difficulty of developing a tutoring system.

The problems associated with model development hinge on the need to refer to recognized experts in the field to be taught by the system (which is to say people who are not only knowledgeable in a specialist field but also in the teaching of that field) and to elicit from them the knowledge that they use in teaching and explaining the subject area (see [9] this volume for an example of this kind of knowledge). Problems include the cost in terms of time and money, the difficulty of recovering knowledge that may not be consciously formalized, the difficulty of translating from the expert's terminology into the formalism required by the system, and the difficulty of ensuring that the information provided by the expert is complete and consistent.

In the design of expert systems, knowledge acquisition is recognised as a non-trivial phase of the design process. Given the time that can be saved during the implementation by the use of off-the-shelf expert system shells knowledge acquisition may even constitute the major part of the design process in terms of time, effort and expense. A number of acquisition methodologies have been developed with a view to making the problem more manageable and improving the results (see [15] for a review of current methodologies). It is reasonable to assert that in the field of ITS design this problem is still more significant as the knowledge that must be acquired is not knowledge about the kind of relatively well-defined domains that most expert systems deal with, but vague knowledge about human reasoning processes.

Given that the model acquisition process represents an obstacle in the path of ITS development, any proposal that appears to offer a means of reducing the size of the obstacle is worth taking seriously. The development of an adequate system for facilitating and rendering

NATO ASI Series, Vol. F 80
Intelligent Tutoring Systems for Foreign Language Learning
Edited by M. L. Swartz and M. Yazdani

more reliable the model acquisition process will be a major step forward for the field of intelligent tutoring systems as a whole. Because second language teaching systems typically make use of tutorial-style interactions (rather than, for example, learning by exploration) the possibility of appropriate and intelligent feedback offered by user modelling makes user-model-based systems particularly suitable for this domain. Accordingly, any enhancement to the model acquisition process will be especially welcome in the specific field of intelligent tutoring for language teaching.

2. The 'Natural Laboratory'

The "Natural Laboratory" methodology [8, 14, 16] referred to in this paper has been conceived as a way of facilitating the acquisition of student models, and of meeting the requirements for knowledge acquisition systems outlined below by:

- permitting specialists to use the terms and concepts that they are familiar with, and performing any necessary transformations from the framework used by the specialist into the formalism required by the system.
- constraining the form in which the expert can express him or herself as little as possible, and, ideally even allowing the experts to choose their own way of working.
- taking an active part in the interaction with the expert and providing contexts for the application of the expert's knowledge, in order to recover the kind of intuitive or unformalized knowledge which would otherwise be missed.

The name of the methodology derives from the fact that the acquisition system is intended to provide, as far as possible, a familiar context for the application of the expert's knowledge, in this case, the activity of diagnosing the causes of student errors. The objective of the methodology is the incremental construction and refinement of student models, and the basic steps to be performed are identified as follows:

1. Definition of the formal knowledge-base representing the field of study to be taught by the tutoring system.
2. Construction by a domain specialist of an initial set of student models. This initial set consists minimally of a model of an idealized 'perfect student' (sometimes referred to as the 'expert model'), but may also include some proposed models of plausible misconceptions.
3. Incremental refinement and extension of the set of misconceptions through a series of dialogues between the system and the expert.
4. Use of the full set of validated misconceptions in the final tutoring system.

The most important part of this methodology is the third stage. In the version of the methodology proposed in this paper, the dialogues referred to are of a specific type, referred to as inverted dialogues, which are described in greater detail below. It is important to note that the third stage is a repeated, incremental process, with the results of each interaction between the system and the designer being put immediately into the tutoring system's knowledge base for use in the next interaction. In this way, although the overhead of constructing a domain representation and an initial set of errors cannot be avoided, it can be very much reduced. Rather than having to construct a complete bug catalogue for the domain by hand, the system designer may define only a minimal set of possible errors, and then use the cycle of interactions as a kind of "bootstrapping" process for refining and enlarging this set of errors. The results of each interaction serve as the basis for future interactions, so that the system steadily increases its knowledge about plausible student misconceptions. The full process is represented schematically in Figure 1 below.

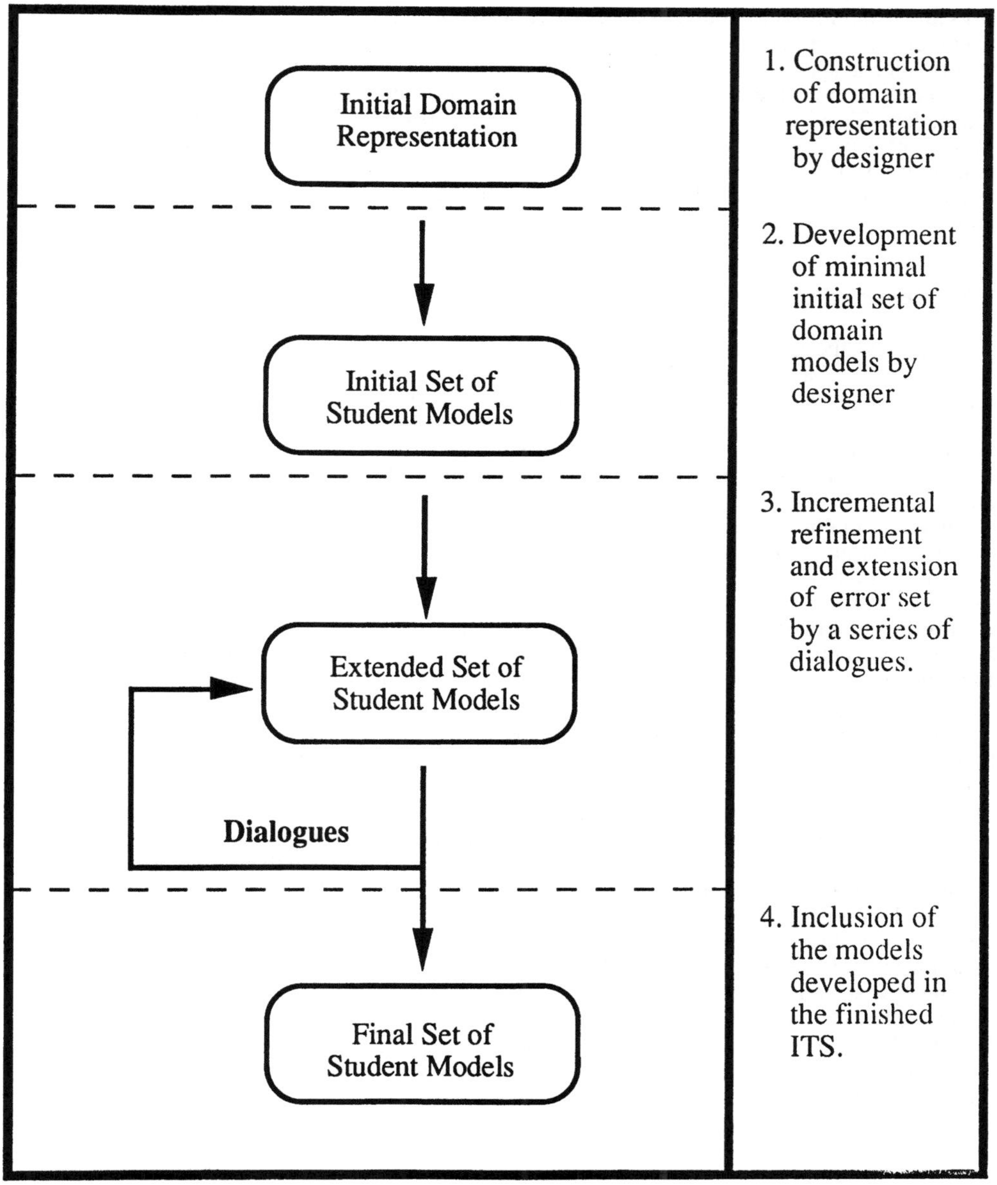

Figure 1. The Natural Laboratory

2.1 Bugs, errors and models

The methodology, at least in its present form, relies heavily on the concept of a *bug*, as defined by Burton [4]:

> "a discrete modification to the correct skills which effectively duplicate the student's behaviour"

Bugs are also referred to in this paper as *misconceptions*. The surface *errors* which are observed in student performances are the visible symptoms of such a bug, deviations from correct performance in specific situations. Errors are said to be caused by a bug.

Models in the context of the Natural Laboratory are computational accounts of the behaviour of a student. That is, they are a representation of the knowledge involved in the activity in which the student is involved. Models may represent the 'correct skills which ... duplicate the student's behaviour' [4], or the skills after modification by a bug. We will follow Brown and Burton [2] in referring to models which describe behaviour that contains errors as *bug* or *misconception models*.

2.2 Inverted dialogues

As mentioned above, the refinement of the set of student models available to the system is carried out by means of a kind of dialogue between the system and the user, known as an inverted dialogue. By *inverted dialogue,* we mean a dialogue in which the usual roles of the participants are reversed or altered, what might be termed a 'non-traditional' use of the system. For instance, when an ITS system is in use, the system normally takes the role of the teacher, and the user has the role of student. In the inverted dialogue counterpart of this type of interaction, the user would adopt the role of a teacher, while the system plays the part of a student.

Inverted dialogues have a number of possible applications throughout the field of intelligent tutoring, ranging from discovery learning to training teachers to diagnose student errors (see [8]), but in this paper we shall be concerned with the application of the concept to the task of model acquisition. The idea is to use inverted dialogues as a means of allowing an expert to acquire an understanding of a model, and to demonstrate that s/he understands the model, without involving him/her in the actual code with which the model is represented. Inverted dialogues for model acquisition are the computational equivalent of talking about something without naming it.

To see how this works, we can consider the simplest form of the Natural Laboratory. In this approach, the models to be included in the tutoring system are developed from the initial model of the 'ideal student' (that is, the model that embodies the system designer's understanding of the knowledge necessary to arrive at a correct answer), for instance by automatic perturbation, and submitted to the expert for examination and approval before insertion in the tutoring system.

Clearly, presenting the expert with listings of the computer code that implements the model is not a practical way to familiarize him/her with the model, and even transcripts of the errors associated with a particular model are likely to be baffling and tiring to examine in bulk. Instead, the Natural Laboratory proposes a two-step process for allowing the expert to examine the behaviour of a model and confirm her/his understanding of it.

In the first step, the expert is presented with some sample errors representative of the model, and then (through the medium of the partially built tutoring system) enters an inverted dialogue of the type described above, in which s/he adopts the role of teacher, and asks questions of the system in its role as a 'student'. The purpose of the dialogue is to allow the expert to identify the nature and cause of the errors, by proposing questions to the system. The expert can experiment with different hypotheses, trying out questions to indicate whether one or other hypothesis is correct.

When the expert has arrived at an understanding of the errors predicted by the model, s/he must confirm that s/he has understood correctly. To achieve this, we use a second type of inverted dialogue, in which the expert takes the student role, and attempts to reproduce the behaviour of the model that s/he has just observed. If the expert's predictions exactly match those of the model, then it can be assumed that the expert has correctly recognized the misconception represented by the model. If the expert then agrees that this is a plausible model, it can be entered into the database of models to be included in the finished version of the tutoring system.

Figure 2. Inverted dialogues in the basic methodology

The purpose of this approach, represented diagramatically in Figure 2, is that the expert should be able to reach and demonstrate an understanding of a misconception represented, without directly inspecting the code that implements a student model. The first part of Figure 2 shows a computer simulating a student's error (a somewhat implausible error - the student appears to have confused the addition and multiplication operators). In the second part, the teacher demonstrates that he has identified the error by producing appropriate behaviour in the context of a different example. Through this process, models proposed by the system designer can be validated by specialists who have little or no knowledge of computer programming.

2.3 Model acquisition by negotiation

In practice, we want to do more than simply verify or reject the models offered by the system designer. The expert should be used as the source for new models, new accounts of the ways in which students can go wrong. For this, we want to look more closely at the cases when the expert and the system disagree in their predictions about the errors characteristic of a particular misconception.

When the expert predicts a different response from that expected by the system, the system should inform him/her of the fact, so that s/he has the chance to check her/his prediction. The system should also be able, on request, to justify its predictions. If, after this, the expert still maintains that his/her prediction was correct, it must mean that s/he is modelling a different misconception from that represented by the system. In such a case, the system should attempt to acquire the model being used by the expert.

The method envisaged is that the expert should be provided with an editing environment to allow her/him to modify existing models to represent the error that s/he has in mind. At first sight, this appears to run counter to the philosophy of the Natural Laboratory, in that it exposes the expert to the underlying representation of the models. However, the problem is less serious than might at first be thought. We can use the context provided by the inverted dialogue and the structure of the models in use to identify the precise area in which the system's model and that being used by the expert differ. We can then restrict the expert's editing activity to that area. Rather than requiring the expert to deal with a complete and arbitrarily complex model we can look at a manageable sub-part of the model.

Another advantage of editing within the context of the Natural Laboratory over editing in isolation is that the inverted dialogue methodology is available to allow the expert to test the models. The expert, having developed a new model, may enter a new inverted dialogue in two stages as above. In the first stage, the expert takes the teacher role, and asks his/her standard set of diagnostic questions to ensure that the model behaves as s/he expects; in the second stage, the system can ask the expert questions to confirm that the model the expert has created really does conform to his/her intentions.

Involving the expert directly in the construction of models is something we would like to avoid, as it carries the risk of introducing inconsistencies to the system, or of confusing the expert. Where it is inevitable, however, the Natural Laboratory methodology can help considerably, by restricting the area under consideration and by providing a means of testing the models created; these advantages, combined with a habitable knowledge-acquisition environment should mean that the acquisition of new models is a practical proposition. The design of such an environment is not a trivial problem but on the other hand it is the subject of a good deal of current research (see [13] for a description of one approach to this problem) so we can reasonably hope that an appropriate environment will be available for our purposes in the near future.

2.4 A wider range of errors: student sessions

A difficulty with using pre-coded error models is that the development of a sufficient set of error models imposes a heavy workload on the system designer. If, on the other hand, the initial model set is not large enough, there is the risk of overlooking significant possible student misconceptions.

A possible solution is to use the partially implemented tutoring system to collect sample errors from real students (see [7] for an example of such an approach). The student's behaviours can be monitored and recorded, and subsequently used as the basis of inverted dialogues with the expert, with the intention of acquiring models to represent the observed behaviours.

The first part of such a dialogue follows the form which should by now be familiar. The expert inspects the list of student answers just as if it were any other model, by asking questions, until s/he is confident that s/he has understood the error being made by the student. The next step is for the expert to confirm that s/he has understood the misconception, by reproducing representative errors in response to the system's questions, exactly as before.

At this point a problem emerges. Even if the expert is capable of identifying and simulating the misconception, there is no model to put into the developing model base. Instead of basing inverted dialogues on the errors generated by an existing model, the dialogues are being based on the errors produced by an actual student with no underlying model.

The solution proposed is to have the system choose from among the models available to it (i.e. the set of models created by the designer of the tutoring system together with any additional models developed during previous inverted dialogues) to find the model that most closely matches the behaviour of the student (or alternatively, to allow the expert to choose an existing model). This model then serves as the basis of a third inverted dialogue, in which the expert continues to simulate the student, while the system matches the expert's behaviours against those predicted by the model chosen. When there is a disagreement, the system enters the edit cycle, asking the expert to modify the model to represent the behaviours of the student. The modified model can then be tested by further inverted dialogues to confirm that it conforms to the expert's expectations. The complete process is represented in Figure 3.

The advantages of this approach are threefold. First, by using real students, the system has the chance of capturing a wider range of real-world errors; there is a risk that if only models generated by the system designer are used, the expert may overlook some plausible misconception in the domain because no existing model is close enough to suggest it. Secondly, the initial model set that must be created by the tutoring system designer can be very small. In the extreme case it is limited to a single model, the designer's model of the 'ideal student' with additional models are built up incrementally in a series of sessions with the acquisition system. Thirdly, using the system with real students may suggest changes that that should be made to the system's model in order to allow it to better represent the knowledge involved in the activity being performed by the student.

3. 'Testing' the methodology: Nobile

The Natural Laboratory methodology described above is being studied as part of the European Community Delta project Nat*Lab (P7004/D1016), a project whose major objective is the definition, evaluation and refinement of the methodology. The evaluation is being carried out with a series of experiments based on prototype systems developed as part of the project. This section describes one of those prototypes, the knowledge acquisition shell *Nobile*[1], which implements the methodologies discussed in this paper.

Nobile has been implemented using Common LISP and the LISP-based knowledge representation languages KRS (see [21,23]) and GTE (see [24]). The existing system was developed using Macintosh Allegro Common LISP on Apple Macintosh computers, making use of the object-oriented Object LISP provided by MACL for implementation of the user interface

---

[1]NOBILE = Nat*Lab Object-Based Interactive Learner Environment.

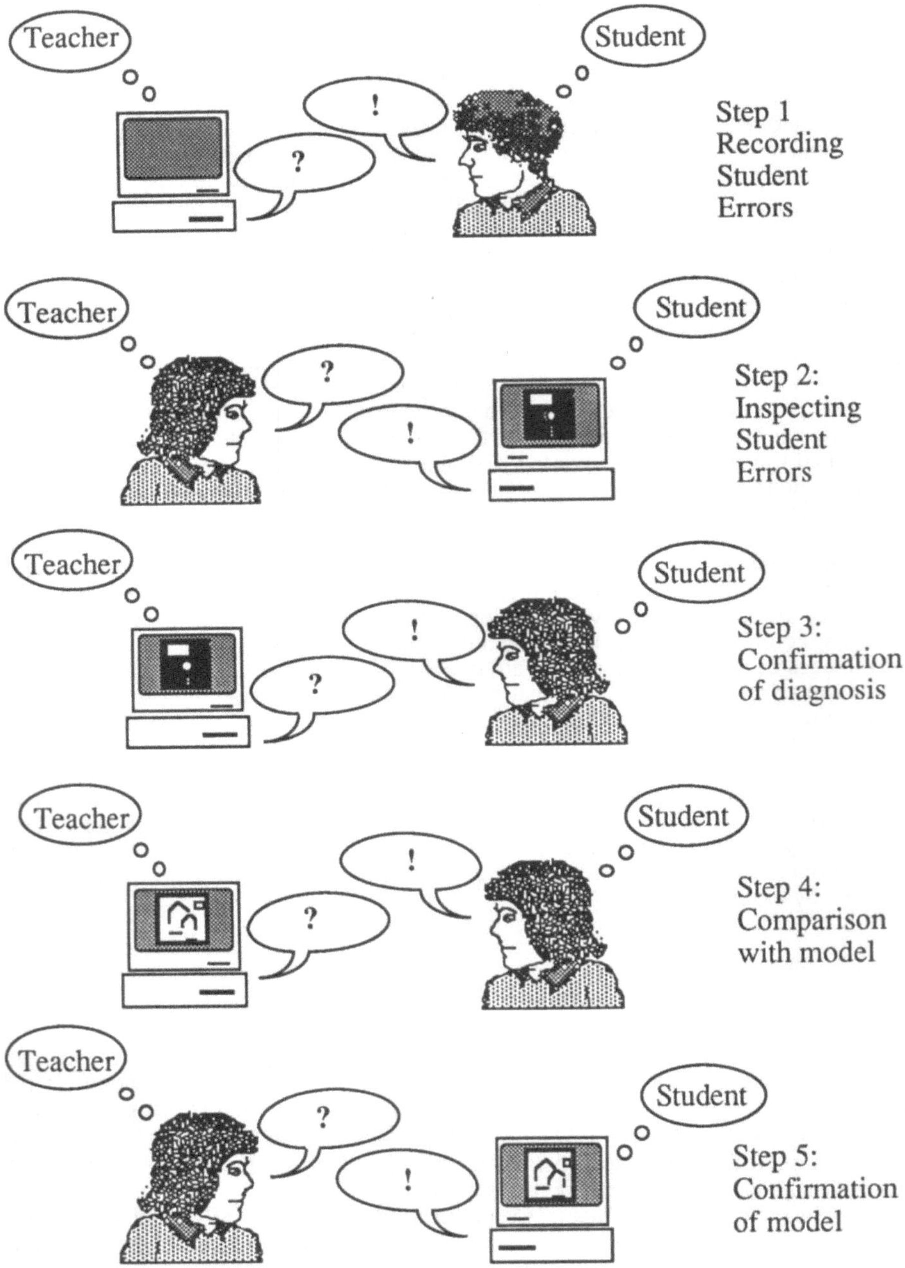

Figure 3. Using Student Sessions for Acquisition

Work is in progress to port the prototype to other environments, Sun UNIX and MS-DOS machines being the current intended targets.

The high-level languages GTE and KRS were chosen in order to allow the knowledge encoded in the system to be made as explicit as possible. The object-oriented representation language KRS is based on intensional logic. KRS is used to represent the factual knowledge available to the tutoring system and also to describe objects in the field of intelligent tutoring systems - models, domains, topics, exercises and so forth. GTE is implemented using KRS and was designed to be used for instructional applications, providing a mechanism for describing activities in terms of tasks and methods. In *Nobile*, it is used to represent the instructional strategies used by the tutoring systems under development, and in the encoding of one type of student model supported by the system - a process-based account of student activities in a domain. Both languages are written in Common LISP and allow access to the full power of the language.

The NOBILE system is a knowledge acquisition shell, into which different tutoring systems can be "plugged in" for knowledge acquisition. The shell provides interface facilities, libraries of instructional methods, and some predefined definitions of important objects in instructional tutoring to be used by the tutoring system. To work with the knowledge acquisition shell, the tutoring system must be designed according to certain guidelines. To allow monitoring of the execution of the system, the didactic strategy of the system must be encoded in GTE and it must make use of some of the definitions provided by the shell - definitions of generic concepts for students, models, and so forth. However, these constraints, at least for the purposes of an experimental system, are not excessively restrictive.

3.1 Implementing inverted dialogues

The Nobile system makes use of the object-oriented programming style supported by KRS to permit an elegant and economical implementation of inverted dialogues. All of the dialogues described above (including the 'non-inverted' interaction between the student and the standard tutoring system) can be described in abstract terms as a dialogue between two agents, one having the role of a teacher, the other having the role of a student . Each individual dialogue type represents an instantiation of the abstract roles by real entities (computer programs, human users etc). The approach taken in "Nobile" is to encode the tutoring system mechanisms to deal with abstract dialogue agents, who are defined in terms of the questions they can answer, and the information that they can be given. For instance, a student might be defined by:

Student

Information

Show a problem

Questions

What is your name?

What is the answer to problem <x> in context <y>?

Do you want to stop now?

During the course of various dialogues, the student role might be filled by different concrete agents - a human student, a record of a past student's answers, an executable student model. Provided that the system provides appropriate definitions for each to carry out the interactions listed above, a tutoring system coded in terms of the abstract interactions can be used transparently with any of them.

The realization of these agents in concrete terms is handled by defining concepts that inherit from the abstract agents, but which include specific definitions of how the interactions are to be handled. For instance, the "What is the answer?" interaction of the abstract student agent would be defined for the various concrete agents thus by:

Real student What is the answer ...	Present problem on-screen Get answer through keyboard or mouse
Recorded student What is the answer ...	Look up answer in a list
System student model What is the answer ...	Execute model

Inverted dialogues can be implemented simply by switching concrete agents. The different possibilities are indicated in Figure 4 below. For more detail on dialogue agents in Nobile, see [6].

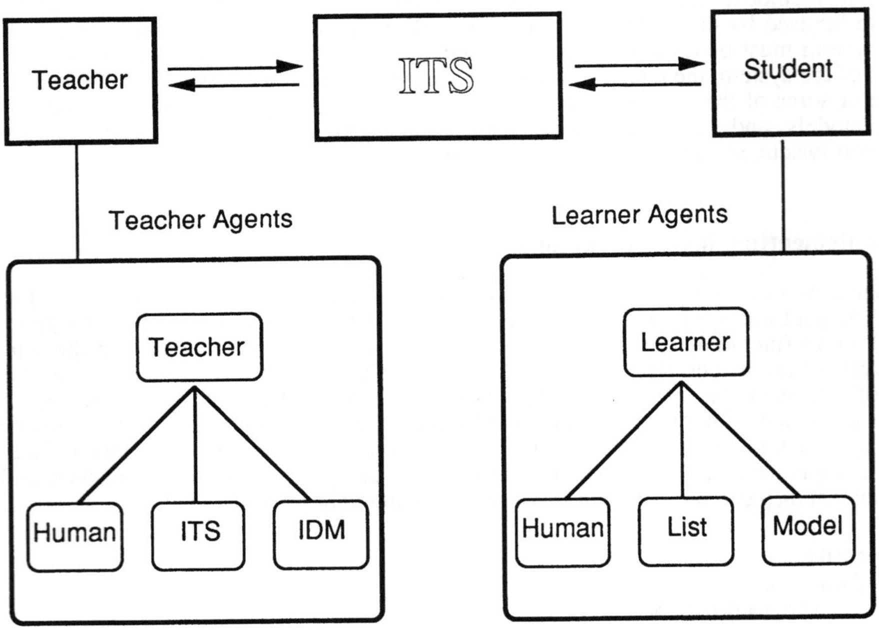

Figure 4. Dialogue agents & the tutoring system

3.2 Models in Nobile

Student models, whose acquisition is the ultimate aim of the system, are realized as a specialization of the abstract learner agent type. The Natural Laboratory methodology requires that models should be:

- generative
- explanatory
- explicit

That is to say, models should be able to be executed to generate new responses (necessary for domains that are not inherently bounded to a fixed set of situations) rather than consisting simply of a list of behaviours. They should be capable of supporting explanation, so that the expert can understand why a model produced a particular response. They should be explicit, in that the knowledge contained in the model should be available for inspection and modification. Moreover, models are expected to conform to some natural structure already present in the domain (see [10-12] for examples), to make the inspection and modification process simpler, and to make use of the terminology and the objects familiar to the expert from his/her knowledge of the domain. In effect, models should consist of small second-generation expert systems (see [20, 22]) capable of (possibly fallacious) reasoning about the domain of study.

The methodology does not make any assumptions about the implementation of such models, and the Nobile system itself only requires that models should be capable of acting as abstract student agents - that is, participating in the range of interactions which define a student. In future, models based on production rules, or scripts, or any other representation that seems appropriate may be developed, but the current implementation of Nobile contains a single class of model, referred to as *hierarchy models.*

Hierarchy models represent an account of the knowledge needed to solve a problem in terms of the activities carried out by the student during the solution of the problem. The structure chosen then is some supposed cognitive structure which might realistically model the student's thought processes, or the steps towards solving a given problem. The implementation uses the task and method paradigm supported by the programming language GTE, where a task is an activity to be carried out ("What to do") and a method is the means to perform the activity ("How to do it"). The underlying factual knowledge about the domain is represented using concepts, the primitive elements of KRS.

The encoding of models as GTE programs fulfils our requirement that models should be generative - solutions are achieved by executing the GTE task hierarchy comprising the model - and also provides for a form of explanation. The execution can be monitored, and variable bindings made during the execution can be displayed to indicate the reasoning process, e.g.

"'Temporal relation' = 'before' in 'Find-temporal-relation'"

The explicit representation of domain knowledge and the well-defined structure of the models helps make the models more intelligible and easier to edit.

4. New Alice: a Nobile tutor for foreign languages

Nobile is not itself a tutoring system, but rather a shell into which purpose-written tutoring systems can be inserted for model-acquisition. In this section we will describe one of these systems, a reimplementation and extension of the Alice[1] Tutoring System [5], to illustrate the components that make up a tutoring system under Nobile.

4.1 About Alice

Alice is a Tutoring System prototype built to "teach" translation of temporal and causal conjunctions from a source language (e.g., Italian, English or French) to a target language (e.g., Italian, English or French). The most important feature of the system consists of the way the knowledge about the subject matter is encoded. Knowledge is encoded in terms of a set of language independent concepts, called *discriminant concepts*, and their realizations in different languages, with the language-dependent and -independent elements connected in a network.

---

[1]ALICE = A Little Intelligent Conjunction Expert.

Readers interested in the idea of discriminant concepts and their implications for teaching should refer to [5] but for the purposes of the present paper a brief example may be useful. One discriminant concept is called DU, and is related to those conjunctions that express the idea of equal duration of the events that they conjoin - *'tant que'* in French, *'finchè'* in Italian, *'as long as'* in English. The reason for using discriminant concepts is that a single word may be ambiguous with respect to two (or more) concepts, and this can be a productive source of errors. As an example, in English the conjunction 'till' is used to instantiate two distinct concepts, termed AD and DS, whereas in Italian each concept is realized by a separate conjunction (DS is instantiated by *'prima che'*, and AD by *'finchè'*). This frequently leads to errors in translations from one language to the other. Figure 5 below shows some of the discriminant concepts making up Alice's knowledge base.

Alice's knowledge about student modelling consists of an overlay model and a bug catalogue (as in [2]). The overlay model is a set of nodes in the net which are known or learned by the student, initially consisting of the nodes of the student's native language. During the session, the net grows to cover those new concepts in the foreign language which are acquired. The bug catalogue is divided into two levels, one of which is concerned with 'bugs' such as literal translation, confusion with adverbs, use of conjunctions not existing in the target language, violation of syntactic constraints, and interference errors (further refined by the second level). The second level of the bug catalogue might be better described as a student model catalogue, and consists of a set of possible incorrect models, each one corresponding to a set of student answers, against which the student's errors can be matched at the end of the session.

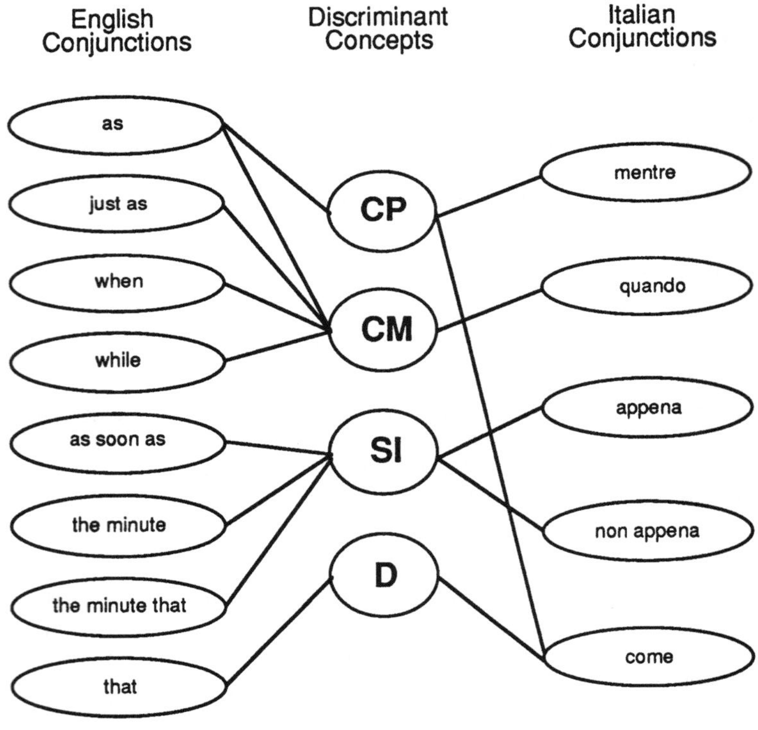

Figure 5. A fragment of Alice's discriminant concept net

The system's teaching strategy involves an exploration of the conceptual net through dynamically chosen exercises designed to test and extend the student's knowledge. The system is also capable of diagnostic dialogues following pre-designed patterns to identify the appropriate student model. The system proved effective at diagnosis, but remediation of errors was not fully explored. The difficulties of effective remediation are discussed in [5].

4.2 ALICE in NOBILE

The Alice domain (temporal conjunctions) and the system's knowledge base have been adopted as the basis for a tutoring system written in GTE and KRS to run under Nobile. This system is in some ways a subset of the Alice program. It deals only with translation of temporal conjunctions, but the scope of the program has also been slightly extended to provide a richer domain for experimentation, so that the system now addresses concepts such as temporal reasoning and tense selection. Alice's contribution to the new system effectively consists of:

- its domain knowledge base
- the 'initial' bug catalogue
- the task of temporal conjunction teaching

The program interacts with the user through a system of menus and textual dialogue windows which are provided as a standard facility by the Nobile shell (optional, but available for use by tutoring systems). The dialogue between system and user is system-driven, made up of problems which are presented textually and answered by the user through menu selections. An example is shown in Figure 6.

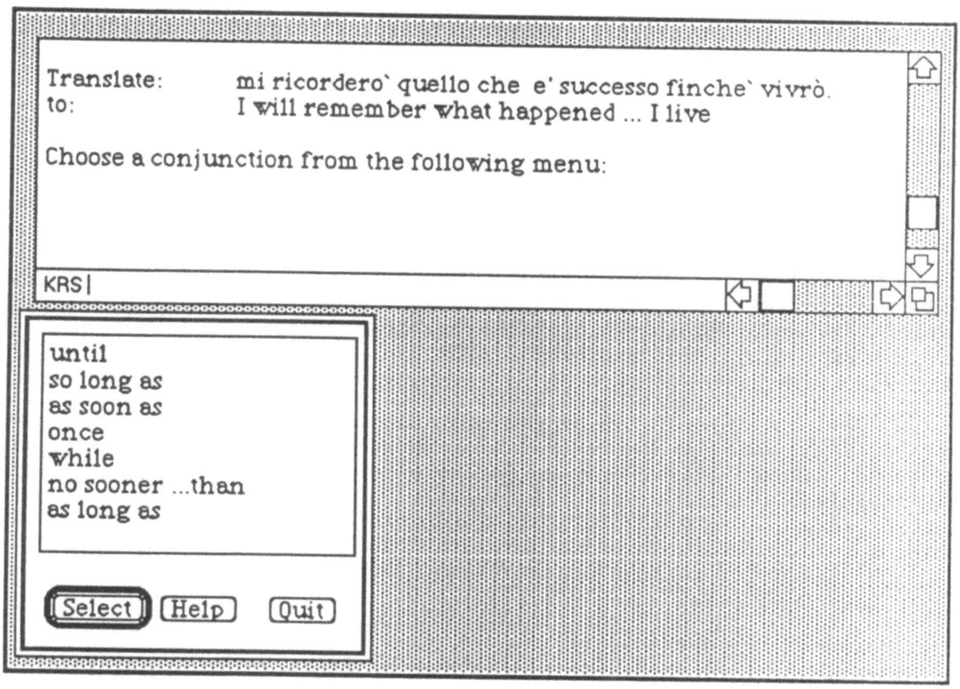

Figure 6. A translation problem in new Alice

As may be obvious, New Alice would win few prizes as an exciting or original tutoring system, and the term 'intelligent' can not be happily applied to the program. New Alice is not intended to be a good tutoring system. It is intended to serve as an experimental platform for model acquisition, so its imperfections can perhaps be excused and the simplicity of the program may be a positive advantage in that it is easier for the expert users to understand.

Despite the rudimentary nature of the system, we can use it to demonstrate how a modular Nobile-compatible tutoring system is written, and, of particular interest, how the knowledge - including the user models - of the system is encoded. In the following sections we will consider four aspects of the system providing examples of each aspect from the new Alice system:

- tutoring concepts
- tutoring strategies
- domain knowledge
- user models

4.3 Tutoring Concepts

The Nobile shell provides a number of pre-defined KRS concepts which are used to describe the building blocks of a tutoring system. Among these concepts are of course the agents described earlier, which are specialized as appropriate by the individual tutoring systems[1]. The concept library also includes concepts for elements such as exercises, topics and domains. Nobile actually proposes a subdivision of exercises into problems - the generic part of an exercise - and situations - a specific context for the application of a problem - and it is the combination of these two elements which creates the exercise presented to the user.

The generic concepts provided by Nobile are refined by the individual tutoring system. For instance, Nobile furnishes a type of problem called a 'Fixed String and Menu' problem, which is characterized by the presentation of a string to a user, and the selection of a response from a menu. The exercise shown in Figure 6 above is based on a specialization of this type of problem, called 'Translate-Conjunction-Problem', which defines how the string and the menu presented should be generated, and what constitutes a solution.

The exercise is created by combining a problem with a situation. The generic Nobile definition for a situation contains very little information and individual tutoring systems must define the structure they require. At present Alice uses a single type of situation which is a KRS concept describing a sentence and its possible translations into three languages. The Alice problems draw on different parts of this context to create the problems. It is worth noting that Nobile encourages the development of situations and problems in a many-to-many relationship. Exercises can be created by the application of different problems to a single situation or of different situations to a single problem. This is used extensively in Alice, where the diagnostic strategy proposes sub-problems of the main problem applied in the same context.

Problems and situations (and the other concepts used) are represented by KRS concepts, which are frame-like objects capable of containing ordinary slot values (possibly other concepts) or function definitions to calculate values, possibly by reference to other concepts in the tutoring knowledge base.

[1]Specialization of agents includes the definition of tutoring strategies (specialization of the system strategy ag addition of enrolment information to student agents and so forth.

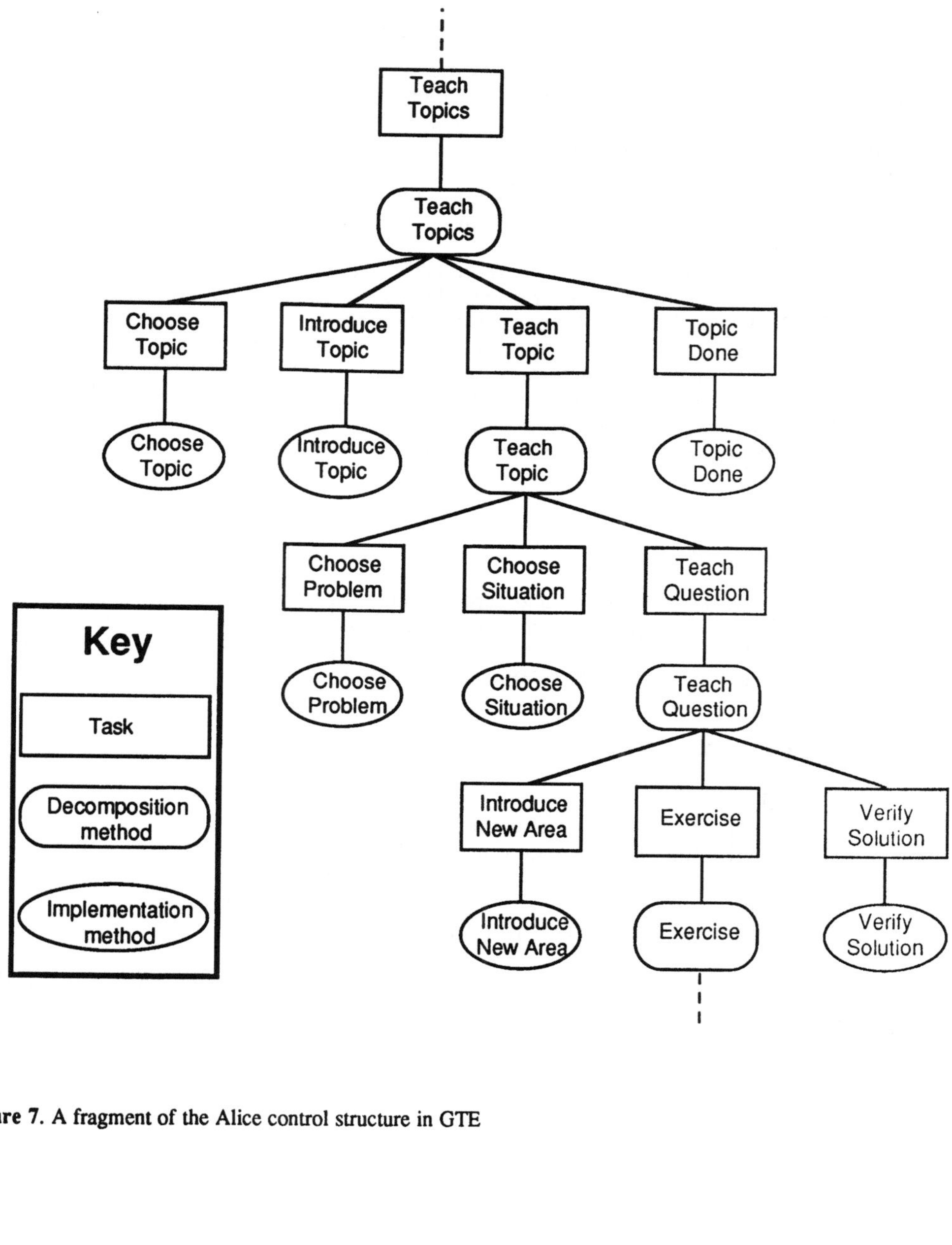

Figure 7. A fragment of the Alice control structure in GTE

4.4 Tutoring strategies

The use of the predefined concepts offered by the system is intended to be optional. Nobile-compatible tutoring systems are required, however, to implement their tutoring strategies according to certain guidelines specifically that these strategies should be encoded in GTE and should make use of the request-passing mechanisms provided by GTE for their interaction with the abstract dialogue agents. The use of GTE permits the monitoring of the system's execution, as well as the agent abstraction needed to implement the inverted dialogues. Figure 7 below shows a part of the Alice control structure, and demonstrates that even simple systems can involve quite complex structures.

The control structures make extensive use of GTE's message-passing mechanisms to direct requests for choices to the current teacher agent. The didactic knowledge of the system thus rests more in the KRS/LISP definitions of the teacher agent for the standard tutoring strategy than in the GTE control structure. In the case of Alice, the strategy is purely diagnostic, attempting to trace the causes for an error by examining the user's responses to subproblems associated with the current problem. The association is encoded in the hierarchical user models included in the system, and Alice's strategy is based on a simple stack-based search mechanism that navigates through the user model of the 'ideal' student to identify sub-activities involved in the main problem-solving activity.

4.5 Domain knowledge

The system's domain knowledge is also represented in terms of KRS concepts which are particularly suitable for the representation of the objects in the world which the tutoring system deals with. In the case of Alice, the main objects represented are languages, conjunctions, discriminant concepts, and temporal relations. The code for a discriminant concept is shown below:

```
(defconcept DC-AD
  (a discriminant-concept
    (realizations
      (italian [list-of-conjunctions finche fino-a-quando])
      (english [list-of-conjunctions until till])
      (french [list-of-conjunctions        tant-que jusqu-a-ce-que
                                           jusqu-au-moment-ou]))
    (temporal-relations [list-of-trs tr-mi])))
```

The semantics of the definition are that the discriminant concept DC-AD is realized in different languages by a variety of conjunctions, and is associated with the temporal relation 'met-by'. These conjunctions and temporal relations are themselves concepts, such as:

```
(defconcept FINCHE
  (a conjunction
    (language italian)
    (name [string "finchè"])
    (translations
      (english [list-of-conjunctions till until
                                           as-long-as before])
      (french [list-of-conjunctions        tant-que jusqu-a-ce-que
                                           jusqu-au-moment-ou
                                           avant-que]))
    (discriminant-concepts
  [list-of-discriminant-concepts dc-ad dc-du dc-ds])))
```

which lists all the possible translations of the Italian word "finchè" (irrespective of the context of use) as well as the discriminant concepts with which it is associated. The network of conjunctions and discriminant concepts is encoded implicitly by these concept definitions.

4.6 Student models

The requirements for student models in the Natural Laboratory have already been described, and their realization by hierarchy models (as one possible class of models) has been alluded to. It remains to illustrate the idea of hierarchy models, giving as an example the model of the 'correct' student developed as part of Alice, illustrated in Figure 8. The model as presented here is very much a first attempt and should not be taken either as a definitive statement on human cognitive processes or as an account of a finalized and validated model. It should serve, however, to clarify some of the ideas involved.

The model breaks down the basic activity of translating a conjunction from one language to another into three sub-activities, respectively the identification of the conjunction in the source sentence, the identification of the associated discriminant concept, and the selection of a translation for the discriminant concept. Some of these activities are themselves decomposed. Because discriminant concepts are associated with temporal relations, the model asserts that the discriminant concept can be identified by identifying the temporal relation between the events described in the conjoined clauses[1] and retrieving the associated discriminant concept. The activity of finding an appropriate realization for the discriminant concept is also decomposed (not shown in the diagram) into processes of retrieving all possible translations of a conjunction and filtering out only those which realize the discriminant concept.

The model serves several purposes. As previously stated, it is used by the tutoring strategy for diagnosis which is made possible by association of problems with task nodes in the tree. If the student has difficulty in translating a conjunction, for instance, the system will attempt to find a reason for this by proposing the problems associated with the sub-activities such as identifying the conjunction in the sentence or finding the temporal relations involved.

The model also serves to generate responses, by a process of information passing, represented by labelled arrows in the tree. GTE context variables are bound and passed into the hierarchy when it is executed (downward arrows), and new bindings made during the execution are used to return the responses predicted by the model (upward arrows).

The model shown is the idealized student model and serves as a basis for student models accounting for particular misconceptions in which parts of the model (including the factual domain knowledge represented by KRS concepts as well as the procedural knowledge encoded in GTE) are altered in order to generate misconceptions. The Nobile system provides tools for graphical editing of models, taking advantage of the structure inherent in the GTE hierarchies to ease the editing task.

---

[1]The model currently uses only Allen's temporal relations, and lacks notions of duration etc. which are important for identifying discriminant concepts, so this is at best a partial analysis.

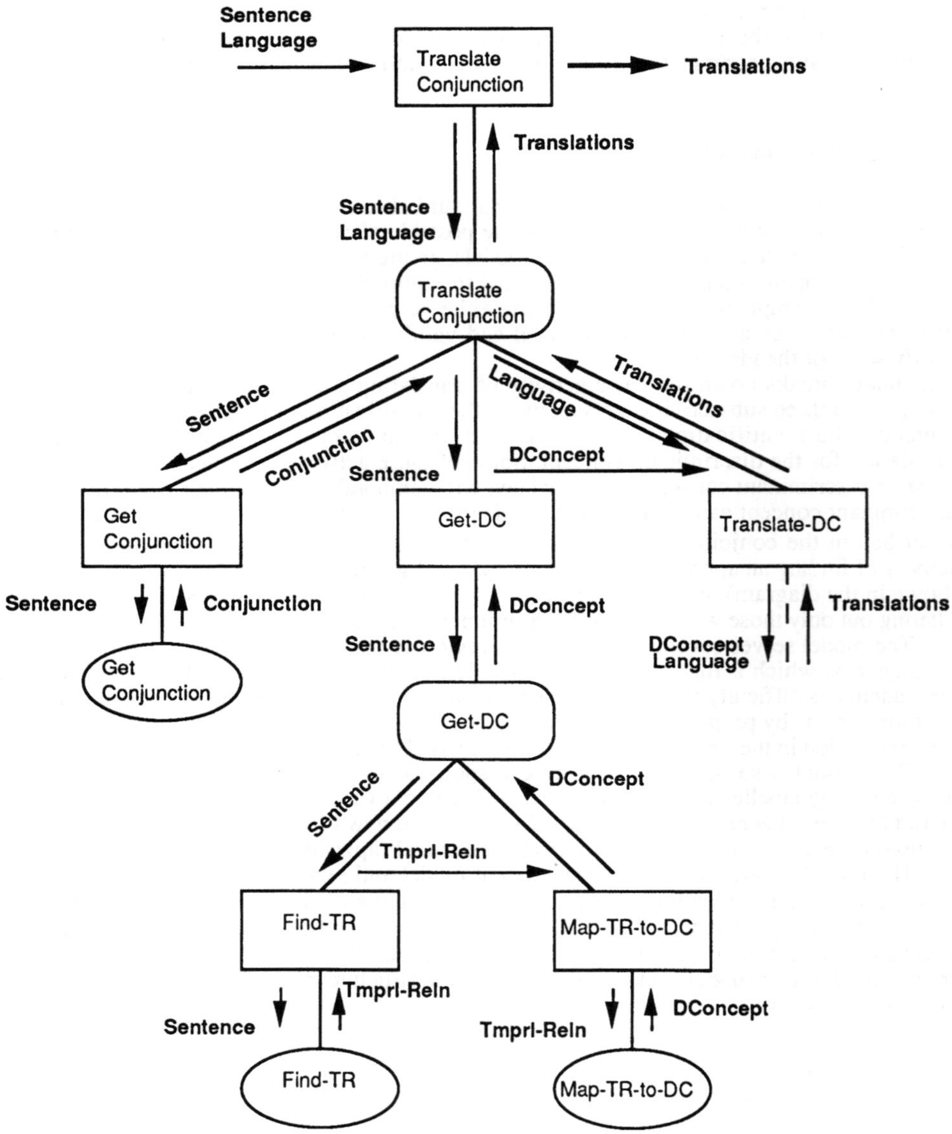

Figure 8. Information flow in a part of the Alice model

5. Conclusion

The Natural Laboratory methodology addresses a problem of significant general interest for those involved in the development of intelligent tutoring systems, namely the acquisition of student models for use in such systems. The methodology proposes a possible way to make this activity faster and cheaper through the use of indirect programming techniques such as inverted dialogues.

The methodology is due to be evaluated and refined through an extensive experimental program in which the Nobile program described here will serve as an experimental testbed. As part of the program, the new Alice tutoring system will be used under Nobile, the objective being to test the acquisition tools and methodologies of the system with respect to the Alice domain of temporal conjunction teaching.

The extensions and implementation style of the Alice system themselves are potentially of interest for workers in the field of second language teaching in that they constitute a detailed examination of one small area of the field. Further, the system provides a realization of that area in terms of the latest symbolic technologies - high-level AI representation languages for encoding knowledge, and the use of student models that are effectively expert systems supporting explanation and deep reasoning.

Acknowledgements: This paper, and the development of the Nobile prototype described herein were made possible by the support given to the Nat*Lab project (Delta P7004/D1016) by the CEC, and by Dida*El s.r.l. The authors would also like to thank the developers of the Laboratorio Naturale project (in particular Prof. G. Magi, and Dott.ssa L. Saetti), the other members of the Nat*Lab consortium - Knowledge Technologies & the Vrije Universiteit Brussel (B), IDSIA (CH), Siemens AG (D), HiTec (GR), the Universities of Udine and Trieste (I) and the Universities of Lancaster & Leeds (UK) - and past and present workers at Dida*Lab (including Philippe Alcouffe, Anna De Censi, Nur Erol, Claudio Guggiari, Marina Salvato, Roberto Serra and Kris Van Marcke) who have given help and suggestions.

References

1. Brachman, R.J. & Levesque, H.J. (eds.). Readings in knowledge representation. Morgan Kaufmann Publishers Inc. (1985)
2. Brown, J.S., & Burton, R.R. Diagnostic models for procedural bugs in basic mathematical skills. Cognitive science (1978)
3. Brown, J.S. Towards a new epistemology for learning. Intelligent tutoring systems at the crossroads of AI and education. Frasson, C. & Gauthiar, J. (eds.), Norwood NJ, Ablex (1989)
4. Burton, R.R. Diagnosing bugs in a simple procedural skill. Intelligent tutoring systems. Sleeman, D. & Brown, J.S. (eds) (1982)
5. Cerri, S.A., ALICE: Acquisition of linguistic items in the context of examples. Instructional science, 18, pp. 63-92, (1989)
6. Cerri, S.A., Cheli, E., & McIntyre, A. Nobile: User model acquisition in a natural laboratory. Proceedings of NATO advanced study institute on "Syntheses of instructional science and computing science for effective instructional computing systems (forthcoming) Calgary, Canada, July (1990)
7. Chanier, T., Pengelly, M. & Self, J. Conceptual modelling in error analysis in computer-assisted language learning systems (this volume)
8. Cheli, E. & McIntyre, A.. "Inverted dialogues" and the "natural laboratory" in user model acquisition. Dida*Lab internal technical report TR90-14 (1990)
9. Demaizière, F. & Blanvillain, O. Learners' intuitions, misconceptions and errors (this volume)
10. Tasso, C., Fum, D., & Giangrandi, P. The use of explanation-based learning for modelling student behaviour in foreign-language tutoring (this volume)
11. Fum, D., Pani, B. & Tasso, C. Naive vs formal grammars: a case for integration in the design of a foreign language tutor (this volume)

12. Miller, G.A. & Fellbaum, C. Wordnet and the organization of lexical memory (this volume)
13. Musen, M.A. Automated generation of model-based knowledge acquisition tools. Pitman, London (1989)
14. Nat*Lab Consortium. Nat*Lab: Student model acquisition in a natural laboratory. Technical Annex. CEC Project 7004/D1016 (1989)
15. Neale, I. First generation expert systems: a review of knowledge acquisition methodologies. The knowledge kngineering review, volume 3 part 2 (1988)
16. Saetti, L. & Cerri, S.A. Maestro! e il laboratorio naturale. Proceedings of didamatica, Bari, Italy (1989)
17. Self, J.(ed.) Artificial intelligence & human learning. Chapman & Hall Ltd., London (1988)
18. Self, J. Student models in CAI. International journal of man-machine studies 6, pp. 261-276 (1974)
19. Shute, V.J. Rose garden promises of intelligent tutoring systems: Blossom or thorn? Presented at the space operations, applications and research (SOAR) symposium, Albuquerque, NM, June (1990)
20. Steels, L. Second generation expert systems, future generation expert systems. North-Holland, Amsterdam (1985)
21. Steels, L. The KRS concept system. VUB AI-Lab technical report 86-1 (1986)
22. Steels, L. Components of expertise. AI magazine, vol. 11. no.2 (1990)
23. Van Marcke K. KRS: An Object-oriented representation language. Revue d'intelligence artificiale, Vol. 1, No.4 (1988)
24. Van Marcke, K. A generic tutoring environment. Proceedings of ECAI-90 (1990)

Language Technology and Language Instruction: Computational Diagnosis of Word Level Errors

Gerard Kempen

NICI, University of Nijmegen, Montessorilaan 3, 6525 HR Nijmegen, The Netherlands

Abstract: Three software packages for grammar and spelling instruction are described, all of them intended to run on personal computers: (1) an 'intelligent' training program which teaches how to conjugate and spell Dutch verbs; (2) a grammar curriculum which covers almost one hundred concepts and terms for describing grammatical structures and includes a training environment for applying them to sentences constructed by the the students themselves; and (3) a student wordprocessor which, in addition to editing facilities, can provide help about the spelling of some 10,000 Dutch words and about the rules governing their inflection. The paper emphasizes the treatment of inflection, agreement, and spelling errors: (1) a search technique which relates manifest inflection errors to points of departure from the formal inflection algorithm; (2) a syntactic parser for detecting syntactic agreement errors; and (3) an accurate spelling checker which can deal with both typographical and orthographical errors ('look-alikes' and 'sound-alikes'). It is concluded that these techniques, which do not aim at full-fledged student modeling, can yield satisfactory results in the context of guided sentence production in first and second language instruction.

Keywords: grammar instruction, spelling instruction, syntactic parsing, error diagnosis, student modeling, guided sentence production, word processing.

1. Introduction

Computational Linguistics and Artificial Intelligence offer powerful methods for detecting, diagnosing, and correcting student errors in written first and second language (L1 and L2) production. This contribution concentrates on three types of word level errors: spelling, inflection, and agreement errors. Word selection errors, a fourth type, is addressed elsewhere in this volume [8]. In three projects we have developed techniques for the computational treatment of such student errors occurring in written compositions or in sentences which were generated under control of a tutorial system.

After brief characterizations of the three projects in Section 1, I will lay out in some detail the three error diagnostic techniques we have elaborated (Section 2). Section 3 (Discussion) introduces two general distinctions between methods of error diagnosis: *descriptive* vs. *explanatory* methods, and *single-error* vs. *multiple-error* methods. Against the background of this typology I then assess the merits of our approaches to error diagnosis in comparison with considerably more complex student modeling techniques. At the outset I wish to emphasize

NATO ASI Series, Vol. F 80
Intelligent Tutoring Systems for Foreign Language Learning
Edited by M. L. Swartz and M. Yazdani

that the projects introduced in Section 1 deal with L1 instruction. However, I believe that our diagnostic techniques can easily be adapted to the requirements of L2 instruction.

2. Three Projects

The Language Technology group of NICI has developed three software packages for grammar and spelling instruction, all of them intended to run on microcomputers of the IBM PC-AT variety:

—an 'intelligent' training program which teaches how to conjugate and spell Dutch verbs

—a grammar curriculum covering almost one hundred concepts and terms for describing grammatical structure, and a training environment for applying them to sentences constructed by the the students themselves, and

—a student wordprocessor which, in addition to editing facilities, can provide help about the spelling of some 10,000 Dutch words and about the rules governing their inflection.

I will discuss these packages in turn.

2.1 Conjugation and spelling of verbs

We have followed a strictly algorithmic approach to teaching the conjugation rules which govern the synthesis of written verb forms of Dutch. The algorithm we devised can be broken down into a *morphosyntactic* and an *orthographical* stage. The former serves to select a 'formula' specifying a string of prefixes and/or suffixes to be attached to the verb's stem. An example is 'stem+*d/t+en*' for regular past tense plural verbs (equivalent to English 'stem+*ed*'; the choice between *d* and *t* depends on the stem's final letter: *d* is chosen iff that letter is a vowel or a voiced consonant). The selection process involves traversing a decision tree whose nodes pose various questions concerning finiteness, tense, number, person, etc. In the latter stage this formula is converted into a character string. After determining the verb's stem and inserting it into the formula at the appropriate place, various other string manipulations are carried out, e.g., (de)gemination of vowels/consonants (as in Eng. *occurred*) and choosing between allomorphs (e.g. *-ed* vs. *-d*). Each stage involves several steps — decisions to be taken or string modifications to be performed.

Since verb forms involving a dozen steps are quite common in Dutch, there are many occasions for systematic or incidental student errors. A special difficulty arises from the fact that, for many verbs, the conjugation rules generate strings which are orthographically distinct but homophonous. E.g., the verb forms *wend* and *wendt* (of infinitive *wenden*, to turn) both end in a voiceless /t/, but the former is first person, the latter third person singular. To make matters even worse, there also exists a third homophonous form *went*, which belongs to the paradigm of the infinitive *wennen* (to get accustomed). Another example is provided by the verb *verkleden* (to change one's clothes) which is homophonous with three forms spelled differently:

verkleden	(infinitive; present tense plural)
verklede	(past participle, inflected)
verkleedden	(past tense, plural)
verkleedde	(past tense, singular)

The two stages of the algorithm correspond to two basic layouts of the computer screen. The morphosyntactic stage is visually displayed in the form of a decision tree whose leaves represent the various formulae. At each non-terminal node a yes/no question is asked about a morphosyntactic feature of the desired verb form (which tense, person, number?). The tree is not shown to the student in its entirety. Instead, the branch leading to a formula unfolds node-by-node in response to the student's answers. For instance, the above formula, which underlies *verkleedden*, is arrived at via the following four questions-and-answers:

Finite verb? Yes
Imperative? No
Present tense? No
Number singular? No.

The steps of the orthographical stage are displayed on successive lines of a sheet of 'scrap paper'. The first line shows the infinitive form, and at each following line the student modifies the character string which the program has automatically copied from the previous line. The operation performed at last line yields the final verb form. The *verkleedden* example involves the following steps:

A. Determine stem of infinitive verb *verkleden*
   Take away -en: *verkled*
   Vowel gemination: *verkleed*
B. Apply formula to stem *verkleed*
   Final consonant of stem is voiced: Add *-d+en*
C. End result: *verkleedden.*

At any step during the morphosyntactic or orthographical stage, as soon as the student makes an error the program gives relevant feedback. At any time, the student can issue requests for information, and is free to shortcut the route through the algorithm by volunteering the final answer to the current exercise.

When preparing a training session with the program, the teacher may select from a menu the type(s) of exercises to be presented to the student (e.g. past tenses and past participles only). S/he can also specify the level of detail at which the student responses will be stored in a logfile. The program guides the student through a random sequence of exercises of the specified type(s). These are selected from a set of almost a thousand. (The teacher can easily add new exercises.) Each exercise consists of a sentence with one position left open, an infinitive verb to fill the blank, and a few codes to indicate the morphosyntactic features of the desired verb form (e.g. 'inflected form of past participle'). The latter are not revealed to the student but serve the program to compute its own answer. The student is requested to reconstruct the morphosyntactic features from the sentence and to type the correctly conjugated form. The program then computes the correct form by applying the inflection algorithm to the infinitive. Whenever its own answer deviates from the student's, it starts up the diagnostic procedure to be discussed below. Usually this results in a proposal to the student to backtrack to a specific step of the algorithm. The program creates the corresponding screen layouts and requests the student to start over from there. For more detailed descriptions of this program and its motivations see [2, 7].

So far we have tested the program on L1 learners only, i.e., on native speakers of Dutch who wish to improve their mastery of Dutch spelling. However, the conjugation algorithm embodied in the program is fully explicit and presupposes no implicit morphological or phonological knowledge of Dutch on the part of the student. This makes it a relatively easy job to adapt the program to the needs of L2 learners of Dutch. We have also begun to explore possibilities of extending the approach to other languages, in particular to German, French and Latin, and are optimistic about the outcome.

2.2 A grammar curriculum

Schools in The Netherlands and in Belgium pay much attention to grammar and spelling instruction. This is due to the rule-based nature of Dutch spelling as exemplified in Section 1.1

on one hand, and to the great importance these countries attach to foreign language skills on the other. We have developed a computer-assisted curriculum which introduces and explains virtually the complete grammatical terminology needed to describe the grammatical structure of non-compound sentences. The grammar theory at the background is Incremental Procedural Grammar (IPG; see [6]), a predecessor of Segment Grammar [3, 4]. The notation and the representation of sentence structure have been simplified and brought in line with pedagogical grammars as typically taught in Dutch and Flemish schools. Sentence structures can be graphically displayed in the form of trees, at a level of detail which is in keeping with the student's current knowledge (see Figure 1).

An important innovative feature of the program concerns the so-called *constructive* exercises it offers. Students familiarize themselves with the grammar terminology and learn to apply them in the course of constructing new sentences out of menus of words or word groups displayed on the screen[1].

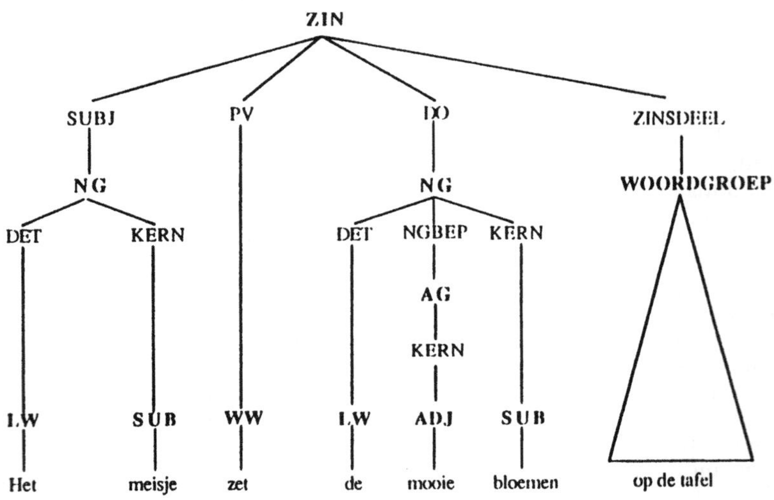

Figure 1. Syntactic tree for a Dutch sentence whose word-by-word translation into English reads *The girl puts the beautiful flowers on the table.* Some non-obvious abbreviations of grammatical terminology: zin=sentence; pv=finite verb; do=direct object; zinsdeel ('sentence part')=constituent; ng=noun phrase; woordgroep=word group; kern=head; ngbep=nominal modifier; ag=adjective group; lw=article; sub=noun; ww=verb. The triangle 'hides' grammatical concepts which have not yet been introduced to the student (prepositional phrases).

These sentences are analyzed by an IPG parser, and the program checks whether the resulting parse trees comply with the current task instruction. The parser is the core of the error diagnosis. It is geared to the evaluation of student responses elicited in the sentence construction exercises, especially errors of syntactic agreement. We will discuss its design in Section 2. For further details of the program I refer the reader to [8].

[1] For another type of constructive exercise see Zock (this volume).

2.3 A student wordprocessor

In order to facilitate the transfer of grammar and spelling training to writing skills, we are building a text editor which supports authors whose mastery of the morphology and orthography of the target language is incomplete. While writing a paper, letter or essay, students can activate various help facilities relevant to a selected word of the text, e.g., provide information about the inflection paradigm and the rules governing it, or about the existence of homophonous lexical entries and their meanings. If the student issues a request for information about a word or wordform which is not listed in the on-line lexicon, the program attempts to analyze it as a compound. In Dutch, the constituents of nominal, verbal and adjectival compounds are written as single words — *wegverkeer* (*road traffic*), *autorijden* (*car driving*), *druipnat* (*soaking wet*) — and one cannot expect all compounds to figure in the lexicon. If this attempt fails, the string is considered a spelling error. The spelling checker which is subsequently activated, then proposes a small set of words as correction alternatives. The method used here, called triphone analysis (see Section 2.3 below) attains a high level of accuracy. Of course, the student always has the option of adding a word to his personal dictionary. In that case, the program initiates a dialog with the student in order to secure all information (word category, stress, irregularity, etc.) needed to compute the complete inflection paradigm. This is then stored in the lexicon and made available to future consultations of the help facility.

3. Error-diagnostic techniques

Although the three software packages were targeted on a hardware platform with limited computational capabilities, we have been able to implement three useful diagnostic tools:
—a search technique which relates manifest inflection errors to points of departure from the formal inflection algorithm
—a syntactic parser for detecting syntactic agreement errors, and
—an accurate spelling checker which can deal with sound-based errors.
The first program has been written in Pascal, the two latter ones in C language.

3.1 Inflection errors

The diagostic module in our training program for verb conjugation is based on built-in morphological and orthographical knowledge. As soon as a student types an incorrect verb form as the final response to an exercise, the program attempts to pinpoint the step in the algorithm where the student was led astray, that is, the point where the student's solution path began to deviate from the correct solution path computed by the system itself. To this purpose the program computes all possible incorrect solution paths which yield the character string typed in by the student. (In the ITS literature this approach is called 'bug generation'; cf. [2, 11] this volume.)

A solution path is incorrect if one or more of the following actions are taken:
(1) an incorrect decision at a node of the morphosyntactic decision tree,
(2) application of an illegal morphosyntactic formula (e.g. using a mixture of past and present tense affixes)
(3) performing an incorrect string modification during the orthographical stage (e.g. adding an incorrect allomorph, regularizing an irregular verb), or

(4) applying the (correct) solution path to an infinitive which is similar to but different from the one propounded in the current exercise (cf. the *wennen/wenden* example in Section 1.1).

Actions of types (2) and (3) presuppose a small list of 'malrules' which the program takes into consideration while generating erroneous verb forms. The malrules we built into the diagnostic module are based on frequent errors of native speakers of Dutch. In a second language teaching context the set should probably be extended, and partly replaced, by malrules based on prototypic errors L2 learners make. When the program embarks on an action of type (4), it chooses from a list of over 1500 Dutch verbs, including all frequent verbs.

If the program establishes several incorrect solution paths to a student response, it selects the path having the earliest point of departure from the correct path, and proposes the student to backtrack to that step of the algorithm. Due to hardware limitations (512 kB of RAM), we have made no attempt to model the student in a formal way: The program is unable to take the student's error history into account, nor is it capable of selecting or generating exercises which could differentiate between alternative diagnoses. Nevertheless, the student is often referred back to a reasonable point in the algorithm. And despite the fact that the search space of incorrect solution paths runs into thousands, the time taken to compute the diagnosis is well below a second except for very unusual and deviant errors.

3.2 Syntactic agreement errors

The grammar curriculum software includes an LR(1) parser — a member of the family of shift-reduce parsers — similar in design to the one developed by M. Tomita [9][2]. Agreement errors are recognized and diagnosed by two special mechanisms as follows. To begin with, the non-terminal symbols of the phrase-structure grammar have been augmented with feature matrices. For example, associated with each of the symbols NP and VP there is a matrix specifying number and person features. When the automaton reduces NP and VP to S (that is, applies the rule S=>NP+VP), it checks whether the features listed in the NP and VP matrices have compatible values. Technically, this involves the execution of a *unification* algorithm to the NP and VP matrices. Unification succeeds not only in case all features match, but also when there are feature violations ('constraint relaxation'). In the latter case, a diagnostic flag is attached to the resulting subtree. For instance, suppose a student assembles the erroneous sentence *Peter word bedankt* (*'Peter am thanked'* ; the correct spelling is *wordt* (Eng. *is*)— *word* and *wordt* are homophonous). The NP and VP matrices now specify incompatible values for the person feature (NP 3rd, VP 1st). Unification nevertheless 'succeeds' and the S node is marked as violating subject-verb agreement. This mark then triggers a feedback message to the student.

The second mechanism for dealing with agreement errors utilizes 'malrules' included in the grammar. For instance, there might be rules saying that a strictly transitive verb may nevertheless occur without direct object, and vice-versa. However, whenever the parser applies any of these rules, an error flag is put up which subsequently elicits a feedback message. The parser's diagnostic component employs a system of numerical error weights in order to obtain a quality ranking within the set of alternative parse trees computed in response to an input sentence. Any feedback messages, including automatic corrections, are based on the highest-quality tree (least errors).

[2]The parser uses a few hundred augmented phrase-structure rules which are converted to a non-deterministic push-down automaton. Parse trees constructed by this automaton (usually several trees for one sentence) are efficiently represented in memory as 'packed forests'. For more technical details see [12].

3.3 Spelling errors

The student wordprocessor employs triphone analysis [13] as the tool for correcting misspelled words. This technique handles both 'look-alikes' (typographical errors, e.g. letter reversals, insertions, omissions) and 'sound-alikes' (incorrect but homophonous spellings). Triphone analysis requires phonological representations of input words as well as of all words in the on-line lexicon. These are provided by a grapheme-to-phoneme converter [3]. Input strings typed in by students are matched against lexical entries in terms of the corresponding phoneme strings rather than the original character strings. The matching algorithm starts out by dividing the phoneme string representing the input word into overlapping segments of three phonemes. An English example is the input non-word *lites* which, after grapheme-to-phoneme conversion, is divided into the following triphones:

(1) # l aI, (2) l aI t, (3) aI t s, (4) t s #.

Each of these triphones is then looked up in a file listing all words whose phonological representation contains that triphone. For instance, the first triphone occurs in *library, light, lights, lying*; the third one is shared by *bytes, lights, writes, heights*. Similarity between input word and a lexical entry is then determined by counting the number of triphones they have in common. For instance, *lites* shares two triphones with *rights*, but only one with *slight* and *sleight*. (I leave out a few additional similarity criteria of lesser importance, e.g. length of the original character strings and left-to-right order of shared triphones.) The result is a small set of correction alternatives (in the order of 1 to 5) for most of the words. The response time is never more than a few seconds.

4. Discussion: word level error diagnosis in guided sentence production

In passing we have touched upon three styles of error diagnosis. The parser and the spelling checker (triphone analysis) aim at what I will call *descriptive* error diagnosis: they characterize the nature of manifest errors without trying to track down bug(s) in the cognitive mechanism which generated them. This style is of great practical importance because it provides the student with relevant and immediate error feedback without imposing heavy demands on hardware and software. However, its impact on the learning process is bound to be rather superficial: treatment of symptoms. In contrast, *explanatory* error diagnosis does attempt to characterize a malfunctioning cognitive mechanism. This style is exemplified by the verb conjugation teaching program.

All diagnostic decisions taken by the systems we have discussed are based on *single errors*. It need not be argued that diagnostic accuracy can greatly profit from considering *multiple errors* made by the current student or by a group of similar students. This applies in particular to descriptive diagnosis. However, multiple-error diagnosis is usually practiced in combination with explanatory error diagnosis and goes by the name 'student modeling'.

Pijls, Kempen & Janner [10] propose to use the 'extended overlay' approach [13, p.347] to student modeling in the context of grammar instruction. Basic ingredient is a 'curriculum network' which specifies didactic dependency relationships between grammatical concepts (cf. [6] on genetic graphs, and [1]). For instance, our grammar teaching program introduces and explains the notion of grammatical subject in terms of finite verb, which in turn presupposes ('is dependent on') the concept of verb tense. By making fully explicit all dependencies implied by the didactic method one arrives at a network of concepts spanning the complete grammar curriculum. The current grammatical knowledge of a student can then be characterized as that part of the curriculum network which s/he has mastered. The network will also include 'maldependencies' which express frequently observed misconceptions concerning the properties and definitions of grammatical concepts (see [10] for some details).

My chief motivation for presenting this 2*2 typology, however, is to emphasize the existence of alternatives to student modeling which uncover much useful error-diagnostic information — maybe most of the information language teachers really need — at a fraction of the cost. Rather than spending inordinate amounts of time and money on student modeling in ITS's for isolated and small-scaled L1 or L2 skills (as is current practice), one can more profilably develop simple diagnostic modules which, through the implementation of special malrules, are attuned to typical errors of well-defined L1 or L2 learner groups.

Such facilities could be installed in language training modules which offer *guided sentence production* exercises, that is, exercises where sentence content, lexical material and/or syntactic form are at least partially under program control. Examples are translation, transformation, sentence combining, sentence completion, cloze test, sentence construction by selecting words or word groups from a menu, picture description, etc. Teachers can arrange such exercises in a way granting students some freedom of shaping their written texts without setting the program diagnostic tasks which, given the limited computational resources available to many schools, would be too difficult.

Acknowledgement: The programs described in this paper have been implemented by the following members of NICI's Language Technology Project: Edwin Bos, Elena Jongen-Janner, Theo Vosse and Ron van Wieringen. I thank them for their invaluable contribution.

References

1. Brecht, B., G. McCalla, J. Greer, & Jones, M. : Planning the content of instruction. In: Proceedings of the 4th International Conference on AI and Education, Amsterdam 1989
2. Chanier, T., Pengelly, M., Twidale, M. & Self, J.: Conceptual Modelling in Error Analysis in Computer-Assisted Language Learning. This volume
3. Daelemans, W.: Studies in Language Technology. An object-oriented computer model of morphophonological aspects of Dutch. Dissertation, University of Louvain 1987
4. De Smedt, K.: Incremental sentence generation. Dissertation, University of Nijmegen 1990
5. De Smedt, K. & Kempen, G.: Segment Grammar: a formalism for incremental sentence generation. In: Natural language generation in Artificial Intelligence and Computational Linguistics. (C. Paris, W. Swartout & W. Mann, Eds.). Boston/Dordrecht/London: Kluwer Academic Publishers 1991
6. Goldstein, I.: The genetic graph: a representation for the evolution of procedural knowledge. International Journal of Man-Machine Studies, 11, 51-77 (1979)
7. Kempen, G. & Hoenkamp, E.: An Incremental Procedural Grammar for sentence formulation. Cognitive Science, 12, 201-258 (1987)
8. Miller, G. & Fellbaum, C.: Wordnet and the Organization of Lexical Memory. This volume.
9. Pijls, F., Daelemans, W. & Kempen, G.: Artificial Intelligence tools for grammar and spelling instruction. Instructional Science, 16, 319-336 (1987)
10. Pijls, F., Kempen, G. & Janner, E.: Intelligent modules for Dutch grammar instruction. In: Research on computer-based instruction. (J. Pieters, P. Simons & L. de Leeuw, Eds.). Amsterdam/Lisse: Swets & Zeitlinger 1990
11. Tasso, C., Fum, D. & Giangrandi, P.: The Use of Explanation-Based Learning for Modeling Student Behavior in Foreign Langauge Tutoring. This volume
12. Tomita, M.: Efficient parsing for natural language: a fast algorithm for practical systems. Dordrecht: Kluwer Academic Publishers 1986
13. Van Berkel, B. & De Smedt, K. : Triphone analysis: a combined method for the correction of orthographical and typographical errors. In: Proceedings of the second conference on applied natural language processing, Austin TX. American Association for Computational Linguistics 1988
14. Wenger, E. Artificial Intelligence and tutoring systems. Los Altos, CA: Morgan Kaufmann 1987

Section Four

Tutoring Knowledge and Learner Control: Knowledge Representation, Computational Strategies, and Environments

The embodiment of tutoring knowledge in a computational model that can be interpreted by a computer system is one of the goals of ITS development. However, the analysis and codification of the constituents of human tutoring poses a difficult problem for the ITS researcher. The particular tutoring strategy that is used in a FL ITS depends on the underlying pedagogical and grammatical theory used [10]. While there are many different theories and approaches to foreign language teaching, communicative language teaching is currently enjoying much attention in the field. However, such a tutoring strategy is difficult to represent in an ITS since it requires representing world knowledge and contextual information.

AI researchers tend to use tutoring strategies that best support their ITS architecture rather than to try and formalize some formal pedagogy. Tutorial dialogues and simulations are two popular tutoring methods. The use of tutorial dialogues to guide learners in constructing sentences in an AI-based language tutoring system has been implemented and tested with some promising results [10]. However, this type of tutoring in a free form language production task is useful for only very advanced learners or as an exercise adjunct closely monitored by the classroom teacher. Other tutoring strategies are needed for learners at varying skill levels. While this FL ITS has not yet addressed a rigorous pedagogy, it has solved some of the difficult AI and NLP problems inherent in developing an ITS, that is to process and remediate learners' ill-formed language.

This type of system is in contrast to much of the CALL systems available that have preprogrammed exercises, but no knowledge bases and reasoning mechanisms from which to correct learners' errors or introduce remedial exercises. Although shy on AI technology, CALL is usually more robust in terms of pedagogy. What we need then is a combination of the best of both approaches to computer-based language instruction in a hybrid tutoring system. An example of such a system has been developed for Japanese at the University of Hawaii by Dr. Crosby and her colleagues. This system uses AI and NLP within an innovative multimedia environment to present language in specific communicative situations.

One important factor for the particular type of tutoring used depends on a learner's skill level. Beginning learners have different learning needs than do more advanced learners similar to the novice-expert distinction in other skill domains. At its most basic level, novices have less well-developed knowledge structures for a language. They are just beginning to acquire a basic grammar structure and are probably still working on formulating the acoustic code for the L2. More advanced learners have a better organized L2 knowledge structure all around, but probably need to automatize their grammar and build a richer lexicon.

What this means pedagogically is that different tutorial strategies are to be used with novices than those used for more advanced learners. Chapter 12 begins with a discussion of an AI-approach to tutoring that supports novice language learners and follows theoretical principles of child language learning. The use of pictures and imagery for teaching novice language learners basic language terms and expressions is well documented [7] and is the tutorial approach developed in this paper. The authors describe a computational method for representing the context surrounding objects depicted in a visual scene. With the addition of

NATO ASI Series, Vol. F 80
Intelligent Tutoring Systems for Foreign Language Learning
Edited by M. L. Swartz and M. Yazdani

sound, this approach illustrates how such a formalism can be used to teach the mapping between the semantics of a contextual image and its linguistic realization (deSausurre's 'signe-signifie-signifiant' [4]).

Chapter 13 shows how principled language tutoring can be accomplished in a learning environment for more advanced learners. The tutorial focus in this work is on vocabulary learning using standard CALL exercises in a hypermedia environment. The author describes the importance of knowledge representation in learning environments when the tutoring knowledge is not formalized computationally. The vocabulary is presented to learners in two different semantic models for lexical knowledge that are described in more detail in Section Two: associative and propositional network models. A preliminary experiment with this form of tutoring indicates that the associative network model is especially useful for influencing word recall and availability in L2.

The tutoring strategy described in Chapter 14 is also for more advanced learners and extends vocabulary learning from the previous chapter to language learning at the sentential level. The tutoring provided in this system is also presented in a learning environment where tools are available to help learners construct well-formed sentences in L2. These tools and the graphical interface are used to guide learners in the mapping of a conceptual structure for an idea they wish to express into a correctly-formed sentence. A propositional representation for the linguistic material is implied by the system and is indeed presented to the learner in graphical form as sentences get constructed and analyzed.

In learning environments, feedback to and guidance for the learner are of critical importance. The papers in Section One have described the language learner as an experimenter who makes continual discoveries in the analysis of the L2. Therefore, providing a means for learner control in automated discovery learning systems is important if the learner as experimenter is to construct and test valid hypotheses about the language. Chapter 15 discusses this issue in the creation of intelligent help facilities for FL ITS that put the learner in control. The author describes a method for separating the task and discussion information from a tutorial interaction so that the system can provide appropriate advice to the learner when needed. A prototype help system based on the design methodology is described to illustrate how the system monitors the learner's actions and provides guidance. Such a technique seems particularly useful for the learning environments described in the previous paper. If the learner as experimenter is to be our model in some FL ITS, then surely we would want to give some type of guidance so that the experimentation with the L2 does not result in misconceptions or ill-formed linguistic mappings for newly acquired material.

Foreign Language Tutoring and Learning Environment

Henry Hamburger [2] and Raza Hashim [1]

1 Department of Computer Science, George Mason University, Fairfax, VA 22030, USA
2 Navy Center for Applied Research in Artificial Intelligence, Naval Research Laboratory, Washington, DC 20375, USA

Abstract: In the FLUENT project, we contemplate and implement immersion-style computational environments for learning a foreign language. Immersion environments encourage the student to use the new language, not analyze or translate it. To this end, the student and the tutor engage in two-way, two-medium communication, where the two media are linguistic and spatial. Our design strategy is to attempt to capture in computational form some of the most effective aspects of the immersive methods that human teachers use with beginning students. The paper provides a rationale for immersion, presents a prototype system, and goes on to delineate component requirements for a full-fledged system.

Keywords: foreign language, language learning, immersion, learning environment, natural approach

1. Goal, Rationale, Strategy and Background

The FLUENT project is an attempt to specify and implement an effective computational environment for learning foreign languages. (FLUENT is an acronym for Foreign Language Understanding Engendered by Naturalistic Techniques). Specifically, it is an immersion-style foreign language tutoring and exploration system. Our design strategy has been to look at the most effective aspects of immersive methods used by human teachers and to attempt to capture them in computational form, to the extent possible. This means having the tutorial system engage the learner in various kinds of dialog where either the system or the learner may, at various times, be communicating either via language or via spatial activities (interactive graphics) on the computer screen.

1.1 Immersion

Immersion, simply put, means using the new language, not analyzing it, not consciously computing formal grammaticality, and not falling back into an already known language. This definition needs a bit of elaboration. First, since one cannot produce language before being exposed to it, reading and listening precede writing and speaking. Also, mere words or sentences, received in isolation, will not magically manifest their meanings. They must appear, initially at least, in physical and social contexts that convey their

NATO ASI Series, Vol. F 80
Intelligent Tutoring Systems for Foreign Language Learning
Edited by M. L. Swartz and M. Yazdani

meanings independently of language, making it at least possible for the learner to infer correctly the intended meanings. Once some language scaffolding is in place, linguistic context can supplement physical and social context in communicating more complex meanings, providing a basis for inferring how complex meanings are constructed in the new language. A further qualification is that, with adults as with children, one tempers the demands of immersion by introducing new aspects of language only gradually.

1.2 Why Immersion?

It is suggestive that gradual immersion occurs and works in pure form for the child learning a first language. This observation has led to many pedagogical proposals in the second language arena, dating at least as far back as the turn of the century [26]. Immersion, suitably modified for adult consumption, has proved successful as a second language technique with human tutors/teachers and has been proposed for computer-based learning [14]. The foreign language classroom methods of "total physical response" and "the natural approach," in effect, immerse adults for the duration of each class period [1, 19]. A prominent aspect of these methods is their use of visible objects and actions, which are directly adaptable to images on the computer screen. These typify the methods that we have attempted to adapt to computational form, by enabling the learner and the tutorial system to communicate in two modes, linguistic and spatial. Note that we will consistently use the word "spatial" to refer to screen activities, in order to remain neutral between pictures and partial animation as well as between input and output. Spatial output is more commonly known as "graphics," which in turn is received by humans as "visual" input.

Substantial success for immersion should not be too surprising, in light of the following age-independent rationale. First, immersion, by its very nature, maximizes the time spent actually practicing the language to be learned, while minimizing potentially disruptive shifts between languages. A subtler but perhaps more crucial point is that immersion may undermine the often strong temptation to use the crutch of understanding by translating from the foreign language (L2) to one's own language (L1). Understanding by translation makes the comprehension of an L2 utterance into a two-step mental process: translation to L1, followed by the usual process of interpreting an L1 input. This compound process would seem likely to foster errors of interference, especially the importation of L1 grammatical constructions. Moreover, with its extra step, it seems bound to be inefficient. Finally, such translation surely must impede what is often called "thinking in a language," regarded by many fluent L2 speakers as a significant breakthrough in their ability. A similar information-processing argument concerning explicit knowledge of grammatical rules is in [21]. Immersion may yield acquisition rates that are slower in some ways than other methods. For example, it has been shown that certain mnemonic devices can speed up vocabulary learning, ostensibly by inducing a three-step process, one that is even more indirect than the two-step one above [3]. But such results are not direct indicators of progress toward the more important long range goal of fluency, for which we believe immersion-style education will be more efficacious.

Adult language learners often have troubles that child first language learners do not share. Though it is possible that biological development and first language interference play a role, note also that adults may try too quickly to put their new language into service in abstract realms. Further, children's immersion is gradual: people speaking to children tend not to inundate the very young with the high seas of advanced syntax, but rather to use short, simple sentences. Both of these properties presumably keep down cognitive load, giving language learning a chance [31]. An ironic related possibility is the hypothesis that adults' greater short-term memory lures them into a combinatorial explosion of language-to-meaning mappings [25]. Finally, close observation reveals that children rarely receive syntactic correction. Some initial tolerance of grammatical errors is also part of our approach, and is supported by observation and argument that go back a long time. A good example is a discussion of "goofing" in a comparison of child and adult second language learning [12]. Consequently, although the system should always conform to standard grammar, we (along with most people talking to children and many foreign language instructors) accord perfect grammar a lower priority than the successful comprehension and communication of ideas at roughly normal speaking speed. The spirit of a naturalistic approach would certainly seem to demand beginning with spoken language (listening and speaking) before written (reading and writing), though to ease technical demands we have begun development in written mode.

1.3 The FLUENT Way

The most distinctive characteristic of FLUENT, even in its current prototype form, is its fine-grain two-medium (spatial as well as linguistic) interaction between student and tutor. Within realistic everyday scenes, coordinated by everyday goal structures, both student and system can both discuss and manipulate objects in meaningful ways. For example, in some dialog modes, the student is empowered to move or alter objects, specifically to do things like making a character's hand turn a faucet on, pick up soap, get it wet, and wash, rinse and dry things, etc. These screen actions alter an internal model, and can lead the tutor to describe an action or its resulting state or to critique an action in terms of a goal structure. These kinds of capabilities, together with an appropriate tutorial module, make possible the immersion approach, in which a student can extend her understanding to include a new language aspect that is introduced in a context that makes its meaning clear. Indeed context and interaction can enhance the effectiveness of visible objects so well that a skilled human teacher can convey abstractions, not just concrete notions, as Berlitz [4, page 4] indicated quite awhile ago: "En introduisant des mots abstraits, il faut ... les employer de facon que le sens soit bien clair par le contexte."

To carry out these objectives, the system requires an internal knowledge representation for storing the properties of the various objects in a discourse, including their physical properties and how to draw them on the screen. The knowledge representation must also make it possible to keep track of what is going on and what has already occurred in the current screen scene. The current implementation does these things in very straightforward ways. The next version will make more extensive use of standard techniques of artificial intelligence and more specifically will draw increasingly upon techniques of intelligent tutoring systems to communicate in a tutorially sound way via its linguistic and spatial (graphic) interfaces.

1.4 Relevant Systems

To place this work in computational perspective, it is well to begin with the pioneering artificial intelligence system for foreign language learning presented in [35]. Though its pedagogy consists only of questions and answers about a small number of texts, theat paper sets out many key issues, opportunities and challenges. Recent work sharing some of these objectives includes sophisticated linguistic diagnosis in an intelligent tutor [13]. Like other natural language processing systems, it has a strategy for constraining the subject matter to reduce ambiguity, relying on linguistic context, as in the task of replacing "write" in "I (write) the letter but I can't find a stamp." Here the intended response is "have written." On the basis of several responses the system analyzes the student's apparent misconceptions concerning tense and aspect.

A more natural task, one that constrains subject matter by the use of pictures, has students of Spanish stating ways in which one picture differs from another [32]. They may try to enter a whole sentence, like "Hay una ventana en casa," and are informed, in L2, of errors such as the missing article before "casa" in this example. Beyond pictures, there is the prospect of incorporating animation. In the FLUENT project, we have experimented with what we will call partial animation. Other projects have already gone to videodisc technology [23, 30]. Sophisticated work on the problem of communicating both linguistically and spatially in the same conversation is reported in [5]; this work also involves multiple applications. For spatial interaction in the educational arena, [22] is of particular interest because of its tools for the composition of spatial primitives. The Kanji City project, which shares some of our goals, has made excellent use of the hypermedia approach to educational software, to teach Japanese in a pictorial environemt with strong continuity [2].

The spatial and linguistic context strategies of constraint can of course both be put to good use, separately or together, focusing on whichever is most effective for a particular purpose. The argument here is only that pictures are especially advantageous for use with beginners, for whom linguistic context would present a bootstrap problem, and that it is indeed feasible to make use of pictures for a broader range of notions than one might casually think. As the student progresses, it gradually becomes possible to rely on linguistic context, and indeed it ultimately becomes important to do so, since it seems quite hopeless to convey pictorially the full range of, say, tense and aspect distinctions.

2. The FLUENT Prototype

To make the discussion more concrete, we now briefly describe the prototype version, FLUENT-1 developed by Tucker Maney, before laying out the planned architecture and conceptual structure in more detail in the next section. The current version, built as a feasibility study, embodies the pedagogical strategy propounded above and to some degree the capabilities that are considered in the next section. Although this work has not yet achieved the degree of breadth, generativity, modularity, student-sensitivity, and complexity of the planned version, the prototype is already sufficiently elaborated to give users a clear sense of the immersion experience and let them learn some Spanish in a memorable way. Users have found it highly engaging.

This version runs on either a Mac-II or a Mac-SE and is written in the language cT. A word about cT may be of interest, given that we found it useful for prototyping. Though intended for authors who need not be expert programmers, this language has the control structures, including recursion, that one generally associates with ordinary procedural programming languages. It is somewhat less satisfying in the data type department, providing strings and arrays, but no pointers (not to mention lists) and no records (or structures, not to mention objects). It does provides a convenient development environment. One of its strengths for educational authors is its capacity for establishing interaction with the learner. However, having our own agenda of interactive techniques, for example the use of partial animation, we made little use of these tools. A key virtue for our purposes was the strength and elegance of the graphics portion of the language, for spatial communication. Finally, cT does not provide easy access to sound, which clearly would be desirable. (cT is a trademark of Carnegie Mellon University. The language was developed principally by Judith Sherwood and Bruce Sherwood, and is now distributed by Falcon Software. A good source is [28].

The three major dimensions of a FLUENT interaction are the dialog mode, the conversational subject matter, and the aspects of language that are in use. The easiest dialog mode for the student is Presentation, in which the tutorial system presents a common noun along with a picture of a prototypical instance of its type, say the word "dog" with an ordinary dog. The student then merely hits a key or button to proceed. Another linguistically undemanding dialog mode is Movecaster, in which the student makes spatial moves in a scene and the tutor describes them; see section 3.2.2. A particularly demanding dialog mode has tutor making the moves and the student expected to furnish the description.

Ideally, the choice among dialog modes, such as those just discussed, would be independent of the choice of a domain or microworld that underlies the conversational subject matter. Although this independence is not achieved in FLUENT-1, four kinds of domains have been developed to various degrees. Collectively these domains support instruction in a considerable range of lexical categories and grammatical phenomena. Moreover, they give the learner practice expressing many useful everyday concepts. Thus, one of the domains deals largely with objects, their attributes and parts; another with location and directions; and a third with numbers and time. These concepts, and others that figure prominently in our domains, are among the objective concepts and attitude categories catalogued in [33].

The most developed of the FLUENT-1 domains stresses actions with goal structures. In it, a human figure can purposefully manipulate objects in a washroom. As in all the domains, the system engages the student in a tutorially appropriate, two-medium dialog, using Spanish at various levels of linguistic difficulty. The domains themselves are not intended to present any new nonlinguistic information or demand any but the most effortless reasoning. They embody only the most ordinary common sense knowledge, such as what faucets and clocks do, and the interface allows manipulation of the objects in very straightforward ways. Thus the student's cognitive effort can be focused on the new language, and new aspects of that language can be understood from the clear context.

The figure in the washroom domain has a movable hand connected to his shoulder by a straight arm that 'rubber-bands' with the hand as the hand moves about on the screen; see Figure 1. The hand can be manipulated by the student or the tutor, depending on the dialog type, to pick up and/or use the other objects in the scene, including faucets, soap, and a light switch. In one dialog type, the student first selects a goal, such as having the figure wash its own face. The student then goes on to carry out suitable moves by controling the partial animation on the computer screen with a mouse, while the tutor makes relevant comments and suggestions, all in Spanish. This kind of dialog requires of the student only the recognition of language. There is another dialog mode, however, in which the student must exercise various degrees of language production ability, from a single word to a phrase to a very short and constrained sentence. The tutor's responses are usually in the form of language, but can include screen moves to perform actions specified by a student who has sufficient production capability to do so. In either case, the tutor is directly responsive to whatever the student has just done or said. The responses can vary according to different levels of general achievement the student may have attained, though no student model has been implemented yet.

Figure 1. An example of a screen from washroom world. The tutor gives a command in Spanish and the student carries it out. This provides comprehension practice and gives the tutor information about how the student is learning.

The language output approach in the current version, which is specialized to Spanish, is to select verbs and nouns that correspond to appropriate operators and operands. The latter hinge in turn on whatever progress the person in the figure has made on various direct or indirect subgoals of the current main goal. A typical main goal is getting washed, and one of its subgoals is to get the face soapy, which in turn requires picking up the soap. The treatment of article takes advantage of the limited context. Since there is only one towel, one piece of soap, etc., definite articles are appropriate throughout the interaction. This simplification allows the student to focus on other aspects of language, and it allows the implementer to focus on other components of the system. We will, however, import and adapt more sophisticated natural language processing capabilities for generation as well as for understanding. Context also helps with pronouns, since whatever the student's role in a dialog, he or she is always interacting with exactly one other agent, whether it is the tutor or the figure on the screen. Consequently, the referents of first person and second person pronouns are always unique, as they would be in a simple real conversation. In a continuing related project with David Canody, we have developed in Common Lisp a more flexible natural language generator that produces descriptions in English for simple objects and states in a part-whole mini-domain. This system takes as its input a frame that is part of a reasoning system with forward and backward chaining, developed in another project [16].

How much of a language can we communicate clearly in the spatial mode? This question is crucial for the success of immersion and gets an encouraging preliminary answer from the experience with the prototype. We find that certain verbs and adverbials that one might not think would be easy to present spatially are made usable and clear by the existence of a common sense goal structure. The system is able, for example, to talk in a natural way about various actions one "needs" to do, or has "not yet" done, or that "help" with the stated current goal. The tutor's remarks, especially suggestions of what to do next, take into account what subgoals have already been achieved. One example of a structured goal is the one mentioned earlier, washing one's face. That particular goal has the subgoals of getting the face soapy, then rinsing and finally drying it. Each of these is further subdivided into primitive screen acts such as turning the hot or cold water faucet on, and later turning it off, picking up the towel and hanging it up when done.

The system keeps track of the location, surface condition, and other properties of objects. It recognizes pursuit of goals by any sequence of the primitive actions, so long as each is possible, and so long as any temporal constraints among subgoals are met. It also allows actions even if they do not progress toward the agreed goal, as long as they are possible, and makes comments accordingly. Once again the rich environment supports immersion-style learning of a surprising range of language constructs. For example, in the bathroom, one naturally encounters the reflexive Spanish verb, lavarse, used for washing one's own hands and face. In this same context but with English as the language we could introduce in a natural way the verb-particle construction with "put down" and "hang up," and adjectival complements to verbs, like "get <NP> soapy.

3. Conceptual Structure of FLUENT

Although the FLUENT-1 system described in the preceding section exhibits many of the external properties called for in the introductory remarks, the ultimate success of the concepts will require a more flexible and complex internal structure, to which we now turn. Several important parts of the planned system architecture for the proposed revised version, FLUENT-2, arise in a natural way in the cycle of communication, beginning with input from the student. The system will carry out these tasks: (i) analyze the student's input linguistically or spatially; (ii) diagnose the linguistic input to update the student model and, in case of errors, to figure out what the student really meant, if possible, to keep the conversation going; (iii) make continuity possible by keeping track of the physical situation and the dialog structure; (iv) make tutorial decisions about what linguistic aspects to use, and what content and dialog structures will permit those linguistic aspects without upsetting continuity; and (v) generate appropriate output, whether linguistic, spatial (graphic), or both. These five capabilities are shown in Figure 2.

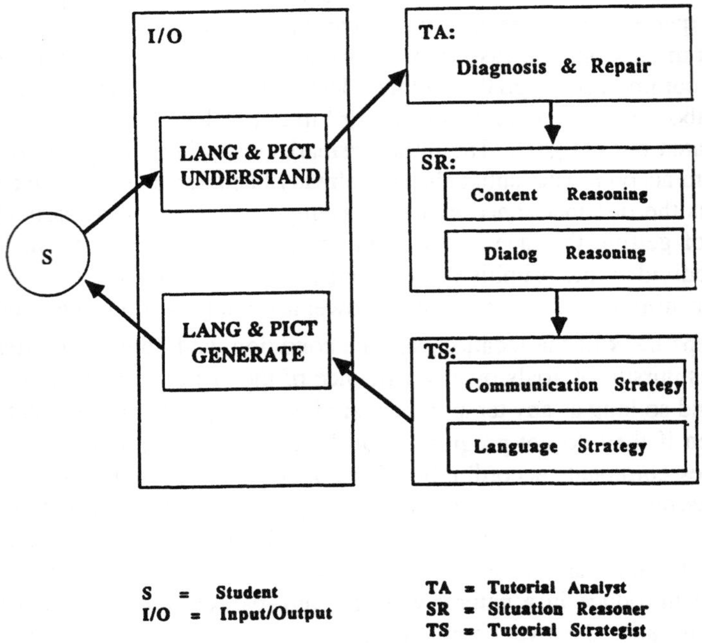

Figure 2. The system architecture for FLUENT.

The discussion is organized into three major sections: representation, communication, and tutoring. Section C.1 presents the representation of ideas in the three forms required by our commitment to immersion: language, pictures and an internal representation system. Section C.2 treats communication, including both the translation among the three representations and an inventory of interactive patterns of communication that are suitable for the language learning experience. Section C.3 is a consideration of such tutoring aspects as construction of a syllabus, maintenance of a student model, and strategies for deciding what to do next. Some of these topics resemble those in generic discussions of intelligent tutoring systems (ITSs). Here, however, the focus is on natural language as the knowledge to be acquired, whereas for other domains of instruction natural language plays at most a role in the interface. The opposite situation holds for the conversational subject matter. This material would be the knowledge to be acquired in a non-language system, whereas here, though crucial for immersion, it is relegated to a lower status: it must be represented, but is not taught.

3.1 Three Representations: Language, Spatial, and Internal

We first state a strategy for tapping into existing achievements in natural language processing. A longer subsection is then devoted to the more unusual aspect of FLUENT, the spatial considerations. Finally we discuss how the spatial concerns influence the internal representation.

3.1.1 Natural Language

Natural language understanding and generation can be monumental tasks if not somehow constrained. Compounding the difficulty of understanding is the learner's propensity to err. There are, however, several sources of constraint that can serve to reign in the problem. First, FLUENT-2 will rely on the natural language processing (NLP) software of the Athena Language Learning Project (ALLP). The intent is to tie FLUENT domains to ALLP interlingual semantic structures in such a way as to benefit from certain potential efficiencies. (ALLP itself has paid significant attention to efficiency [20]). By providing a limited domain at any particular time, FLUENT can eliminate much lexical ambiguity. By providing a context constrained by the spatial interaction and previous discourse, it can cut down referential ambiguity, smoothing the path from logical form to final meaning in context. Such ambiguity reductions are usually pursued for the sake of the understanding side, but are relevant to generation too, since what one generates for the learner should be uniquely interpretable.

Another contributor to manageability of the natural language problem is that in the early stages of learning, one only needs a sharply curtailed grammar and vocabulary, though these do increase with progress. Even for the errors, there is a source of containment, namely the propensity of various learners to make similar mistakes, which can therefore be to some extent anticipated. These errors may be oversimplifications of the target language or inappropriately imported aspects from a particular native language. The ALLP system already deals gracefully with some of these, by means of a best-first parsing strategy that tends to favor parses containing popular errors. Even fluent speakers make mistakes; [8] provides a useful taxonomy of strategies for ill-formed input.

Some styles of interaction also diminish the problems. For example, yes/no questions require only a word of response and wh-questions only a noun phrase; commands even accept a purely spatial response. By selecting these particular dialog modes in the early stages, the tutor can minimize not only the demands on the learner's language production but also on the system's ability to understand. On the generation side, one aspect of the natural language processing problem, that of deciding what to say, can be decided essentially by fiat, by choosing a particular dialog mode, such as Movecaster (section 3.2.2), in which the tutor describes student actions and resulting state changes.

3.1.2 Spatial representation

At first glance, a mouse and a computer screen may not seem up to the task of providing the rich spatial interaction we need for immersion. The above description of the prototype may give some confidence on this matter. Still, a few remarks are in order about the power of pictures and mouse maneuvers to convey movement and change in continuing everyday scenes. First, the spatial medium, like the linguistic, is bi-directional, with objects manipulated within scenes by both learner and tutor, enabling the two to maintain mutual understanding. From the mouse primitives of movement and buttoning, with suitable conventions about how to interpret them, one can build up a spatial communication repertoire that permits the student to express such notions as: selecting an object or a part of one; connecting two objects or parts to each other; operating on an operand; and moving something to a point or to a region. We plan to investigate the usefulness of recognizing movement according to certain types of trajectories, such as circumnavigating or passing through something, moving back and forth, or following a route. In the prototype system we used a simple but highly effective form of partial animation: letting a hand perform movements while its arm behaves as a rubber band from the shoulder.

Turning from the mouse to the content of pictures, we now try to show that the range of concepts suitable for spatial communication (hinging on visual recognition on the part of the learner) is sufficiently broad to make FLUENT work. We will mention a few lexical categories and syntactic aspects and look at the promise and problems of conveying each of them spatially. The categories of noun, adjective and verb all have members that submit to spatial presentation. There are straightforward techniques for proper as well as common nouns. Reasonably straightforward spatial treatment is also possible for the functionality of spatial prepositions, plurals, and possessives.

Consider first the common nouns, which should be the simplest category to present. A recognizable object typically conveys a common noun that represents a natural type to which it belongs. (On this and related points, see [29]). Moreover, although there is some flexibility about how high in the type hierarchy to look, there is often a convention about the choice. For example, if the system presents a picture of a dog, presumably that is to convey the common noun "dog," even though what the picture shows is in fact more precisely a terrier or less a precisely a member of the canidae, a mammal, an animal, etc. However, a dog and a cat together can create the conditions for speaking about a higher type to which both belong. Again there is a conventional level at which to look, here "animals" rather than "mammals" or "physical objects." So pictures would seem to have broad potential for common nouns, provided that the new language disagrees only rarely with the learner's first language on what is in the type hierarchy and on the conventions about where in that hierarchy to look when picking appropriate common nouns for talking about ordinary objects.

Except in the case of common nouns, however, a picture out of context does not convey a unique word or phrase, so tutoring is not just a matter of something so simple as presenting picture-phrase pairs. To get a quick idea of how crucial context can be for presenting verbs, for example, note that a hand moving back and forth can be an instance of wiping, waving, drawing or combing (etc.) depending on what the hand is holding, if anything, and on what its owner's goals are known to be. That a context with goals will be helpful should be clear from the earlier discussion of the verbs in the bathroom scene. Interestingly, a type ambiguity problem similar to that just discussed for common nouns also shows up with verbs and also must be dealt with by the use of context and/or multiple uses. If, for example, John is shown "going" somewhere, he will necessarily be going in some particular way, like walking. This ambiguity can ultimately be resolved if the learner's processing is complex enough to take advantage of seeing a ball, as well as a person, executing "going" at various times, since a ball does not walk or run (though it may roll or bounce). "Go" is more abstract than "walk" in two ways: it tolerates a broader class of arguments and it covers different forms of locomotion.

Having discussed a couple of lexical categories, we now touch briefly on some exercises for syntax in FLUENT-1. Few if any grammatical aspects are directly picturable, so the issue is how effective indirect methods can be. Take the relationships between adjectives and their head nouns, with respect to agreement and relative order. First of all, note that some adjectives even in linguistic isolation can be conveyed pictorially by a variant of the "cat plus dog equals animals" technique mentioned above, for example, presenting "black" with black objects of disparate type. Once some adjectives and nouns are known, FLUENT-1 presents by picture a concept that in language is represented by an adjective and a noun. Once again context plays a key role: to make the use of the adjective pragmatically necessary, the system requires the student to distinguish objects of the same type, hence requiring the same noun, but with differing attributes, distinguishable by adjectives. With a sufficient variety of such pictures, each associated, in context, with corresponding language, we hypothesize that an adult will learn, as a child does, to conform to the grammatical constraints, and to do so fluently, unencumbered by conscious grammatical computation, even though an adult may learn grammar explicitly as a back-up capability.

3.1.3 Internal representation

It is appropriate to use an object-oriented representation, not only to benefit from the reduced data entry effort and storage efficiency that inheritance permits, but more significantly because the system needs the appropriate knowledge of how objects are related in order to converse properly. FLUENT-2 will have one hierarchy for things and another for activities, with type constraints on arguments. Two such hierarchies are related in that an event can change the state of an attribute of an object. Most clearly in need of representation are the physical objects whose images appear on the screen.

These objects have visible attributes like size, color, and image shape, as well as non-visible ones such as surface condition and movability. Some of these properties have unchanging values, but others may vary. The surface condition of an object, for example, can be in various states like dry, wet and soapy at different times. Interestingly, the surface condition attribute itself has an attribute with respect to visibility, specifically that it is unchangingly invisible. In addition to the attributes of individuals and of attributes themselves, there are relationships between objects, like part-whole and the ability of one to support another. As noted, common sense goal structures can be useful for coordinating learner-tutor dialog. Thus we need and/or goal trees and some temporal ordering constraints. At the leaves of a goal tree are simple activities some of which correspond to spatial primitives.

3.2 Communication

Communication is a fundamental activity in FLUENT; indeed from the viewpoint of the learner, it is really the only activity. We discuss communication at two levels. To communicate in two media, the system translates between them, via its internal representation, as discussed in 3.2.1. These capabilities are building blocks, from the higher level viewpoint of the tutorial component of the system, which must arrange that the translations be performed at appropriate times, that is, according to tutorially useful patterns of interaction, taken up in 3.2.2.

3.2.1 Translation among representations

Four kinds of translation are needed: in both directions between the internal knowledge representation and each of the external representations, linguistic and spatial. Translations of various subsets of English to model-theoretic semantics have been presented by various authors; especially relevant here is [11], because of its attention to context and spatial relations. Spatial representations must also be translated to and from the internal representation.

To begin on the spatial side, our general strategy for spatial output will be to attach simple graphics procedures to the lowest level actions in the goal structures alluded to above. For example, drying one's hands, though a subgoal in the example above, includes subgoals of its own, like picking up a towel, which includes moving a hand to the towel, a spatial primitive. Turning to the input or understanding side of spatial communication, for the washroom scene we have designed a rule system with over twenty generic rules for updating the internal representation in response to events that the learner instigates on the screen. Seven of these rules concern the surface condition of objects like dirty hands, a soapy face, or a dry towel. The one that concerns wetting things under the water spout looks like this:

Preconditions: Mobile-hand : holding = X
X unequal Soap
either Hot-faucet : activity = on
or Cold-faucet : activity = on

Action: X visits Water-spout

Results: Mobile-hand : surface = —w→
X : surface = —w→

The preconditions and results all concern the internal representation. The action of the hand is an abstract screen event, but is defined in terms of concrete (quantitative) variables like mouse states and the numerical locations and sizes of the objects. The notation, "—w→," lets the rule be generic. The "w" mapping specifies how to update the value of the surface attribute from each possible state, say from dirty to muddy or from soapy to wet. There are other mappings of this sort. This notation enables us to simplify the preconditions, which otherwise would need information about the surface state of both the object (X) and the mobile hand. The consequence would be a proliferation of rules and loss of clarity.

We now turn from the spatial to the linguistic realm. Section 3.1.1 touches on the input or understanding side, specifically the pervasive issue of disambiguation and how some aspects of this application may assist with it. Here we will comment only on the output side. Natural language generation (NLG) can be divided into (at least) two parts: deciding what to say and determining how to say it. The ALLP software can already carry out the second of these, provided it is given as input an idea expressed in terms of its interlingual semantic structures. The core of this representation is the predicate-argument structure, but information about time, reference and mood is also encoded Consider what FLUENT-2 will have to do to provide that semantic input when, for example, it is describing to the learner what s/he has just done in the washroom scene. There are various levels in the goal structure at which to view an act. Each level can have its own semantic predicate-argument structure. The high level activity that is ultimately expressed in English as "get X clean" (where X is some object) includes lower level ones expressed as "get X soapy," "rinse X" and "dry X," that in turn have finer grain parts, ultimately associated with specific state transitions like that from soapy to wet. The selection of which of these levels to express will have to be determined within FLUENT-2, by reasoning about context and goals.

Further, the states and transition in the FLUENT-2 knowledge representation will have to make contact with the ALLP lexicon and semantic representation system. In the bathroom example, the states need predicates that are typically be associated with adjectives like "wet" or "dry." More subtle is the role of words like "make" and "get" that express the idea of doing some unspecified activity to bring about the resulting state. Important NLG information also comes from the particular current dialog mode, which determines the mood (question, imperative, etc.) of the output and, in the case of a command, which entity fills the syntactic role of second person. For English, the sentences that describe the transitions and the resulting states take forms like those listed just below, where <agent> is the screen character whose hand is performing the actions on some <theme> or object, possibly itself or some part of its body.

<agent> "make" <theme> <Adj>

<theme> "get" <Adj>

<agent> <Verb> <theme>

3.2.2 Interactivity

A pedagogy can be characterized in part as a collection of dialog modes and a way of choosing among them according to circumstances. A Socratic dialog, for example, uses a dialog mode that involves questions from the tutor. In contrast, the foreign language pedagogy of "total physical response" requires dialog modes that call for visible physical action, by either the teacher/tutor or the learner. Dialog modes differ in their difficulty for the learner, suitability for different cognitive styles and the clues they can supply about what the learner knows. In one interaction mode, Movecaster, the tutor is like a sportscaster telling what is happening on the field of play. Here, the field of interest is the computer screen and the events are the moves by the learner, who can make arbitrary legal moves. The Movecaster then makes a comment, which may be simply a statement of what action has just occurred. Alternatively, the comment may describe a changed aspect of the situation, or specify how the change relates to a previously established goal. The Movecaster mode has the desirable property that it keeps language flowing, and keeps it clearly synchronized with meanings. Also, it gives the opportunity for the beginner to practice comprehension skills before having to produce language. Movecasting provides even non-beginners the opportunity to explore a new domain, to gain familiarity with ways of expressing its new relationships, before going on to more demanding dialog modes. Finally, this mode does not require the NLG system to make micro decisions about what to say.

In the prototype, we have experimented, using template-style NLG, with limited versions of several other dialog modes that we call Presentation, Command, Execute, Delegate, Query, and Answer. Each brings together ideas and the corresponding language. For Presentation mode this is done directly by presenting a phrase or sentence in L2, along with a spatial representation of its meaning, both chosen by the tutor. A Command interaction begins with the tutor telling the learner, in L2, to do something by manipulating screen objects. The converse activity is Delegate mode, in which the learner has the initiative. In this case a palette of verbs and physical objects is available to help to learner compose her thoughts and equally to constrain the natural language understanding capability that the system will require. Delegating begins with the tutor commanding a high level goal which the learner is to decompose into subgoals and give as lower level commands to a screen character.

3.3 Tutoring

3.3.1 Syllabus

Syllabus issues include most prominently the language aspects themselves; we shall return to these shortly. Also of concern is the conversational subject matter via which the student can possibly be exposed to the language. The subject matter, though not the central issue, must nevertheless be chosen with care, so as to include useful topics as well as support the introduction of the crucial grammatical constructs. The Waystage project [33] has outlined a single set of concepts intended to suffice for a variety of languages, and has catalogued the key grammatical constructs of English that express these concepts. That project does not endeavor to impose an order on either the concepts or the corresponding aspects of English grammar. Still, it does turn out to be a highly suggestive resource, cataloguing general objective concepts (temporal and spatial notions, existence, quantity, attributes, relations, etc.), speaker attitudes toward those concepts (assistance, suggestion, possibility, likelihood, emotional stance, etc.), and a listing of some particularly appropriate domains.

Turning to the core of the syllabus, the language aspects to be taught, one needs a substantial array of capabilities, even for a modest system. It seems reasonable to demand explicit representation of lexical categories, lexical features, particular lexical items, phrase structure (dominance and ordering) rules, verb subcategorization and case marking, various kinds of constraints, including agreement, and rules about the semantic properties and consequences of the foregoing. Given the known complexity of devising all these correctly, it is tempting to think of letting the role of syllabus be filled by the language knowledge of an existing NLP system, taken off the shelf. It is instructive to see why it's not that simple; we note several obstacles. First, experience with intelligent tutoring systems suggests that the knowledge in a performance-oriented expert system is not sufficient for communicating knowledge to a student [10]. This is true even when the rules are in non-technical (glass box) form. The problem is worse if the rules are in technical (black box) form; see the distinction made by [9]. Next, unlike other systems FLUENT does not teach grammatical and morphological rules explicitly, though it does need to have them in declarative form for student modeling. A further difficulty arises if the application end of the chosen off-the-shelf system is specialized for a different knowledge representation. Finally, the syllabus must include for each language a partial ordering of its rules.

Such an ordering is important for any subject, since it helps the system to introduce material at a time when it is pedagogically reasonable to do so. One justification for introducing an aspect relatively early is that it is logically a prerequisite of other aspects. A related but distinct property is how intrinsically easy an aspect is to learn, as determined by studying the natural course of acquisition, in L2 where possible [7]. A third consideration, noted above, is an aspect's practical role in expressing needed concepts. Finally, of special concern here is the possibility of constructing picturable phrases and establishing spatial interaction. Textbooks that teach pictorially, such as [18], may be credited with implicitly attempting to strike a balance among all these criteria. Unfortunately, such books provide little explicit pedagogical reasoning, but we have been able to do some reverse engineering. In partially pictorial books, like [27], the grammatical intent is clear, but the many pictures are seldom pedagogically independent, relying instead on explanation and heavy use of cognate vocabulary.

3.3.2 Individuation

Once the syllabus is established, the tutoring system needs to move around in it in response to the apparent abilities of a particular student. To do this, the tutor also needs to choose a scene that supports use of the specific language aspects the student would work on. We have devised a method of scene selection that can roughly be characterized as inverting an index to scenes, though it is somewhat more complex than that. Within a scene, a tutor can, even without recourse to a student model, be responsive to the student's current response. In effect, the tutor reasons, "Since you said that, you need to know (or do) this next." Such immediate responsiveness is all we expect to achieve in the near term, and the prototype does not contain an individual student model. Generally, of course, a defining aspiration of ITSs is to gain a longer term picture of what a student is up to, in order to respond to general tendencies or to put the current response into a broader perspective, the better to understand the underlying bases of a superficial misperformances. A relevant idea that emerged in the 1960s among child language acquisitionists is that the child has her/his own grammar, which may include rules not to be found in a correct adult grammar, but that may in some cases be simplifications of adult rules. This approach, perhaps best exemplified in [6], may be regarded as a precursor of the ITS work on bugs and malrules. One must of course allow for the fact that L2 learners share some kinds of L1 bugs, typically avoid others, and bring new ones related to their own L1.

3.3.3 Tutoring Principles

A tenet of ITSs favors the declarative expression of tutorial principles and techniques as an explicit set of rules accompanied by an interpreter that reasons with them to reach tutorial decisions in particular situations. We mention two techniques that can be formulated as sets of rules. One is the constraint of introducing only one new thing at a time, for reasons discussed in [17] in the context of language learning, and [34] in terms of machine learning. The consequences of this principle are strongest when the rules are of fine grain, as in the delineation of twelve steps on childrens' paths to a correct relative clause [15]. Another technique that appears to facilitate language learning is the use of expansion of a learner's sentence or partial sentence into an appropriate longer form [24]. Some tutorial principles can, however, most appropriately be built directly into the conceptual organization of the system. For example, our emphasis on the pairing of linguistic and spatial communication is built into several of the dialog modes. Also essentially built-in are the pedagogical decisions to avoid explicit discussion of grammar and to downplay dependence on the student's first language.

Acknowledgement

We gratefully acknowledge the helpful insights of Tucker Maney, who developed the implementation discussed in section B at the Navy Center for Applied Research in Artificial Intelligence, a part of the Naval Research Laboratory, which has supported much of this work.

References

1. Asher, J.J.: Learning another language through actions. San Jose, CA: Pajaro Press (1977)
2. Ashworth, D. and Stelovsky, J.: Kanji City: An exploration of hypermedia applications in CALL. Calico Journal, 6, 4, 27-38 (1989)
3. Atkinson, R.C.: Mnemotechnics in second language. American Psychologist, 30, 821-828 (1975).
4. Berlitz, M.D.: Deuxieme livre pour l'enseignement des langues modernes: Partie francaise pour adultes. New York: Berlitz 1925
5. Bobrow, R. J., Resnik, P. and Weischedel, R.: Multiple underlying systems: Translating user requests into programs to produce answers. Paper presented at BBN Natural Language Symposium, Cambridge, MA, Nov. 29 - Dec. 1 1989
6. Bowerman, M.: Early syntactic development: A cross-linguistic study with special reference to Finnish. Cambridge, England: Cambridge University Press 1973
7. Broselow, E.: Second language acquisition. In Newmeyer, F.J., Linguistics: The Cambridge survey, v.III. Cambridge: Cambridge University Press 1988
8. Carbonell, J. and Hayes, P.J.: Recovery strategies for parsing extragrammatical language. American J. of Computational Linguisitics, 9, 3-4,123-146 (1983)
9. Chanier, T., Pengelly, M., Twidale, M. and Self, J.: Conceptual modelling in error analysis in computer-assisted language learning systems. (This volume)
10. Clancey, W. J.: Knowledge-Based Tutoring: The GUIDON Program. Cambridge, MA: MIT Press 1987
11. Crangle, C. and Suppes, P.: Context-fixing semantics for instructable robots. Int. J. Man-Machine Studies, 27, 371-400 (1987)
12. Dulay, H. C. and Burt, M.: You can't learn without goofing: An analysis of second language 'errors'. In Richards, J.C. (Ed.) Error Analysis: Perspectives on Second Language Acquisition. London: Longmans Group Ltd 1974
13. Fum, D., Giangrandi, P. and Tasso, C.: ET: An intelligent tutor for foreign language teaching. Proceedings of the Conference on Intelligent Tutoring Systems, Montreal, 462-468 1988
14. Hamburger, H.: FLUENT: Foreign language understanding engendered by naturalistic techniques. Internat. Wkp. on ITS for Foreign Language Learning. Trieste, Italy, November 28-29, 1988
15. Hamburger, H. and Crain, S.: Relative acquisition. In Language development: Syntax and semantics. S. Kuczaj (ed.). Hillsdale, NJ: Lawrence Erlbaum Associates 1982
16. Hamburger, H., Lodgher, A., Maney, T., Jardine, C. and Siff, F.: A Decentralized AI System for Transcript Applications. Proceedings of IEEE/AISIG, May 9-11 1990
17. Hamburger, H. and Wexler, K.: A mathematical theory of learning transformational grammar. Journal of Mathematical Psychology (1975)
18. Ibarra, F.: Look and learn Spanish. New York: Dell Publishing Co 1962
19. Krashen, S.D. and Terrell, T.D.: The natural approach. Oxford: Pergamon Press 1983
20. Malone, S. and Felshin, S.: GLR parsing for erroneous input. In Tomita, M. (Ed.), GLR Parsing (to appear).
21. McLaughlin, B., Rossman, T. and McLeod, B.: Second language learning: An infommation-processing perspective. Language Leaming, 33,135-158 (1983)
22. Munro, A. and Pizzini, Q. A.: Direct manipulation authoring of object behavior in an interactive graphical modeling environment. Proceedings of the IEEE International Conference on Systems, Man and Cybemetics, Los Angeles, November 4-7 1990
23. Murray, J.: Humanists in an institute of technology: How foreign languages are reshaping workstation computing at MIT. Academic Computing, September (1987)
24. Nelson, K.E.: Facilitating syntax acquisition. Paper presented to the Eastem Psychological Assn New York, April 1975
25. Newport, E.L.: Maturational constraints on language leaming. Cognitive Science, 14, 1, 11-28 (1990)
26. Richards, T.C. and Rodgers, T.S.: Approaches and methods in language teaching. Cambridge: Cambridge University Press 1986
27. Sacks da Silva, Z.: Persona a persona. New York: Macmillan Publishing Co 1982
28. Sherwood, J.: The cT reference manual. Champaign, IL: Stipes Publishing Co 1988
29. Sowa, J.: Conceptual Structures. Reading MA: Addison Wesley 1984
30. Swanson, C.W.: Deutsch in Deutschland: repurposing a foreign language videodisc. Academic Computing, 4,1 (1989).

31. Sweller, J.: Cognitive load during problem-solving: Effects on learning. Cognitive Science, 12, 2, 257-286 (1988)
32. Underwood, J.: When the music stops: A review of "Using computers in language learning." Calico Journal, 4, 3, 35-50 (1987)
33. Van Ek, J.A., Alexander, L.G. & Fitzpatrick: Waystage English. Oxford: Pergamon Press 1980
34. VanLehn, K.: Learning one subprocedure per lesson. Artificial Intelligence, 31, 1, 1-40 (1987)
35. Weischedel, R.M., Voge, W.M. and James, M.: An artificial intelligence approach to language instruction. Artificial Intelligence, 10, 3, 225-240 (1978)

Issues for Tutoring Knowledge in Foreign Language Intelligent Tutoring Systems

Merryanna L. Swartz[1]

Vitro Corporation - Advanced Technology, Silver Spring, MD

Abstract: The tutoring approach and the representation of the expert knowledge in a foreign language ITS depend on the particular skill being taught (grammar, dialogue, vocabulary). Rule-based knowledge representations are appropriate for grammar tutoring. Scripts or semantic network representations may be more useful when learning language in context. Pedagogical contexts for the tutor and several knowledge representation schemes useful for foreign language learning are discussed in this paper. Research on developing a discovery learning environment for vocabulary learning as an alternative to planned-based rules in the tutor model is presented. The environment used both associative and propositional network models to represent lexical knowledge in different contexts. Preliminary data from a study comparing the effect of each model on word recall suggest that an associative network representation for the lexicon is effective for vocabulary tutoring with more advanced learners. The word usage results suggest that either representation influences communication skills when the vocabulary is already known by the learner. Contrary to what was predicted, the use of a more complex representation (propositional network) did not influence word usage positively.

Keywords: discovery learning environment, semantic network models, tutoring knowledge, vocabulary learning

1. Introduction

The development of the tutor model in an intelligent tutoring system (ITS) still remains a perplexing problem despite the many recent advances in ITS research. The problem is exacerbated when we consider complex and ill-understood domains such as foreign language learning.

Two different pedagogical contexts for the tutor model in ITS have been proposed: opportunistic and plan-based [29]. The opportunistic context takes advantage of tutoring opportunities as they arise during learner-system interactions. This pedagogical context supports discovery learning where learners interact with the instructional material in a learner-controlled sequence. Thus the opportunistic approach is well suited to tutoring 'in situ' [29] when learners solve problems in learning environments. In plan-based contexts, instructional goals are used to dynamically control the learner-system interaction. Learners follow a specific sequence that is controlled by knowledge in the tutor model. Therefore, this approach lends itself more to formal rule-based representations in the tutor model and less toward open learning environments.

Learning environments support discovery learning. They do not control the instructional interaction with planning techniques and generally do not have a separate tutor model when they are used in an ITS. Tutorial dialogues, hints, and coaching [25, 30, 31]

[1] This work was begun while the author was at the U. S. Army Research Institute.

NATO ASI Series, Vol. F 80
Intelligent Tutoring Systems for Foreign Language Learning
Edited by M. L. Swartz and M. Yazdani

have generally been used to control or guide the discoveries learners make. The tutoring in these systems comes about by a careful representation of the instructional material so that learners will discover appropriate knowledge structures in the domain. Thus it is important to be mindful of good tutoring principles and knowledge structures for the domain skill when developing these systems.

The use of a learning environment in an ITS is one alternative to tutoring and may be especially useful for foreign language learning. This work examines how a learning environment uses psychologically valid knowledge representations to organize vocabulary instruction as an alternative to more formal, rule-based approaches to tutoring in an ITS. This paper will discuss foreign language tutoring and the general problem of representing foreign language knowledge in an ITS. We then discuss the two semantic models used for representing the vocabulary knowledge, and the learning environment developed. The last section of the paper discusses the results of a study that compared the influence of the two models on word recall and word usage.

The principal argument presented in this paper stresses the need to investigate components of tutoring knowledge that are grounded in sound psychological and foreign language learning principles. Research based on these principles is important for three reasons: 1) We know very little about how to represent and use tutoring strategies in ITS, 2) Research on tutoring strategies that is theory-driven may shed light on the cognitive processes involved in foreign language learning outcome, and 3) Theoretical frameworks can facilitate the development of knowledge-based tutoring for language learning, especially when discovery learning environments are used.

2. Foreign Language Tutoring

The teaching of a foreign language is different from other types of complex skills because there are so many dimensions involved (phonological, semantic, syntactic, sociocultural) in the skill. Many of the teaching principles and practices are unique in foreign language learning. For example, in order to properly encode another articulatory system, imitation as a form of practice plays a critical role in the acquisition of near-native performance (See [17] this volume). This kind of practice may not be appropriate for other non-language skills. Imitation can be acquired through application of the language teaching principles 1) repeating language behavior at appropriate intervals and 2) varying exercises to internalize linguistic patterns (See Table 1). These kinds of principles need to be incorporated into the tutoring knowledge in the system so that the instructional interaction can be managed properly.

Some tutoring methods will be better than others for language learning on a computer; still others will be preferred when a specific language skill is the focus of the instruction (i. e., grammar versus dialogue skills). Selecting a particular tutoring method for ITS depends on the approach used to teach the language and the particular skill (reading or writing for example). The approach used in this research is based on communicative competency and adheres to many of the teaching principles presented in Table 1.

Communicative language teaching has recently received much attention in the field of applied linguistics [15, 16, 21, 22]. In this paradigm, language learning is viewed more as the ability to communicate meaningfully in a target language than as the ability to manipulate various grammatical structures correctly. A basic prerequisite for communicative competence is the ability to express propositions properly in the target language [17]. Yet, communication is much more than simple proposition generation. Efficient communicators in a foreign language are those that can process the situation in which they are involved by deciding what knowledge is to be shared between the speaker and listener [22]. The argument that required mappings between form and function will not occur unless adequate semantic content is provided is proffered in this volume [17]. It is the situation in which language occurs that provides this semantic content in communicative language teaching.

Table 1

Principles for Foreign Language Teaching*

Principle	Rationale
1. Language behavior is learned through experience	Practice makes permanent
2. Present language in context	Promotes authentic language behavior
3. Present language in its natural order (receptive to productive)	Supports basic patterns before derived patterns
4. Teach the most frequent, high utility items first	High utility factor supported
5. Teach simple to complex	Promotes generalization
6. Exploit communicative situations	Improves motivation; promotes generalization
7. Support instruction with declarative explanation	Facilitates understanding and orientation to the language
8. Repeat language behavior at appropriate intervals	Spaced practice improves learning
9. Vary practice exercises to internalize patterns	Periodic reinforcement instills automaticity
10. Teach grammatical form through patterns in the language	Provides useable, salient models

*These principles were developed during meetings held at the National Foreign Language Center (NFLC), Washington, D.C. Participants included expert language pedagogues, Eleanor Jorden, Ron Walton, Galal Walker, and Ralph Ginsberg.

Three primary assumptions[2] behind the development of foreign language instruction that are important for ITS are 1) language is learned from the environment (situation), 2) the elements composing the environment can be isolated and identified, and 3) language learning is experiential. These assumptions are supported by the set of teaching principles presented previously. From these assumptions it follows that one of the goals for creating a foreign language ITS that promotes communicative language competencies is to present the language in appropriate situations or experiences. And we have proposed doing so by developing a learning environment to present various linguistic situations to the learner. Below several candidate knowledge representations useful for presenting the semantics of

---

[2] I am grateful to Galal Walker, Chinese professor at Ohio State University, for pointing out the importance of these assumptions.

different situations to learners are discussed; then we discuss those representations chosen to develop the learning environment.

3. Knowledge Representations and Models for the Communicative Aspects of Language

In order to present language in specific situations, the tutoring knowledge must "know" about them. The use of a knowledge representation formalism to codify the features that define the situations and link these features to the appropriate linguistic elements is one solution. However, the representation of semantic or world knowledge in natural language understanding systems is not an easy problem. Yet in language tutoring systems that support communicative competency teaching, including such world knowledge into the knowledge base is essential for deriving the meaning of utterances typed into the computer in some student-computer exchange.

The ITS tradition has used knowledge-based representations to codify knowledge for the instructional domain. This is also the case for learning environments since knowledge bases are also a part of those systems. These representations have generally included rule-based models and semantic networks [25]. One group of ITS researchers [2] argue for the use of knowledge-based tutoring that represents students' problem solving behavior (the student model) as a partial goal hierarchy structure of the expert model. They designed such a system using IF-THEN rules (a production system model) to represent the goal structure for the skill. This type of instruction is adequate for procedural skill domains such as computer programming or command languages. However, in domains that aren't as easily or completely defined as procedural skills such as language learning, other types of models may be necessary. One exception though, is the teaching of grammar. A production system model can very nicely represent the rules for various linguistic structures in a language. This type of tutoring is currently receiving attention in the foreign language ITS community [5, 10]. However, representing the expert knowledge in production rules alone may not be appropriate for learning vocabulary, dialogue, or reading skills in realistic language experiences or situations.

What we must now discover is what representations are useful for teaching these other language skills. Many different kinds of knowledge representations for describing the underlying structure of discourse (dialogue or text) have been examined by psychologists: schemas [23]; scripts [24]; discourse goals [11]; associative networks [14]; and propositional networks [13]. Research on designing foreign language instruction for teaching dialogue skills has suggested using scripts to represent the essential features of the situations in which a dialogue occurs [26]. The individual features of the situation codified in a script representation are what define the required linguistic output. For example, the discourse goal, events, social roles, setting, and time are used to define a prototypic utterance for each participant in an exchange. However, this proposed design was never implemented in a language tutoring system.

Current work on codifying tutoring knowledge in foreign language ITS has drawn from some of the above knowledge representations. A more formal representation of tutoring rules in a separate tutoring model is used by [6] in this volume. Rules that embody discourse goals for prototypic conversations have been used to represent the semantics of conversations in a dialogue exercise for English [31]. Another approach in this volume [12] uses production rules to define the actions associated with the language elements that describe a pictoral scene to immerse beginning learners in a stereotypic situation. In another paper in this volume, [32] the system tutors students using a propositional representation to aid learners in the construction of simple sentences. Some of these approaches use the particular knowledge representation displayed in the environment to support communicative language teaching. Some of them also use rules in a plan-based context to control the tutoring interactions. Our research on teaching foreign vocabulary in a discovery learning environment [27] uses two semantic network models, one of which is a propositional network representation similar to [8, 32], to represent the words to be learned; the other an associative network similar to [20]. Next we discuss the two semantic models used to organize the vocabulary and the rationale for using the learning environment being developed.

3.1 Semantic Situations for Foreign Vocabulary Tutoring

Building a good vocabulary is an essential prerequisite for acquiring communicative competency in a language. However, the learning should involve more than simple vocabulary item memorization. Eight assumptions to consider when developing instruction for vocabulary learning are proposed [22] (See Table 2). These assumptions support communicative language teaching and the use of both associative and propositional networks for representing the different semantic situations in the LEXNET-INSITU system. Below we discuss how these assumptions were used to develop a learning environment for advanced learners that presents vocabulary in two different semantic models.

Table 2

Assumptions for Vocabulary Teaching (from [22])

1. Native speakers continue to expand their vocabulary in adulthood, whereas there is comparatively little development in their syntax.

2. Knowing a word means knowing the degree of probability of encountering that word in speech or print. For many words we also know the sort of words most likely to be associated with it.

3. Knowing a word implies knowing the limitations imposed on the use of the word according to variations of function and situation.

4. Knowing a word means knowing the syntactic behavior associated with the word.

5. Knowing a word entails knowledge of the underlying form of a word and the derivations that can be made from it.

6. Knowing a word entails knowledge of the network of associations between that word and other words in the language.

7. Knowing a word means knowing the semantic value of a word.

8. Knowing a word means knowing many of the different meanings associated with a word.

Foreign language pedagogues have recognized the value of teaching vocabulary to advanced learners based on the semantic and categorical structure among concept groups [4, 7, 18]. The sixth assumption in Table 2 also indicates the importance of vocabulary learning in associative contexts, and we have seen above that associative networks have been used to represent discourse. Cognitive scientists have long been interested in how associative knowledge structures of lexical items are acquired and stored in memory [1, 9, 28]. This organizational structure, when used to present words to students, may have an effect on how vocabulary is learned and retained. Thus we have support for the use of an associative network as one semantic model in which to present new words to learners.

In order to use words in a language, however, learners need to understand and use them and their associates in a variety of communicative situations. Presenting vocabulary in realistic situations provides learners with a rich context that provides adequate semantic information to support communication skills. Different language situations elaborate upon various semantic and pragmatic meanings for a given lexical item and present the learner with different experiences. Assumptions 3, 7, and 8 (Table 2) also suggest the importance of presenting words in more communicative situations. Moreover, research shows that advanced learners benefit from vocabulary learning in discourse contexts that teach these kinds of relations between words [18].

A good model for lexical knowledge includes representing phonological, morphological, semantic and pragmatic relations among lexical concepts [19]. The primary knowledge representation used in this model for realizing the semantic relations between words is an associative network (See [20], this volume for a current discussion of this model). This type of model stresses the relations between concepts and their lexicalizations in a foreign language. In order to introduce morphologic and pragmatic relations between words, a richer model is needed. A richer model proposed in this volume [8] suggests the use of a propositional network to teach comprehension skills in a foreign language. A propositional model can teach relations between words in the context of natural text or discourse that are not available in the associative network model. Thus this model is useful for teaching the pragmatics of language in use.

This research draws from these two semantic models for representing the lexicon and examines their role in word learning. The theory on lexical organization in memory described in [20] serves as the primary framework for organizing the vocabulary in the learning environment described below. A propositional network model [13] for organizing discourse served as the framework underlying the texts used to present the vocabulary. The rest of this paper describes how a principled design for a foreign language learning environment can provide implicit tutoring that supports communicative language teaching through the presentation of two different representations for the lexicon: an associative network and a propositional network. The learning environment (LEXNET-INSITU) uses these models to teach foreign language vocabulary by combining sequenced lesson modules with embedded discovery learning.

4. Learning Environment Development

LEXNET-INSITU is the system being developed. This name was chosen to signify the two knowledge representations used to present vocabulary to the learner. LEXNET refers to the associative network representation used to organize the vocabulary to be taught. INSITU refers to the propositional network representations used for presenting the vocabulary in a particular situation. Details on the theoretical framework for this system are discussed elsewhere [27]. The use of hypermedia was included in the environment so that learners could have access to supplemental information about the words not presented directly by either of the two models (pronunciation, grammar explanation, translation, illustrative sentence). There are five instructional modules for the vocabulary that provide different kinds of information for words and exercises to practice word use. The first two modules are the two models used in which to present vocabulary to learners. The last three modules are instructional activities designed to strengthen word learning.

4.1 Vocabulary Knowledge Base

The LEXNET-INSITU system has a separate knowledge base for the vocabulary items. There are only nouns and verbs in this version of the system with 166 entries with all associates included. Most of the words are nouns (133) with the rest verbs. Each word type in the knowledge base has a unique entry in a word frame with specified slots for word features, link-typed associates (the synonyms, antonyms, hyponyms for each word), and syntactic information. Nouns have slots that specify the required markers for gender, case, and number. Verbs have slots for three tenses: simple present, simple past, and future.

The system accesses this knowledge base when different instructional modules are used by the learner. When learners read the texts (several stories that present the target vocabulary) and select a target word to get additional information on it, the system goes to the knowledge base and reads in specific information depending on which menu item is selected (See Figure 1). The structure of the associative network is realized visually in the graphical interface used to display portions of the network in the second module (See Figure 2). Learners preselect word and link type before they enter this and the next two instructional modules. In the last three modules that present exercises to the learner, the system again accesses the knowledge base with a pattern matcher to analyze how learners use the words in different contexts. Feedback is provided based on matches of the student behavior and the word information stored in the knowledge base. The feedback presented is stored statically and does not offer true student modeling at this stage of development.

While the present implementation does not use sophisticated artificial intelligence techniques for modeling the learner and adapting feedback, the use of a separate knowledge base for the vocabulary lends itself to future enhancements of this type. In addition, the modular structure of this system makes the addition of new words and texts very easy for language teachers.

4.2 Vocabulary Tutoring in LEXNET-INSITU

The tutoring in this system is implicit. That is to say, the environment is structured so that a student can discover the various knowledge structures for words by exploring the system. The tutoring principles in Table 1 were used to guide the design of the learning environment. The tutoring is embodied in the presentation of the vocabulary in the two different network models: associative and propositional, rather than by using formal tutoring rules to move learners through the lessons. This feature distinguishes the learning environment from a formal tutoring system with adaptive, goal-based instruction. Because the system supports communicative language teaching theory, students always have access to words in a variety of communicative contexts (sentences, texts). The system is organized in a lesson sequence designed to take students from simple to more complex activities (principle 6 from Table 1) if a more structured approach to learning is desired. However, the student is also free to browse the system in a discovery-like mode while learning the vocabulary. This puts the learner in control of his/her own learning and supports the role of 'learner as experimenter' [15].

4.2.1 Instructional Modules

The first module presents vocabulary within the context of narrative texts taken from newspaper articles in "Le Monde", a French newspaper. This is the propositional network and provides learners with rich, specific situations for the vocabulary items. This lesson upholds principles 1, 2, 3 & 11 from Table 1 and assumptions 2, 3, 4, & 7 from Table 2. These texts were propositionalized following a well known model [13]. This allows a codification of the texts in order to see where the target words to be learned occurred within the propositional structure. A pop-up menu is displayed when students click on a target word. The menu provides students with choices of various lexico-semantic elaborations for the word. The student can get a direct translation, be sent to the associative network structure for the designated word so associates of the target word can be studied and reviewed, get a grammar point presented about the target word, hear the word's pronunciation, and see an additional illustrative sentence using the target word as shown in Figure 1.

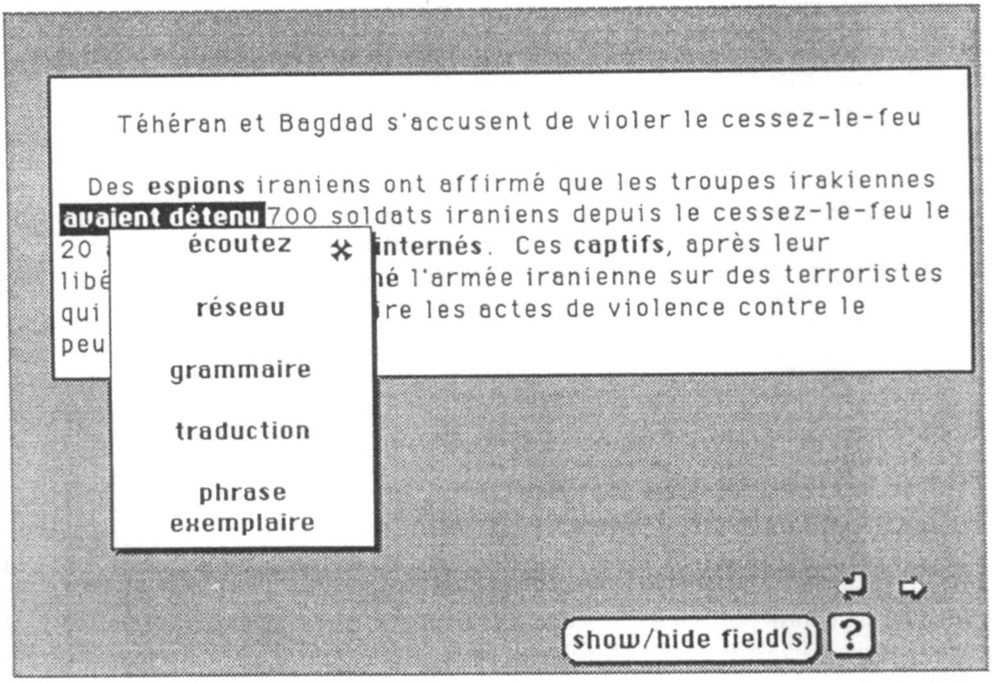

Figure 1. This figure shows what the learner sees when reading the stories. When a highlighted word is selected, a menu pops up that makes additional information about the word available.

The second module presents the target lexicon in an organized, associative network based on the portion of the theoretical framework that describes how the mental lexicon is organized in memory. This situation is less rich than the propositional one; word associates for the target word make up the situation in this context. This lesson upholds principle 2 from Table 1 and assumptions 6 & 8 from Table 2. The vocabulary covered two word classes (nouns and verbs) and three relations between constituents in the network: hyponymy, synonymy, and antonymy. The relations between verbs in the network are used pedagogically to present learners with words that "go together" or are "opposite" in meaning and thus stray somewhat from the formal organization of the verb hierarchy discussed in this volume [20]. Although the entire lexicon with all associates is over 160 words, the student is only presented with a small 'chunk' of the network, as shown in Figure 2, at any one time. By clicking on a word or icon, students can have access to direct translations, pronunciation, and an illustrative sentence for each word.

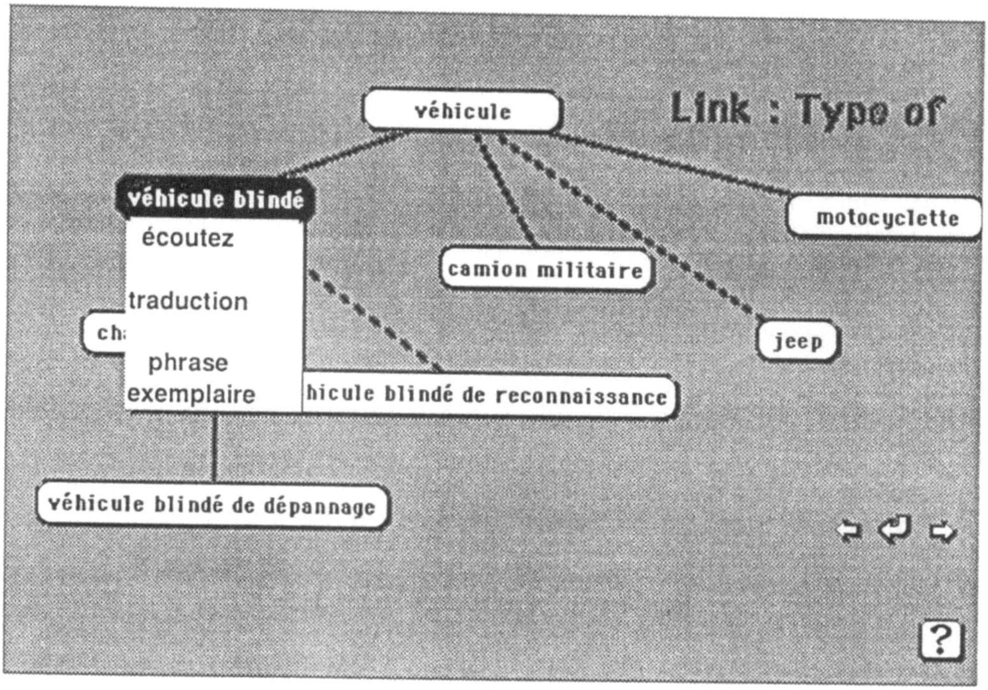

Figure 2. This figure shows what the learner sees when exploring the network structure. Similar to figure 1, when a word is selected, a menu pops up that makes additional information available to the learner.

The third module tests whether students have learned the relations among the lexical items they memorized in the organized network presented in the previous module. This lesson upholds principle 10 from Table 1 and assumptions 6 & 7 from Table 2. A semantic grouping strategy is used to reinforce this instructional goal. Students select a particular relation and are presented with a mixed list of words they have already learned in modules one and two. They are to organize the words into network-like clusters according to 'how the words go together. Each example has a correct grouping and an incorrect grouping. Feedback is provided so that students may check their knowledge about relationships between words.

The fourth module uses a cloze exercise (fill in the blank) to assess whether students can use the words appropriately in sentence contexts. This lesson upholds principles 1, 2, 3,

7, 10 & 11 from Table 1 and assumptions 3, 4, 7 & 8 from Table 2. This activity takes the student from the network structure, the weak context, and introduces a first level of enriched context (sentences) for the words. This module presents the learner with a noun network and a verb network. Learners select a candidate from each 'tree' and uses the item to fill in sentence templates that are shown on the bottom of the computer display. Feedback is provided so that they may check their knowledge about using words to create meaningful sentences.

The last module presents students with narrative texts (discourse) of paragraph length similar in structure to the texts presented in the first module. This lesson upholds principles 1, 2, 3, 7, 10 & 11 from Table 1 and assumptions 3, 4, 7 & 8 from Table 2. This module has two modes: explore and test. Paragraphs, analyzed propositionally as described above, are available with carefully placed cloze items that can be used to test word understanding. The explore mode is designed to encourage broad use of the lexicon and its related associates in the paragraphs. A list of candidate words for each paragraph is provided with a menu that allows students to go to the network structure of the selected word. Feedback on choices is provided so that students can check their understanding. In the test mode, students are not allowed to explore word associates in the semantic network as they fill in the blanks.

One of the research questions we are examining is if one type of representation (associative or propositional network) has an advantage over the other on recall, use, and retention of the vocabulary. Empirical evidence for the utility of one or both of these models would provide support for the use of these types of representations in ITS knowledge bases. Preliminary results from a study to assess the instructional use of these two models are presented below.

5. Empirical Support for the Tutoring in LEXNET-INSITU

A pilot study that compared two semantic models on vocabulary learning as measured by word recall, word usage, and word retention was conducted. Twenty-seven French language students from the U. S. Defense Language Institute participated in the study [3]. These subjects were in the end of their first year of full-time study in an immersion program. A self rating questionnaire showed they were all at a 1+ or 2 proficiency level (intermediate students). A 3 (learning condition) X 6 (language task) X 2 (retention interval) mixed design was used. Three groups were formed for the learning condition: 1) network context, 2) text context, and 3) combined (network and text) context. The language tasks and retention intervals were analyzed as repeated measures.

Students studied 54 French vocabulary items taken from the LEXNET-INSITU system. The organization of the experimental network was validated by a word sorting study (N= 13) and used four hierarchical, hyponymic network structures to organize the words. Each structure had a single superordinate and two subordinate levels of word associates. The narrative text used in the discourse context was a "walk-through" of this network. Each of the superordinate words from the four networks were presented in the first paragraph of the text as topic headings for the rest of the text. As the "walk-through" continued, each of the other 50 words were introduced in the text closely following the placement of the words in the network structure. In both the network and discourse contexts, 18 words were underlined. These words were tested in the pre- and posttests and used as a measure of word learning.

The pretest, a French-to-English translation task, was administered first. After studying the words in one of the learning conditions for five minutes, and following a brief

---

[3] I would like to thank Kirk Thor, research assistant at the U. S. Army Research Institute, for his help with the data reduction and analyses.

distractor task (math problems), students engaged in five recall tasks (one free, four cued). The four superordinate words from the hierarchical network structure were used as the cues in the cued recall tasks. Next a posttest, similar in format to the pretest, was administered. Students translated 48 words taken from the the pool of 54 words, including the 18 pretest words. This was followed by a cloze exercise that required students to complete sentences using words they had just studied. These sentences were different in form from those in the discourse context but similar in meaning. The students were then asked to translate these sentences into English. Some of these measures (recall tasks, posttest, and cloze task) were collected from the subjects in a second trial after a one week interval. None of the study materials were presented in the second trial. The results from these tasks were intended to reflect the effects of the different contexts on long term memory for word recall and retention.

5.1 Results

The results from this preliminary study present a somewhat confusing picture with regard to word learning in context. However, the data clearly show that cued and free recall are improved much more by the network alone than by text alone or text and network combined. The text condition appears to add some ambiguities to the ability to translate words, and to the clearcut network structure that facilitates recall.

Overall, the words used in this experiment were known to the subjects *a priori* as measured by the pretest. Subjects in the network condition were able to recall more words when compared to the other groups in both trials as predicted. However, contrary to what was predicted, no such differences among groups were found in the cloze tasks. Summary results from both trials for the underlined words in the recall tasks are shown in Table 3. Results from the pre- and posttest, and the cloze tasks for both trials are shown in Figure 3.

An analysis of variance with trial as the repeated measure was conducted for each of the recall tasks. There was a significant group effect for the free and first two cued recall tasks with the third cued recall approaching significance (See Table 3). The trial effect was significant for all recall tasks ($p < .001$). These results suggest that for learners who have some knowledge about the language, studying words in an associative network facilitates word retrieval and word availability both immediately after study and following the delay interval. This finding suggests that the same cognitive processes used in a native language to recall word hierarchies [3] are used in a foreign language. The reliable decline in the number of words recalled in all groups after a one week interval is also consistent with research on memory retrieval mechanisms [1].

Studying words in discourse contexts appears to support initial word learning and word retention over time. Subjects knew most of the words as measured by the pretest (see Figure 3); subjects in the text condition made the greatest gain in word learning. No significant gain in word knowledge resulted in the other two conditions. A significant interaction in the comparison of the pretest with posttest 1 suggests that studying words in text passages influences word learning positively. The comparison between the posttest 1 and the posttest 2, administered a week later, also resulted in a significant interaction. While subjects in the conditions that studied words in both text passages (text and combination) were able to remember the meaning of the same number of words after a week, those in the network condition were not.

The nonsignificant result between groups in the cloze tasks was surprising. We had predicted that the text group would make fewer errors in the cloze tasks. It is well known in the psychological literature that learners perform better at test when the context is the same as the one used for study. This would predict that the text groups would perform better on the cloze tasks. However, all three groups performed about the same on this task.

Table 3

Mean Number of Words Recalled (out of 18) in a Foreign Language as Function of Retention Interval

Recall Task		Learning Condition: Network	Text	Combined
Free				
	Immediate	16.37	11.87	11.22
	Delay	9.12	5.87	6.44
Group = $F(2,22)$ = 3.88, p = .03; Trial = $F(1,22)$ = 29.53, p < .0001				
Cue 1				
	Immediate	11.25	9.87	8.33
	Delay	9.00	4.12	4.77
Group = $F(2,22)$ = 4.35, p = .02; Trial = $F(1,22)$ = 22.40, p < .0001				
Cue 2				
	Immediate	12.37	7.75	10.55
	Delay	9.50	4.25	5.88
Group = $F(2,22)$ = 4.34, p = .02; Trial = $F(1,22)$ = 27.22, p < .0001				
Cue 3				
	Immediate	13.37	9.00	12.55
	Delay	9.87	5.37	7.22
Group = $F(2,22)$ = 3.07, p = .06; Trial = $F(1,22)$ = 31.32, p < .0001				
Cue 4				
	Immediate	15.00	10.12	11.55
	Delay	7.12	4.12	6.55
Group = $F(2,22)$ = 2.53, p = .10; Trial = $F(1,22)$ = 73.61, p < .0001				

One explanation for this lack of difference is that the context cues from the sentences themselves were sufficient for facilitating language independent, conceptual processing to understand the test sentence (cf. [8] for more discussion). Also, we have seen already that the performance of the network group is superior under cued conditions. The cloze task also provides these superordinates as context cues and should have a similar effect. Perhaps the observed result was affected by the similar conditions of learning and retrieval in the text group. The combined condition should be best and it was, although not reliably so.

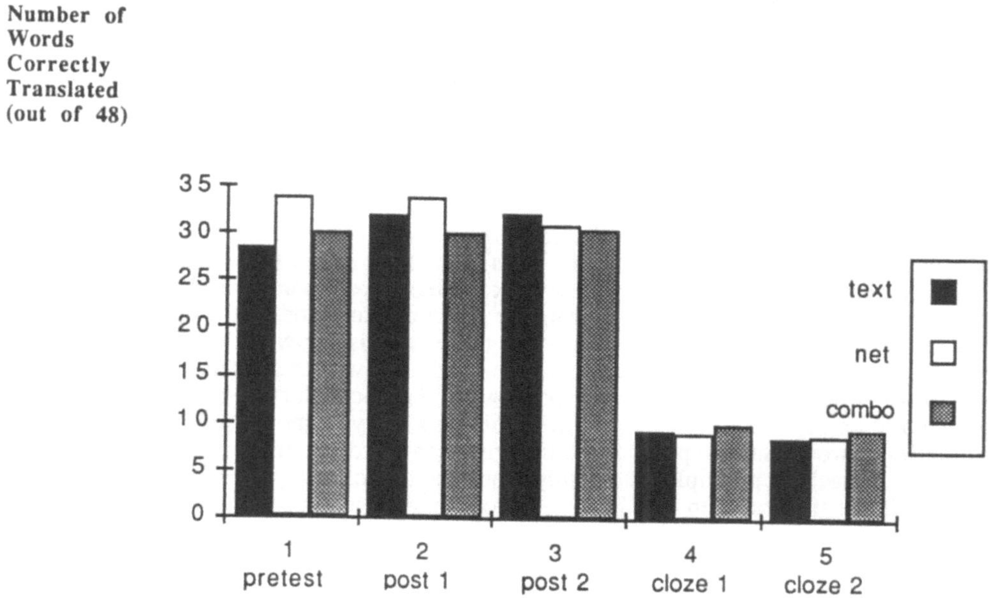

Pretest with Post 1
Group X Trial = $F(2,22)$ = 5.16, p = .01

Post 1 with Post 2
Group X Trial = $F(1,22)$ = 3.39, p = .05

Figure 3. Comparison of a). mean number of words known at pre- and posttest (post 1 is immediately after the study session; post 2 after a one week delay) and b). mean number of words used correctly in cloze problems (cloze 1 is immediately after the study session; cloze 2 after a one week delay).

Another explanation may be that they may have been guessing what the right word should be. Two single word gaps were left in each 10 to 12 word sentence leaving ample contextual cues for the learners to use to aid this kind of guessing or inferencing. A better test of word meaning and usage might have been to give the subjects two words from the stimulus set and instruct them to construct a meaningful sentence.

Finally, since the subjects knew all of the stimulus words *a priori*, it may be that an associative network context is all that is needed to support memorial processes for retrieving and using words in sentences when learners have some level of proficiency. What was not tested in this experiment was the effect of the different contexts on word learning for unknown words. With unknown, noncognate words, the effects of studying them in context may become evident.

More detailed analyses of the results are needed to understand their implications for word learning. What these preliminary data suggest is that associative networks influence recall processes positively in a foreign language when the words are known or are cognates, and when learners are at an intermediate level of proficiency. Although facilitating word availability is not equivalent to facilitating word learning, it is a prerequisite. Propositional networks seem to be important for strengthening word retention skills. Thus we can argue for the use of both kinds of network models for representing the knowledge in a vocabulary learning environment.

6. Implications for Tutoring Strategies in Foreign Language ITS

This research has described a knowledge-based learning environment that can serve as an alternative for codifying formal tutoring rules in the tutor model for some tutoring system. The environment used two semantic network models to represent lexical knowledge. The preliminary data from a study comparing the effect of each model on word recall suggest that an associative network representation for the lexicon is a powerful tutoring strategy for teaching word meaning. The cloze exercise results showed that either representation is useful for supporting communication skills when the vocabulary is known. The use of a more complex representation (propositional network) may be more useful for teaching the subtleties of word usage in particular situations when words are unknown.

A set of teaching principles and assumptions about vocabulary learning were offered to assist ITS researchers when they build the tutor model or learning environment for an ITS. Incorporating teaching principles from foreign language pedagogy will enhance the type of sequencing and remediation a system can provide and improve the overall instructional interaction for a student. Although the present LEXNET-INSITU system does not incorporate any artificial intelligence techniques for adapting the instruction or for allowing parsable input, these enhancements are possible in future developments. At this stage of the research, we wished to demonstrate the utility of a discovery learning environment for promoting communicative competencies based on a principled design.

Tutoring knowledge in foreign language ITS's depends just as much on the representation of expert knowledge as it does on the embodiment of appropriate tutoring rules and principles for the domain. How the expert knowledge is represented in a foreign language ITS depends on the particular skill being taught (grammar, dialogue, vocabulary). This research suggests that learning environments with psychologically valid knowledge representations for the lexicon are useful for vocabulary tutoring.

The work presented here is a small beginning in the examination of teaching language skills on a computer that follow communicative language teaching theory. We need to explore further what kinds of representations are optimal for tutoring different language skills, whether these representations can be implemented and manipulated in an ITS, and if they facilitate the learning of languages.

References

1. Anderson, J. R. & Bower, G.: Human associative memory. Hillsdale, NJ: Lawrence Erlbaum Associates 1974
2. Anderson, J. R. , Boyle, C. F., Farrell, R. G., & Reiser, B. J.: Cognitive principles in the design of computer tutors. Proceedings of the Sixth Cognitive Science Society Conference. Boulder, CO., pp. 2-8 1984
3. Bower, G., Clark, M. C., Lesgold, A. M., & Winzenz, D.: Hierarchical retrieval schemes in recall of categorized word lists. Journal of Verbal Learning and Verbal Behavior, 8, 323-343, (1969)
4. Carter, R. Vocabulary and second/foreign language teaching, Language Teaching, 2, 3-16, (1987)
5. Chen, L. & Kurtz, B. L.: XTRA-TE: Using natural language processing software to develop an ITS for language learning. 4th International Conference on Artificial Intelligence and Education, Amsterdam, May, pp. 54-63 1989
6. Criswell, E., Byrnes, H. & Pfister, G.: Intelligent automated strategies of teaching foreign language in context (this volume)
7. Cornu, A-M. The first step in vocabulary teaching. Modern Language Journal, 63, 262-272 (1979)

8. Frederiksen, C., Donin, J., Hoover, M., & Décary, M.: Semantic discourse processing and tutoring systems for second language learning. (this volume)
9. Forster, K. I.: Accessing the mental lexicon, in R. J. Wales & E. Walker (Eds.), New Approaches to Language Mechanisms, Amsterdam, Netherlands: North-Holland Publishing Company 1976
10. Fum, D., Pani, B. & Tasso, C.: Naive versus formal grammar: A case for integration in the design of a foreign language tutor (this volume)
11. Guindon, R.: A multidisciplinary perspective on dialogue structure in user-advisor dialogues. In R. Guindon (Ed.). Cognitive Science in the Applications for Human-Computer Interaction (pp.163-197). Hillsdale, NJ: Lawrence Erlbaum Associates 1988
12. Hamburger, H. & Hashim, R.: Foreign language tutoring and learning environment (this volume)
13. Kintsch, W. & van Dijk, T. A.: Toward a model of text comprehension and production. Psychological Review, 85, 363-394 (1978)
14. Kintsch, W.: The role of knowledge in discourse comprehension: A construction-integration model. Psychological Review, 95, 163-182 (1988)
15. Legenhausen, L. & Wolff, D.: Storyboard and communicative language learning: Results of the Düsseldorf CALL project (this volume)
16. Littlewood, W.: Communicative Language Teaching. London, UK: Cambridge University Press 1981
17. MacWhinney, B.: The competition model and foreign language acquisition (this volume)
18. Meara, P. & Ingle, S.: The formal representation of words in an L2 speaker's lexicon. Second Language Research, 2, 160-171 (1986)
19. Miller, G. A., Fellbaum, C., Kegl, J., & Miller, K.: Wordnet: An electronic lexical reference system based on theories of lexical memory. Révue Québecoise de Linguistique, 17, 181-213 (1988)
20. Miller, G. A. & Fellbaum, C.: Wordnet and the organization of memory (this volume)
21. O'Maggio, A. C.: Teaching Language in Context. Boston, MA: Heinle & Heinle Publishers, Inc 1986
22. Richards, J. C.: The Context of Language Teaching. New York, NY: Cambridge University Press 1985
23. Rumelhart, D. E.: Notes on a schema for stories. In D. G. Bobrow & A. Collins (Eds.), Representation and understanding. New York, NY: Academic Press 1975
24. Schank, R, & Abelson, R..: Scripts, Plans, Goals, and Understanding. Hillsdale, NJ: Lawrence Erlbaum Assoc.iation 1977
25. Sleeman, D. & Brown, J. S.: Intelligent Tutoring Systems. New York, NY: Academic Press, Inc 1982
26. Swartz, M. L. & Russell, D. M.: FL-IDE: Hypertext for structuring a conceptual design for computer-assisted language learning. Instructional Science, 18, 5-26 (1989)
27. Swartz, M. L. : Development of a hypermedia foreign language learning environment. Technical Report, Alexandria, VA: U. S. Army Research Institute (1989)
28. Tulving, E. & Donaldson, W.: Organization of memory. New York, NY: Academic Press 1972
29. Wenger, E.: Artificial intelligence and tutoring systems. Los Altos, CA: Morgan Kaufmann Publishers, Inc 1987
30. Wolf, B. & McDonald, D. D.: Context-dependent transitions in tutoring discourse. Proceedings of the National Conference on Artificial Intelligence, Austin, TX: August 6-10,1984
31. Yamamoto, H., Kai, K., Osato, M., Shiino, T., & Inui, M.: A Structure for an Intelligent CAI System for Training Foreign Language Conversation Skills Based on Conversation Simulation. Paper presented at the International Conference on Advanced Research on Computers in Education. July 18-20. Gakushuin University, Tokyo, Japan 1990
32. Zock, M.: SWIM or sink: The problem of communicating thought (this volume)

SWIM [1] or Sink : The Problem of Communicating Thought

Michael Zock

LIMSI, Langage & Cognition, B.P. 133, 91403 Orsay / France

Abstract : The goal of this paper is twofold (a) to present a system which aims to allow students to learn in an intuitive, meaningful and intelligent way to produce sentences in French; and (b) to describe a methodology for solving a particular problem that arises with this system : the control of conceptual input. Since SWIM is an attempt to mimic natural learning, —it is the student who asks the questions and the system which answers them,— we are faced with a communication problem. How can we ask the system "how does one say <x>?" , if we don't know in what terms to specify, hence convey the content of x (meaning, message) ? In other words, how can we communicate thought without using a natural language? We shall discuss in this paper a first attempt to solve this problem. More precisely, we shall present the sketch of an interface, —a semantically driven message editor,— that should ultimately allow even naive users to communicate complex thoughts in a natural way .

Keywords : Intelligent Tutoring System, sentence generation, control of conceptual input, conceptual graph editor, semantic interface, meaning-form relationship, intermediate structures

1. Introduction

A common problem in foreign language learning is that one knows *what* to say (idea), but one does not know *how* to say it (form). While native speakers or teachers know *how* to translate the intended message, they rarely know *why* one uses a specific form. People, unlike computers, do not usually have access to their knowledge base, telling them what rules govern form. Since computers can translate messages as well as justify why the system generated a specific form, it is tempting to use them as learning tools.

2. Historical Background

The system described here is such a tool. Actually, it is the natural outgrowth of a smaller system [15] whose task is to assist students in inductively learning [2] a set of rules to generate sentences in French. While the goal of the preceding system was restricted to the learning of personal pronouns in French, the goal of this system is to cover a much wider subset of the French language, i.e. complex noun-phrases, relative clauses, etc.[3]

As we will see below, when generalizing from the smaller system to the larger one we had a problem with the conceptual component, i.e., the range of facts the system would allow the user to talk about. In consequence, we had to think of ways to enhance the power of the

1 **SWIM** is the acronym of **See What I Mean** ? The system has been implemented by A. Laroui in LeLisp on a MacIntosh. I would like to thank Lary Taylor from Apple Europe for the support of this work.

2 Please note that we are dealing in this paper with *learning* not with *teaching*. It is the *user* who controls the process. It is he, and not the teacher or the system, who asks the questions.

3 So far the system can only produce simple sentences. Most of our efforts have been put into the graphical rather than the linguistic component.

NATO ASI Series, Vol. F 80
Intelligent Tutoring Systems for Foreign Language Learning
Edited by M. L. Swartz and M. Yazdani

conceptual component so as to allow the user to communicate ideas of arbitrary complexity in any order.

Before getting into the details of the problem and the solution we propose, we will start by describing the system's underlying philosophy.

3. Goals of the System

The major goal of the system here described is to provide a "natural" environment [4] for learning in an intelligent [5] and meaningful [6] way to produce sentences in French. In order to achieve this goal several subgoals have to be attained.:

Goal a : The student should be maximally integrated into the process, that is that he should be active rather than reactive (talk only when being asked), as he usually knows best what his needs are.[7] In consequence, the student should be encouraged to ask questions rather than simply answer them. The system allows the student to ask the following questions [8]:

(1) How does one say	**< idea > ?**
(2) Can one say	**< linguistic form > ?**
(3) How should one say	**< idea > ?**
(4) Why does one say	**< form-1> and not <form-2 >?**
(5) What would happen if	**< conceptual modification > ?**
(6) What would happen if	**< syntactic modification > ?**
(7) What would happen if	**<word y>instead of<word x >?**
(8) What is the difference between	**< form x > and < form y > ?**

All these questions may occur at one moment or another in a natural setting (learning situation). They correspond to different strategies or learning needs. [9]

The first communication-mode (how does one say <idea>?) raises an interesting problem : how to control conceptual input, that is, how to tell the computer *what* one wants to say (message) since one doesn't know *how* to say it in this particular language. The fundamental question here is in what terms to code and communicate thought. Should one use words, [10] images, or abstract categories (primitives, metalanguage), or a hybrid form of knowledge representation ?

---

4 A computerized learning environment is said to be *natural*, if new knowledge can be acquired as a by product of another goal directed activity. We walk to get somewhere, not to learn to walk. We learn languages to communicate, not to learn grammar. Natural learning is typically empirical (hypothesis testing) and unsystematic : we observe or produce certain changes and draw conclusions on the basis of the regularities between a set of covariations.

5 The words *intelligent learning* are used to distinguish between rote- and inductive learning (learning by exploration, hypothesis-testing). Only the latter is said to be intelligent, or productive.

6 "Meaningfulness" refers to the fact that the learner is given relevant information, that is, information he may need at a specific moment.

7 This goal is in accord with research on learners' misconceptions. See [1].

8 For the time being only the modes 1, 5, 6 and 8 are implemented.

9 Unfortunately I don't know of any empirical work substantiating this claim. It would be interesting though to investigate which questions are dominant for a given learner type at a given level of competency.

10 For example, one could use one's mother-tongue, in which case we would be faced with a translation problem.

Goal b : In order to enable the system to answer the question "How does one say <x>?" one must know of a method of telling the system the meaning of <x>. This means, in our case, that we have to provide the user with an interface that allows him to communicate his thoughts.

Since messages or thoughts can be of arbitrary complexity, and as their constituent elements (ideas) may come into our mind in any order, we need a powerful, yet flexible conceptual component. The ideal would be to have a tool that allows us to build conceptual structures of arbitrary complexity incrementally and in any order.

Goal c : Learning a language requires not only learning words and learning how to combine and shape them (syntax and morphology), but it also requires that one learns the conditions under which to use each of these forms. As linguistic forms may vary as a function of (a) conceptual, (b) linguistic and (c) pragmatic choices, it is important to learn how each one of these variables affects form.[11]

While our long-term goal is to show how all these choices are reflected in the linguistic form, we restrict the discussion in this paper to the relationship between meaning and form. [12] We will now give a short description of the system and show how it works.

4. Description of the System

The dialogue is initiated by having the user specify the language in which he wants to communicate his thoughts, and the communication mode. Let us assume that the chosen language was English and that the communication mode was "How does one say <idea> ?". In that case the system traverses, the tree in Figure 1 top to bottom left to right.

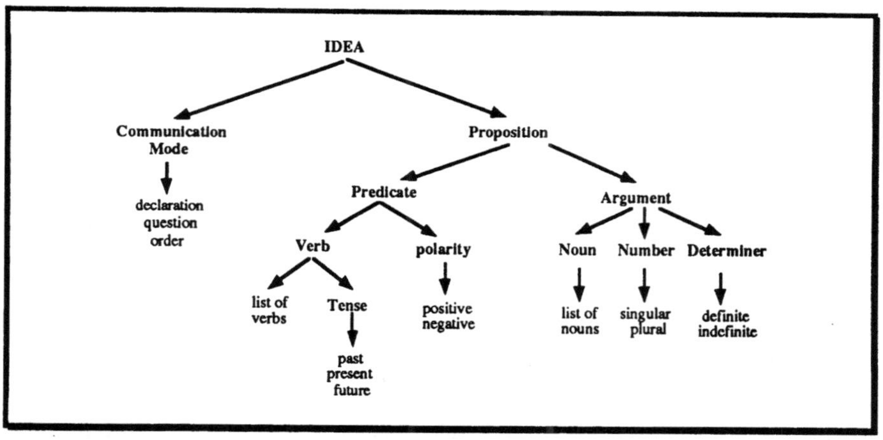

Figure 1. A primitive interface to communicate thought

11 *Conceptual choices*: different meanings yield different forms (he sings vs. he sang).
Linguistic choices : the same meaning can be expressed by different words or syntactic forms (paraphrases);
Pragmatic choices : different linguistic means serve different discourse purposes, i.e., different forms are used to achieve different goals (active vs. passive voice, etc.).

12 For a discussion of how form may be affected by rhetorical choices like topicalisation, framing, etc. see [14].

Obviously, the student doesn't see the tree. He is given a menu from which he has to choose. By choosing (clicking) specific values from a set of attributes, the user tells the system what he wants to say. As the dialogue develops, the system builds the underlying meaning in the form of conceptual graphs [13]. It then invites the user to try to express this meaning, after which it will output its own form.

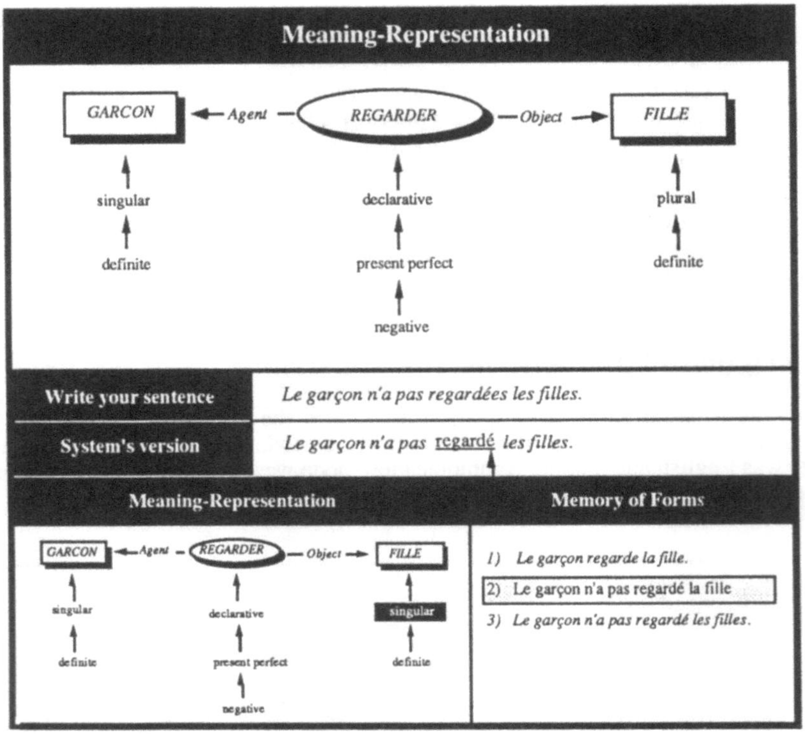

Figure 2. An interface to learn empirically about the meaning-form relationship

As you can see from Figure 2, the screen is divided into five parts. The large window at the top of the screen represents the underlying meaning of the message a student is trying to convey. The next two windows contain respectively the user's attempt to express this meaning and the system's version. Possible mismatches between these two versions are highlighted on the screen. This allows the system to draw the student's attention to errors. In the example given the student made a mistake in the verb-agreement ("regardées" instead of "regardé").

Finally, the window at the bottom, called "memory of forms", is an incrementally built data base (trace) containing all of the sentences encountered so far. [13] The window to the left, called "meaning representation", is a device for displaying, hence to recall the underlying conceptual representation of a specific sentence chosen from the *memory of form window*.It is activated by clicking any of the forms contained in the data base.

The idea behind this separation is to allow the user to make a contrastive analysis of meaning and form between two sentences. (See the communication mode 8: *What is the difference between* `<form x>` *and* `<form y>` ?) Choosing a sentence in the "memory of form"

13 It is planned to allow the user to organize this database according to his needs. One could also automatize this process of classification on the basis of linguistic or conceptual criteria. For example, all sentences in interrogative-negative form may be grouped together, irrespective of the order in which they were constructed. This last part is not yet implemented.

window gives a representation of the sentence's meaning in the "meaning representation" window. By comparing the surface form and the underlying meaning of two sentences, the user can appreciate the relationship between meaning and form.[14] The critical feature, the one that is responsible for the difference of form, is highlighted by the system. In our example it is the value "singular".

This is the basic cycle. Past this point, the user has various options : either he continues in the basic communication mode (*How does one say* <idea> ?), or he changes the kind of question he wants to ask. Let us suppose that he wants to build a completely different sentence. In this case he could either go through the whole routine as depicted in Figure 1, which is quite cumbersome, or he could perform the conceptual changes directely on the graph. Obviously, this latter method is much faster.[15]

Actually, everything you see on the graph, except deep-case relations, is considered by the system as a variable whose value may be changed directely by the user. In order to do so, he clicks on any of the shown attributes (verb, tense, mode, etc.) and chooses a new value. For example, if he clicks on the verb "regarder" (to watch) the system answers by displaying a list of verbs from which one must choose. By clicking on the feature "present", the system shows different values (present, past, future, etc.) of the variable *tense*. Everytime the system is given some piece of information it will change the meaning representation accordingly, and, if asked, output the corresponding form .

For example, if one started from sentence (a) asking the system to change the number of the direct object from "singular" to "plural" it would produce (b). If one asked it to change the tense from "present" to "past perfect", it would produce (c), etc. (See Figure 3):

(a) Le garçon regarde *la fille*	(the boy watches the *girl*)
(b) Le garçon regarde *les filles*	(the boy watches the *girls*)
(c) Le garçon *a regardé* les filles	(the boy *has watched* the girls)

As one can see, this method allows for local as well as for global changes. Actually, the dialogue described corresponds to the communication mode 6. If one changes only one value each time, asking the system to tell right away how this meaning change is reflected in form, one can very quickly build and explore a large search space. Actually, this kind of dialogue between man and machine is much faster and less tedious than it would be between a student and a teacher. The change of meaning and the system's generation of the corresponding form take about a second, even for an untrained user.

Another communication mode the system allows for is called: `What would happen if` <syntactic change>?. This mode allows the user to perform certain transformations such as *passive voice* or *pronominalization.* In the latter case, the system will ask the user to specify which element he wants pronominalized (the boy, the girl, or both). Assume that, starting from the conceptual structure underlying sentence (a), the user wants to pronominalize respectively the agent, the object, and finally both arguments (See Figure 4). In these cases he would get the following output :

---

[14] Obviously, this mapping of meaning onto form is fundamental to language learning. As psychologists and linguists have often noted, people compare structures not only within but also between languages. See [9, 10, 11, 18].

[15] Actually, that is one of the major advantages of abstract representations compared to, let us say, icons. Another advantage is that this kind of representation shows on-line how conceptual, linguistic or pragmatic choices affect the intermediate structure, hence more or less directly the final form. In consequence, by displaying on-line the way that the intermediate structure changes after each choice, we have a means of moving from a black box to a glass box. The former only shows how changes of the input (conceptual choices) are reflected in the output, whereas the latter also shows how pragmatic (discourse choices : topicalisation, focus) or linguistic choices (words choice), etc. affect the intermediate levels. For more details see [16, 17, 19]. Finally, graphs are very efficient means not only for coding thought, but also for providing cues for the language user : the latter may recognize potential syntactic structures on the basis of conceptual configurations (direction of the arcs, nature of the object pointed at, etc.). For more details, see [18].

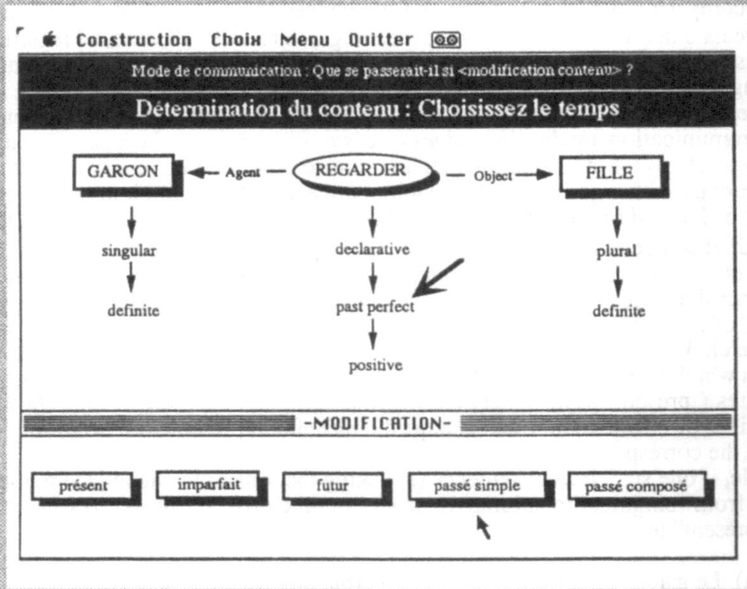

Figure 3. Meaning changes by direct manipulation of the conceptual structure

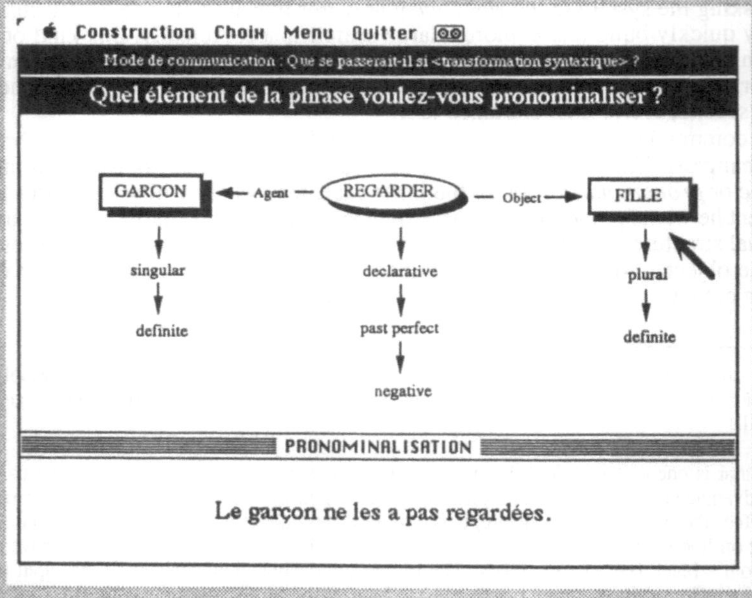

Figure 4. Changes of the syntactic structure

Il regarde la fille.	(*He* watches the girl)
Le garçon *la* regarde.	(The boy watches *her*)
Il la regarde.	(*He* watches *her*)

We hope that by experimenting with the system, that is, by exploring and contrasting the different possibilities, the user will learn how variations of meaning are reflected in form.

5. Discussion

When Figures 1 and 2 are considered, the system's weakest point is clearly evident : its conceptual component. However there are other weak spots :

(a) the *linguistic coverage* is extremely small : only very simple structures can be used;

(b) the *size* of the discourse universe : one can only talk about a very limited range of facts; [16]

(c) the conceptual interface is a *surface* rather than a *deep-structure* component (it already contains the lexical items and it knows which syntactic categories to use, i.e., the program thinks in terms of the target language);

(d) the conceptual structure is built incrementally. Yet this progressive building of the conceptual structure is not shown on-line. Hence the user may get lost, not knowing what he has built so far.

(e) the *rigidity* of the conceptual component : the order in which the meaning is conveyed is defined a priori. Verbs have always to be chosen before nouns.

(f) the terminology used (*metalanguage*) may be inaccessible to the linguistically innocent user;[17]

In the remainder of this paper I will mainly be concerned with two of these points: the problems of the power and flexibility of the conceptual component.

6. A Possible Solution

When the points describe above are considered, it becomes obvious that what is needed is an interface that allows one to build dynamically, in any order (flexibility) conceptual structures of arbitrary complexity. For example, such an interface must allow for recursive structures. What we describe below is not meant to be the ultimate solution to the problem; rather it points in a direction where we hope to find the solution.

Figure 5, below, can be considered as such a conceptual interface. It starts from the assumption that all complex thoughts (texts, paragraphs, compound sentences) can be decomposed into a set of simple thoughts or propositions [7], that is, into a list of predicates

16 Looking at point (b), one may be tempted to add new words. However, adding vocabulary would not fundamentally enhance the system's expressive power, i.e., range of conceptual and linguistic structures. Furthermore, adding new words would still not solve the weakness of the lexical component (point c). Finally, with the power of the lexicon (size) come the problems of access. The bigger the lexicon, the more efficient must be its organization (flexibility of access). Decision trees guiding the user when lexicalizing a given conceptual fragment (see 5), or simple hierarchies are probably not sufficient. A lattice type organization is probably more appropriate (content adressable memory).

17 For a proposition of how to visualize such abstract notions as time, tense and aspect see [8].

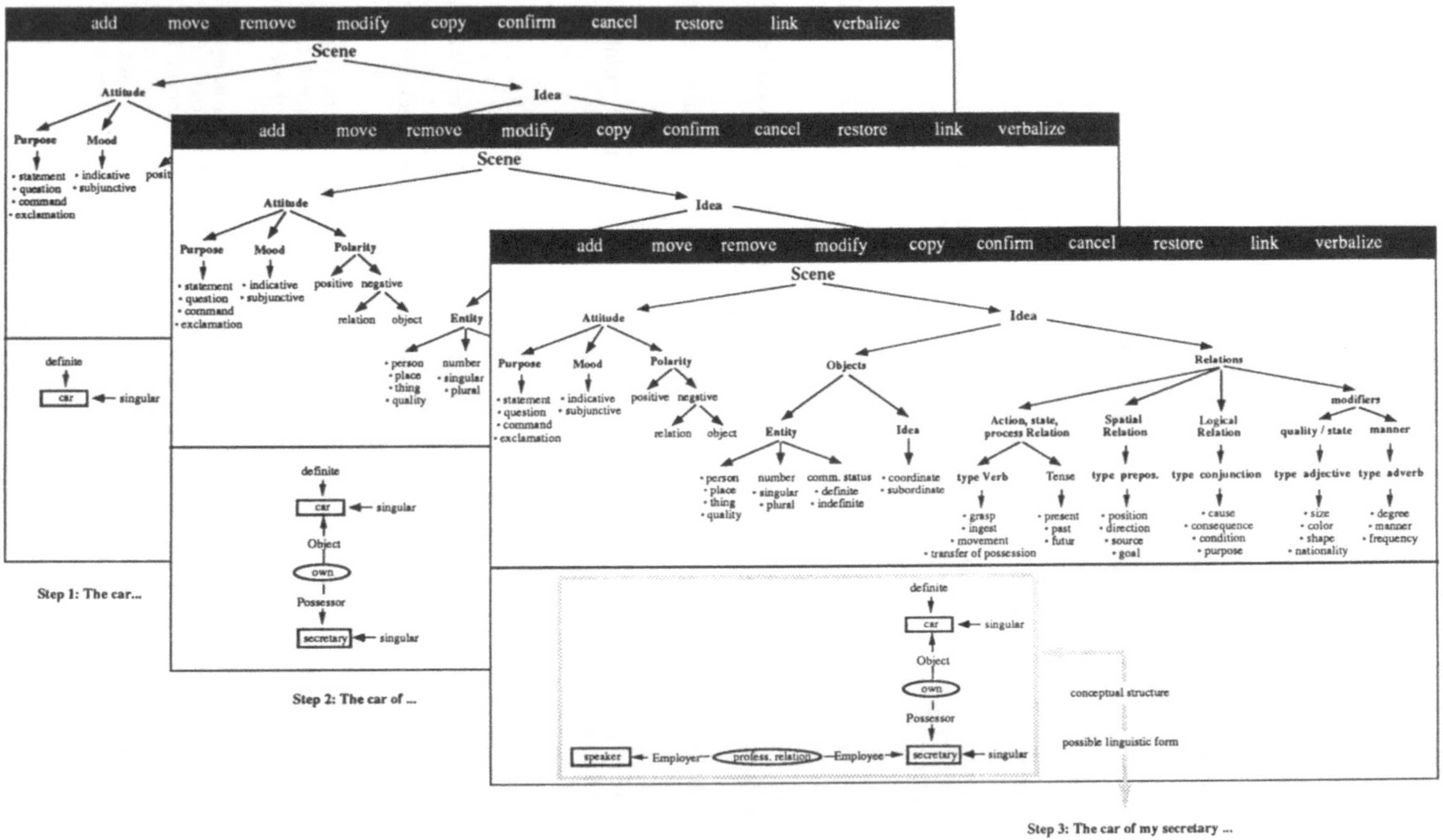

Figure 5. An interactive conceptual graph editor

(relations) and arguments (objects) which are related to each other in various ways (coordination, subordination, embedding).[18] Another assumption, related to the former, posits that all thoughts consist basically in predicating something about something else (argument). Predications can be made of arguments of any complexity : simple arguments (nouns), predicates (adjectives, verbs), propositions, paragraphs, or entire texts.[19] Finally, all sentences are used for specific purposes; that is, one has to signal whether one is making a statement, asking a question, or giving a command.

Figure 5 encodes these kinds of assumptions. Actually, what is shown on this figure can be conceived of as a *conceptual graph editor*. On the top appear the editing modes (add, move, link, copy, etc.). Directly below are the meaning components (objects and relations) from which one must choose in order to convey thought.

While the building of conceptual structures (message) is driven by the user, —he chooses what he wants to say— the process is controlled by the system: the latter specifies what can be said, or what is meaningful. The conceptual grammar behind the conceptual graph editor specifies what objects are relevant in a given culture and what objects can be linked in what way. Apart from these two operations (choose an object and link it to another in a specific way) there is no way to be culturally meaningful. [20]

Finally, at the bottom appears the linguistic output. As the user chooses among the possible conceptual components, the system builds the corresponding structure on-line. If the latter were fed to a generator like IPG [4, 6], we could produce the corresponding form piece by piece.

6.1 Example of an incrementally built Conceptual Structure

Let us see how this kind of interface might be used to produce the underlying meaning of a complex sentence like:

"The car of my new secretary, who you met last Saturday at the party, has been stolen."

In Figure 6 below, we present a schematic dialogue between the user and the system. As one proceeds in the dialogue, [21] the system builds incrementally (by unification) the corresponding graph (See Figure 7) :

18 See [2, 3] for a similar interface using propositional representations for the semantic analysis of sentences.

19 In consequence, these predicates may surface as adjectives or verbs, as nouns and adverbs.

20 In other words, we believe that the components and their assembly are culture specific.

21 Actually the dialogue is much simpler than it looks here. The user clicks directly on the relevant parts of the conceptual tree shown in Figure 5.

SYSTEM :	**USER'S CHOICE :**
1) Choose your communication mode !	How does one say <idea> ?
2) Specify the content : what do you want to start with : an object (argument) or a relationship (predicate) ?[22]	object : car
3) Specify the number and the determiner !	number: singular determiner: definite
4) What kind of relation do you want to connect: ?[23]	type verb : possess
5) «Possession» has the following case-frame : *possess (owner, object).*	
Specify the *owner* !	secretary
Specify the *object !*	car
6) What kind of relation do you want to connect: ?	type verb : professional relationship
7) «Professional Relationship» has the following case-frame : *Relationship* (*employer*, *employee*).	
Please specify the *employer* !	speaker
Please specify the *employee* !	secretary
	etc.

Figure 6: System-user dialogue sample for constructing the sentence, "The car of my new secretary, who you met last Saturday at the party, has been stolen."

22 This choice does of course have certain consequences. Whereas starting with a relationship (predicate) is mor efficient from a computational point of view, as one immediately knows the associated case-frame, —that is probabl the reason why this approach is used in most work on natural language generation,— starting with the argument i intuitively more natural, since, in order to predicate something about something else, the discourse object (referent has to be already present in the speaker's mind.

23 Please note that, unlike in step 2, the system asks only for the connection of a predicate (relationship), that is, th system assumes that one does not want to build an incoherent structure. Of course, one could easily allow for suc imperfect structures. In principle it is quite conceivable that at a specific moment of this structure building process a object is not connected. As the graph is built on-line, this fact will be immediately recognized by the user.

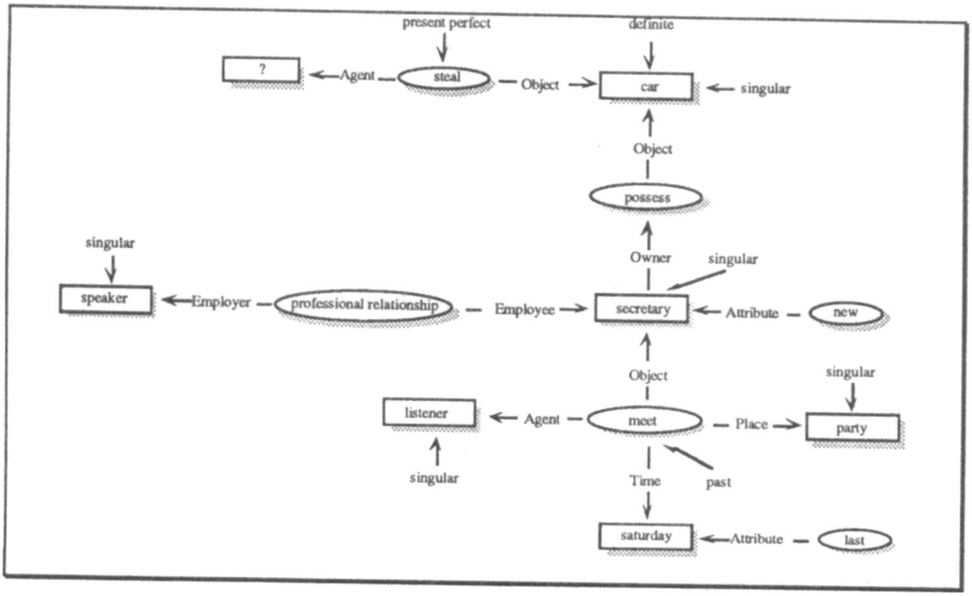

Figure 7: Conceptual representation of the example sentence given above

7. Discussion

The design of a conceptual interface along the lines discussed here has various interesting features. Such an interface is:

- *powerful*: it allows, at least in principle, for the building of conceptua structures of arbitrary complexity;
- *flexible* : the order of processing is fairly free : graphs can be expanded in any direction, that is, one can start either by determining the predicate or the argument; [24]
- *efficient* : information can be accessed, and hence communicated, very quickly. As the user signals his choices by clicking specific parts in the conceptual tree, he can access the relevant information directly without having to browse through the hierarchy from top to bottom.
- *explicit* : as the conceptual structures are built on-line, the user becomes immediately aware if his thoughts are not connected, that is, the system makes explicit missing links (lack of coherency).

---

[24] The building of conceptual structures is fairly flexible. That is, the order in which the processing takes place is syntactically much less constrained than for natural language. While the former are relational, the latter are linear due to the channel constraint. In consequence, it is nearly always possible to add some information to an existing conceptual structure, —the order in which the graph is built is mainly a function of the order in which new ideas spring to mind—, it is not always possible to add a new word to the right hand side of the linguistic structure built so far. Conceptual structures and linguistic structures do not obey the same constraints.

Finally, the graph notation also illustrates quite nicely the relationship between meaning and form. A given meaning can be expressed by different forms (paraphrase). Take for example the sentence above. The same meaning can be expressed either by a series of short sentences (a-f), or by one long sentence (g) :

(a) I have a secretary.	(d) This party took place last Saturday.
(b) She is new.	(e) She has a car.
(c) You met her at a party.	(f) It has been stolen.

(g) The car of my new secretary, who you met at the party last Saturday, has been stolen.

Conversely, different meanings may map onto identical linguistic forms.

The key of the door	[part of]
The car of my friend	[possession]
The father of my brother	[family relationship]

In conclusion, if the interface integrates a number of interisting features, it still does not meet two important objectives : it does not cover very much yet, and as it stands, it is not well adapted for the naive, metalinguistically innocent user. This will be work for the future.

8. Conclusion

We have described a computerized learning environment whose design is motivated from a cognitive point of view. The qualities of this approach lie in the facts that

- the system decomposes the process and visualizes the nature and implications of a set of choices. In doing so it provides the learner with a setting that allows him to gain empirically certain insights about the structure and the process of producing language (What determines what ? How to map meaning onto form ?). In reducing the learner's mental load, we also increase his control.

- the user is maximally integrated into the process. He is active rather than reactive. He asks the questions and the system answers them (user-centered approach). The consequences of this insightful, exploration-based learning are that (a) the questions asked are related to the user's goals, hence they are relevant and meaningful (intrinsic motivation); (b) the student learns not only a language, that is, to produce a set of well formed linguistic structures, but he also acquires a method of learning in an intelligent way (efficient learning strategies).

- the system allows for self-instruction (private tutor).

We have also discussed a problem that arises in interactive natural language generation, conceptual input. How (in what terms) to specify the message one intends to convey ? Though very important, in particular for man-machine communication, this problem has never been addressed. It raises many interesting problems both from a theoretical and from a practical point of view: how are thoughts coded, organized and accessed? Can thoughts be communicated without recourse to a natural language ? What kind of interface and grammar are needed in order to allow for the generation of well formed thought ?, etc.

We have proposed a method for editing well formed conceptual graphs incrementally and in free order. That is what we mean by *controlling conceptual input* (what to say).While we believe that the ideas underlying the conceptual graph editor are of the right sort, we are also aware of the fact that much more work is needed on the conceptual side to make the system work.

References

1. Demaizière F. & Blanvillain, O.: Learners' Intuitions, misconceptions and errors. This volume
2. Frederiksen C.,& M. Décary: Cognitive Discourse Analysis, Technical Report, McGill Univeristy, Laboratory of Applied Cognitive Science 1989
3. Frederiksen C., Donin J., Hoover M. & M. Décary: Semantic discourse processing and tutoring systems for second language learning. This volume
4. de Smedt K. & Kempen G. Incremental sentence production, self-correction and coordination. In Kempen G. (Ed.), *Natural Language generation : new results in Artificial Intelligence, Psychology & Linguistics*, Dordrecht , Boston : Martinus Nijhoff 1987
5. Goldman N.: Conceptual generation. In Schank R. (Ed.), *Conceptual Information Processing*, North Holland, Dordrecht 1975
6. Kempen,G. & Hoenkamp, T.: An Incremental Procedural Grammar for Sentence Formulation, Cognitive Science, 11,
7. Kintsch W.: The representation of meaning in memory. Hillsdale, NJ: Lawrence Erlbaum Associates 1974
8. Ligozat G. & Zock M.: Generating temporal expressions from icons. In *25th Colloquium of Linguistics*, Paderborn 1990
9. Mac Whinney B.: The competition model and foreign language acquisition. This volume
10. Nogier J. & Zock M.: Lexical choice as a process of matching definitions on an utterance graph. In *5th Workshop on conceptual graphs*, European Conference of Artificial Intelligence, Stockholm 1990
11. Richards J.: Error Analysis: Perspective on Second Language Acquisition. Longman 1984
12. Schank R.: Conceptual Information Processing. North Holland, Dordrecht 1975
13. Sowa J.: Conceptual structures : Information processing in mind and machine. Reading, MA: Addisen-Wesley 1984
14. Zock M.: Natural languages are flexible tools : that's what makes them hard to explain, to learn and to use, in Zock M. & Sabah G.: Advances in Natural Language Generation: an interdisciplinary perspective, vol. 1, Norwood, N.J.: Ablex Publishers 1988
15. Zock M., Laroui, A. & Francopoulo G.: Language Learning as problem solving: Modelling logical aspects of inductive learning to generate sentences in french by man and machine, In *Proceedings of the 12th Coling*, Budapest, (1988)
16. Zock M.: If you can't open the black box, open a window! or, How to visualize dependency relationships when mapping meaning onto form ? In *Proceedings of COGNITIVA*, Madrid 1990
17. Zock M.: Comment transformer une boîte noire en boîte de verre, ou, l'utilité des structures intermédiaires comme moyen d'explication du fonctionnement du français (How to transform a black box into a glass box, or, how intermediate structures may help the language learner to understand the functioning of french ?). In *Proceedings of the Journées de Cachan*, L'explication dans l'enseignement et l'EIAO, Paris 1990
18. Zock M.: Sentence generation by pattern matching : the problem of syntactic choice. In Gargov G. & Staynov P. (Eds.), *Explorations in Cognitive Linguistics*, Benjamins, North Holland, Dordrecht 1991
19. Zock, M.: How to transform a black box into a glass box ?, or, Why use intermediate structures in computer assisted language learning. In Walker, D. (Ed.) Proceedings of the 7th Annual Apple European University Consortium conference, Paris 1991

Invoking and exploring HELP in a decoupled task<->discussion level environment for second language learning*

Roland Sussex

Centre for Language Teaching and Research, The University of Queensland, Queensland 4072, AUSTRALIA

Abstract: Research into Intelligent Tutoring Systems has paid a great deal of attention to the performance of the student. The question of modelling the human instructor has been less studied, particularly in the ways in which the human instructor's interventions relate to the implementation and provision of intelligent HELP. By decoupling the task and discussion levels, it is possible to investigate how the HELP system can emulate the human instructor in providing advice and "discussion" level direction without requiring an encyclopaedic knowledge of student-machine interactions at the task level.

Keywords: intelligent educational systems, intelligent help, language learning, computer-based tools, hypermedia

1. Introduction

Most Intelligent Tutoring Systems ("ITS"; for a survey see [37]) have suffered from a particular difficulty of conceptualization and design: if genuinely intelligent, such systems have usually been non-generic, in the sense that they have not been readily adaptable to learning applications for other tasks. On the other hand, if they have been generic, as with the case of some authoring shells, it has usually been difficult to adapt them to the purposes of domain-specific learning. In both cases the size of the software engineering task which they require has tended to deter both users and implementers. And there has been insufficient attention paid to the cognitive issues of instructor-learner interaction.

Rather than building a single monolithic system, Geoff Cumming (La Trobe University, Melbourne) and I approach the question instead through a tools metaphor, where the computer provides the learner with a set of tools. Much of the initiative and intelligence then resides with the learner. The system looks on as the learner explores the various materials, forms hypotheses, and applies the hypotheses to different questions and bodies of knowledge.

But what happens when learners finds themselves in difficulties? Traditional intelligent HELP systems have usually required a deep and detailed knowledge of the current problem, the student model and the current student's learning history, as well as the state of the current process and the goals of the lesson. This can be accomplished in highly structured domains, as the Leeds research on the Eurohelp project has shown [2, 17-18, 24]. But this is not what the human instructor does: with a less encyclopaedic and detailed knowledge of all these task factors, he/she is able nevertheless to provide help, guidance, advice and support in a range of

* The ideas presented in this paper owe a great deal to Geoff Cumming, who is the co-investigator on this project. Rosemary Baker has provided important input in the area of repair theory, and Merryanna Swartz & Masoud Yazdani have suggested many improvements. Infelicities in the paper are my responsibility.

Funding for the investigation of issues of expert-systems based learning environments in the EXCALIBUR Project [14], from which many of the ideas presented here ultimately derived, was provided by the Australian Research Council under grant A5 8716345.

NATO ASI Series, Vol. F 80
Intelligent Tutoring Systems for Foreign Language Learning
Edited by M. L. Swartz and M. Yazdani

learning contexts. In particular, instructors are able to "take another angle" on the learner's current problem; to attack an issue from another direction, to provide "discussion level" interaction, as opposed to "task level" support.

The project which we are working on seeks to model this kind of interaction between the human instructor and the learner. By decoupling the task and discussion levels we can pose questions concerning the nature of HELP interventions, the kinds of intervention which can be provided at the discussion level, and the kinds of information which must pass between the learner and these two levels for the HELP system to function successfully.

In terms of second language learning, this means facilities like writing and reference tools as applications on the screen, and systems for tracking the student's actions, invoking help, and navigating between the levels. These interactions provide a handle on a range of cognitive and modelling issues in second language learning.

2. Language Learning, Artificial Intelligence & Expert Systems

Early explorations and applications in CALL ("Computer-Aided Language Learning") were strongly oriented towards the drill-and-practice, test-and-branch models. This is hardly surprising, given that many of the lesson authors were language teachers with a modest command of BASIC, and an *idée fixe* with arrays and data-structures. Of itself such a development would have been essentially neutral. But at the same time - the late fifties and sixties - language learning and applied linguistics were moving energetically away from these traditional models in the direction of communicative-functional approaches to language learning, where the forms of language were subordinated to their information-passing function in inter-personal situations. As a result, applied linguistic theory has tended to move further from CALL practice, since the communicative-functional approach requires sophisticated software with advanced abilities in handling open-ended input, parsing, and semantic judgements to relate language forms to messages and contexts. In addition, the logical structuring of such CALL materials presented what were at the time insuperable problems, since free-form interaction in a functional context is practically impossible to handle with conventional procedural programming techniques: if it is to be successful, it has to be driven by intelligent architectures working with goal-driven algorithms.

The advent of parsing engines of adequate power but more modest hardware requirements is likely to shrink the distance between contemporary applied linguistic theory and CALL, especially since there has been a move away from the more radical communicative-functional emphasis in the direction of methodology in language teaching [27]. This shift of emphasis sits well with attempts to expand the range of traditional CALL into more powerful modes of interaction with the learner. Many intelligent tutoring systems over the past decade have used more advanced software architectures, where intelligence has been defined in terms of all-or-nothing properties of the system as a whole. If it did not have a syntactic parser to handle input, or if it did not have an inference engine to handle decisions and deductions from the domain data-base, the system was not intelligent. These restrictions have placed strong restraints on the application of advances in intelligent tutoring systems to CALL, where much of the non-formal language domain has not lent itself easily to formalizing in terms of data-structures or knowledge-bases. It is difficult, for instance, to build intelligent data-structures for interactional language use, even in the terms of a model like Halliday's Systemic Grammar, used by Winograd for Shrdlu [38] and widely regarded as one of the few models which allows the transfer of formal language structures to non-formal language use in communicating and social contexts.

These factors, combined with a shortage of quality courseware in the CALL area, have contributed to delaying the introduction of intelligent tutoring into the CALL area. There have been some happy exceptions to this generalization. Some delicate language-based software [9, 12] has provided a proof-of-concept that intelligent CALL is possible in structured language domains [25, 26, 29, 30, 32, 36]. But in general, the attempt to build broadly based intelligent systems for language learning has been hampered by the very complex nature of the domain itself, and the problems of modelling learning and learners' approaches to learning in this area. A particular area of neglect has been the concept and implementation of HELP, whether conventional or intelligent. There have also been rather few attempts at modelling the cognitive processes and heuristics of second language learners using CALL or other learning materials. And we know of no attempts explore the cognitive issues of intelligent HELP systems in second language lexical learning. All these factors have tended to isolate CALL from studies of cognition and learning in the Computer-Aided Learning and Intelligent Computer-Aided Learning area, and to leave a great deal of CALL a long way behind some of the research and development in computer-aided learning in other domains.

2.1 The tools metaphor

The approach which we have adopted to solve this problem for CALL system building involves the tools metaphor [7, 10]. Rather than providing an intelligent shell to manage the learner's progress, we are seeking to supply a scalably intelligent learning environment. In the context of Intelligent HELP for language learning, this means a basic desk-top with reading and writing applications (and in some implementations, hearing and speaking applications where appropriate audio equipment is installed); monolingual and bilingual dictionaries, especially those like WordNet with a structured knowledge base [15-16, 22]; grammar reference sources; and text corpora which can be searched with keyword-in-context and concordancing software. The learner is effectively free to explore the domain, moving from explicit local tasks to discussions of the tasks, and the wider links of the tasks with other kinds of knowledge [5-6]. Much of the initiative and control for the direction, speed and navigation of the learning rests with the learner, and the role of the system is more to watch, guide and offer help, rather than to retain a close and formal control over the interactions.

These resources and tools are principally passive – sources of information which the student explores, following an agenda determined by the current learning task. The intelligence of such environments lies in the guidance mechanisms which advise the student's explorations. But this microworld is not entirely like those of Papert [23] or Lawler [19], since there is a variable dimension of interaction between the student's current activities and the environment, in the form of active grammar checkers like LINGER [40]. Such systems provide the student with a powerful means of validating orthographic, morphological and syntactic aspects of the language they are working with. They also constitute not only a bridge between the more passive nature of the static environment, and the more active nature of parsing engines; but also a moving window of expertise, since the growing sophistication of LINGER-like systems allows the incremental addition of more intelligence to the environment. This architecture represents a combination of the microworld and intelligent tutoring systems, resembling the proposals of Feuerzeig [11] for a dual-purpose (active/passive) LOGO microworld for learning mathematics. It also echoes the more language-oriented proposals put forward by Lawler [20].

2.2 Task level and discussion level

We have presented the basic architecture of this component elsewhere [33]. The idea was originally proposed by Cumming & Self [30], and involves the separation of the task level, which is the level at which the learner undertakes specific learning interactions, from the discussion level, the level where more abstract, treatment of the learning problem takes place. For instance, a student working on a comprehension exercise may have missed one or more of a sequence of cues in the development of the text on which the questions are based. The task level involves the identification of the textual material relating to the question, and the analysis of the problem on the basis of information available to the learner. The discussion level could concern heuristics (for instance, how to go about recovering information from an imperfectly understood text), strategies in answering comprehension questions (how much information to include, how to direct relevant information to the specific question at hand), and questions of textual coherence and sequence of arguments.

In terms of traditional CALL the discussion level can be seen as a HELP facility (Figure 1). The student is able to access HELP for each question, either a specific HELP message ("help #1") or a general HELP message and information. After using the HELP facility to locate the required information, the student returns to the task level and completes the current task. HELP can be invoked by the student, or can be invoked by the system as a result of an analysis of the student's inputs and behaviour, resulting in a diagnosis of "thrashing" or impasse [34]. It is normally the student who decides when to return to the task level to complete the current task.

HELP is not always implemented as a separate level. Some HELP messages fit neatly into question/answer interactions as hints and expansions of the current task. More general and background HELP, however, is usually handled as a separate module, with different traffic handlers managing the transitions between the task and the HELP. Such an arrangement is suitable for background reference information like lists of vocabulary, grammatical rules and examples, and examples of problems similar to the task currently in progress.

The division between the task and discussion levels is partly an empirical issue, and partly a theoretical one. The empirical aspect concerns the comprehension of the question or learning task, the analysis of the information and rules relevant to its solution, and the steps required to reach a satisfactory response. The theoretical aspect has been less studied, but includes the question of the division of information between the task and the discussion levels, and in particular the information which is needed for the student to invoke HELP, or for the system to invoke HELP; and the nature and volume of information which is relevant to effective operation at the HELP level, and for the system to know when to transfer the learner back to the task level, or to know when to allow the learner to opt to return to the task level.

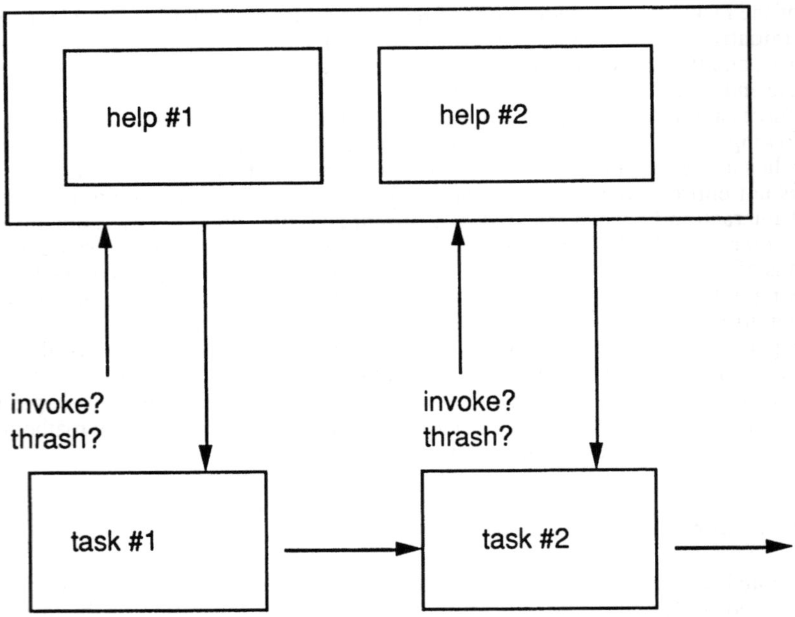

Figure 1. Traditional HELP

3. Invoking HELP

The model which we are using to drive the investigation of this question is the human instructor in the classroom, or perhaps looking over the shoulder of the learner, either in an electronic classroom or metaphorically looking over the student's shoulder by means of a network connection. Investigations of CALL systems to date have dealt extensively with the learner and student modelling, and with system architectures and software design. They have not devoted a lot of time to modelling the actions of the human instructor, nor to emulating the performance of the human instructor in either question/answer interactions, or more discovery-driven learning. This aspect of language learning, and instructor-learner interaction, presents a great deal of interest for modelling learning processes.

HELP is traditionally invoked in two principal ways: by the student, and by system intervention when it is determined that the learner is thrashing (a piscatorial metaphor) at an impasse. *Student invocation* of HELP is usually handled by function keys or mouse events, and presents no particular ergonomic problems, though the kind of HELP offered, and the learner's navigation through the HELP material, raises issues which we discuss below ("Providing HELP"). It is often motivated by the student's perception of impasse, and often occurs at a very specific juncture in the process of solving a task. On the other hand, students also want from time to time to stand back from a current series of learning events, and to consider wider issues, other approaches, the formation of tentative generalizations, the creation of links between current and previous knowledge, and so on. Such instances involve student reactions like

> Hey, I think this has something to do with the problems we were dealing with last week. Is it true that this problem is showing us a new way of using the patterns we learnt before? I'd like to look at those again ...

"HELP" is the wrong name for this kind of intervention in a learning sequence; "DISCUSS?" is a more appropriate prompt, and we are working on the description, taxonomy and modelling of the kinds of cognitive events and structures which are represented by this type of interaction between the instructor and the learner.

Instructor invoked HELP, in distinction to student invoked HELP, is either an imperative intervention ("Stop! You've got confused. Here is what you need to know ...") or a proffered intervention ("I think you're going round in circles. Do you want a hint now, or would you prefer to try to solve it on your own?"); the learner can either accept or decline the offer. In either instance the instructor has often what is effectively total knowledge of the task in hand. However, this not always the case. The human instructor, whether present in the classroom or monitoring learners' actions over a network, may have a fuller but not necessarily encyclopaedic knowledge of the domain being learned. And depending on the nature of the learning task, the number of learners in the group, and the number and nature of interactions with each learner, the instructor will have a more or less full knowledge of the progress of each learner, and an impression of the progress of the group. The reasons which will move the instructor to intervene in the learning activities will be varied. He/she may need to intervene, in the manner of traditional HELP facilities, to rescue the student from impasse or to provide hints and directions. HELP interventions of this kind will be prompted by familiar patterns of student interactions, and often take a fairly specific approach to correcting the current difficulty. But there are also HELP interventions which are less directly prompted by local impasse, for instance if the instructor feels that the group as a whole is having trouble with attacking a problem, or that the group is now past a specific learning area and needs guidance to determine and attack the next goal, and so on. And there are classes of HELP interventions which have to do with exploratory knowledge acquisition, where the instructor is concerned with guiding the formation and testing of learners' heuristics and hypotheses.

In conventional CALL materials, learners who invoke HELP often want specific, task-related information, the minimum which will enable them to solve the current problem. If anything, this is even more true of instructor/system driven HELP interventions, where the task error is detected by pattern-matching routines, and the required information is provided in the form of prompts, hints and missing information, often accompanied by scoring penalties. The effectiveness of these HELP approaches is an empirical matter, and one not entirely without interest. But the issues which concern us more are the discussion level HELP facilities, and the kinds of information and conceptual structures which they support and encourage.

3.1 Providing intelligent HELP

Local, task-based HELP, whether invoked by the student or the instructor, has a great deal to do with impasse or thrashing. There is already a considerable literature on impasse in learning, how to define it, and what kinds of action to take as a result. One approach to this question in language learning involves "repair theory" [1, 13]; for an ITS-oriented concept of "repair" see [3-4, 31, 35]. The parameters of repair are determined fairly tightly by the current learning problem, and involve an attempt by the student to use his/her current resources, which either are insufficient to solve the problem or have been misapplied to the problem, to find another way around it. It is possible to formalize such learning problems in terms of goals and resources, perhaps as a Goal-Task Hierarchy with multiple solution paths [28]. Typical examples involve the learner embarking on a structure without full control of the grammatical or lexical demands which are about to be made:

> I think that next we have to ... um ... [cannot remember "avoid"] ... find another way to solve this problem [lexical repair]

> I think that we will have to get this difficulty over ... um ... [problems with word order and separable verbal particles] ... have to get over this difficulty

Repair is one way in which a learner can negotiate a learning problem. It is not inconsistent with local help, which involving specific guidance on aspects of a task-level problem, which can be supplied by specific advice ("You have forgotten that this verb has an irregular past tense: shot"); by providing reference sources like lists of words, constructions, formulae and examples, which the student browses through in search of relevant information; by a diagnostic dialogue; and so on. But repair has the great merit of the student seeking to implement and adapt existing knowledge to solving the task. It is a part-step towards the discussion level HELP, which in this case could involve tools and advice on the browsing process, or would constitute a part of the diagnostic dialogue and the heuristics, strategies, rules and analysis of the problem which the student is trying to formulate. Modelling and encouraging repair strategies are particularly relevant to language learning, since they occur so often in everyday linguistic interactions, and they represent a relatively tractable, and communicatively rich, means of implementing a discussion-level HELP. It also represents a bridge between formal language learning and communicative-functional language learning.

Less local, task-driven HELP, in contrast, is much more discussion-level in nature. It involves a large set of possible avenues of exploration and advice (Figure 2). This architecture presents many opportunities for exploiting current research into hypermedia and multimedia. It also allows us to concentrate on the analysis and modelling of instructor-learner interactions, and on HELP-driven interventions, focusing on the students' ability to formulate hypotheses and search strategies and heuristics through grammatical and lexical materials, both in the classroom and on some prototype tools; and on the nature, timing and extent of instructor interventions in language learning tasks.

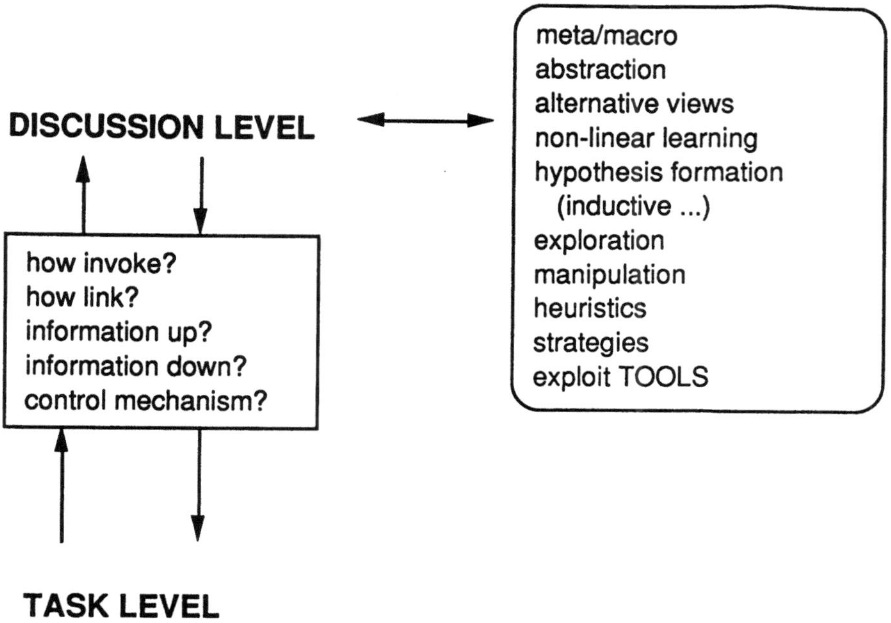

Figure 2. Implementing Discussion-Level HELP

There are certain aspects of second language lexical learning tasks which provide a particularly convenient means of access to the kinds of questions we are asking about the nature of HELP systems and their implementation in the context of this architecture. We have already discussed the potential of Repair, which has a number of attractive procedural and heuristic aspects, since the student is able to recover from impasse in a restricted, and therefore controllable, context. A second domain which is relatively tractable for the purposes of investigating discussion-level help in language learning is structural semantics. Lyons [21] has already established major taxonomies of lexis, and ways of relating lexical items in systematic structures. Many of these lend themselves to computational implementation, whether in semantic nets, matrices, trees or other formalisms.

We are particularly interested in the ways second language learners access their lexis: through cues in the first language, or in the second language? Through phonological or semantic (or other) triggers? How do they establish heuristics of search, in both study tools like dictionaries and in reference works, and how to they apply these heuristics to mental search? For instance, what are the best strategies when a learner is faced with a lexical gap, where the target language offers no ready translation equivalent, or when the target language offers multiple solutions to a search for a single lexical translation equivalent? How can learners effectively check for the presence of a possible *faux ami,* the case where a word misleadingly appears familiar (e.g., French *fameux* 'notorious', Polish *karawan* 'hearse')? What strategies will locate a possible idiom, and what kinds of strategies will then deliver a viable translation equivalent?

Training students in these strategies is not something which is normally part of second language teaching. But developing these skills is something which second language learners badly need. And the kinds of strategies which can be applied to their learning fit well with the model of task<->discussion level dichotomy which we are proposing as the architecture for an intelligent help system. To begin with, when lexical search breaks down learners exhibit impasse phenomena which can often be modelled explicitly in terms of semantic targets and failed goals. It is possible to determine, either by the learner's interactions or through diagnostic dialogue, just where the search has fallen over. The help which then intervenes can be structured in a number of ways which can reflect either the fine-grained nature of the task level, or, to varying degrees, more abstract and other-viewpoint aspects of the discussion level. For instance, students who fail to find an unambiguous lexical equivalent in the target language can be encouraged to try to find an equivalent for a synonym in the source language:

	Source language	Target language
Step 1:	'sophisticated'	Russian: izjaščnyj, izyskannyj ...
Step 2:	'recherché'	Russian: izyskannyj

Alternatively, learners who are confused by situations where a word translates as two words in the target language can be reminded of other kinds of grammatical combinations for this phenomenon:

	Source language	Target language
Step 1:	'(to) clap'	Russian: bit' v ladoši (lit. "beat on the palms")
Step 2:	'desk'	Russian: pis'mennyj stol (lit. "writing table")

The nature of discussion level treatments of translation equivalence, indeed, serves to show an interesting property of the task<->discussion distinction: it is not always easy to determine whether a given HELP intervention is operating at the task level or the discussion level. The semantic/grammatical metalanguage which we find at the discussion level can be implemented in a more data-driven way at the task level, sometimes with equally effective results, at least in terms of the solution of the present task problem. It is both a theoretical and an empirical question whether the task<->discussion distinction turns out to be a matter of gradients, or whether they have characteristics which serve to draw a clear line between them.

The more lexical decision problems can be described and modelled in terms of structural semantics, the easier it is to build a semantic net or other intelligent data-system/inference engine to drive the HELP system. With context-sensitive issues, however, the question of lexical decision becomes much more complicated, and the HELP system will have more difficulty in determining the factors affecting lexical choice in the individual case. However, even here a significant number of factors can be handled in terms of diagnostic dialogue with the learner. In a sentence like "the wind was from the north, and so warm that John took off his coat" will make different sense depending on whether the action is in the northern or southern hemisphere, and how close to the equator John happens to be. The general emphasis of the task<->discussion level approach is to put the burden of intelligence and initiative more on the learner. The learner should be able to work out, for instance, that the north wind in the northern hemisphere is not usually warm, except close to the equator.

Ultimately the intelligent HELP ("IHELP") architecture will meet up with psychological-cognitive research on the human management of the lexicon. There is, of course, a good volume of research already completed or under way on aspects of first language lexical storage and retrieval, and to some extent on related issues in the much smaller volume of work on second language lexical storage and retrieval. In the longer term the findings on second language lexical search in intelligent help systems will join with the computationally tractable aspects of this work on cognitive psychology and cognitive linguistics. Our immediate goal, however, is to plot what second language learners currently do in lexical search and retrieval in reference works, to derive a pattern of strategies from these searches, and then to incorporate this knowledge into an intelligent help system which will encourage the learners to explore, experiment [39], try out hypotheses, practice, discuss, and eventually to solve problems of lexical equivalence, access, storage and reinforcement in second language learning.

4. Intelligence in the intelligent HELP system

What makes such a system intelligent, and how can this intelligence be modelled and developed? In particular, what issues of software engineering are relevant to the construction of a system of this kind, and what lessons are there from this process for the generation of generic intelligent CALL courseware?

A central role of the IHELP system is to monitor the learner's actions, and to provide input and guidance, as well as dialogue and resources, and hints on their efficient exploitation, when the learner needs it. Navigation hints and guidance are a major task when the learner is searching data-bases and reference tools. The formation of viable heuristics, and the exploration of strategies, together with comments on their likely and actual effectiveness for each specific case, are important features for IHELP. The discussion level provides a means for other-angle approaches to problems, and the system does not need an encyclopaedic knowledge of the task level event and the student's learning history to make an appropriate intervention.

A further attractive aspect of the IHELP approach is that it provides a handle on one area of the mapping and modelling of the learner's knowledge in terms of command of the domain, and in terms of mastery of the skills needed to search data-bases and reference tools, and to exploit them for specific language learning purposes. IHELP does not, in our understanding, aim for the kind of exhaustive modelling which is possible in highly structure Intelligent Tutoring systems. There have been some important recent advances in student modelling [22-23], but this area remains a difficult one. IHELP offers opportunities for tackling the modelling of student knowledge, specifically procedural knowledge and search strategies, using independently validated taxonomies and rules of structural semantics and related semantic systems. IHELP's goal is to help learners to learn, and to focus on features like the conceptual navigation between knowledge and metaknowledge.

A key underlying issue of intelligence in IHELP, however, is to determine what kinds of information are required for the effective invocation of HELP, how little information the task level needs from the discussion level in order to function, and what information states and criteria are to be met for the learner to return from the discussion level to the task level. One aspect of this problem depends on system architecture; the other, however, is accessible through empirical observation of practising language teachers, and from the protocols of students engaged in task analysis and repair.

4.1 Implementing the HELP system

We have built prototypes of part of IHELP in Hypercard and Authorware. The goal of this implementation was to test some of the design, architecture, and navigation concepts which IHELP raises, and to determine the parameters for the implementation of the major components of the system.

This prototype has been encouraging in its tolerance of incremental development. As we remarked above, one of the more serious problems with intelligent tutoring systems is the necessity to construct elaborate support structures, data-structures and rule systems for the system to function at all. The IHELP approach, on the other hand, permits a gradualist, scalable approach to implementing both intelligent HELP, and the incorporation of discussion level interventions. If this indication is substantiated by further practice, we shall be able to pursue in more detail the gradual transfer of initiative and intelligence from the learner to the system, and to examine the balances between task and discussion level support which turn out to be appropriate and effective for different learners.

5. Conclusion: aspects of learning in non-proximate systems

There is a widespread development under way in Europe, North America and Australasia towards distance education. This will be particularly important in the European Economic Community where, after 1992, the learning of foreign languages will be significantly expanded. Since there is no obvious source of teachers to fill this sudden need, distance education will have to play a major role in supporting language learning. The IHELP model presents one of the kind of scalably intelligent tools which would be able to support this kind of development in language learning.

It is also safe to predict that there will be a major increase in open-access learning. There is a distinction to be drawn between open-access learning, which is characterized by non-timetabled access, and distance learning, which is specifically at a physical distance, with or without the presence of the instructor on telephone or other communication systems. Intelligent language learning support systems like IHELP have the potential to make a notable contribution to this area as well.

The problem is that the time lines are tight. There is a very large demand for superior CALL courseware in many parts of the globe, particularly in Asian and strategic-European languages (French, German, Spanish, Russian). Intelligent tutoring systems, particularly those with advanced tutoring capacities, require extensive development time. On the other hand, intelligent components of such systems, like grammar checkers, provide significant extensions to the microworld+tools concept. It is for this reason that we believe that intelligent learning tool systems, with more exploratory learning and supported discussion, but also with hybrid combinations of intelligent language-validation tools, will provide a viable component among the many which will be needed to support language learning, and research into language learning.

References

1. Bialystok, E. & Fröhlich, M.: Oral communication strategies for lexical difficulties. The Interlanguage Studies Bulletin, 5, 1, 3-30 1980
2. Breuker, J.A., Winkels, R.G.F. & Sandberg, J.A.C.: Didactic goal generator. University of Amsterdam, ESPRIT 280 Eurohelp Report 07 1986
3. Brown, J.S. & Burton, R.B.: Diagnostic models for procedural bugs in basic mathematical skills. Cognitive Science 2, 155-192 1978
4. Brown, J.S. & van Lehn, K.: Repair theory: a generative theory of bugs in procedural skills. Cognitive Science 4, 379-426 1980
5. Chanier, T., Dillenbourg, P., Hartley, R., Hintze, D., Nichols, D., Pengelly, M., Self, J. & Twidale, M.: A prototype for the acquisition of rule-based student models. University of Lancaster: Computing Department, AI Report #40 1990
6. Chanier, T., Pengelly, M., Self, J. & Twidale, M.: Conceptual modelling in error analysis in computer assisted language learning systems (this volume)
7. Collins, A. & Brown, J. S.: The computer as a tool for learning through reflection. In: Learning issues for intelligent tutoring systems (Heinz Mandl & Alan Lesgold, eds). pp. 1-18. New York: Springer-Verlag 1988
8. Cumming, G. & Self, J.: Intelligent educational systems: identifying and decoupling the conversational levels. Instructional Science 19, 11-27 1990
9. Emirkanian, L. & Bouchard, L. H.: Towards a knowledge-based tool for correcting French text. In: Computers in education (F. Lovis & E.D. Tagg, eds), pp. 583-588. Amsterdam: North-Holland Elsevier Science Publishers 1988
10. Ercoli, P. & Lewis, R. (eds). Artificial Intelligence tools in education. Amsterdam: North-Holland 1988.
11. Feuerzeig, W.: Algebra slaves and agents in a Log-based mathematics curriculum. In: Artificial intelligence and education. Volume 1: learning environments and tutoring systems (Robert W. Lawler & Masoud Yazdani, eds), pp. 27-54. Norwood, N.J.: Ablex Publishing 1988
12. Fum, D., Pani, B. & Tasso, C.: Naive vs. formal grammars: a case for integration in the design of a foreign language tutor (this volume)
13. Færch, C. & Kasper, G.: Process and strategies in foreign language learning and communication. The Interlanguage Studies Bulletin 5, 1, 47-118 1980
14. Girle, R. A.: Report of the first Round Table Conference. Australian Educational Expert Systems Project. Brisbane, University of Queensland, Project EXCALIBUR Publications 1986
15. Handke, J.: Natürliche Sprache. Theorie und Implementierung in LISP. Hamburg: McGraw-Hill 1989.
16. Handke, J.: A multiple-purpose AI system based on AI-techniques (this volume)
17. Hartley, J.R. & Smith, M.J.: Question answering and explanation giving in on-line help systems. In: Artificial Intelligence and human learning. Intelligent Computer-Aided Instruction (John Self, ed.), pp. 338-360. London & New York: Chapman & Hall 1988
18. Hartley, J.R. & R.M. Pilkington: Software tools for supporting learning: intelligent on-line help systems. In: Artificial Intelligence tools in education (P. Ercoli & R. Lewis, eds), pp. 39-66. Amsterdam: North-Holland 1988
19. Lawler, R.: Computer experience and cognitive development. New York: John Wiley, Inc. 1985

20. Lawler, R. P.: Learning environments: now, then, and someday. In: Artificial intelligence and education. Volume 1: learning environments and tutoring systems (Robert W. Lawler & Masoud Yazdani, eds), pp. 1-25. Norwood, N.J.: Ablex Publishing 1988
21. Lyons, J.: Semantics. Cambridge: Cambridge University Press 1977
22. Miller, G. A. & Fellbaum, C.: WordNet and the organization of lexical memory (this volume)
23. Papert, S.: Mindstorms: children, computers and powerful ideas. New York: Basic Books 1980.
24. Pilkington, R., Hartley, R. & Tattersall, C.: Instructional design management. University of Leeds, CEC ESPRIT p-280 Eurohelp 1988
25. Polson, M. C. & Richardson, J. J.: Foundations of intelligent tutoring systems. Hillsdale, New Jersey: Erlbaum 1988
26. Psotka, J., Massey, L. D. & Mutter, S. A.: Intelligent tutoring systems. Lessons learned. Hillsdale, NJ: Erlbaum 1988
27. Quinn, T.J.: Functional approaches in language pedagogy. In: Annual review of applied linguistics 5 (Robert B. Kaplan et al., eds), pp. 60-80. Cambridge: Cambridge University Press 1984
28. Richards, T., Webb, G. & Craske, N.: Object oriented control for computer-assisted learning systems. In: Artificial Intelligence tools in education (P. Ercoli & R. Lewis, eds), pp. 203-219. Amsterdam: North-Holland 1988
29. Self, J.: Artificial Intelligence and human learning. Intelligent Computer-Aided Instruction. London & New York: Chapman & Hall 1988
30. Sleeman, D. & Brown J.S.: Intelligent tutoring systems. New York, Academic Press 1982
31. Sleeman, D.H. & Smith, M.J.: Modelling students' problem solving. Artificial Intelligence 16, 171-187 1981
32. Sussex, R.: Issues in Computer-Aided Language Learning: towards an expert-systems learning environment. In: Language, learning and community. Festschrift in honour of Terry Quinn (C.N. Candlin and T. McNamara, eds), pp. 91-104. Macquarie University, Sydney: National Centre for English Language Teaching and Research 1989
33. Sussex, R.D. & Cumming, G.D. : Intelligent tools and lexical support for the language learner: providing advice at task and discussion levels. Paper presented at the World Conference on Computers in Education, Sydney, August 1990. In: Computers in Education (A. McDougall & C. Dowling, eds), pp. 459-464. North-Holland: Elsevier Science Publishers B.V. 1990
34. van Lehn, K.: Toward a theory of impasse-driven learning. In Learning issues for intelligent tutoring systems (Heinz Mandl & Alan Lesgold, eds): pp. 19-41. New York: Springer-Verlag 1988
35. van Lehn, K.: On the representation of procedures in repair theory. In: The development of mathematical thinking (H.P. Ginsburg, ed.), pp. 197-252. New York: Academic Press 1983.
36. Weischedel, R. M., Voge, W. M. & James, M.: An Artificial Intelligence approach to language instruction. Artificial Intelligence 10, 225-240 1978
37. Wenger, E.: Artificial intelligence and tutoring systems: computational and cognitive approaches to the communication of knowledge. Los Altos, CA.: Morgan Kaufmann Publishers 1987
38. Winograd, T.: Language as a cognitive process. Reading, MA: Addison-Wesley 1983
39. Legenhausen, L. & Wolff, D.: STORYBOARD and communicative language learning: results of the Düsseldorf CALL project (this volume)
40. Yazdani, M.: Steps towards an intelligent language tutoring shell (paper presented at the Workshop).

Section Five

Computer Systems and Evironments for Foreign Language Learning

In the previous sections of the book we have been shown the importance of knowledge acquisition research to uncover prototypic errors, the diversity of different formalisms for representing linguistic knowledge in different knowledge bases in the the expert and learner models, how parsing language learners' interlingua is a unique NLP problem in FL ITS, and how important language teaching principles and innovative learning environments are for the tutoring knowledge in a FL ITS. This section presents a suite of papers that describe working prototypes of language tutoring systems. None of these systems are true FL ITS, but they do demonstrate the potential for working systems, and they incorporate many AI technologies not available in traditional CALL. After we review the current state of the art, we close the book with an encouraging view of the technology promise for the next generation FL ITS.

Chapter 16 opens this section's overview of prototype foreign language tutoring systems with a discussion of existing NLP techniques and tools which may serve the purpose of developing such environments. Ongoing research at the Computing Research Laboratory is exploring machine translation, robust parsing algorithms, and automatic dictionary extraction tools. These technologies should prove useful in developing FL ITS, but as the author warns, a "hodge podge" of advanced technologies does not by any means guarantee success. During our working group sessions, we explored this notion of combining each others' contributions (someone's parser with another's student modeler with yet another's tutoring technique) into one system, but rejected the notion as untenable. Advanced technology tools may be helpful in developing ITS, but only with careful thought as to their use. The author of this chapter suggests how the tools listed above, with some work, could be used to develop an instructional aid for learners of Japanese who need to write business letters.

As a next step toward developing FL ITS, Chapter 17 discusses a research effort that is developing a computational strategy for sentence generation exercises in Turkish. In this paper, the author first describes the need to develop a generative grammar, and then gives an overview of Turkish linguistics to illustrate the detail required in the grammar. We are introduced to a meaning frame used by the grammar knowledge base to represent features in the grammar and which can be used by learners to construct sentences. While this system is only a first step toward a FL ITS implementation, it demonstrates how AI techniques can be used for translating sentences as well as useable practice exercises for a less commonly taught language.

The author of Chapter 18 describes a general instructional system that uses AI techniques to provide some 'intelligence' in the system. While this system is not an ITS (it has no formal student model or tutor model), it does represent an effort to perform effective natural language analysis. Although no principled instructional approach is followed, WIZDOM does provide a wide range of exercises and games for the learner. And the system runs in a DOS environment. The author discusses how the natural language analyzer handles degraded input, an important issue discussed elsewhere in this book.

The next working system described in Chapter 19 attempts to implement ITS-like techniques (learner-sensitive feedback, NLP, automated tutoring), but does not formally represent knowledge in the three essential ITS modules (expert, student, tutor). Nevertheless, this German tutoring system provides contextual instruction and good use of

NATO ASI Series, Vol. F 80
Intelligent Tutoring Systems for Foreign Language Learning
Edited by M. L. Swartz and M. Yazdani

In this book, we have looked at language learners, psycholinguistic and computational theories for FL ITS, and computational approaches for the implementation of linguistic and tutoring knowledge. We have said earlier that the promise of combining AI and NLP in one hybrid tutoring system was a realistic goal. Now, after reviewing the current state of the art, we close this book with an enthusiastic view of the future of FL ITS. Chapter 20 reviews all of the technologies and tools currently employed to develop FL ITS: robust parsers, natural language analysis techniques, semantic networks, and hypermedia. As these technology advances show, the reality of a working ITS in language domains seems imminent. However, those of us active in the field also realize that many hard problems still exist and much continued research is needed. Nevertheless, we persevere, and encourage others in the FL ITS community to join us in this endeavor.

Building an Intelligent Second Language Tutoring System from Whatever Bits you Happen to Have Lying Around

Yorick Wilks and David Farwell
Computing Research Laboratory, NMSU, Las Cruces, NM 88003.

Abstract: The Computing Research Laboratory (CRL) at New Mexico State University is currently engaged in the design of language teaching software, based on previously developed mature artificial intelligence and machine translation technologies within CRL. Our approach is unique because it uses the robustness of a natural language processing (NLP) system which incorporates both general world knowledge and task domain knowledge (Metallel), beliefs ascription (ViewGen), and semantic parsing techniques (PREMO) in the service of better student-system interaction.

Broadly stated, the central theoretical goal of our project is to investigate the uses of participant modeling through belief ascription in the development of an intelligent tutoring system (ITS) for second language learning, not only for the purpose of improved student-system interactions, but for the purpose of monitoring student performance and planning corrective intervention. We aim to produce a sophisticated, flexible, NLP-based tutoring system that will, on the one hand, help students acquire and maintain second language skills and, on the other, function as a workstation for investigating issues in second language acquisition and pedagogy.

Keywords: Intelligent Tutoring System, Belief Systems, Machine Translation

1. Introduction

A rational way to begin research and development into such an ITS would be to start from first principles. The problem, then, lies in deciding which theories of language and pedagogy may prove useful to us. We shall begin with a brief survey of NLP techniques/theories that form the foundation of our system.

The following NLP technologies have been tested for a possible role in ITS. These specific NLP modules and techniques were all developed at CRL:

1) a machine translation (MT) system, ULTRA [6] a modular, five-language, interlingual MT system successfully working with vocabularies of approximately 10,000 words per language.

2) robust parsing techniques which use semantic structures and notions such as "preference" for extracting the most plausible interpretation from well or ill-formed linguistic utterances: the PREMO [2] and OSCON systems [8].

NATO ASI Series, Vol. F 80
Intelligent Tutoring Systems for Foreign Language Learning
Edited by M. L. Swartz and M. Yazdani

3) procedures for manipulating and generalizing large machine lexicons of the kind that will be needed for an adequate ITS package [29]: using technologies for extracting both symbolic frame-like structures and weighted network clusterings of word sense associations from learners' dictionaries like LDOCE and Cobuild.

4) an approach to belief modeling, based on the ViewGen System [2]: a default-based system for constructing plausible belief-set models of and about agents, to any level of nesting (of beliefs about beliefs) required by some given situation.

5) an approach to the pragmatics of cultural difference in solving the problem of translating documents (such as a business letter) from one language/culture to another (English or Spanish to Japanese, for instance), [4].

It is important to notice that, although they are all tools, these programs also imply AI theories of language and communication. In other words, although they have performance capabilities, they are more than mere peripherals, displays, windows and interfaces (the specifics of which will be discussed later). Understanding the underlying theory of these programs is crucial.

2. NLP Tools for ITS

We are adopting a language teaching approach that assumes three commonly hypothesized levels of analysis, apart from simple grammatical knowledge: notional [25], functional [9] and situational [24]. The notional aspect of communicative competence is essentially semantic, i.e. a description of the speaker's intended message. It includes references to such notions as frequency of occurrence, motion, location, and so on, and is relevant to MT. The functional level concerns the speaker's goals, describing a situation, requesting information, agreeing with so-and-so's viewpoint, disagreeing, and so on, and is relevant to beliefs modeling. The situational aspect concerns the world context surrounding the communication, i.e. when the event concerns a business interaction, a travel interaction, a shopping interaction, etc., and is relevant to intercultural translations. We expect that all three must be taken into account in the construction of our ITS.

The following is a discussion of the theoretical and practical relevance of each of the five NLP modules mentioned above to ITS, in turn:

I) Translation: Since the object in learning a second language is not to translate back into one's first language, but learn to understand and generate wholly within the new language, and thereby achieve fluency (as one did in the learning of one's original language), we believe the development of a language-independent system for representing linguistic utterances would be central to an ITS.

The case for the relevance of MT is twofold: firstly, multilingual NLP is already available to us. Secondly, that form of MT makes the assumption that there is some underlying universal element in translation which makes the process possible by human or machine: virtually all theories of second language learning make this assumption, and this has also been the focus of CRL's multilingual ULTRA MT project [6], [28].

It follows that although to learn a second language is not necessarily to translate, the processes of second language learning and translation are parallel: we assume there to be a common world (physical or conceptual) that provides a crosslingual, or interlingual element in both situations. In our own MT work, this hypothetical interlingual element is made explicit; in the ULTRA program, all translations pass through a common linguistic representation which is independent of both the source and target languages. In ViewGen, we assume a common world of beliefs which are also independent of language (see below).

II) Robust parsing: robust processing has been a focus of virtually all of the NLP projects at CRL. At the core of this effort is Preference Semantics [26], [27], an approach to natural language understanding that is based on the notion that language should be understood as a maximally coherent structure (in a defined sense), independent of syntax. The basic unit of analysis is therefore the utterance, rather than its syntactic counterpart, whether that be that a word, a phrase, a sentence or some larger textual unit. The framework for analysis is built upon both semantic/notional categories and structures, and discourse pragmatic/functional categories and structures.

A variety of parsers and generators have been developed within the preference semantics (PS) approach. They include the Semantic Definite Clause Grammars of English for the XTRA English-Chinese machine translation system [10] and Meta5 system, an implementation base for Collative Semantics [7]. Programs for parsing sentences when the input is ill-formed have also been developed within the PREMO paradigm [21].

These systems, while observing language-specific syntactic constraints through the use of feature unification, completely integrate syntactic, semantic and pragmatic processing with the result that no syntactic level of representation can be identified. This is a crucial feature for ITS, we believe, because that field has been limited, until now, by the unavailability of a computational parser for the ill-formed sentences learners may produce. This gap has usually been filled by slot-filling techniques in most available language teaching software (cf. critiques in [5, 22].

By using semantic parsing methods such as those embodied in PREMO, which are relatively insensitive to grammatical error in the source text, a pedagogical technique can be developed. Such a facility would yield a meaning-based, rather than a grammar-based, analysis:

(a) It would employ such a facility only when the syntactic parser (such as the ULTRA parser, see above) fails, on he assumption that that indicates a grammatical error by the student.

(b) It would then pass the structure derived by the semantic parser through a generator for the second language and print it, with some such rubric as:

You should write (Corrected Second Language Sentence)

(c) and would perhaps pass the same representation through the MT system and generate a correct version in the student's native language adding:

On the assumption that you mean (First Language Sentence).

III) Automated Dictionary Extraction: we are investigating, in particular, the use of dictionary-derived semantic networks and clusterings as possible aids to the student in vocabulary acquisition. We believe that the results of such empirical methods may prove superior to handcrafted lexicons on "psycholinguistic principles" such as WordNet [15].

For several years, CRL has been engaged in an NSF-supported project to extract semantic information from dictionaries such as LDOCE on a large scale, in order to increase the size and performance of NLP projects. An assumption of that work is that both explicit-symbolic and implicit-statistical information can be extracted from dictionaries and corpora, and that both forms of information can strengthen one another.

More importantly for our purposes here, since such dictionaries were not intended for computational linguists, but learners of English, it seems natural that the contents of such a dictionary (in this case, one with a basic two-thousand word vocabulary) be made available to a student of English for consultation at a screen, as well as in a book.

In combining our ULTRA MT work with methods of extracting information from LDOCE that include parsing the dictionary itself, as well as resolving the definition words to their appropriate senses, we have gone one step further: using the basic senses of LDOCE as an interlingual prototype for MT. Moreover, this interlingual translation method does not compromise the linguistic and cultural diversity of possible languages in any way.

We would like to extend this method, and use it to compensate for the temporary lack of such dictionaries in other languages. We will do this by tuning English-derived sense entries against foreign language texts like Japanese in order to adjust the semantic entries to the actual syntagms encountered in the second language texts, as in the case of actual (as opposed to predicted) classes of entities that function as verb objects. A similar procedure for hand-coded lexical entries is described by [1].

Another closely related form of dictionary research at CRL complements this: a group of colleagues [20] has been empirically building networks of words and word senses from dictionaries, corpora, and closeness information about concepts derived from native speaker informants, using a weighted network construction technique called PATHFINDER.

These techniques are relevant to ITS because they explore a range of clustering algorithms in search of the best concept clusters, and are in no way English-based. They could demonstrate that colocar-poner-meter is a group of closely associated Spanish verbs, as easily as that partisan-terrorist-guerilla is a set of closely associated English nouns. The crucial feature of this method is its ability to show relatedness, presented in a simple network form which is immediately comprehensible to a student, as well as a structure derived from the second language sources. In contrast, systems like WordNet [15] provide only relatedness without contrast, and do so by extension from English rather than from the corpora of the language being taught.

IV) ViewGen [2] is a program based on a default algorithm for constructing "environments" that represent the beliefs of others, down to any level of recursive nesting (e.g. "John's view of Joe's view of ...", and so on). Of particular importance is the ability to ascribe beliefs through this system. By constructing a complex model of individual belief spaces, the system can identify and respond to the mistaken or differing beliefs of others. This allows the tutoring system to construct a representation of the student's views of the task being performed, the overall goal of the task, the roles of the student and tutor in performing the task and, above all, the task domain knowledge.

On the assumption that a "common world" of shared beliefs is necessary for understanding and communication, ViewGen would be an appropriate tool for modeling beliefs and goals predicted by the system about the student user, possibly including (one level lower) the system's beliefs about the student's beliefs about the system itself.

In the big picture, ViewGen assumes a common world of knowledge (e.g. physical and technical) which all educated adults share. In any practical context of language learning, as in AI, it is axiomatic that shared representations of knowledge of the world indeed exist between agents and learners, contrary to skeptical theoretical models of communication [23]. Indeed, we could not communicate at all if we did not unconsciously make very large numbers of assumptions about what other people believe about the world (such as "the sun rises in the east", etc.). And modeling these belief environments explicitly could also aid us in teaching a second language.

From this simple principle, considerable complexity follows when any kind of expertise is introduced, and we can no longer assume a common world of shared knowledge by default. If, for instance, the speaker is a doctor and the listener is not, no shared expertise can be assumed, nor can one assume on a more mundane level that one's self-knowledge is necessarily shared by others.

In a similar way, for any subject being taught, the expertise of the teacher cannot be assumed by default. Hence, in the case of language teaching, the expert (computer or human) can only assume the student has that knowledge for which it has evidence, either because its retention is confirmed by questions, or because it follows by generalization from what has already been taught.

All this suggests a fairly rigid separation of knowledge of language from knowledge of the world in the system's model of the student. But in fact, such separation is not necessary, since it remains only to determine which belief sets are marked as expertise to be "run" or evaluated by accredited individuals (which may eventually include the user himself). Indeed, the system may simultaneously be teaching non-linguistic material (such as Japanese social customs as regards the sending and receiving of letters) and linguistic material.

We now turn to our main topic: a passive and active pair of modules that will provide the core of our system.

3. The Importance of Stick Man and Woman: The Passive Component

Anyone who has seen ITS demonstrations has encountered a stick man and woman who perform various tasks to provide a visual aid to language learning. As part of the linguistic theory that underlies our ITS design, their importance is more than historical.

To go back in time, language theory was influenced by Wittgenstein's "Picture Theory of Truth" [30], a notion that contributed to a theory of situation semantics [3], both theories providing a notion of reference or meaning outside language. Another influential concept was that of languages as games, with different cultural standards of inference, proof, evidence, etc., games you had to know "from within" (like cricket) before you grasped their point. If that was the case, could you form a new game from a cross-section of words from a given language, as Ogden and Richards did by creating the notion of Basic English [16], a "mini-English" of a thousand words sufficient for all expression? And what of the visual equivalent of such a tool? One such tool was devised by Richards, who turned Wittgenstein's Picture Theory into a neat little volume called ``English Through Pictures" [17] that has stood the test of time, and has been a bestseller ever since. As many theorists prefer, with this method, one learns a new language without referring to one's native language. Here is the beginning of French Through Pictures [18]:

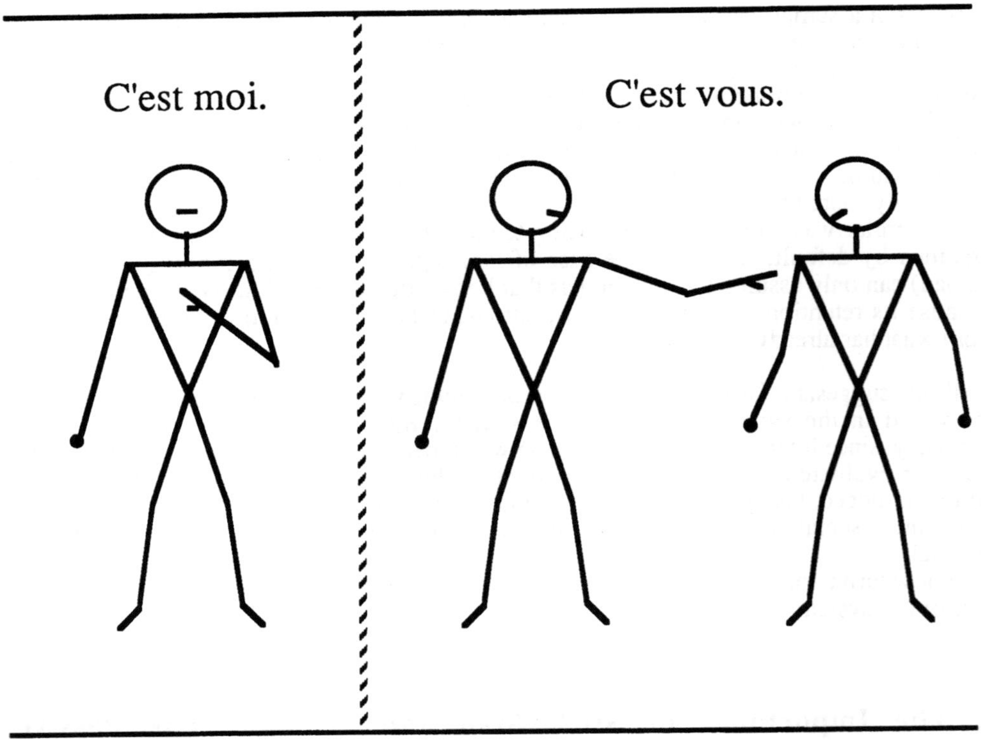

This is reminiscent of Wittgenstein's problem with the notion of a negative fact. Unlike most modern uses of stick people there is in fact a very complex structure underlying the sequence of pictures, based on binary contrasting of pairs. In the first pair above, the French sentences are apprehended as wholes, but the contrast is "moi" (me) versus "vous" (you), and so on for every pair. In a sophisticated philosophical analysis of this work Masterman [14] once argued (to an audience of astonished and largely uncomprehending philosophers) that there was a simple, primitive language of contrasts underlying the whole book, which formed a strictly hierarchical structure.

The purpose of this brief philosophical excursion is partly to remind readers where stick man and woman came from, and their long, honorable and lucrative role in second language teaching from what can seem a curiously modern set of assumptions about immersion in the second language. Their use was, for Richards, structured, not casual.

In a strange remark in the introduction to the French version, Richards complained about people all over the world who were stealing the book by pasting in strips of words from other language and creating a new version, and claimed, by contrast, that this French version was "by no means a mere translation of the English Pocket Book". I think he must have meant it was authentic, done with his blessing, because, what else could it be but a translation?

In some clear sense, the assumed universality and comprehensibility of the pictures across cultures, or at least close cultures, virtually defined a notion of translation: the stick pictures represent directly the meaning that the differing language strings have in common, and those strings could be said, by definition, to be translations of each other in virtue of that fact.

That does not require that every language book use the same pictures: only in the French version, for example, were there pictures of France. Indicating women by their skirts might have caused problems in Greece and Scotland. In fact there is good evidence [12] that schematic pictorial representation is no more truly universal than, say, onomatopoeia (and the notorious French "Patatras" for the sound all English speakers know to be "Crash"). It would be easy to construct deeper problems as to the universality of the pictures:

The dog is behind the tree.
Mbwa ni mbele ya mimi.

The dog is in front of me.
Mbwa ni mbele ya mimi.

Here we have two pictures that could be used to teach the two English sentences The dog is behind the tree (from the speaker, since he is speaking) and The dog is in front of me. If the contrast of me and dog had already been introduced, this pair could be used to introduce the contrast pair in-front-of/behind.

Interestingly, the pair could not be used in Swahili Through Pictures to make such a contrast, since "mbele ya" (roughly corresponding to "in front of," appropriately inflected for noun class) would occur in both, given conceptualization of position in that language from the front of the speaker forward and not interrupted by intervening objects.

What follows from this is not the radical (and possibly destructive) conclusion that the pictures are language dependent, in a way that Richards' universality implicitly assumed was not the case, but that the contrasts made by given pairs will be language dependent in a small number of cases. Indeed, it may be that no real assumption of universality of concepts/pictures is required to explain how the system works as well as it does, and that would certainly suit its Wittegensteinian roots better. All that may be required is some universality of contrast (such as the pairs give) and that there is some functionally constructible set of such contrasts sufficient to establish, monolingually, how a term is used.

Why bring back all this old stuff; surely computer-based ITS must have killed the sales of these books. Probably not, in fact. Certainly, one motive is to say that the stick people have a longer and more structured history than many realize. Another is to seriously propose such courses as Richards' as prime candidates for automation, as we are doing, minus certain conventions that the possibility of screen movement makes redundant, e.g. the ghost figures who have left the room. However, the system also supports conventions quite strong enough to support the introduction of notions like belief structure, so as to underpin communication.

Such courses as Richards' are, in our view, prime candidates for automation. Such a system could support the introduction of notions like belief structure, as in the following example:

In this illustration, the dialogue can only be understood if one assumes certain beliefs of the man, about what the woman is doing.

Such a course is universalist and translation-based, even though the student is wholly passive (he only has to answer questions and tests every few pages as to the status of the stick people's situation: "Who left the room?", "Where is the hat now?", etc.). Since our central assumptions about language learning are basically those of the Communicative Language Teaching approaches [19], [13], [11], in particular that learning and maintenance of second languages is best achieved through meaningful language use, unlike such one-sided approaches to teaching, we expect our ITS to support a full range of activities. They will include passive activities (such as responding to commands, identifying important people on the basis of descriptions, and picking out or drawing pictures on the basis of descriptions), restricted active exercises (such as responding to yes/no questions or WH-questions, filling out charts or forms, and using simple one word/phrasal descriptions or conversational formulae) and finally, fully active exercises (such as cooperative problem solving tasks, and role playing and open-ended discourse in which the learner is expected to contribute personal opinions, evaluations and information).

4. An Active Pragmatic Component for Writing

We propose to use an updated version of Richards' passive course, based on structured contrasts, and possibly allowing the student a translation as a last resort in a way the book could not. This aspect will be supplemented by a pragmatic and active program which will be based on an existing prototype at CRL, designed to teach writing in another language/culture, which uses stereotypes and templates to generate Japanese business letters for Americans who know no Japanese.

In its intended use as a letter generator, it teaches no Japanese whatever to the American, who would never see the final product. Instead, it displays a retranslation, through the ULTRA interlingual system (see above), turned back into English, possibly different from the original, but close enough. If it is deemed satisfactory, it can be mailed with confidence, even though the sender knows no Japanese at all! It is clear that the making explicit of such intermediate translation processes would be beneficial to any language tutoring system.

5. Implementation

How will our ITS be implemented, and what pedagogical techniques will it employ? Initially, we are developing materials for adult learners who obtain an introduction to the fundamentals of the second language through the stick pictures and then go on to the active pragmatic component. The initial implementation of the prototype will focus on teaching, maintaining or improving standard English or Spanish. It will do this through the explicit task medium of writing business letters over a range of topics or occasions. As in our Japanese language prototype, the central content of the exercises will include the norms of business politeness and interaction in the second language culture, as well as the relevant linguistic expertise.

Long-term planning of activities and their internal sequencing will be based on the system's model of the student's second language knowledge, the system's second language knowledge, and the system's view of "natural sequencing", vis a vis notional and functional contexts of the task at hand. While initially such orderings will be programmed automatically, the system will eventually be able to infer the optimal order on the basis of general pedagogical principles. Although our focus will be on reading and writing, we believe these methods will be equally applicable to listening and speaking, and eventually hope to integrate both areas of language pedagogy.

5.1 Interface

The primary functions of the interface will be to provide a rich learning environment for the student, and a sophisticated channel of communication between student and system. More specifically:

- the system will employ user-friendly authoring tools to develop CD-ROM audiovisual instructional materials, as well as to extend and modify both the second, and native language systems.

- the system will operate within a sophisticated, multi-media, hypermedia environment, and

- the linguistic and audio-visual channels of the interface will be optimally integrated.

The primary objective of adding graphics, sound, or video will be to create a fun, fanciful, and motivating learning environment. Thus far, we have developed a general interface prototype which allows us to gradually integrate multi-media techniques, and evaluate their utility in the context of actual student/instructor interactions. We have also explored the possible use of CD-ROM video display, sophisticated graphics, speech synthesis, speech analysis, the use of hypermedia techniques in learning activities, and the possibility of networking systems to allow for interaction with more than one student at a time.

5.2 Didactics

Given that the student and the tutorial system will be engaged in some sort of purposeful task, we believe the system should be careful when correcting the student, so as to be as unintrusive as possible. We feel that most correction should be masked in the form of clarifying and corrective dialog, such as "do you mean ...?", or, "don't you mean..?"; "in other words ..."; "for example ...", and so on. Another tactic would be explanatory dialog, such as "wouldn't it be better if ...?", or, "but if ... then..."; "since you think ..., then ...", etc. Such dialogue is a normal part of performing a cooperative task; to the student, it would appear to be no less than a natural response to an error from an agreeable partner.

6. Conclusion

A major benefit of such a pragmatic approach is its great capacity for adaptive, individualized instruction. Since the system will have broad conversational capabilities (over a number of limited task domains), and will be equipped with multilingual capabilities, its ability to communicate with the student will be quite rich. Furthermore, it will be able to perform a variety of tasks, which include monitoring the student's performance and modeling his second language knowledge, diagnosing errors in order to guide intervention, and tailoring instructional technique to the student's individual needs.

The strong foundation for our ITS in both natural language processing and pedagogical techniques, as well as its grounding in current research at CRL, makes this project a promising development in the field of translation and second language teaching.

References

1. Annick, P., and Pustejovsky, J.: Knowledge acquisition from corpora. In: Proceedings of the 13th international conference on computational linguistics (COLING-90), Helsinki, Finland 1990
2. Ballim, A., and Wilks, Y.: Artificial believers. Hillsdale, NJ: Lawrence Erlbaum Associates 1991
3. Barwise, J., and Perry, J.: Situations and attitudes.Cambridge, MA.: MIT Press 1983
4. Candelaria de Ram, S. and Yasuda, S.: Cultural effects in the machine translation of Japanese business letters. Paper presented at the Western Conference of the Association for Asian Studies, Long Beach, CA 1989
5. Cook, V., and Fass, D. Natural language processing by computer and language teaching. System, 14(2), 163-170, (1986)
6. Farwell, D. and Wilks, Y.: Ultra: a multilingual machine translator. Memoranda in computer and cognitive science, MCCS-90-202, Computing Research Laboratory, New Mexico State University, Las Cruces, NM 1990
7. Fass, D.: Collative semantics: a semantics for natural language processing. Memoranda in computer and cognitive science, MCCS-88-118, New Mexico State University, Las Cruces, NM 1988
8. Guthrie, L., McKevitt, P. and Wilks, Y.: OSCON: An operating system consultant. In: Proceedings of the 4th annual Rocky Mountain conference on artificial intelligence. pp. 103-113. Denver, CO 1989
9. Halliday, M.: Learning how to mean: Explorations in the development of language. London: Edward Arnold 1975
10. Huang, X-M.: Semantic analysis in XTRA, an English-Chinese machine translation system. Computers and translation, 3(2), 101-120 (1988)
11. Johnson, K.: Skill psychology and communicative methodology. Seminar at the Regional English Learning Centre, Singapore 1984

12. Kennedy, J.: Metaphor in pictures. Perception, 11 (1982)
13. Littlewood, W.: Foreign and second language learning: Language acquisition research and its implications for the classroom. Cambridge, UK: Cambridge University Press 1984
14. Masterman, M.: Translation. In: Proceedings of the aristotelean society 1961
15. Miller, G. and Fellbaum, C.: WordNet and the organization of lexical memory. (This Volume)
16. Ogden, C., and Richards, I.: The meaning of meaning.London: Routledge & Kegan Paul 1936
17. Richards, I.: The pocket book of basic English (US version of English through pictures). New York: Pocket Books 1945
18. Richards, I.: French through pictures. New York: Pocket Books 1950
19. Savignon, S.: Communicative competence: Theory and classroom practice. Reading, MA.: Addison-Wesley 1983
20. Schvaneveldt, R., (ed.). Pathfinder associative networks. Norwood, NJ.: Ablex 1990
21. Slator, B., and Wilks, Y.: PREMO: Parsing by conspicuous lexical consumption. In Advances in parsing technology, M. Tomita (Ed.). New York: Morgan Kaufman 1990
22. Weischedel, R., Voge, W. and James, M.: An artificial intelligence approach to language instruction. Artificial intelligence, 10, 225-240 (1978)
23. Whorf, B.: Language, thought and reality: Selected writings of Benjamin Lee Whorf (J. Carroll, ed.). New York: Wiley 1956
24. Widdowson, H.: Teaching language as communication. Oxford, UK: Oxford University Press 1978
25. Wilkins, D.: Notional syllabuses. Oxford, UK: Oxford University Press 1976
26. Wilks, Y.: A preferential pattern-seeking semantics for natural language inference. Artificial intelligence, 6, 53-74 (1975)
27. Wilks, Y.: Making preferences more active. Artificial intelligence, 11, 75-97 (1978)
28. Wilks, Y. and Farwell, D.: A white paper on research n pragmatics-based machine translation. Memoranda in computer and cognitive science, MCCS-90-188, New Mexico State University, Las Cruces, NM 1989
29. Wilks, Y., Fass, D., Guo, C-M., McDonald, J., Plate,T., and Slator, B.: Machine tractable dictionaries as tools and resources for natural language processing. Journal of machine translation (1990)
30. Wittgenstein, L.: Tractatus Logico-Philosophicus. London: Routledge & Kegan Paul 1922

Drill and Practice for Turkish Grammar

H. Altay Güvenir

Computer Engineering and Information Science Department, Bilkent University, Ankara 06533 TURKEY

Abstract: This paper describes ongoing research project to develop an intelligent tutoring system for teaching Turkish grammar as a foreign language. The teaching strategy is based on drill and practice. The learner is expected to translate a given meaning into a sentence in Turkish. The meaning to be translated is either randomly and meaningfully generated by the system or set up by the learner. To be able to evaluate the learner's translation, or explain how to translate a meaning into a Turkish sentence, the system must be able to generate the correct sentence in Turkish as well. The paper describes a generative grammar which is both easy for human learners and suitable for computer generation of sentences in the Turkish language. The grammar developed here is based on the agglutinative structure and the vowel harmonic feature of the Turkish language.

Keywords: CALL, Intelligent Tutoring, Sentence Generation, Turkish, Grammar

1. Introduction

The aim of this research is to develop an intelligent tutoring system for teaching Turkish as a second language. The knowledge base of the system consists of a generative grammar representing the rules of the Turkish language. The teaching strategy is based on drill and practice. Drill-and-practice can be very effective in teaching foreign language grammar if it is equipped with Artificial Intelligence (AI) techniques. An Intelligent Drill-and Practice (IDP) system for foreign language teaching can incorporate AI techniques in two main areas.

Firstly, the knowledge about the sentence formation rules of the natural language being taught has to be encoded as a knowledge base. This is necessary because an IDP system must be able to construct sentences in the target language as answers to the questions posed by itself or by the learner. Also it is important that the construction of the sentences is explained to the learner in an explicit and structured way using basic concepts and operations. The DRIP program described in this paper stores in its knowledge base the grammar representing the rules of Turkish language. These basic concepts and the associated operations are given to the learner in a classroom or by book and DRIP provides a computerized learning environment to master them. The student is allowed to learn through exploration, by testing his/her hypotheses.

Secondly, AI techniques can be used in the analysis and diagnosis of errors in the students' sentences, in monitoring the performance and modeling the competence of the individual student, and finally planning an appropriate strategy according to the needs of the student.

NATO ASI Series, Vol. F 80
Intelligent Tutoring Systems for Foreign Language Learning
Edited by M. L. Swartz and M. Yazdani

In its function as tutor, the drill and practice application is considered as a major component of Computer-Assisted Instruction (CAI) [5, 9]. Drill and practice software is intended to reinforce instruction that students have already been given by the teacher. Although criticized by some people, as being a 'lesser form' of CAI, drill and practice is destined to be one of the main uses of CAI, as long as people have to learn routine and repetitive tasks of any nature. There are many areas where some form of drilling is necessary in order to develop basic skills or to reinforce essential knowledge. No one learns a foreign vocabulary without the need to practice and repeat the words [11, 13-14]. There are many commercial Computer-Assisted Language Learning (CALL) products that apply drill and practice as their teaching strategy. These programs are generally designed as computer games to teach vocabulary or correct sentence formation in a foreign language. The shortcoming of the drill game programs is that they are designed for a specific context. However, if the program is to be general, the representation of sentence formation rules of a foreign language becomes important, so that the computer also constructs the sentences correctly. To be of instructional value, the program has to be able to explain how it constructed the sentence as well. Thus, the representation of knowledge about a natural language grammar plays a crucial role in the design of an Intelligent Tutoring System (ITS) for foreign language teaching.

In this paper we describe a grammar for Turkish language and a computer program called DRIP (DRIll and Practice) that uses this grammar to teach Turkish as a foreign language. The learner is expected to translate a meaning, given as a frame, into a sentence in Turkish. The meaning frame is either randomly and meaningfully generated by the system, or set up by the learner. The system allows the learner to change and fix the values of some of the frame slots. That is, if the learner needs to practice only the questions in future tense, he or she can fix those slots so that the frames generated by the system are in future tense and in question mood.

The student's translation is compared to the correct sentence derived by the system. If the two do not match, then a message indicating the position of the error with the possible cause is given. To be able to evaluate the student's sentence, the system has to derive the correct sentence in Turkish, as well. This requires that the system "knows" the grammar of Turkish language. That is, the rules of the language are represented in a way that is both easy for human learner to understand and suitable for computer to generate the basic sentences in Turkish.

A generative grammar has been developed to represent the Turkish language. This grammar is based on the agglutinative structure and the vowel harmonic features of Turkish. Of course, representing a natural language completely is almost impossible. Instead, we try to represent only the basic transitive sentence structure. A transitive sentence is composed of three main components, which are subject, verb and object. Although this sentence structure is simple, composed of two or three words, it is rich enough to represent a substantial portion of the Turkish grammar when tense, polarity, object case, number and mood information are incorporated.

2. Turkish Language

Morphologically, Turkish is classified as an *agglutinative* language, that is, each morph realizes only one morpheme [3, 7]. In such a language every word can be segmented into units, each of which has a single meaning. Another example of an agglutinative language is Japanese. In these languages, the morphemes are arranged loosely together, with little or no inflection [4, 10, 12].

Turkish is written in Latin alphabet, and the Turkish spelling system is nearly phonemic. It is well known that English spelling does not adequately reflect English pronunciation. For example, the three words 'pare', 'pear', and 'pair' are all pronounced exactly the same way while the words 'present' (gift) and 'present' (to make a gift to) are spelled the same way but pronounced differently. In Turkish, the situation is considerably better, since the Turkish spelling system is much more nearly phonemic than that of English.

The Turkish alphabet has six new symbols. These symbols and their corresponding phonetic representations are 'ç' /tʃ/, 'ğ', 'ı' /ɯ/, 'ö' /ø/, 'ş' /ʃ/, ü /y/. The letter 'ğ' merges the pronunciations of the vowels before and after it.

2.1 Vowel Harmony in Turkish

Turkish suffixes change according to the rules of vowel harmony, which have the effect of causing the vowels of a word to assimilate to one another [2, 15, 16]. Therefore it is instructive to look at the vowels of Turkish first.

Vowels pronounced with the tongue in the front of the mouth are called *front vowels*; those made with the tongue in the back of the mouth are called *back vowels*. The vowels of Turkish can be grouped in frontness as follows:

Front vowels:	e	i	ö	ü
Back vowels:	a	ı	o	u

Vowels made with the tongue high and close to the roof of the mouth are called *high vowels*; those made with the tongue low and jaw open are called *low vowels*. Turkish has four high and four low vowels, matched in pairs as follows:

High vowels:	i	i	u	ü
Low vowels:	a	e	o	ö

Vowels made with the lips forward and rounded are called rounded vowels; those made with the lips drawn back are called unrounded vowels. The vowels of Turkish can be grouped in terms of rounding as follows:

Rounded vowels:	o	ö	u	ü
Unrounded vowels:	a	e	ı	i

Turkish exhibits what is referred to as "palatal" or front-back vowel harmony. According to this rule words of the language have only front or only back vowels. Harmony in Turkish is in general root-controlled, in that suffix vowels alternate to agree with root vowels, while root vowels never alternate to conform to the vowels of the suffix. An exception to this rule occurs in the case of present continuous tense suffix, which may change the last vowel of the root verb. This situation will be shown with examples later.

There are two main vowel harmonic variables that occur in Turkish grammar. These variables arise only as part of an abstract suffix. The first variable, represented as *E*, alternates between 'a' and 'e' to stay in harmony with the previous vowel (the first vowel to the left of the variable *E*) in frontness, as shown in the following table:

previous vowel	value of *E*
a, ı, o, u	a
e, i, ö, ü	e

The other vowel harmonic variable, *I*, alternates between the high vowels assimilating into the previous vowel in frontness and rounding, as shown in the following table:

previous vowel	value of *I*
a, ı	ı
e, i	i
o, u	u
ö, ü	ü

Both of these vowel harmonic variables also change the preceding character, if it is 'k' or 'p', in the following way:

preceding letter	change to
k	ğ
p	b

For example, 'kayık'-E is 'kayığa /to the boat', and 'kayık'-I is 'kayığı / the boat'.

There are other languages whose phonology include vowel harmony rules. These languages are classified in the Ural-Altaic language family and include languages such as Hungarian, Mongolian and Finnish. The debate over the proper treatment of vowel harmony is of strong interest to phonologists [8].

2.2 Consonant Harmony in Turkish

The Turkish language possesses not only vowel harmony but also consonant harmony. The initial consonant of some suffixes assimilates into the preceding consonant with respect to voicing. That is, if the suffix is attached to a voiceless consonant, the suffix-initial consonant becomes voiceless, while if the suffix is attached to a voiced consonant or vowel, the suffix-initial consonant is voiced [2, 16]. The voiceless consonants in Turkish are 'ç', 'f', 'h', 'p', 's', 'ş', and 't'; all others are voiced. The past tense suffix, for instance, is *-DI*. Here *D* is a consonant harmonic variable which has the value 't' if the preceding character is a voiceless consonant and 'd' after either a voiced consonant or a vowel.

3. Meaning Frame

The objective of the student here is to learn to translate a meaning frame into a sentence in Turkish. Currently, in the DRIP program only the transitive sentence structure in active voice is used. A transitive sentence has two nouns and a verb. One of the nouns functions as the *subject*, the agent of the action. The second noun of a transitive sentence performs the function of *object* . The object represents the undergoer of the action, the object towards which the action is directed. For example, 'çayı içtin / you drank the tea' is a transitive sentence with the pronoun 'sen[1] / you (singular)' functioning as the subject, the second noun 'çay / tea' functioning as the object of the sentence. The object can be singular or plural in its number, and may require some case information as described further in this section. The verb 'iç / drink' functions as the action predicator in this sentence.

A sentence can be positive or negative in its polarity and declarative or interrogative in its mood. The transitive sentence example given above is a positive and declarative sentence. The negative declarative sentence of the same action would be 'çayı içmedin / you didn't drink the

[1]Note that 'sen' does not appear in the sentence. The suffix 'n' in 'içtin' conveys 2nd person singular.

tea'. We chose only the yes/no type questions for the interrogative mood. This selection is due to the more complex sentence structure of yes/no type questions. The information type questions are easily formed by replacing the answer word in the answer sentence by the corresponding question word. For example, the information question 'neyi içtin? / what did you drink?' is easily obtained from the above sentence by replacing the word 'çayı / the tea' by the question word 'neyi / what'. The positive yes/no question of the above action would be 'çayı içtin mi? / did you drink the tea?'. Similarly, the negative question of the same action is 'çayı içmedin mi? / didn't you drink the tea?'.

All those components of a transitive sentence are gathered into a *meaning frame*. A meaning frame (or frame), therefore, is composed of eight functional places or *slots*: subject, predicator (or simply verb), tense, polarity, object, object case, object number, and mood. An example frame is shown in Figure 1. This frame is simpler than the two proposed by Abeille [1]. The slots of a meaning frame in DRIP can be filled by certain categories or types of item. In the following subsections we will look at the possible values for each of these slots in detail.

3.1. Subject

The subject slot of a frame can be filled by a noun, a pronoun, a noun phrase, or an embedded sentence. We are going to use only pronouns functioning as subjects, since grammatically nouns are realized as 3rd person (singular or plural) pronouns. Noun phrases and embedded sentences would require the expansion of the frame structure.

```
Frame
Subject     : biz / we
Predicator  : it / push
Tense       : şimdiki / progressive
Polarity    : olumsuz / negative
Object      : kutu / box
Object case : belirtme / accusative
Number      : çoğul / plural
Mood        : bildirme / declarative
```

Figure 1. An example frame

The Turkish language has six distinct personal pronouns, three singular and three plural. Those pronouns are 'ben / I', 'sen / you (sing.)', 'o / he, she, or it', 'biz / we', 'siz / you (pl.)', and 'onlar / they'. In Turkish the 2nd person is distinguished as both singular and plural pronouns. Note that there is no distinction in gender, neither in singular nor plural 3rd person pronouns.

In Turkish, person is marked in the verb by means of a suffix. A pronoun representing the person may also be included in the sentence to emphasize the person. For, example,

'Çay içtim / I drank tea'
'Ben çay içtim (Diğerleri ne içti bilmiyorum) /
I drank tea (I don't know what others drank)'.

The grammatical rules in DRIP include only the first case, that is, the subject is not emphasized. In some cases the form of the personal morpheme may intersect with the tense morpheme in the verb word. For example, the 1st person plural morpheme is

-Ik for past tense,
-Iz for all other tenses.

The complete list of the pronouns and their corresponding morphemes are given in the following table:

	pronoun	morpheme
1st sing.	ben	*-Im*
2nd sing.	sen	-[*s*]*In*
3rd sing.	o	Ø
1st pl.	biz	-*I*[*k*/*z*]
2nd pl.	siz	-[*s*]*InIz*
3rd pl.	onlar	*-lEr*

The [*k*/*z*] in the 1st person plural morpheme indicates that a 'k' or 'z' will replace its value depending on a value from the frame, in this case the tense information. We will use square brackets to represent the variables whose values depend on frame values. The [*s*] in the 2nd person morphemes is also such a variable. Its value is the letter 's' if the frame is in any tense other than past tense, Ø (null) if the frame is in past tense.

3.2. Predicator

The predicator slot of a meaning frame is always filled by a verb. Thus, we will simply use the term *verb* for predicator, although predicator is a "function" of a sentence and verb is a "category". Verbs refer to "events". Events could be actions, processes, happenings or states.

The verb roots are bound, since they are followed by a polarity morpheme (if the sentence is negative), then by a tense morpheme and a person morpheme functioning as subject. The pattern, or the ordering of the morphemes of a verb word in a transitive declarative sentence can be shown as

verb + polarity + tense + subject

In Turkish, the verb root and the following suffixes are independent of each other. That is the verb root is always the same no matter what polarity, tense or subject are involved. In English, on the other hand, the verb 'go' has three different forms (go, went, gone) depending on the tense. We believe that this feature of Turkish makes it easier to learn as a foreign language, since the student does not have to memorize several different forms of the same verb.

3.3. Tense

One piece of information that languages often encode with relation to events is the time when they take place, specifically either before the time of speaking, at the time of speaking, or after the time of speaking [6]. These real-world time differences are encoded in the language by means the grammatical category of *tense*. In Turkish, tense is marked by suffixes in the verb.

Four different tenses are included in DRIP. They are '*geçmiş / past*', '*geniş / present*', '*şimdiki / progressive*', and '*gelecek / future*'.

The past tense suffix is -DI. Here, D is a harmonic consonant variable which alternates between 'd' and 't'. It has the value 't' if the preceding letter is a voiceless consonant, the value 'd' otherwise. For example,

'kapıyı çaldım / I knocked the door'	(verb: 'çal / knock')
'kapıyı açtım / I opened the door'	(verb: 'aç / open').

The suffix of the *progressive* (*present continuous*) tense is -*!Iyor*. This tense normally corresponds to the English '*is -ing*' tense but sometimes corresponds to the English present. For example,

'kapıyı açıyorum / I am opening the door'	(verb: 'aç / open')
'dergi okuyorun / I am reading a journal'	(verb: 'oku / read')
'su istiyorum / I want (some) water'	(verb: 'iste / want').

Note that in the second example the last letter before the progressive suffix is 'u' which is already a high vowel (*I*). Therefore, no extra vowel is inserted for *!I*. On the other hand, the last vowel 'e' of the verb root ('iste'), in the third example, is changed to an 'i', the appropriate high vowel. This is the difference between the harmonic variables *I* and *!I*: if the preceding letter is a vowel then *I* disappears, whereas *!I* forces it to be a high vowel. Therefore, we will call *!I* as dominant *I*. Also *!I* does not modify the preceding consonant if it is 'k' or 'p' as *I* does.

The *future* tense suffix is -(y)*!EcEk*. A letter 'y' is inserted if the verb stem ends in a vowel. Some examples in future tense are

'süt içecekler / they will drink milk'	(verb: 'iç / drink')
'kutuyu taşıyacaksın / you (sing.) will carry the box'	(verb: 'taşı / carry')
'okuldan geleceğim / I will come from the school'	(verb: 'gel / come').

Here, the -*!E* is similar to the -*!I*, in that it does not modify the preceding consonant if it is a 'k' or 'p' as -*E* does.

The present tense is the only complicated tense in Turkish. The suffix to be used depends on the polarity of the meaning frame first. The present tense suffix for a positive sentence is -*Ir* if the previous letter is an 'l' or 'r'; -*Er* otherwise. Some examples of positive sentences in present tense are:

'çay içerim / I drink tea'	(verb: 'iç / drink')
'okuldan gelirler / they come from school'	(verb: 'gel / come').

On the other hand, if the sentence has negative polarity, the present tense suffix depends further on the mood of the sentence. If the sentence is a negative question then the negative suffix -*mE* is followed by the letter 'z'. Some examples are:

'çay içmez misin? / don't you drink tea?'	(verb: 'iç / drink')
'et yemez mi? / doesn't she eat meat?'	(verb: 'ye / eat')

If the sentence is in the negative declarative mood, then the present tense suffix depends on the subject: Ø (null) if 1st person singular, 'y' if 1st person plural, 'z' otherwise. Some examples are:

'çay içmem / I don't drink tea' (verb: 'iç / drink')
'çay içmez / he doesn't drink tea'
'çay içmeyiz / we don't drink tea'
'çay içmezsiniz / you (plural) don't drink tea')

As it is seen from the above examples, there is no single suffix for the present tense in Turkish. The choice of the suffix depends on the polarity, mood and the subject of the meaning frame.

3.4. Polarity

We distinguish two polarities, namely 'positive' (affirmative) and 'negative'. In Turkish, negative polarity is realized by the negative morpheme *-mE*, which is placed just after the root and before the tense in the verb word. No extra morpheme is used if the sentence is in the positive mood. Some examples are:

'dergiyi okudum / I read the journal'
'dergiyi okumadım / I didn't read the journal'
'dergiyi vereceğim / I will give the journal'
'dergiyi vermeyeceğim / I will not give the journal'

The negative morpheme is independent of any other information from the frame; its value is determined based only on the vowel harmony with the verb root.

3.5. Case

Case is a grammatical category which is marked in the noun. The function of case is to signal the grammatical and semantic relationship between the noun and the verb. Six cases of nouns are possible in the transitive sentence structure.

Nominative case, in Turkish, is used to mark the noun as indefinite.[2] The nominative case is realized by a null case suffix; all other cases require their own suffixes. For example, the noun 'elma / apple' is in the nominative case in the sentence 'elma yedim / I ate an apple'.

Accusative case is used to mark that the noun is a definite one. In this case the noun has already been introduced into the discourse. For example, the noun 'elmayı / the apple' is in the accusative case in the sentence 'elmayı yedim / I ate the apple'. The accusative case is realized by the *-(y)I* suffix. Here, the character 'y' is required if the last letter of the preceding noun is a vowel. This consonant 'y' is necessary because, in Turkish, a vowel is never followed by another vowel.

Dative case is used to indicate that the preceding noun is the place to or toward which motion is directed. The dative case is realized by the *-(y)E* suffix. For example, the noun 'bankaya / to the bank' is in the dative case in the sentence 'bankaya gittim / I went to the bank'.

Locative case is used to indicate the place at which an action occurs. For example, the noun 'evde / at home' is in the locative case in the sentence 'evde oturuyorlar / they are staying at home'. The locative case suffix is *-DE*. Here *D* alternates between 'd' and 't' according to consonant harmony.

Ablative case is used to indicate the place from which motion proceeds. For example, the noun 'bankadan / from the bank' is in ablative case in the sentence 'bankadan geliyorum'. The

---

[2]Note that the Turkish language does not have articles.

ablative case is realized by the suffix *-DEn*. Here *D* and *E* are harmonic variables as defined above.

Instrumental case is used to indicate the instrument with or by which the motion proceeds. For example, the 'fırçayla / with brush' is in instrumental case in the sentence 'fırçayla boyayacak / he will paint with the brush'. The instrumental case suffix is *-(!y)lE*. Here, the optional harmonic variable *(!y)* is replaced by the letter 'y' if it is preceded by a vowel, otherwise it is dropped.

3.6. Number

Number is the grammatical category applicable to nouns. In Turkish, as in many other languages, singular nouns are not marked for number. Plural nouns in Turkish are made only by the *-lEr* morpheme. Some examples are:

'kutular / boxes'	(noun: 'kutu / box')
'şehirler / cities'	(noun: 'şehir / city')
'yapraklar / leaves'	(noun: 'yaprak / leaf')
'adamlar / men'	(noun: 'adam / man')

There are no exceptions such as 'criteria' (plural of 'criterion') or 'men' (plural of 'man') in English. Also, mass nouns like 'mud' or 'information' do not have a plural form in English. This is not the case in Turkish; the plural of each noun can be formed if the context requires it.

3.7. Mood

A sentence can be in one of two moods: *declarative* (*affirmative*) or *interrogative*. Here we are only interested in polar questions as the interrogative mood; that is, questions with 'yes' or 'no' answers. In Turkish, polar questions are realized by the particle *mI*. There are two possible patterns of transitive polar questions. The choice of the patterns is determined by both tense and subject values. The first pattern,

object verb+subject *mI* ?

is used if the sentence is in the past tense, or the subject is 3rd person (singular or plural). Note here that the question particle *mI* is not a suffix; rather it is a word itself. The other pattern

object verb *mI*(y)+subject ?

is used for all other cases. Here the value of the high vowel *I* is determined based on the vowel harmony of the verb word. The symbol (y) signals an optional 'y'; a 'y' is needed if the first letter of the subject morpheme is a vowel.

4. Grammar

We define here the generative grammar used by DRIP. The terminals of the grammar are the symbols of the Turkish alphabet, since the individual vowels and consonants are required to determine the values of harmonic variables in the morphemes. This grammar has three types of variables: pattern variables, frame variables, and harmonic variables. For each of the variables there exists exactly one corresponding rule which determines its value.

Pattern variables are used to represent fixed constituent structures, that is, the fixed order of words or morphemes. A pattern variable can be replaced by the corresponding pattern, which is given in the form of a rewrite rule, called *pattern rule*. These rules are also called *phrase structure rules* in the literature [12]. A pattern, which constitutes the right-hand side of a pattern rule, may consist of any type of variable or terminal symbols. For example, a declarative transitive sentence in Turkish has the pattern "object verb+subject." This pattern of declarative sentence is represented as:

<declarative> → <object><verb>[?subject].

Here, angle brackets are used to identify the pattern variables. The pattern for the <declarative> variable introduces two more pattern variables, and a frame variable. The complete list of the pattern rules in DRIP is shown in Figure 2.[3]

```
<sentence=[?mood]
<declarative>=<object> <verb>[?subject].
<interrogative>=[?subject&tense]
<questionA>=<object> <verb> <question>[?subject]?
<questionB>=<object> <verb>[?subject] <question>?
<object>=[object][?number][?case]
<verb>=[verb][?polarity][?tense]
<question>=m{i}{y}
<negative>=m{e}
<plural>=l{e}r
<nominative>=
<accusative>={y}{i}
<dative>={y}{e}
<locative>={d}{e}
<ablative>={d}{e}n
<instrumental>={!y}l{e}
<past>={d}{i}
<present>=[Pr?polarity]
<prsntPos>={?lr_ei}r
<prsntNeg>=[PrNg?mood]
<prsntNegQue>=z
<prsntNegDcl>=[PrNgDc?subject]
<progressive>={!i}yor
<future>={y}{!e}c{e}k
<ben>={i}m
<sen>=[?tense_s]
<o>=
<biz>={i}[?tense_kz]
<siz>={i}[?tense_s]{i}n{i}z
<onlar>=l{e}r
```

Figure 2. The complete list of patterns in DRIP.

[3]In the text file containing the pattern rules the symbol '=' is used for '→'.

Frame variables are used for references to the meaning frame. A frame variable can be replaced by either a pattern variable or a terminal symbol. The value to be replaced is determined by the corresponding frame rule. Square brackets are used to identify the frame variables. For instance, the frame variable [?tense_kz] in the pattern variable for the 1st person plural pronoun <biz> indicates a decision to be made based on the tense slot of the frame. The frame rule for [?tense_kz] is defined as:

[?tense_kz] → k if tense = past
z otherwise

That is, the frame variable [?tense_kz] is replaced by the terminal symbol 'k' if the frame is in past tense, by the symbol 'z' otherwise. The value of the frame variable [?number] is determined based on the number slot of the frame by the following rule:

[?number] → <plural> if number = plural
Ø otherwise

As a convention, a question mark is used in the name of a frame variable to indicate a decision point. Other frame variables simply copy a value from the corresponding slot of the frame. For example, the frame variable [object] in the pattern for the variable <object> is simply replaced by the value of the object slot of the frame.

Harmonic variables are used for the letters whose values are to be determined according to the vowel or consonant harmony rules. The value to be replaced is determined by the corresponding harmonic rule. Curly brackets are used to identify the harmonic variables. For example, the harmonic variable *E* is represented as {e}. Thus, the harmonic variable {e} in the plural pattern "l{e}r", is replaced by the vowel 'e' if the previous vowel is front, 'a' if it is a back vowel. The harmonic rule corresponding to {e} is given as

{e} → a if previous vowel is a, ı, o, or u
e otherwise

A harmonic variable can be replaced by a terminal symbol or by another harmonic variable, and it is replaced only if its value can be determined. The harmonic variables {e} and {i} are dropped (replaced by Ø) if they are preceded by a vowel already. Harmonic variables may have a side effect on the preceding terminal symbol. For example, the harmonic variables {e} and {i} change the preceding 'k' to 'ğ' and 'p' to 'b', as explained in section 2.1. The dominant harmonic variables {!e} and {!i}, on the other hand, remove the preceding vowel in order to enforce an 'a' or 'e', and a high vowel in their positions, respectively. The dominant harmonic vowels, however, do not change the preceding consonant.

The harmonic variable {y} is replaced by the terminal symbol 'y' only if it is preceded by a vowel and also it is expected to be followed by a vowel; otherwise it is dropped. It is enough to have a preceding vowel to replace the dominant harmonic variable {!y} by the terminal 'y'; it is dropped otherwise. The harmonic variable {?lr_ei}, used in the positive present tense pattern, is dropped if it is preceded by a vowel, replaced by the harmonic variable {!i} if it is preceded by a 'l' or 'r', and replaced by {!e} any other consonant.

```
<sentence>
Replacing the pattern <sentence> by [?mood] results in
[?mood]
End of one pass!

Replacing the frame variable [?mood] by <declarative> results in
<declarative>
End of one pass!

Replacing the pattern <declarative> by <object> <verb>[?subject].
results in <object> <verb>[?subject].
End of one pass!

Replacing the pattern <object> by [object][?number][?case] results in
[object][?number][?case] <verb>[?subject].
Replacing the pattern <verb> by [verb][?polarity][?tense] results in
[object][?number][?case] [verb][?polarity][?tense][?subject].
Replacing the frame variable [?subject] by <biz> results in
[object][?number][?case] [verb][?polarity][?tense]<biz>.
End of one pass!

Replacing the frame variable [object] by kutu results in
kutu[?number][?case] [verb][?polarity][?tense]<biz>.
Replacing the frame variable [?number] by <plural> results in
kutu<plural>[?case] [verb][?polarity][?tense]<biz>.
Replacing the frame variable [?case] by <accusative> results in
kutu<plural><accusative> [verb][?polarity][?tense]<biz>.
Replacing the frame variable [verb] by it results in
kutu<plural><accusative> it[?polarity][?tense]<biz>.
Replacing the frame variable [?polarity] by <negative> results in
kutu<plural><accusative> it<negative>[?tense]<biz>.
Replacing the frame variable [?tense] by <progressive> results in
kutu<plural><accusative> it<negative><progressive><biz>.
Replacing the pattern <biz> by {i}[?tense_kz] results in
kutu<plural><accusative> it<negative><progressive>{i}[?tense_kz].
End of one pass!

Replacing the pattern <plural> by l{e}r results in
kutul{e}r<accusative> it<negative><progressive>{i}[?tense_kz].
Replacing the pattern <accusative> by {y}{i} results in
kutul{e}r{y}{i} it<negative><progressive>{i}[?tense_kz].
Replacing the pattern <negative> by m{e} results in
kutul{e}r{y}{i} itm{e}<progressive>{i}[?tense_kz].
Replacing the pattern <progressive> by {!i}yor results in
kutul{e}r{y}{i} itm{e}{!i}yor{i}[?tense_kz].
Replacing the harmonic variable {i} results in
kutul{e}r{y}{i} itm{e}{!i}yoru[?tense_kz].
Replacing the frame variable [?tense_kz] by z results in
kutul{e}r{y}{i} itm{e}{!i}yoruz.
End of one pass!

Replacing the harmonic variable {e} results in
kutular{y}{i} itm{e}{!i}yoruz.
Replacing the harmonic variable {y} results in
kutular{i} itm{e}{!i}yoruz.
Replacing the harmonic variable {i} results in
kutuları itm{e}{!i}yoruz.
Replacing the harmonic variable {e} results in
kutuları itme{!i}yoruz.
Replacing the harmonic variable {!i} results in
kutuları itmiyoruz.
```

Figure 3. Construction of the sentence "kutuları itmiyoruz" from the frame in Figure 1.

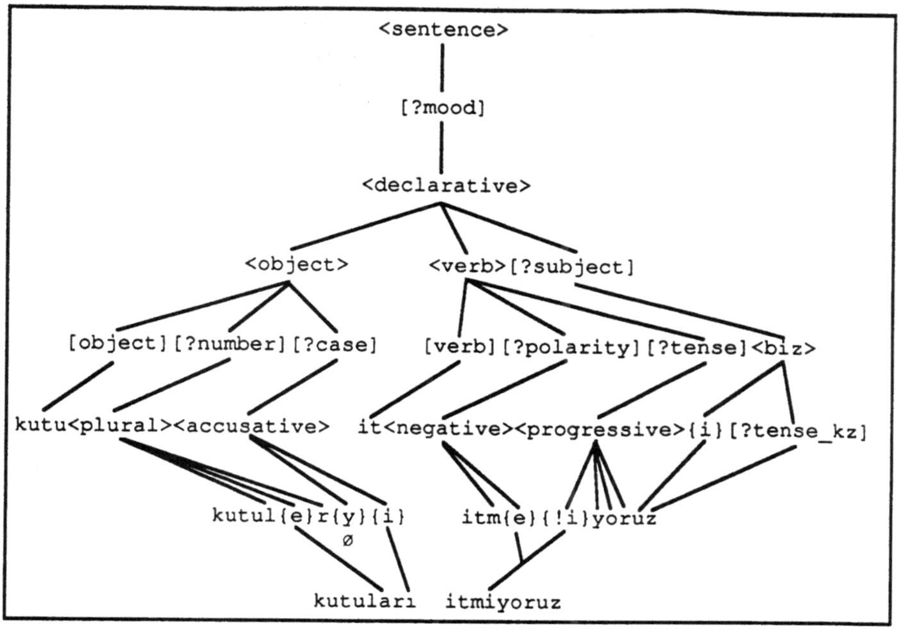

Figure 4. The derivation tree for the sentence 'kutuları itmiyoruz'.

Construction of a sentence using this grammar starts with the pattern variable <sentence>. Depending on the mood of the frame two patterns are possible: declarative or interrogative. That is, to construct a sentence, one has to look at the mood of the sentence first, and choose the right pattern accordingly. This choice is performed by the frame variable [?mood], which is replaced by the pattern variables <declarative> or <interrogative> according to the value in the mood slot of the meaning frame. When there are two or more variables, the left most variable is replaced first. This is due to the fact that the vowel harmony in Turkish is a left-to-right process operating sequentially from syllable to syllable. The step-by-step construction of the sentence "kutuları itmiyoruz" from the frame given in Figure 1 is shown in Figure 3.

The tree representation of the construction of the same sentence is illustrated in Figure 4. Replacement of the variables is a breadth-first and left-to-right process. Each level of the tree corresponds to one pass of the replacement process.

The generative grammar presented here is both easy for a human learner to understand and suitable for computer construction of sentences in Turkish language. The process of the generation of a sentence is controlled by a meaning frame. Through the frame variables appropriate pattern variables are called upon, which in turn, invoke the corresponding phrase structure rules. The patterns introduced by these rewrite rules consist of further pattern variables, frame variables or harmonic variables. Since there is exactly one pattern rule for each pattern, the construction process is deterministic. Therefore, for any given meaning frame, the sentence representing that meaning is unique.

In learning a second language using a generative grammar, it is important to understand why a particular phrase rule is selected, and under what conditions it is applicable. Since, in the grammar presented here, the decision points in the construction of a sentence are separated on the basis of pattern rules, frame decisions and harmonic values, the learner can easily see what the fixed structural patterns are, when and how these decisions are made.

5. DRIP

DRIP[4] is a prototype intelligent tutoring program designed for the drill and practice of Turkish grammar learning. The objective of the learner is to translate a given meaning frame into a Turkish sentence. In this sense, our approach is similar to Zock's [17], but DRIP goes beyond the meaning-form mapping to explain details of the translation process. The frames are either generated randomly by DRIP or set up by the learner. The program is interactive, in that both the program and the learner can initiate a translation problem. When computer is translating, it explains each step of the translation process. Each variable being replaced and the values they are replaced with are shown in order. If the learner is to translate, his/her sentence is analyzed and the position of the possible error is indicated.

Drill-and-practice is based on the idea of repeatedly performing essentially the same operations with slight modification. DRIP allows the learner to fix some of the slot values of the frame to the particular values that he/she wants to practice. If the learner feels a need for practicing a particular tense and a particular verb, for example, he/she can change and then fix the values of those slots. Then any further frames generated by DRIP will have those fixed values in the corresponding slots. Those fixed slots are highlighted in the frame window.

The program has a fixed screen layout which is divided into four windows as shown in Figure 5. The upper-left window, called *frame window*, displays the contents of the current frame to be translated. The list of possible actions the learner can take is shown in the upper-right window as a menu. The value in any one of the slots, except object and object case, can be changed to any reasonable value. For example, if the subject slot is to be changed then the new value must be one of the six pronouns. The learner is expected to enter the new value in Turkish to give him further practice with the Turkish vocabulary and grammatical terminology. The learner can fix any combination of those slots to their current values shown in the frame window. Similarly, those slots can be released so that DRIP can assign different values to them.

5.1. Selection of new frames

When the learner gets a new setup of the frame slots, all the slots that are not fixed are randomly assigned a new value. The fixed slots maintain their values. The values of the object and object case slots are determined according to the value of the verb slot, so that the verb, object and object case slots form a meaningful combination. For example, a sentence such as 'kutulara yemedik / we didn't eat to the boxes' would confuse the learner further. Therefore, the lexicon is organized as a list of verb and object case pairs. Along with each entry a list of possible objects is given. A sample portion of the lexicon is shown in Figure 6. The experimental lexicon currently consists of 34 transitive Turkish verbs and 93 objects organized in 38 verb / object case entries. Some verbs can be used with different sets of objects, since their meanings are different; some verbs can be used with more than one object case.

5.2. Construction of sentences

Whether the learner or DRIP is translating, the construction of the sentence must be performed. If the program is showing the translation, each step of the process is displayed to the learner, in the *transactions window* at the bottom. If the variable being replaced is a pattern or a frame variable, the corresponding pattern or the value obtained from the frame is shown, respectively.

---

[4]DRIP is written in Pascal language and runs on DOS-compatible computers.

```
frame
Subject : biz / we
Verb    : it / push
Tense   : şimdiki / progressive
Polarity: olumsuz / negative
Object  : kutu / box
Object case: belirtme / accusative
Number  : çoğul / plural
Moods   : bildirme / declarative

Menu
Change a slot
Fix a slot
Release a slot
New frame
Let me translate
Show its translation
Quit
Option: Showing the translation

Sentence
kutu<plural><accusative> it<negative><progressive>{i}[?tense_kz]

Transactions

Replacing the pattern <progressive> by {!i}yor results in
kutul{e}r{y}{i} itm{e}{!i}yor{i}[?tense_kz].

Replacing the harmonic variable {i} results in
kutul{e}r{y}{i} itm{e}{!i}yoru[?tense_kz].

Replacing the frame variable [?tense_kz] by z results in
kutul{e}r{y}{i} itme{e}{!i}yoruz.
```

Figure 5. The screen organization of DRIP.

```
   ...
aç / open ; belirtme / accusative
   kapı / door
   pencere / window
aç / turn on ; belirtme / accusative
   radyo / radio
   televizyon / TV
   ışık / light
   ...
gel / come ; araçlı / instrumental
   tren /train
   otobüs / bus
   uçak / airplane
   bisiklet / bicycle
gel / come ; çıkma / ablative
   ev / home
   okul / school
   alış veriş / shopping
   park / park
   ...
```

Figure 6. A portion of the lexicon.

The sentence is constructed using the generative grammar described in Section 4. At the end of each pass the developing sentence is shown in the *sentence window* in the middle. Student can follow how the variables are being replaced from left to right.

When the learner is translating, his/her sentence is read from the sentence window. At the same time DRIP starts its own translation process, and the learner's sentence is compared with the sentence obtained at the end of each pass. Only the terminal symbols, that is letters, are matched. If a mismatch is encountered, the evolving sentence obtained at the end of the last pass is shown to the student. By comparing it with his sentence, the student can figure out the wrong replacement of the variable that caused the error. Also the letter causing the mismatch is highlighted on his/her sentences.

6. Future Work

The grammar and the DRIP program described here are the initial part of ongoing research on developing intelligent tutoring systems for teaching foreign languages. The planned future work can be grouped in two areas. First, the class of sentences that can be derived is to be increased by extending the grammatical knowledge base. The second area of improvement is the evaluation and modelling of the learners.

To increase the educational value the coverage of the language has to be increased. The sentence structure is currently limited to transitive sentences. The meaning frame has to be extended by a slot which indicates the sentence structure, that is, whether it is transitive or intransitive. This would also require the identification of verbs as transitive, intransitive or both. Currently, the sentences are constructed in active voice. The grammatical knowledge base can be extended to include the pattern rules for passive voice structure as well. This would also enable the learner to transform a sentence between active and passive voice, which is a common exercise in learning a foreign language. Another possibility for deriving more complex sentences is to expand the nouns by demonstratives (*this*, *that*), the possessives (*my*, *your*, etc.), and by adjectives referring to color, size, shape, etc, in accordance with the noun. Other grammatical structures can also be included in DRIP. All this expansions would require a more complex frame structure with more slots.

Evaluation of the students translations and diagnosing any possible errors is an area that requires the incorporation of more AI techniques. Based on the results of some form of diagnosis, the weaknesses of the student can be determined and the frames can be generated to focus the student on these weak points. The weaknesses could be classified based on the use of particular values of the frame slots that are grammatically important, the corresponding patterns, and the determination of the values of the harmonic variables. Here it is important to distinguish errors that are made regularly and systematically from the mistakes that are made occasionally and not systematically. The mistakes can be corrected by the learner himself. However, the learner will need extra help to correct the errors. Therefore, error analysis is very important in the success of any ITS project.

7. Conclusion

Drill-and-practice, although criticized by some educationalists who claim that it trivializes learning, can be very effective in teaching foreign language grammar if it is equipped with AI techniques.

An intelligent drill-and-practice (IDP) system for foreign language teaching encodes in its knowledge base the knowledge about the sentence formation rules of the natural language being taught, so that the system can construct sentences in this language as answers to the questions posed both by itself or by the learner. Also using this knowledge base, the sentence construction process can be explained to the learner in an explicit and structured way. The knowledge base of the DRIP program described in this paper stores a grammar representing the rules of Turkish language. In the grammar proposed here, the rules are structured around three different forms: pattern rules, frame rules and harmonic rules. These rules are given to the learner in a classroom or by a book, and DRIP provides a computerized learning environment to master them through exploration, by testing his/her hypotheses.

We have asked several faculty members, who have come to Bilkent University from the USA or Britain and were interested in learning Turkish, to try and evaluate the prototype DRIP program. They found it difficult to visualize the concept that the frame window described, in the first try. However, they became comfortable with it after a few translations. A series of experiments are planned to validate the grammar proposed here, and evaluate intelligent drill-and-practice in the context of learning a foreign language grammar.

References

1. Abeille, A.: A lexicalized tree adjoining grammar for french and its relevance to language learning (this volume)
2. Aksan, D.: Her yönüyle dil, Ana çizgileriyle dilbilim, Vol. 2, Ankara: Turk Dil Kurumu. 1980
3. Banguoğlu, T.: Tükçenin Grameri. Ankara: Turk Dil Kurumu. 1986
4. Brown, E K. and J. E. Miller: Syntax: A Linguistic introduction to sentence structure. London: Hutchinson Education. 1980
5. Costanzo, W. V.: The electronic Text: Learning to write, read, and reason with computers. Englewood Cliffs: Educational Technology Publications. 1989
6 Fum, D., Pani. B., Tasso, C.: Naive vs. Formal Grammars: a case for integration in the design of a foreign language tutor (this volume)
7. Gencan, T. N.: Dilbilgisi, Ankara: Turk Dil Kurumu. 1979
8. Hare, M. L.: The role of similarity in Hungarian Vowel Harmony: A connectionist Account. Department of Linguistics, University of California, San Diego, CRL Technical Report 9004, January 1990
9. Howie, S. H.: Reading, Writing, and Computers: planning for integration. Boston: Allyn and Bacon 1989
10. Jackson, H.: Discovering Grammar. Oxford: Pergamon Press 1985
11. Kenning, M. J. and M-M. Kenning: An Introduction to Computer Assisted Language Teaching. London: Oxford University Press 1983
12. Lehmann, W. P.: Language: An Introduction. New York: Random House 1983
13. Romiszowski, A. J.:Developing Auto-Instructional Materials from programmed texts to CAL and interactive video. (Instructional development; 2). London: Kogan Page 1986
14. Stevick, E. W.: Teaching and Learning Languages. Cambridge: Cambridge University Press 1982
15. Underhill, R.: Turkish. In: Studies in Turkish Linguistics (D. I. Slobin and K. Zimmer, eds.) John Benjamin Publishing Co. 1986
16. Underhill, R.: Turkish Grammar. Cambridge: The MIT Press 1976
17 Zock, M.: SWIM or sink: the problem of communicating thought, How can I tell you how to say it, if you can't tell me what you want to say? (this volume)

WIZDOM
A Multiple-Purpose Language Tutoring System Based on AI Techniques

Jürgen Handke, University of Wuppertal, West Germany

Abstract[1]: This paper discusses some possibilities of implementing an Intelligent Language Tutoring System (ILTS) on the PC. On the basis of WIZDOM, a tutorial system developed by a team of programmers conducted by the author, the organization of such a system will be evaluated. It will be shown that specific implementation techniques are required and compromises between Natural Language (NL) ability and realization principles have to be made.

Keywords: Intelligent Language Tutoring

1. Intelligent Language Tutoring, Theory and Realization

In recent years Artificial Intelligence (AI) techniques have played an increasingly important role in the research of Intelligent Computer-Assisted Instruction (ICAI) / Intelligent Tutoring System (ITS):

"Computer-based educational devices which do not incorporate some form of artificial intelligence programming may include very sophisticated models of concepts and operations in their subject domain, but do not actually comprehend anything about the student, material or pedagogical approach. Instead, the machine is a mindless method for delivering to the learner a series of symbols which the student attempts to interpret and assimilate into his or her existing knowledge." [3,329].

This is especially true in the area of elementary programming, algebra, geometry or geography where a number of advances have been made. These systems, for example ALGEBRALAND or GEOMETRY TUTOR [2,4ff.], the LISP Tutor, the PROUST system or WEST [5,143ff.]; [12,209ff.] consist of the following basic modules:

- a knowledge base,
- an evaluation/problem-solving component,
- an "interaction" component,
- a "user-modelling" or "cognitive diagnostics" component.

In general, such ITS rely on the following basic strategies: They present the tutorial material in some way or other, apply some skills of error analysis and error remedy and thus assess the educational level of the student.

While these components and strategies are relatively easy to implement for domains whose syntax is precisely defined such as arithmetic or elementary programming, their realization is extremely complicated in the area of language teaching. Let us compare two examples.

---

[1] I am grateful for helpful remarks by Klaus Deiß, one of the programmers of WIZDOM, and Colin Foskett (both University of Wuppertal).

NATO ASI Series, Vol. F 80
Intelligent Tutoring Systems for Foreign Language Learning
Edited by M. L. Swartz and M. Yazdani

(a) Elementary Programming in LISP

In a LISP Tutor domain one will have to deal with list selectors such as CAR, CDR, CONS etc., a natural source of programming errors. However, the types of error can be easily predicted:

- wrong parenthetical structure, e.g. *(CAR '(A B C)))
- illegitimate argument types, e.g. *(CDR 'A)
- illegitimate argument structure, e.g. *(CAR 'A 'B)
- incorrect spelling of a primitive, e.g. *(CONZ 'A '(B C))
- trouble with variables and constants

Even though a few additional errors could occur (for example, argument position), the number of possible errors is clearly limited and can thus be determined in advance. Hence, the concept of "error libraries" [12,209] makes sense.

(b) Natural Language Analysis, Example: Verb Groups

By contrast, an ILTS would run into deep trouble with lists of anticipated errors. A common exercise type in the process of language teaching makes use of text gaps which have to be filled with the missing elements. Here is an example:

If Drake _______________ the Armada to the Netherlands first, it wouldn't have had so many problems.

Figure 1. Verb Groups in Gap Exercises

It is certainly possible to predict a number of possible errors:

*hasn't taken - wrong tense
*haven't taken - wrong number and tense
*had taken - positive instead of negative
*had not taked - wrong verb form
*could take - modality error
*is taking - aspectual error
*is takeing - orthographic error

However, depending on the problem it may not be possible to predict all of the possible errors, since their number is unlimited. Theoretically, any verb, even semantically illegal ones, could be chosen as the main verb of the VG and would have to be evaluated (had not sent, had not sailed, had not driven, had not lead, *had not gone, *had not become etc.). The anticipation of even such possibilities would lead to a combinatorial explosion of the error library. Hence, two alternatives are available:

(a) Reject an error with no corresponding entry in the error library as wrong.
(b) Try to evaluate an error and display a helpful comment.

In order to realize the latter option the concept of error libraries must be given up in an ILTS and be replaced by powerful analysis and generating procedures.

1.1 Natural Language (NL) Analysis in an ILTS

The analysis capability of an ILTS must be extremely robust. The system must not only be capable of analyzing input, but also of handling degraded input and displaying helpful error messages. Deviation from the expected input, however, can occur at different levels:

(a) Orthographic Deviation
Words such as *carrys or *freind should be recognized by the system and accompanied by a message about the correct orthography of the word.

(b) Internal Syntactic Deviation
Inputs such as *hadn't taking should not simply be rejected as "illegal", but the problem the analyzer faces should carefully be evaluated with a corresponding error analysis such as "-ing forms can only occur if some form of be is contained in the Verbal Group (VG)".

(c) External Syntactic Deviation
An input error such as *hadn't gone in the problem of Figure 1 is different from an internal syntactic error since it does not violate the internal syntactic structure of the VG, but the subcategorization facts of the head verb (go is intransitive and doesn't fit in the syntactic context). The analyzer should take account of this fact.

(d) Contextual Semantic Deviation
Over and above the syntactic analysis, semantic evaluation routines should assess the contextual adequacy of inputs such as *hadn't known (see Figure 1) and inform the student about the contextual (il)legitimacy of the input.

In order to fulfil these and other demands, an ILTS must be equipped with extremely powerful NL-modules whose ability lies beyond those of a bare Natural Language Processing System (NLPS). They must be able to analyze correct and incorrect input and display helpful comments in the latter case.

1.2 Components of an ILTS

According to Schwind [13,392] the following modules have to be added to elevate an ITS to an ILTS:

- a grammar knowledge base
- an exercise execution component
- a natural or graphic interface
- an error explication component

In other words, an ILTS can be seen as an expert system within an ITS. Its tasks are to analyze input, to provide detailed error analyses and explanations and to interface the NL-components with the ITS.

Even though there are attempts to make ILTSs available, many aspects of theoretical and computational linguistic theory are far from being solved. For this reason an ILTS for the whole range of NL teaching with a fully-fledged dialogue component is far from being realized, let alone on a small computer system.

"Currently, most Intelligent Computer-Assisted Instruction (ICAI) programs run on expensive LISP machines. However, such programs should eventually run on relatively inexpensive 68000- or 80386-machines. However, as we have already described, it is unlikely that such machines will find their way into schools until well into the next decade. Thus, developers of ICAI programs have two choices. They can either develop prototypes while they wait for the educational market to mature, or they can create ICAI programs that address issues (e.g. understanding statistical concepts) and/or populations (e.g. poor readers) within the school system that are sufficiently important that at least some schools will be motivated to acquire the machines required to run the program." [9,346].

We have chosen a third alternative: See what is possible in the area of ILTS and implement it on a small and cheap computer system. Since most computer-systems in Europe, especially those in schools, run under DOS, we have decided to make our tutorial system available for DOS-compatible computers, preferably for 80x86-machines.

1.3 Implementation Techniques

In order to implement the components of an ILTS on a small computer system, a number of requirements have to be met. These concern the choice of an adequate programming language, its ability to properly administer the enormous amount of tutorial data and the choice of algorithms capable of performing efficient search and processing. Only a few programming languages can handle these demands.

One argument which strongly influences the choice of the programming language in an ILTS is its efficiency to organize the storage capacity available. Since an ILTS will have to administer amounts of data too large to fit in working memory, it will have to rely on external devices (floppy disks, hard disks etc.). Hence, operations which quickly read these data are key operations within an ILTS. The data itself can be declarative (lexical frames, comments etc.) or procedural (programs and modules). Due to memory limitations an efficiently organized ILTS cannot afford to activate all modules and program parts at the same time. For example, word generating procedures are only required if the normal evaluation routines fail to manage word recognition. For this reason techniques for automatic activation and deactivation of parts of the ILTS are of extreme importance.

Obviously, one language alone cannot manage all these aspects. While typical AI-languages such as LISP or PROLOG can be used to deal with the NL-aspects of the program, these languages have a large number of weaknesses in other areas (I/O operations, file operations, graphics, menu support, interaction with the operating system etc.). For this reason we argue for a combination of several languages each applied to its specific domain. We recommend implementing an ILTS using a combination of LISP and C[2].

While LISP is used to handle most of the AI-aspects, esp. NL-analysis and NL-generation, C deals with all those aspects where LISP is extremely slow or inefficient. In order to realize the (de)activation of modules and program parts we have implemented object-oriented programming techniques [7,4ff.] which access LISP-functions and modules when required[3]. The techniques of combining programming languages are described in [4].

---

2 The following interpreters/compilers are used in WIZDOM: Turbo C (Borland), muLISP-86 (Soft Warehouse).

3 At present our systems also incorporate a number of Assembler routines. However, in order to achieve a high degree of portability, these routines will be dispensed with as soon as possible.

1.4 A First Summary

A comparison between ITS and ILTS shows that enormous efforts (see 1.3) and a number of compromises (see 2.2.1) have to be made in order to develop an ILTS. Not all NL-components required in an ILTS can be realized nor are adequate computer systems for the implementation of ILTSs available. One could follow Kurland's [9,346] suggestion and wait until these deficiencies have been sorted out. However, we suggest that a constrained ILTS can already be made available irrespective of the machine used. Such a system will certainly be far more efficient than the primitive Computer-Assisted Language Learning (CALL) systems around. WIZDOM is our proposal in this respect.

2. WIZDOM

WIZDOM is a tutorial system for CALL that satisfies the needs of professional software and realizes a large number of AI-principles as well as of computational linguistics. WIZDOM/Version 1.0 uses English as its target language. It can be run on a normally configured PC/AT under DOS (3.0 upw.) with a minimum RAM capacity of 512 KB.

The fundamental idea behind WIZDOM is that on the basis of a professional text editor, exercises should be created, processed and evaluated by the machine on the basis of its linguistic knowledge, thus combining the needs of word processing with linguistic support and tutorial software. WIZDOM is highly modular and has the system architecture as shown in Figure 2.

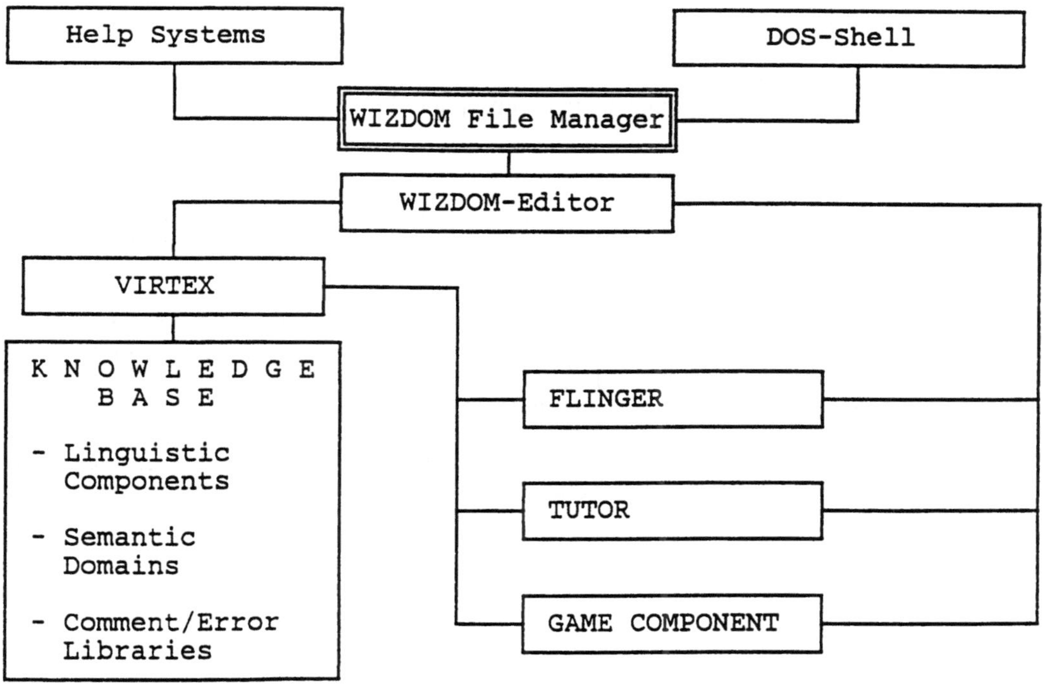

Figure. 2. WIZDOM's system architecture

2.1 WIZDOM's Basic Components

(a) The Editor
The Editor cooperates with Virtual Lexicon (VIRTEX) and Flexible Language Generator (FLINGER) and can handle texts of up to 30 pages length. It is menu and function key driven and by and large satisfies the needs of professional word processors.
(b) VIRTEX, the Lexicon
The heart of the system is a powerful lexicon. VIRTEX provides the user, at request on-line, with information about isolated words or about words in context. In the latter case words are syntactically disambiguated (2.2.1).

VIRTEX contains 7,500 entries (stems). To achieve fast lexical access, the lexicon is represented as a cohort-based discrimination network external to the program[4]. On a hard disk drive the average access time for an inflected word is 400 msecs. The lexicon can be extended by the user using an additional module, the interactive lexicon editor. Specialized databases (business, medical language, etc.) can also be added to the kernel lexicon.

With the help of VIRTEX the user can apply specific search routines to texts, for example, searching for past tense verbs, adverbs, ambiguous words etc. VIRTEX will mark them or write them into a file. Furthermore, the search-target "all words" can be used as an efficient spell-check.
(c) FLINGER, the Exercise Generator
FLINGER cooperates with WIZDOM's linguistic components and allows automatic or interactive generation of the following exercise types:
- orthographical restoration,
- vocabulary building,
- gap exercises,
- synonym exercises,
- translation exercises,
- multiple choice exercises,
- syntactic exercises (verb groups, noun groups, phrasal verbs)
- morphological exercises,
- text reconstruction,
- restricted question answering.

Needless to say, FLINGER, like "ordinary" CALL software allows teacher-based anticipation of possible errors including didactic comments, hence the realization of the concept of error libraries.
(d) TUTOR - the Interactive Tutorial Component
Once exercises have been created by WIZDOM all sorts of help facilities are at the student's disposal. The TUTOR can offer help based on morphology, syntax, synonyms or can give the translations into German of word-based exercises.

Apart from interactively guiding the student through an exercise the TUTOR evaluates the student's performance on the basis of linguistic input analyzes, error heuristics and its own linguistic knowledge. At the end of an exercise WIZDOM presents a detailed error protocol which can serve as a precise diagnostic of the student's linguistic capabilities.

---

4 The term "cohort-network" has been borrowed from theories of the mental lexicon [12], where the initial number of possible word candidates is narrowed down until only one or no word candidate is left. VIRTEX's network structure allows similar access techniques.

Evaluation of the exercise EXAMPLE1.EXR	
Lexicon activated	: 5
Word/Phrase structure shown	: 2
Translation shown	: 1
Synonyms offered	: 4
Teacher help shown	: 0
50% of word structure shown	: 0
Looked at original text	: 2
Looked at all words	: 0
Total number of problems	: 22
Correct solutions	: 14
Incorrect solutions	: 6
Correct solutions (2nd Go)	: 5
Correct guesses	: 0
==> Structural errors	: 2
==> Errors with tense, etc.	: 1
==> Meaning errors	: 2
==> Spelling difficulties	: 1
Overall result	: 72%

Figure. 3. Final Protocol (overview)

(e) The Game Component
WIZDOM's game component can be seen as an integrated vocabulary trainer. Depending on the semantic domain active, WIZDOM can enter into a dialogue about various topics (presently available: animal games, a quiz about Britain, a quiz about the United States). WIZDOM will ask questions, which the student has to answer. All general facilities are active in this component (lexical retrieval, word generators, general database information etc.). Hence, the student can retrieve lexical information, grammatical help, general information, or information about domain-specific terms.

(f) Further Facilities
WIZDOM has numerous innovative utilities, the most important among them being the various help systems dealing with general aspects of handling the program, grammatical terminology, and evaluation comments. The language of these help systems (presently available: English and German) and their difficulty level can be changed at any time. For users keen on entering the DOS-level from WIZDOM a constantly active DOS-Shell and a system-clean-up option are also included.

2.2 The Realization of WIZDOM's Linguistic Components

WIZDOM (see Figure 2) heavily relies on its lexicon (see 2.1.(b)). In most exercise types, the lexical analysis of input words and the generation of adequate comments on the basis of the analysis is fully sufficient. However, in a large number of tasks further linguistic components have to be activated. The implementation of these components illustrates the conflict between the desirable NL-ability of an ILTS and the demands of the tutorial process.

2.2.1 Disambiguation, a Compromise between NL Ability and Tutorial Demands

The basis of all linguistic analysis and generation capabilities is VIRTEX, WIZDOM's lexical component. It enables the system to retrieve information about words in isolation or directly from within a text. The latter possibility would not be very helpful if all possible interpretations of a word were presented. Here is an example of such a case:

(1) He had cut his hand.

He = Pronoun, had = Auxiliary or Copular Verb, cut = Verb or Noun, his = Determiner or Possessive Pronoun, hand = Noun or Verb.

In order to disambiguate the words in (1) morpho-lexically (i.e. work out the correct category) the linguistic context has to be incorporated. The ideal procedure to do this is to implement parsing algorithms which integrate lexical with syntactic and semantic knowledge and build up a conceptual representation of the sentence. Such a technique, however, is far too costly in an ILTS, since it would consume an enormous amount of processing time and thus drastically slow down the tutorial process.

For this reason, we have chosen an alternative way which enables the system to disambiguate words within milliseconds. In (1), for example, the context AUX/COP (had) followed by N/V (cut) followed (DET/PRON) (his) allows only one interpretation:

(had)	(cut)	(his)		(had)	(cut)
[AUX/V]	[N/V]	[DET/PRON]	==>	[Auxiliary]	[Verb]

Since the sentence is not finished at this point (no punctuation after his), his is to be interpreted as a Determiner and hand as a Noun. We do not claim that this method covers all possibilities of morpho-lexical ambiguity, however, the vast majority of contexts can be disambiguated with this technique. Since the disambiguation techniques are implemented as external discrimination networks and make use of the general cohort-based discrimination net techniques (see section 2.2.2), the standard lexicon accessing algorithm can be made use of, and - like the main lexicon - the disambiguation networks can be expanded infinitely.

The implementation of these networks, which also incorporate subcategorization facts, is a good illustration of the compromise we have to make between total NL-ability of an ILTS and the implementation of psychologically and linguistically inadequate but technically realizable principles. It is clear that true disambiguation is only possible if the entire context is analyzed linguistically. However, this would have to be done at the expense of processing speed (In an ILTS one cannot wait several minutes for the result of the analysis).

2.2.2 Morpho-Lexical Analysis

VIRTEX contains the following subcomponents:
- the main lexicon (7,500 entries)
- the disambiguation lexicon
- the language-specific grammatical entry lexicon (420 entries[5])

---

[5] The grammatical entry lexicon translates linguistic features such as V1, TEMP or CS into words which the student can understand: V1 = intransitive, TEMP = temporal, CS = subordinating conjunction. In addition to this it contains helpful information about these terms, for example: "A subordinating conjunction is a word such as if, although etc. Here is an example: ..."

- the analysis/generation component
- the morphological lexicon
- the orthographic automata
- the search component
- the phonetic symbol generator

Lexicon, disambiguation lexicon and grammatical entry lexicon are all implemented as cohort-based discrimination networks realizing the architecture described in [4,IV/V]. They are all unrestricted in their size. The physical file sizes of their main networks (those that are bound to variables in RAM) are:

- main lexicon: 18.1 KB
- disambiguation component: 0.2 KB
- grammatical entries: 1.4 KB

Entries from all three networks are retrieved using the same algorithm. While words have to be analyzed morphologically and orthographically, entries from the grammatical terminology lexicon and the disambiguation lexicon can be retrieved without the application of orthographical and morphological procedures. The morphological component consists of an affix lexicon which can handle inflectional and some derivational variants (e.g. -able, -er, -less alternants). A restricted number of compounds can be generated via pointer lists in the lexical datafile. In order to analyze orthographic variants (dying ==> die+ing, getting ==> get+ing etc.) a module using the principles of two-level morphology has been implemented.

Two further lexical components are worth mentioning:

(a) collective search strategies
The search component allows collective search strategies to be applied to texts, for example, "Find and mark all Prepositions!". This enables WIZDOM to generate word-class based exercises fully autonomously.

(b) phonemic transcription
In a number of cases WIZDOM has to access the phonemic transcription of a lexical entry. For example, the generation of determiners in the game component (2.1.(e)) cannot be carried out without phonemic information (a penguin, an ostrich, a useful animal etc.). To make the phonemic information available not only for the process of word generation but also for the tutorial process, symbol generators that transfer an arbitrary internal code to actual phonemic transcription using the principles of the IPA had to be developed.

2.2.3 Syntactic and Semantic Analysis

All syntactic and semantic rule systems are implemented as networks. The process of syntactic analysis is controlled by a Cascaded Augmented Transition Network (CATN), which like the lexical networks is external to the system (the main net requires only 0.2 KB RAM). It is used to parse partial input such as VGs or NPs and to analyze questions asked by the student in the game component. In WIZDOM version 2.0 the CATN incorporates domain-specific semantic information, for example knowledge about animals, the United Kingdom, etc. This knowledge is represented in terms of semantic frames in conjunction with domain-specific semantic networks.

2.2.4 Further Linguistic Components

In order to exclude numbers from the lexicon, a number generator was added to the system which analyzes and generates numbers of up to 15 digits. Apart from the ability to retrieve numbers directly from the text and present them in various languages, the number generator is made use of in the guessing games, when WIZDOM asks for the altitude of mountains, the population figures of towns etc.

Whenever input words are spelt incorrectly but the deviation still allows lexical access (e.g. *carrys, *geting, *hoofs etc.) WIZDOM regenerates the correct structure, applying its word generator. This technique allows comments on orthographical errors, and does not involve aborting the analysis.

2.3 Some Snapshots of WIZDOM at Work

The following figures illustrate some of WIZDOM's possibilities. Figure 3 is a snapshot of WIZDOM's exercise generator (FLINGER) at work. The generation of an exercise is extremely easy. After loading a text into the editor one simply activates the exercise menu and WIZDOM's exercise generator FLINGER automatically decides what to do. While in the exercise types 1 to 7 (Figure 4) FLINGER interacts with the user (making lexical suggestions, internally holding the linguistic analyzes), exercise types 8 to 10 are created fully autonomously on the basis of WIZDOM's search heuristics. Since WIZDOM has access to the lexical information about each word, entirely new exercise types are possible. For example, one can create a gap exercise where all Prepositions and all Verb forms are blanked out, thus creating text reconstruction with morphological knowledge. Note that even in these automatically created exercise types WIZDOM can offer morphological help and a translation into German (see Figure 5).

```
 To be processed: hadn't sent

                                       Admiral of the English Crown
   FLINGER Exercise Menu
                                       onal sentences III
   1 Word-based Gap Exercise       [W] rm of the verbs.
   2 Verbgroup Gap Exercise        [V]
1  3 Noungroup Gap Exercise        [N] n Drake long ago if he
   4 Free Editing Exercise         [F]  pirate in his younger years.
   5 Exercises with phrasal verbs  [P]
2  6 Multiple Choice General       [M]  told their pupils so much
   7 Multiple Choice Orthography   [O]                 such
   8 Removing specific word classes [C]
   9 Word Reconstruction Exercise  [S]
3 10 Text Reconstruction Exercise  [R] ght have landed successfully
                                        his admirals different
   orders.

4. If he hadn't sent the Armada to the Netherlands first,
   it wouldn't have got so many problems.
```

Figure 4. FLINGER's Exercise Generating Menu

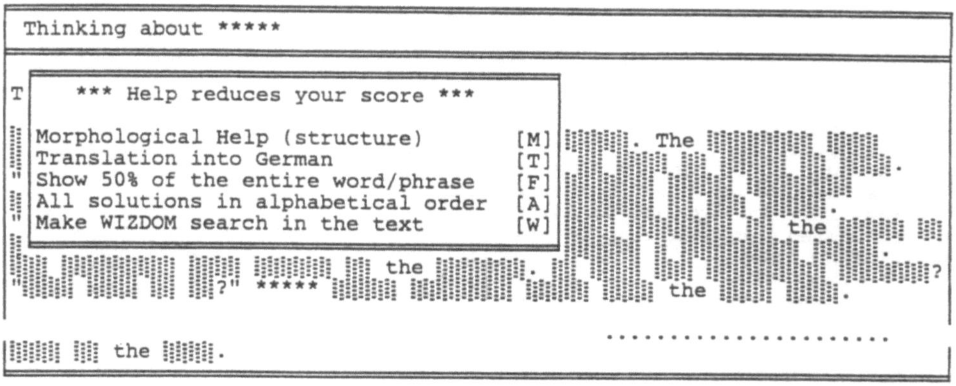

Figure 5: Help in Text Reconstructions

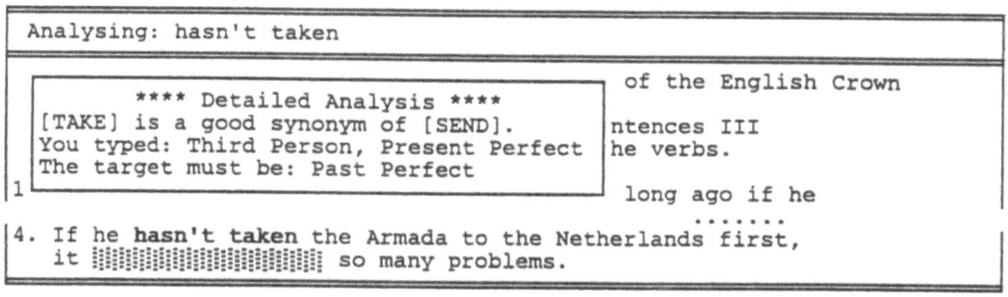

Figure 6. Evaluation in Syntactic Groups

Well-known text reconstruction exercises can now be augmented with linguistic information. Due to its linguistic knowledge WIZDOM can make available a variety of information about each word hidden. Figure 6 illustrates these new facilities.

WIZDOM's power can be documented most efficiently in a syntactic exercise such as "Insert the correct Verb Form". With its linguistic components WIZDOM can analyze the input and compare it with the automatically generated features of the target and provide detailed error analyses. Note that lexical information is available. The student can freely move around in the text and retrieve the translation, synonyms, the pronunciation or information about the structure of a word whenever desired.

The final example illustrates the interaction between WIZDOM (WIZDOM asks) and the user:

```
                    <WIZDOM ASKS ABOUT ANIMALS>

Can the animal expel poison? No.
Have you chosen a vertebrate? Yes.
Is it correct that it is able to suckle its offsprings? Yes.
Is my assumption right that it has a brain? Yes.
May I assume that it has got many bones? Don't know!
Is my assumption right that it has a lung? Yes.
Am I right in thinking that it is a mammal? Yes.
Have you chosen a mammal that eats anything? Don't know!
Does it bring luck? __
                    ..........
```

Figure 7. Guessing Games (Animals, WIZDOM asks)

The questions which WIZDOM asks are randomized ones partly generated by the system. For example, Noun Phrases are fully generated by an interaction between the semantic component and the lexicon. This allows plural forms and Article/Noun concord to be generated.

3. Summary

As desirable as the augmentation of traditional CALL-Software with the principles of AI may be, it is an extremely complex task. Theoretical issues, programming demands and hardware requirements (such software should run on a normal PC!) constrain the implementation to a large degree. Tutorial systems, which satisfy these and additional requirements (for example, dialogue capability) cannot be made available within the near future. For this reason, we have to confine ourselves to those areas where reliable rules and principles as well as commonly accepted programming concepts exist.
WIZDOM is a first step into this direction. It is not a true ILTS since its dialogue capabilities are limited. However, WIZDOM has an enormous analysis capability. It does not have to rely on human instructions about possible input errors in the tutorial process, but it applies its linguistic knowledge to human input. This not only allows the free editing of exercise texts but also offers completely new exercise forms, for example, text reconstruction where the system is in full charge of the structure of each word. Thus, terms such as error anticipation/libraries or constrained text editors such as authoring systems should definitely belong to the past.

4. References

1. Bumbaca, F.: Intelligent computer-assisted instruction: a theoretical framework. International Journal Man-Machine Studies 29:227-255 (1988)
2. Collins, A. & Brown, J.S.: The computer as a tool for learning through reflection. In: Mandl & Lesgold (eds.): Learning issues for intelligent tutoring systems. New York, NY: Springer-Verlag 1988
3. Dede, C.: A review and synthesis of recent research in intelligent computer-assisted instruction. International journal man-machine studies 24/(4):329-353 (1986)
4. Deiß, K., Handke, J. & Meyer, B.: Professionelles Programmieren mit LISP. Hamburg: McGraw-Hill 1990
5. Fischer, G.: Enhancing incremental learning processes with knowledge-based systems. In: Mandl & Lesgold (eds.): Learning isues for intelligent tutoring systems. New York, NY: Springer-Verlag 1988
6. Handke, J.: Natürliche Sprache: Theorie und Implementierung in LISP. Hamburg: McGraw-Hill 1989
7. Keene, S.E.: Object-oriented programming in common LISP. New York: Addison-Wesley 1989

8. Kunz, G. C. & Schott, F.: Intelligente Tutorielle Systeme. Göttingen: Verlag für Psychologie 1987
9. Kurland, D.M.: Computer applications in education: A historical overview. Annual review of computer science, 1987/2: 317-358 (1987)
10. Lesgold, A.: Intelligenter Computerunterstützter Unterricht. In: Mandl, H. & Spada, H. (eds.): Wissenspsychologie. München: Psychologie Verlagsunion 1988
11. Mandl, H.. & Lesgold, A.: Learning isues for intelligent tutoring systems. New York, NY: Springer Verlag 1988
12. Ohlsson, S.: Some principles of intelligent tutoring. In: Lawler, R./Yazdani, M. (eds.). Artificial intelligence and education, Vol 1: Learning environments and tutoring systems. New York, NY: Norwood 1987
13. Schwind, C.B.: Overview of an intelligent language tutoring system. Proceedings of the 2nd international conference on AI, pp. 389-407 1986

Intelligent Automated Strategies of Teaching Foreign Language in Context

Eleanor Criswell[1], Heidi Byrnes[2], Guenter Pfister[3]

[1] Science Applications International Corporation, Intelligent Technology Division, 1710 Goodridge Drive, McLean, VA 22102
[2] Georgetown University, German Department, Washington, DC 20057
[3] University of Maryland, German Department, Jimenez Hall, Room 3215, College Park, MD 20742

Abstract: Trends in foreign language teaching for instructional settings are fundamentally motivated by our understanding of the essence of language, characteristics of human learning, and a human's capacity to learn a language other than the native language. Following from our understanding in those areas, we have developed a prototype intelligent, automated, foreign language tutoring system, based on principles of contextualized, communicative language teaching. Our system emphasizes the exclusive or near exclusive use of the foreign language in meaningful situations, interactive instructional sequences, highly sensitive computer responses to the inputs of individual students, including the use of a natural language processing system to evaluate free text inputs, and the use of a variety of different types of practice exercises and media. We are building a system for developing lessons that function like a gifted teacher, and at the same time, are useful as research testbeds.

Keywords: Intelligent Computer-Assisted Instruction, Foreign Language Training, Contextualized Language Teaching, Communicative Language Teaching, Natural Language Processing, Hypermedia.

1. Contextualized Language Teaching

1.1 The affective domain in language learning

Language is the fundamental medium through which communication takes place, and is the bearer of the culture in which students have to maneuver adeptly. Language is no mere codification system, no mere interface for the use of static units of discrete and manageable bits of meaning. It is a very human and personal phenomenon. In our attempts to teach foreign language, we may be apt to forget the personal nature of the phenomenon we are dealing with.

Learners are human beings whose actions are motivated by a diverse array of affective-psychological factors. Students are not learning machines, but people with likes, dislikes, talents, questions, and personal concerns. These cannot be dismissed as irrelevant to the objectives we wish to achieve; on the contrary, human characteristics must be channeled and used to their greatest effect in the process of teaching a foreign language.

NATO ASI Series, Vol. F 80
Intelligent Tutoring Systems for Foreign Language Learning
Edited by M. L. Swartz and M. Yazdani

Effective foreign language learning occurs within a framework which recognizes that information must be converted into the ability to function effectively in a specific environment. All of our learning takes place within a continuing process of constructing reality. Each individual constructs his or her reality from the building blocks at hand, chiefly, one's native language. This reality is a product of expectations which we develop when we become aware of the norms which structure our society and its values. Thus, each of us is constantly involved in a process of fulfilling and/or adjusting our expectations based on our experience of the world around us. Language serves a multitude of communicative needs for human beings in the real world, a fact that must not be forgotten as we seek ways of enhancing language learning.

1.2 Bringing in extra-linguistic context

Foreign language instruction must first and foremost find a way for bringing extra-linguistic context to play in the acquisition of a foreign language. This is necessary for accessing the student's potential, interest, and desire for any learning at all, but also for safeguarding the essential character of language as a means for communication, as contrasted with an aggregate of forms. Obviously it is impossible to create in the classroom all the extra-linguistic background phenomena that define communication. Thus, a workable substitute must be found that approximates the role these contexts play in real-life communication. The following principles characterize this pedagogy [see 10, 16 for complementary principles]:

1. Establish the extra-linguistic context through language tasks. Language use involves choices about what tasks we wish to accomplish in a given communicative setting. Contextualized language teaching is teaching on the basis of tasks. By sketching out tasks for our students which they need to accomplish, we activate their desire to communicate, we build on their ability to call up entire scenarios or domains which help organize reality, we set in motion their strategic competence to manage conversations, and we give them criteria for differentiating the important from the ancillary features of the communicative setting which they are asked to create as a mental image.

2. Relate the hierarchy of tasks to the hierarchy of form complexity. A hierarchy of tasks is postulated, based on the formal complexity of the language most likely to occur with these tasks. Tasks associated with typical transactional exchanges pertaining to such notions as place and time, or inquiring about goods and services in daily life, require the speaker to have a basic command of sentence-level syntax, simple questions and answers, and a sufficiently elaborated vocabulary range to cover the high-frequency vocabulary of daily life. By contrast, narration and description require the speaker to be able to process language beyond the sentence level, engaging in backgrounding and foregrounding, using markers of cohesion and coherence, expanding the sentence beyond its kernel, not to mention being able to access a more elaborated vocabulary and a system for indicating temporal relationships.

3. Analyze the learner's place on the task/complexity hierarchy. The individual instructor or the overall program of instruction must have a keen awareness of the learner's place along the task/complexity hierarchy. It must allow for just the right amount of stretching, reaching, and challenging, but must also offer time for solidifying, automatizing, and reorganizing previously acquired features. That is the essence of the concept of i + 1, locating instruction at the learner's current level of comfort, but pushing and probing to the next higher level.

4. Aim at the progression from context-embedded to decontextualized forms. Extralinguistic context and linguistic form together accomplish communication in complementary distribution in inverse relation. That is, the more defined the communicative exchange, the more embedded into a highly specified context, the lower the need for elaborated language forms. Or conversely, the more open-ended the context, the more elaborated are the language forms necessary to handle the contingencies which inhere in this communicative setting. Thus, one might summarize increasing facility with the language as one that allows the learner not only to handle context-embedded

communicative situations, but an ever-increasing range of situations where language-related capabilities are the only way to master the tasks.

5. Use an inverse relationship between task and language levels. The pedagogy of tasks benefits from and exploits the special dynamic of the inverse relationship between task and language levels. For example, one might say it is not so much language forms that make a reading comprehension text difficult, but the tasks a learner is asked to perform as a result of having worked with specific language material.

6. Respect the acquisitional hierarchy of different language modalities. The different modes of language use -- listening, reading, writing, and speaking -- differ in the kinds of tasks typically associated with them and also in the ease with which learners are likely to be able to handle them. Thus it is a well known fact that we can comprehend more in reading and listening than we can produce in writing and speaking. That being the case, and assuming that comprehension is a critical factor in learning, even a language program that aims at speaking ability, the most difficult mode to master in most European languages, must regard the advantage of catching a student's intellect by presenting him or her with comprehension work.

7. Create an instructional context by interrelating the different language modalities. The pedagogy of tasks not only acknowledges the acquisitional hierarchy among the language modes. It creates an instructional context within which all four modes are interrelated. Individual learners approach learning in different ways, responding more favorably to one or the other mode of language use. Thus inherently, a broader palette of offerings which connects different language modalities together with their likely tasks has a higher chance of meeting the needs of a larger learner group. In addition, it replicates much of what we do with language in daily life. In every case, tasks are being accomplished that are based on certain contexts, linguistic as well as extralinguistic, and call for certain kinds of language performance.

1.3 Contextualized foreign language learning strategies

One view of appropriate language learning strategies which follows from this notion of the importance of the communicative goals of language learners as individuals [2,3,9,11,13,14,15] is that language learning strategies should require the learner to control the learning process, to control his or her construction of reality. Language must be taught within its cultural environment, to include authentic cultural elements and language. The ultimate goal of language learning is an integration of a foreign language with the learner's identity so the learner can function in another culture at the highest levels.

Language learning strategies must foster the development of personal, communicative, foreign language use. Language learning strategies are designed to bring a student from a state of minimal communicative involvement to a point where language and communication in the foreign language are part of the student's identity. First, the learner is prepared or motivated to learn. Positive attitudes toward the target culture need to be developed. Then the learner demonstrates that he or she is interested in learning. Language learning strategy supports this by including activities with short term goals. Accomplishment of longer term goals is supported by providing real life situations reflecting the culture of the language. The student comes to value the target language only if the language is used in nonartificial ways. Next, the learner comes to understand the members of the target language community. The learner must empathize with the target community, not view it critically. Finally, the language becomes internalized. The student now has acquired a new mode of thinking and a new culture.

Contextualized foreign language lessons may begin with a narrative or dialogue selection about the foreign culture. Narratives might concentrate on differences between the native and foreign cultures while dialogues might highlight interactions between people. The selections in the lesson get the learner to listen to, read, and speak about the foreign culture, increasing in difficulty so as to allow the student to practice further what has already been mastered, but also to acquire new facilities.

The contextualized lesson should include asking and answering questions arising from the narrative or dialogue selections. A learner's natural curiosity plays an important role in these exercises. Questions posed to the student may require factual answers from the narrative. However, from an affective perspective, students are also interested in their own lives and concerns, perhaps even more so than in mere factual information. Therefore, posing personalized questions to the student is helpful. Question and answer activity represents a most important means of guiding learning: through it, learners can control what information they need to prune from the narrative or dialogue.

Communication is spontaneous and requires quick response. Therefore it must be practiced in exercises that allow the student to use and apply the requisite grammatical structures. By identifying recurring patterns, learners form rules and generalizations about the structure of the foreign language, thereby improving both their intake of new material as well as their output. A key to this approach is the realization on the part of students that they as individuals control the amount and rate at which they will acquire new information for further competence in the foreign language.

2. Intelligent Automated Language Tutoring

2.1. Overview

Using what we know about the importance of contextualized language training, as well as other work conducted during the course of this multi-year project [8], we developed generalized characteristics for a computerized foreign language teaching system. Obviously a computer can not function with the moment to moment flexibility and expertise of a gifted, pedagogically aware teacher, but we wanted our system to come as close as possible. Even more important, we wanted our system to reflect sound foreign language pedagogy, not simply showcase adventures in computer technology.

The most central characteristics of our system are: (1) exclusive or near exclusive use of the foreign language in meaningful or contextualized situations, (2) interactive instructional sequences which require language production on the part of the student, (3) highly sensitive computer responses to the inputs of individual students, and (4) use of a variety of different instructional exercises. We then implemented these characteristics in the context of a complete, language lesson development system, which runs on a PC-type computer. Figure 1 shows the architecture of the language teaching system. The interested reader may consult other sources [8] for a full description of the project and system. However, the remainder of this paper focuses on the automated tutor component of the system (see Figure l) as well as on the design of one lesson we have implemented in German.

2.2. Artificial intelligence in the system

Achieving the high degree of sensitivity to student inputs and flexibility in instructional methods required the use of artificial intelligence concepts and programming techniques. The system is intelligent in two of its fundamental functions: the tutor and natural language processing functions. These two functions represent two expert models: one in teaching and one in language.

Intelligence in the automated tutor

First, the tutor is intelligent in its highly interactive sequences and sensitivity to individual students. The intelligent automated tutor functions much like a human instructor that sizes up an individual student and tailors instruction to suit the individual. The intelligent tutor uses a student's history to

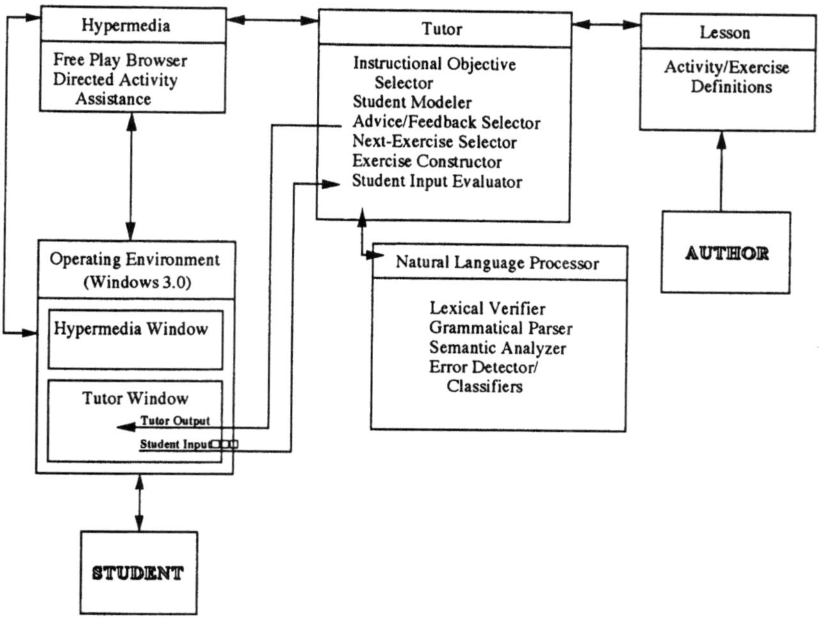

Figure 1. Language teaching system architecture

select instructional activities. It is as if the automated tutor thinks "Oh, I know you, and I think I know why you said `to est' instead of `to the east'. I've seen you stumble on similar points before. I won't worry about the misspelled word right now, I'll focus on your understanding of the phrase expressing direction. I know that showing you a picture usually helps you figure things out. I also know that you are a fast learner, and you don't need much help. So I'll show you a picture right now."

Additionally, the tutor is intelligent in its ability to use a variety of instructional methods, much like a human teacher with an imaginative mind and a variety of classroom aids. The automated tutor offers approximately 10 types of activities (new activity types are authorable), each of which has multiple iterations (called practice exercises) at varying difficulty levels. Also at the disposal of the automated tutor is a hypermedia system that provides aural, graphic, and textual information about the foreign language words used in the lesson.

In contrast, a conventional automated tutor has only a limited range of instructional methods, most notably drill, and routes anyone making an error down a similar path, and there are not many paths to choose from. For example, anyone answering "to east" when the answer should have been "to the west" is routed to the same canned remedial activity, regardless of the individual history and characteristics of the student. Obviously, receiving canned remediation on the use of "to" plus definite article, for example, misses the mark when the student error was really a problem with "east-west." The paths in conventional automated instructional systems typically contain only true-false, multiple choice, or short fill-in-the-blank exercises.

Intelligence in the natural language processor

The second use of artificial intelligence in the system lies in the natural language processing component. A sophisticated foreign language training system must be able to evaluate free text inputs from the student, markedly distinguishing it from systems that can only handle true-false, multiple choice, or canned fill-ins. Sole reliance on simple exercises will not support acquisition and maintenance of real communication in the foreign language. The natural language component contains the expertise in the foreign language against which free text inputs are judged. This component evaluates language inputs for lexical, grammatical, and semantic correctness. Evaluation results are sent to the tutor component that decides what to do with the information.

The interested reader may consult [1] or [8] for more information about the natural language processing system. In summary, the natural language processing system was designed to handle a number of crucial requirements, e.g., must identify all errors -- lexical, grammatical, semantic -- within a single sentence, must run on a PC-type computer, must be adaptable to multiple foreign languages.

Incorporating these system requirements, the natural language processing component was designed around the Government-Binding approach [4] that includes construction-independent rules and constraints which provide a highly compact grammar representation. This compactness is directly related to its use of language independent universals. Construction-non-specific formulae are grouped into interacting modules. These modules are then parameterized, making it possible to represent different languages by specifying their respective parameter values [1]. Thus, large parts of the natural language processing system are re-usable across languages.

The natural language processor evaluates sentence length inputs. As mentioned earlier, the system presents a variety of instructional activities to the student; some student inputs are parsed conventionally by the tutor itself. However, whole sentences completely or partially generated (as in a fill-in-the-blank within a sentence) by the student are evaluated by the natural language processor. The natural language module first checks that its on-line lexicon contains all the words used in the sentence; the system invokes a lexical assist if unknown words are found to allow the student to select words from the existing lexicon. Next, the sentence input is evaluated for grammatical correctness. Next, a semantics module ascertains if the sentence input is contextually appropriate. Finally, the natural language processor sends to the automated tutor component a list of errors found. The automated tutor then decides what to do with this information, based on interactions among its multiple knowledge bases as described below.

2.3. Knowledge bases in the tutor component

The tutor component in this system assumes the functions of the tutor model of pedagogical knowledge found in many intelligent tutoring systems [5,12]. However, our automated tutor differs from other intelligent tutors in two ways. First, we have dramatically increased the complexity of the tutor component to increase the tutor's sensitivity to the actions of individual students. As mentioned earlier, we are trying to make the automated tutor act as much like a gifted human foreign language teacher as possible.

In addition, we have implemented the tutor component in modular fashion to permit experimental manipulation within and across modules. Each module, corresponding to a tutor function, contains rules for tutoring that are authorable. Thus, the modular tutor component provides an uncommon opportunity for us to conduct research on multiple aspects of tutoring expertise.

Previous analyses of tutoring [6,7,8] led us to the notion that an automated intelligent tutor should be designed in five knowledge bases which correspond to its main functions: instructional objective selector, student modeler, next-exercise selector, advice/feedback selector, and exercise constructor. Designing the tutor in separate knowledge bases allows us the opportunity to manipulate rules for purposes of experimental comparisons among rules. The knowledge bases are shown in Figure 2. The tutor also contains a student input evaluator capability (shown in Figure 1). These components of the intelligent, automated tutor are described below.

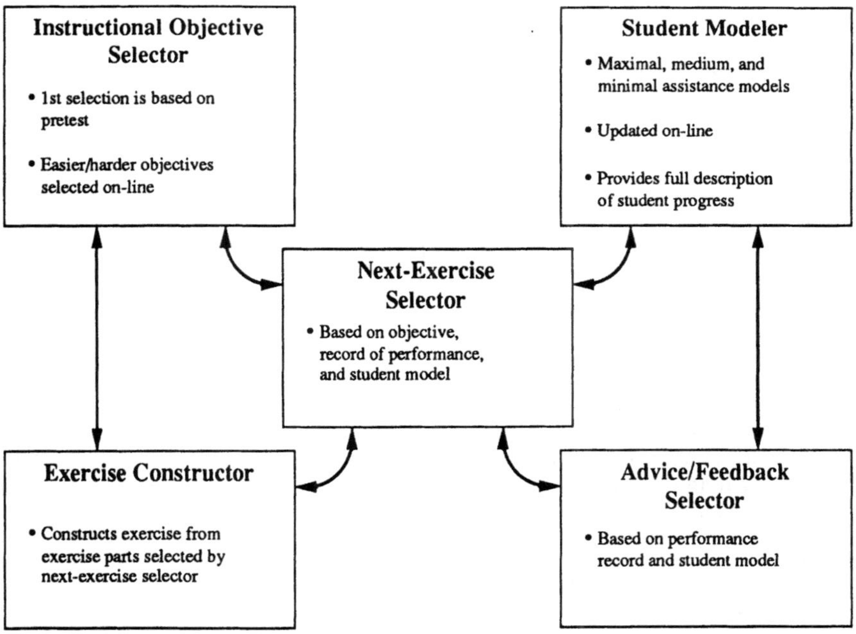

Figure 2. Rule Bases for Intelligent Automated Tutoring

Instructional objective selector

The rules in the instructional objective selector choose instructional foci based on their location along a difficulty hierarchy and student test scores. The first instructional objective is selected based on pretest scores reflecting proficiency levels, for example, any objective at 50-70% strength might be eligible for selection as an instructional focus. During the lesson, the system provides feedback and advice related to that objective. If the system detects a threshold of errors in a previously mastered objective, the student is advised of the problem; if the problem continues, the lesson focus switches to the problem objective. If the system detects errors in objectives not yet undertaken, no feedback or advice is given, but the errorful baseline data are retained for use in later analysis.

Student modeler

Student models are descriptions or representations of the student. The student model characterizes a student's progress, or what the student does and does not know, and explains that progress, in its whys and hows. Student models, then, critically contribute to the automated tutor's instructional decision making for individual students. (See papers in the section on Student Modeling, this volume, for other approaches to this problem.)

We have chosen to model three types of students: students requiring minimal, medium, and maximal amounts of assistance. This modeling parallels what a human teacher might do, giving help to those that need it and leaving the others relatively alone until they ask for help. Rules in these models designate the amount and type of help available as well as progression/remediation criteria. In general, minimal assistance students are moved through the lesson very quickly, and maximal assistance students are allowed to move through more slowly. The student model updates itself on-line. For example, if a maximal assistance student is progressing well, the model will reclassify the student as one requiring medium assistance to provide more freedom from tutor intervention.

The student modeler contains the student's performance levels on all instructional objectives, what the student knows. In addition, the student modeler attempts to determine "why" a student knows something, by comparing the student's performance on multiple instructional objectives and practice exercises. For example, the system might calculate that a student gave an incorrect input "to east" because he or she has not mastered the use of "to" plus definite article as opposed to not knowing the difference between "east" and "west." This calculation would be made using scores on previous exercises. In this case, these scores would show no error history for "east" versus "west," but would show an error history on use of "to" plus definite article.

The student modeler in our system is advanced over some student modelers, but could be improved to infer diagnoses based on more or deeper reasoning than described in the previous paragraph. As an example, adding deeper inferencing might entail adding rules that allow the tutor to hypothesize about the nature of the student's problems, then test those hypotheses. The current automated tutor does not test its own hunches in the way a human teacher might. We would like to add deeper inferencing capabilities to this aspect of the student modeler, then evaluate the benefits of using contrasting approaches to student modeling.

Next-exercise selector

The next-exercise selector in the automated tutor can be set to reflect differing pedagogical approaches to selecting the next activity. For example, in a current lesson, a maximal assistance student receives more exercises per instructional objective than a minimal assistance student. Maximal assistance students receive remedial attention earlier than minimal assistance students, reflecting the notion that we can ignore certain unpatterned errors with our advanced students but need to catch even unpatterned errors with our maximal assistance students.

A contrary view may also be supportable. Maximal assistance students might be given more instances for trying out their hypotheses about how certain messages are conveyed or how certain language forms work. Assuming that maximal assistance students have many areas in which their language is flawed, the intelligent tutor makes the decision not to correct all errors, but to focus instructional emphasis only on certain errors, while ignoring others. Following through with this view, we might hypothesize that advanced students already possess such a good command of the language system that it is possible to help them eliminate remaining errors quickly with immediate interventions. These notions are all testable.

Advice/feedback selector

Rules in the advice/feedback selector component of the automated tutor prescribe how often and what type of feedback and advice to present. In one lesson in German for example, these rules vary depending on the student model. For example, maximal assistance students are given more frequent and elaborate feedback on the specific instructional points than minimal assistance students. The advice/feedback component draws heavily on the error report received from the natural language processing module. This component determines how much information from the error report will be given to the student.

As with the other tutor components in our system, differing approaches may be compared experimentally. For example, we can address such questions as: under what conditions should the automated tutor inform the student that an error was made (feedback), or inform that an error was made and give the location of the error in the sentence (feedback plus one type of advice), or inform that an error was made and provide additional information about the nature of the error (feedback plus another type of advice)? Research using the advice/feedback selector module can address some of the compelling instructional questions of the day.

Exercise constructor

Practice exercises are not built in advance and stored somewhere in the system. Rather, the exercise constructor builds on-line the next exercise specified by the next exercise selector. Exercises differ in type (e.g., true-false, generate sentence) and difficulty (e.g., easy, medium, hard) as well as content (e.g., geographic locations, prepositional phrases). Each exercise is specified along several dimensions, and the rules in the exercise constructor build the next exercise using appropriate values along the dimensions. For example, exercises are timed. The next exercise to be constructed might be one in which the slowest time tolerated is 30 seconds, and that value would be incorporated into the exercise.

Student input evaluator

As mentioned earlier, the system supports use of a variety of practice exercises, reflecting system instructional flexibility and motivational capability. The automated tutor component evaluates some types of exercises, and the natural language processing component evaluates others.

In the tutor component, true-false, multiple choice, point to (a location on a map, for example), and sorting (e.g., placing items under correct column headers) exercises are evaluated using conventional techniques for parsing inputs. These techniques involve comparing the student's input to prespecified correct inputs. In our system, many of the lesson author's prespecifications do not have to be exact; this is an advance over the authoring techniques required by many conventional computer-based instructional systems. However, artificial intelligence techniques are not needed to parse student responses to conventional exercises, such as true-false, multiple choice, point to, and sorting types of exercises. Subsequently, the evaluation produced by the exercise evaluator component of the tutor is used by other tutor components to make instructional decisions.

By contrast, fill-in-the-blank and enter-complete-sentence exercises are evaluated by the natural language processing system. We designed the system such that all complete sentences are analyzed by the natural language processor. The main benefit, of course, is that the system can evaluate complete sentences entered by students. We also get benefits by having the natural language component evaluate fill-in-the-blanks. Assuming that the system-generated portion of a sentence is correct, any errors found by the natural language processor would have to be in the student's fill-ins. Because the entire sentence is sent to the natural language processor, we can effectively generate numerous fill-in-the-blank exercises using the same sentence, simply by automatically changing the component left blank. The natural language component can evaluate student inputs where many correct answers are possible, both in entire student-generated sentences as well as fill-ins. For example, in the sentence "Schlitz is located ________ Fulda," several correct answers are possible, e.g., "north of," "north and east of," "near the city of." The results of the natural language analysis are sent to the tutor component for decision-making regarding what to do next.

3. Sample Contextualized Lesson in German Reading Comprehension

3.1 The scenario

Using the prototype system, we have developed a lesson that incorporates a computerized version of contextualized foreign language teaching. The lesson focuses on German expressions of location and direction which are important for military personnel (our students in this project) and difficult grammatically for English speakers of German. The backdrop to the lesson is a series of paragraphs that first describes a look at a map of Europe, then a look at a map of Germany. The student uses these paragraphs in listening comprehension exercises. Thus prepared, the student moves on to a reading comprehension lesson which focuses on a scenario describing a view of a specific region from the top of a 400-meters high hill. The student is to imagine he or she is standing on the top of the hill, looking all around, noticing cultural and man-made terrain features. The scenario contains three paragraphs with about 325 words.

Figure 3 shows a student interface for a reading comprehension/vocabulary usage lesson in German. The scenario is displayed in the lesson text window; this window enlarges to take up the entire screen, if the student wishes. Maps and graphic images related to the scenario are available in the hypermedia window. Practice exercises and interactions with the material occur in the tutor window, except exercises that require the student to point to a location on a map. Even for point-to exercises, system judgments on student inputs appear in the tutor window.

3.2 Practice exercises

Activity groups

In order to graduate to the next instructional objective, the student must successfully pass through a series of activities. These range from simple, straightforward activities such as indicating which phrases illustrate directions, to sorting location and direction statements into two lists, to fill-in-the-blanks (e.g., We are standing on a hill to the ___ of Lauterbach) to enter-complete-sentences (e.g., Where is the city of Schlitz in relation to Lauterbach?). Of course, the range of activities used by a human teacher is much wider than that available on a computer; nevertheless, we are able to

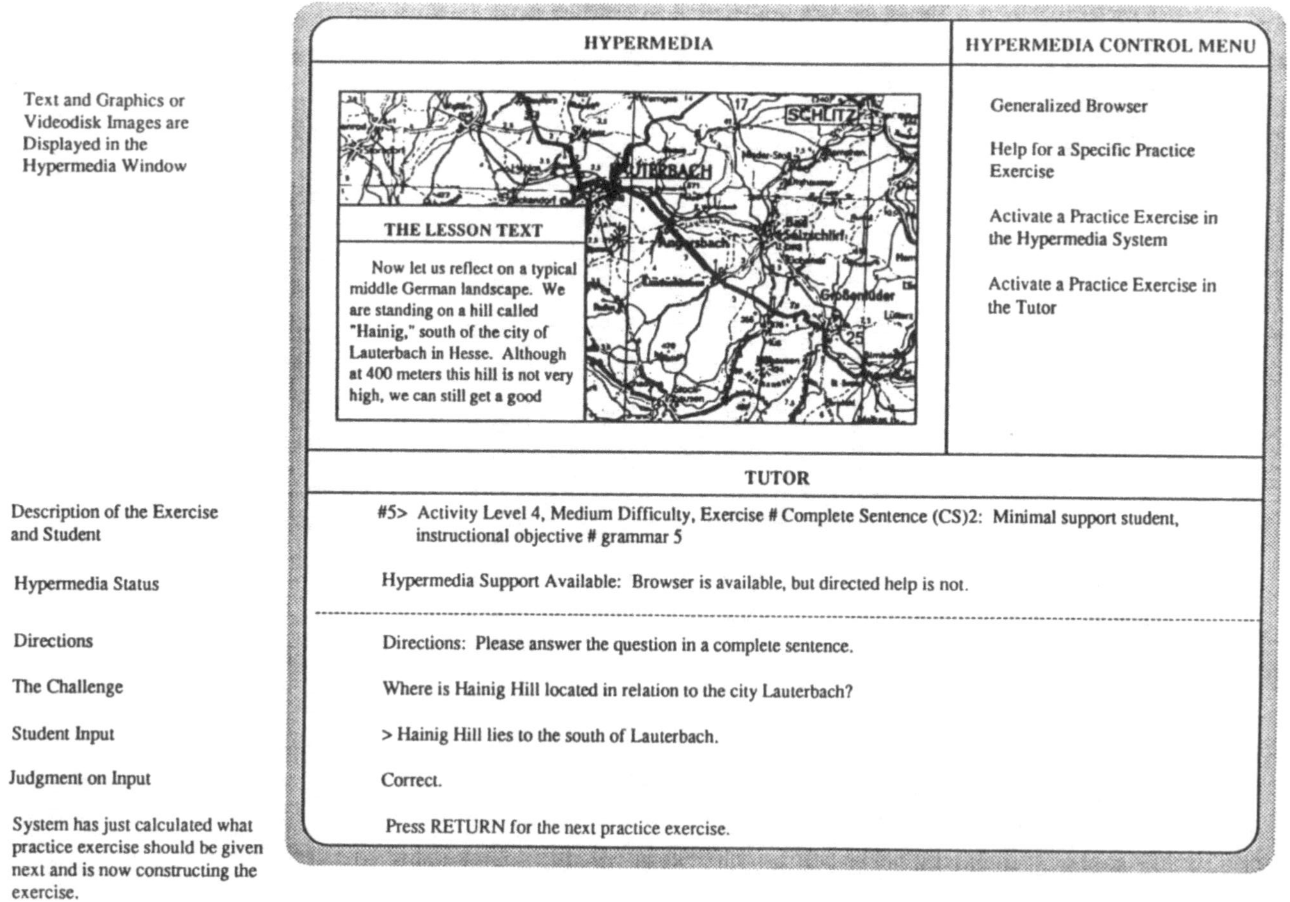

Figure 3. Student Interface for a Reading Comprehension/Vocabulary Usage Lesson

implement many more different types of activities than those usually implemented in a computer training system.

Difficulty levels

For each activity we developed practice exercises that vary in difficulty. Thus any activity can be administered as a practice exercise of easy, average, or high difficulty. Variables affecting difficulty are degree of accuracy required, time constraints, and help available. For example, an exercise requiring a precise input, in a short amount of time without additional help such as is available in the hypermedia system, is more difficult than one satisfied with only imprecise inputs, and offering generous time limits with additional help.

4. Future Work

Near-term work on the automated tutor component of this project focuses on (1) conducting experimental evaluations of aspects of tutor effectiveness and (2) implementing a lesson in another language (Arabic) using the modular shell system.

Our research program will be aimed at comparing the instructional effectiveness of different combinations of rules reflecting differing pedagogical approaches. For example, we hope to answer questions such as: what type of feedback and advice for what type of language errors for what student characteristics are associated with more effective learning? Our research program will be directed at identifying specific aspects of instructional intelligence associated with contextualized language training that lead to such effectiveness. The modular design of the system supports such experimentation.

We have begun implementing a lesson in Arabic, to parallel as closely as possible the lesson developed in German. Using the lesson in the second language, we will be able to see, among other things, which, if any, instructional effectiveness variables are language-independent. For example, does graphic illustration heighten instructional effects for one language more than others, or does detailed advice provide better instruction for grammar errors of particular types, or does a maximal assistance student in German require more detailed feedback than a maximal assistance student of Arabic. We will be able to use the system to evaluate instructional variables within and across languages.

Acknowledgements

This paper describes part of a large project called "Applications of Artificial Intelligence to Foreign Language Training" funded by the U.S. Army Research Institute, Training Research Lab, Alexandria, VA, Melissa Holland, Technical Monitor, Contract MDA-903-89-C-0033 to Science Applications International Corporation, McLean, VA, USA.

References

1. Azadegan, S., Martin, J., Merlo, P., and Weinberg, A.: Experimental natural language representations for intelligent computer-assisted instruction. Technical Report for U.S. Army Research Institute. McLean, VA: Science Applications International Corporation 1989

2. Bragger, J.: The development of oral proficiency. In proficiency, curriculum, articulation: The ties that bind (A. O'Maggio, ed). Northeast Conference Reports. Middlebury, VT: The Northeast Conference 1985

3. Canale, M., and Swain, M.: Theoretical bases of communicative approaches to second language teaching and testing. Applied Linguistics 1, 1-47 (1980)

4. Chomsky, N.: Lectures on government and binding. Cambridge: Foris 1981

5. Criswell, E.: The design of computer-based instruction. New York: Macmillan 1989

6. Criswell, E., Boyer, M., Canody, D., and Miller, L.: Student-initiated interactions in a conventional CBI lesson. Journal of Computer-Based Instruction 17 (2), 61-65 (1989)

7. Criswell, E., Byrnes, H., Rapaport, B., Dukes, M., Miller, L., and Blascak, D.: Analysis of foreign language requirements for military interrogators. Technical Report for U.S. Army Research Institute. McLean, VA: Science Applications International Corporation 1989

8. Criswell, E., Weinberg, A., Miller, L., Byrnes, H., and Blascak, D.: Applications of artificial intelligence to foreign language learning: Analysis, design, and initial prototyping. Technical Report for U.S. Army Research Institute. McLean, VA: Science Applications International Corporation 1989

9. Legenhausen, L., and Wolff, D.: STORYBOARD and communicative language learning: Results of the Düsseldorf CALL project (this volume)

10. MacWhinney, B.: The competition model and foreign language acquisition (this volume)

11. Omaggio, A.: Teaching language in context. Boston, MA: Heinle & Heinle 1986

12. Rickel, J.: Intelligent computer-aided instruction: A survey organized around system components. IEEE Transactions on Systems, Man, and Cybernetics 1, 40-57 (1989)

13. Rivers, W.: The principles of interactive language learning and teaching. NFLC Occasional Papers, February 1989

14. Stevick, E.: Teaching languages: A way and ways. Rowley, MA: Newbury House 1980

15. Swaffer, J., Arens, K., and Byrnes, H.: Reading for meaning: An integrated approach to language learning. Englewood Cliffs, NJ: Prentice Hall 1991

16. Swartz, M.L.: Issues for tutoring knowledge in foreign language intelligent tutoring systems (this volume)

The Technological Promise of Second Language Intelligent Tutoring Systems in the 21st Century

Joseph Psotka[1], Melissa Holland[1], and Stephen Kerst[2]

[1] U. S. Army Research Institute, ATTN: PERI-II, 5001 Eisenhower Avenue, Alexandria, VA 22333-56
[2] The Catholic University of America, Department of Education, Washington, D.C. 20064

Abstract: The technologies useful for second language teaching are changing rapidly, opening many new directions for developing intelligent tutoring systems. Two artificial intelligence (AI) technologies that promise to improve teaching by combining the best components of immersion and grammatical instruction are hypertext and natural language parsing. Each is suited to a different kind of language learning. Parsers offer broad sensitivity to syntactic and morphological forms of language, but they process semantic components only superficially and arbitrarily, with no sign of dramatic improvement in the foreseeable future. Hypertext offers an easy way to add semantics -- not to the parser, but to the visible environment the student enters. Specifically, hypertext enables three methods of representing the semantics of a language: pictures, lexical browsers, and the emerging technology of cyberspace. The most important goal for language teaching in the 21st century is to exploit these methods of representing meaning and to integrate them with syntactic parsers to create enriched environments for second language acquisition.

Keywords: Syntactic parsers, hypertext, semantic network browsers, second language acquisition, imagery, hierarchical dictionaries, intelligent tutoring systems, AI.

1. From Syntactic Parsers to CyberSpace

As demonstrated by several papers in this volume [1, 24, 18], natural language parsers have been extensively developed and fruitfully applied to second language instruction. By offering broad sensitivity to syntactic and morphological forms of language, these parsers improve grammatical instruction. However, to meet a central objective of second language instruction -- that of approximating naturalistic immersion in our teaching technologies -- we must add a strong complement of meaning to currently available parsers. In this paper we argue that the most practical technology by which to create a comprehensive semantics is hypertext. First, hypertext supports the construction of lexical network browsers that show in graphical form how words are conceptually related. Second, hypertext offers convenient ways of attaching pictures to text, informing the symbolic component of language with the referential and context-setting power of images. Finally, a new generation of technology, called cyberspace, carries hypertext into apparent three-dimensional environments for expressing meaning.

Parsers and hypertext provide related but distinct ways of characterizing what goes on in language processing -- one involves syntax, the other semantics. For researchers of second language instruction, these characterizations describe different levels of linguistic knowledge that can help to guide and assess what students are learning. In this paper we will review briefly the limits and strengths of syntactic parsers, then look at the possibilities of hypertext -- in particular, at 3 forms of semantic representation enabled by current and emerging technology: lexical networks, referential pictures, and cyberspace.

We have found it epistemologically useful to compare these forms of representation. They provide different instantiations of our knowledge that can help us reflect on how we understand. In the case of

NATO ASI Series, Vol. F 80
Intelligent Tutoring Systems for Foreign Language Learning
Edited by M. L. Swartz and M. Yazdani

semantics, the divergent views given by networks, pictures, and cyberspace can be contrasted to explore what meaning is and how to teach it. Thus, the value of the representational techniques exploding from new computer and cognitive science technologies lies not only in the instructional environments they make possible, but in the insights they yield about syntax and semantics. Before delving into hypertext representations, we will take a closer look at the limitations of current natural language parsers.

1.2 Limitations of Parsers for Teaching and Modeling Students: The Need for Semantic Representations

While natural language parsers show promise on a number of fronts, they also have a pervasive limitation. Most parsers are syntactic in scope and fail to represent deeper levels of language processing, such as semantics, pragmatics, and topical knowledge. Let us consider how this limitation affects two uses of parsing technology in second language instruction.

First, parsers can be used to teach a second language by exercising and critiquing students' production of sentences. However, parsers without semantics can evaluate only grammatical aspects of what students write and not whether it is sensible or appropriate. Moreover, they cannot show students the subtleties of word meaning and interrelationships. Finally, parsers without semantics cannot approximate the immersion environments called for by theories of communicative language teaching [25, 6, 3, 29]. Because parsers lack connection to a knowledge base of facts, scenarios, and contexts of use, they cannot represent or respond to real communicative needs. As noted both by Yazdani [58] and by Frederiksen [18], the sentence production and critiquing activities that parsers support must be semantically motivated if they are to be useful for instruction. Otherwise, students practice blind generation and analysis of sentences without learning how to use language to communicate.

A second use of parsers is to build models of students' knowledge of the second language -- their emerging grammars -- so as to direct and tailor individual instruction and to support intelligent language tutoring. Specifically, the computational techniques used in parsing double as a way to model students' syntactic competence -- to track students' errors and to infer automatically the underlying knowledge gaps and distortions that need to be remediated. These inferences can be aided by extrapolations from students' knowledge of their first language, also described in the form of parsing rules and data. For a range of grammatical constructions, learners appear to transfer the rules of their first language to their second language [33, 42, 51]. Thus, as argued by Lytinen and Moon [32] and rearticulated by Yazdani [58], computational descriptions of a student's knowledge of the first language make a powerful metric for explaining the student's errors in learning a second language.

Despite the promise of parsers to support intelligent tutoring through student modeling, this effort is again limited by current natural language processing technology. The narrow description of semantics and its relation to syntax limits the diagnostic power of the parser: Interactions between syntax, lexicon, and meaning that pervade the linguistic system go unrecognized. Moreover, syntax-based parsers cannot account for the roles of perception and higher order thinking skills in students' language production. It appears to us that any attempt to model and explain students' errors, with an eye toward better diagnosis and remediation, must consider semantics, perception, and conception as well as syntax. Existing parsing systems may be of little help in identifying the status of competence, sources of error, and the nature of differences among cultural and linguistic groups.

Thus, syntactic parsers appear to fall short both for motivating communicative language learning and for modeling students' linguistic knowledge. To support intelligent tutoring, we need techniques for representing semantics in as useful a way as parsers currently represent syntax.

1.3 A Beginning Semantics: Parsers for Propositional Analysis

The beginnings of semantic structures can be added to syntactic parsers using some of the knowledge representation techniques pioneered by artificial intelligence, as seen in the CODA-X system developed by Fredriksen [18]. This system uses a rule-based semantics that derives propositional analyses of sentences based on the syntactic analyses produced by the parser. Propositional analyses are explicitly limited to the specification of truth value and propositional content, with content decomposed into semantic cases (object, location, etc.) assigned to each argument of the proposition. A long term goal of the tutor, not yet realized, is to construct conceptual representations that tie propositions to memory, thought, and discourse. At this point in its development, the system shows students how to map between the syntactic trees produced by a grammatical analysis and the semantic trees produced by a propositional analysis.

Development of rule-based semantic systems such as CODA-X is clearly an aid to second language acquisition. However, these systems typically stop with case assignment and basic logical description. When deeper conceptual and knowledge base connections are developed, these necessarily encompass only very small domains. Moreover, semantic parsers are notoriously brittle and inextensible, demanding hand-crafted functionality that is just as narrow as current techniques for representing domain knowledge. Finally, semantic parsers are at best only symbolic additions that do little to take advantage of the power of situations and frames to set contexts and motivate communication. We turn, therefore, to the techniques enabled by hypertext to represent semantics.

2. Beyond Parsers: Three Techniques for Semantic Representation

As the "situatedness" of learning becomes better understood [10], technologies for language teaching must increasingly take advantage of the perceptual interpretive skills that humans possess to communicate and understand meaning. Learning and perception must be integrated through systems that manipulate pictures and scenes as easily as sentences. Fortunately, the technologies of multimedia digital representation and hypertext afford unprecedented opportunities for building computer programs with dynamically linked lexical information, manipulable pictures, and 3-dimensional images, whose use in second language instruction can then be explored.

Below we consider the representational forms enabled by hypertext and its extensions. We examine lexical networks, pictures, and cyberspace, illustrate their pedagogical uses, describe technologies for implementation, and raise critical questions for research. We then look at how to integrate these forms with each other and with parsing systems.

2.1 Semantic Representations in the Form of Lexical Networks

Displaying links between words. We first consider semantic representations in the form of lexical networks, meant specifically for teaching word meanings and their interrelationships. A network is a system of nodes and links, well suited for describing words (as nodes) and the semantic relations between them (as links), as illustrated in Figure 1. Networks of words can be graphically displayed and presented to students as a browser or adapted to more directive instruction. Before examining how to construct these graphical displays, let us consider why we would want to use them in second language teaching. Do links between words play a role in human memory? Are they important in native speakers' use of language?

A research rationale: The role of lexical links in word recall, sorting, and priming tasks. Decades of psycholinguistic research suggest that words in human memory are connected along systematic semantic dimensions. Most recent is the research on models of semantic memory (our memory for word meanings) in cognitive science, which depict words as linked in ways that are more or less standard across speakers [2, 11, 17, 27, 37, 50, 53]. The structure of words and links takes the form of networks, reflected for a small domain in Figure 1. Supporting these network models is a history of experimental research in which semantic links demonstrate powerful and uniform effects.

First is a body of work in verbal learning that views words in memory as related by learned associations [15], which are demonstrated in several experimental paradigms. In tests of word association [15, 45], people are asked to respond freely to a stimulus word. The response words tend to be consistent across people and to reflect principled semantic relationships to the stimulus word. For example, "dog" frequently elicits "animal" as a response (a class-inclusion relationship, also called hyponymy) and "wet" frequently elicits "dry" (antonymy).

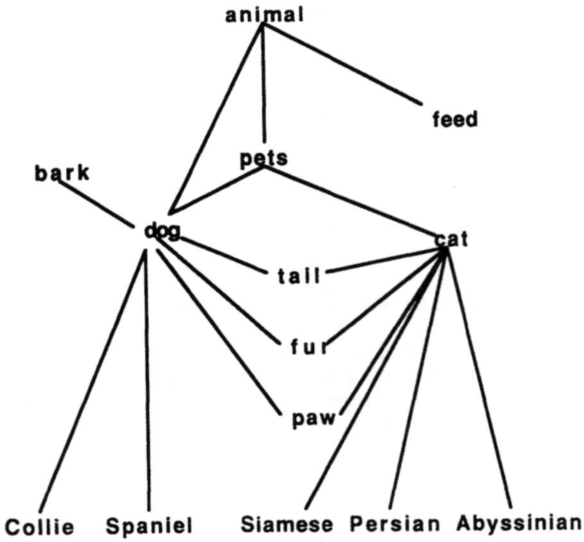

Figure 1. An hypothesized network structure for a sample of lexical memory

In studies of free recall of words [5, 35, 56], people are asked to recall a list of words in any order. Words that are conceptually related in the list tend to cluster together in recall, regardless of how the words were sequenced in the original list. For example, words referring to animals might be recalled adjacently and separately from words referring to plants; under animals, words referring to birds might be recalled separately from words referring to dogs.from words referring to dogs. Clustering is inferred to arise because related words have prior links in memory and thus serve as direct cues for one another in a retrieval task. Not only do the clusters reflect principled semantic dimensions, but they also reveal what appear to be natural hierarchies in the mental lexicon.

A final paradigm that demonstrates systematic links between words in memory involves people's judgments of semantic relatedness, as revealed in word sorting tasks [28, 38, 40]. People are asked to sort words together into groups on the basis of meaning. Statistical analyses apply to show the average tendency and shape of word groupings across people. Adults are typically found to group words hierarchically and along the same principled semantic dimensions revealed in word association and free recall. They also tend to agree in their groupings, suggesting canonical organizations of word knowledge shared by speakers of a language.

Beyond their importance for learning and sorting sets of isolated words, lexical links appear critical for natural uses of language, such as listening and reading. Listening and reading require accessing the meanings of presented words, as approximated in tachistoscopic studies of word recognition [11, 12, 17, 26, 37, 55, 57]. A typical paradigm is to have viewers make decisions as quickly as possible about whether a stimulus ("cat" vs. "cak") is or is not a word. These decisions go faster when viewers see a related word ("dog") immediately before the stimulus. Thus, presented words tend to prime or activate related words, making them easier to find in memory. A single word can prime a whole set of linked words through "spreading activation" [2]. Priming results add to the evidence that conceptually related words are tied together in memory, forming semantic networks.

The effect of anticipatory priming arguably extends to reading and listening under real-world conditions. Discourse analyses of authentic text and talk reveal that semantically related words co-occur densely [22], creating a natural role for priming. If semantic associates of an initially encountered word like "cat" are activated automatically, they should be easier to recognize and retrieve when they appear in immediately following portions of a text or discourse. Of course, not all the words in an activated network will appear in an episode of text or talk, but many of them will if the episode is coherent. A pre-activated network of semantic associates constrains the reader/hearer's expectations about what comes next in a sentence or utterance. These constrained expectations not only facilitate reading and listening, but enable them to proceed at the fast pace we are used to [36, 38, 40, 41].

A final set of data supporting network models of memory come from studies of brain physiology. It is well known that visual information from the retina maps to the cortex through topographic and non-isomorphic projections, and that these projections are multiply linked and successively organized into hierarchical structures [4]. Not only does cortical architecture support the reality of network representations, but networks may provide a useful metaphor for the topographic and hierarchical structures of the brain.

Implementing lexical networks. The experimental evidence points to the importance for native speakers of a structured lexicon with dense interconnections that guide expectations and anchor retention. The evidence also reveals how the lexicon is structured in some domains. It is a logical step, then, to hypothesize that learners of a language can move toward acquiring lexical structure by seeing explicit presentations of lexical links, such as Figure 1. To implement such presentations, we need computational structures by which to encode and display connections among words. Uniquely suited to providing these computational structures is the technology of hypertext: a systematic approach to structuring and delivering linked information.

Vannevar Bush [8] is generally credited with the basic ideas of hypertext systems. However, it is only recently that computers with high bandwidth graphical displays have been able to implement these ideas in an acceptable way [21]. A central feature of hypertext systems is the "hotspots" that appear on a computer screen surface, such as a text interface. These visible invitations to explore and navigate the text can be activated to bring up nodes of information that have been linked to the hotspot. The web of nodes and links can be made directly visible and interactively inspectable through a directed acyclic graph, semantic network, or tree, which is displayed graphically on the screen.

Using lexical links in vocabulary instruction. Given the goal of presenting lexical links in a second language, we hypothesize that they should mirror the conventional lexical organization of native speakers of that language, as derived from analyses of semantic memory. We further hypothesize that sets of linked words should be presented without mediation by first language words, so as to foster direct associations between words in the second language. In this way, inter-word associations should become robust enough to occur rapidly and relatively automatically, helping learners of the language to understand naturally paced speech and to read at efficient rates. Of potential use in designing lexical presentations are two theoretical approaches to modeling semantic memory: (1) models that encompass all meaningful associations between words, both logical and functional or coincidental, as analyzed by Kintsch [26, 27], and illustrated in Figure 1, and (2) models that isolate selected relationships, such as the logico-semantic links identified by Miller [38]. We have found the selective approach of Miller more practical in developing lexical networks to assist second language acquisition.

Miller identifies primary relations among nouns, verbs, adjectives, and adverbs in an extensive program of lexical description, implemented in an on-line lexical reference system called WordNet [39]. The primary semantic relations include hyponymy ("a collie is-a dog"), meronymy ("a paw is-part-of a foot"), synonymy, and antonymy. Some of these relations (hyponymy and meronymy) give rise to semantic hierarchies ("a collie is a dog, a dog is an animal, an animal is a living thing"). The WordNet project has laid out the structure of these relations among thousands of English words, and is beginning to develop parallel structures in other languages.

To exploit these structures in vocabulary instruction, we have developed prototypical learning environments using Apple's HyperCard system. The first attempt [7] resulted in a vocabulary program for English called HyperLexicon, which includes a conceptual design and sample lexical networks based on WordNet. For example, words for parts of the body are depicted in parallel "is-part-of" hierarchies referring to humans and animals (Figure 2). The display of such hierarchies provides a kind of universal graphic communication that minimizes the need for mediation by a student's first language

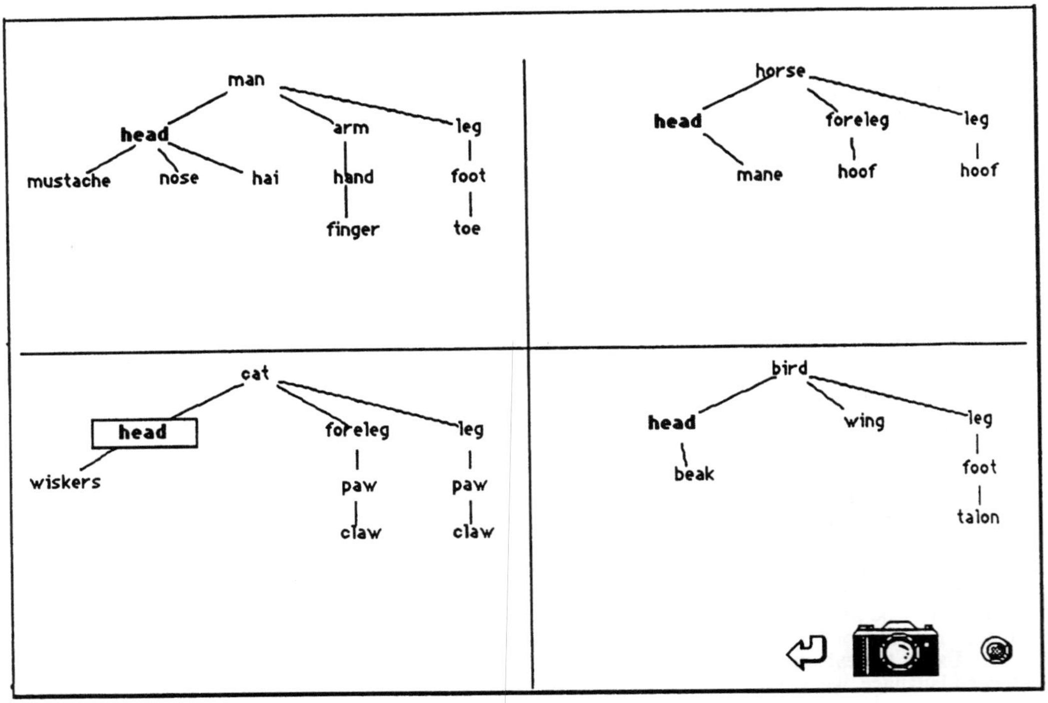

Figure 2. A hypertext display of a part-whole hierarchy for "man" with analogous hierarchies for "horse", "cat", and "bird"

Networks of words such as in Figure 2 might be used in several ways. In HyperLexicon they are presented to students for free and unguided browsing. HyperLexicon does allow limited interaction (e.g., when students button on a word, corresponding words become highlighted in parallel hierarchies; also, students can use hotspots to get further information about words); however, there are no directive exercises that require responses and return feedback. The system's goal is to organize lexical knowledge via hierarchies, which students can then access directly. The pedagogical assumption is that hierarchical displays will make lexical connections transparent and graspable, and that students will internalize and strengthen these connections by browsing through the hierarchies.

A second use of networks is to make them accessible from text to provide extra infomation about words, as demonstrated in Swartz's LEXNET-in-Situ [54]. Thus, students see words in authentic paragraph contexts and can optionally access word networks while reading or doing other work with paragraphs.

A third use of networks is to have students generate their own. This practice is intended to build productive and flexible use of words as students remember learned links and forge new ones. Generation can proceed along prescribed semantic dimensions, as in LEXNET-in-Situ, or can be entirely unconstrained, as in the popular method used to teach foreign vocabulary -- semantic mapping [43]. In semantic mapping, students given some specific topic freely generate associated words. These are written down in concentric maplike patterns that resemble an associative network. The pedagogical assumption is that students must learn to link words in new and shifting alignments in response to ever changing discourse topics and purposes.

Questions for research. The availability of lexical networks through hypertext raises critical questions about their instructional use. First, the cognitive goals of presenting networks need to be made clearer and tradeoffs articulated: to teach the meaning of new words vs. the integration of already known words; to build automaticity in traversing fixed links, as in WordNet and HyperLexicon, vs. to build flexibility in creating new links, as promoted by semantic mapping. Lesson designers must consider how to coordinate the constrained lexicon of Miller with the unconstrained connections of Kintsch.

Second, more work needs to be done to develop and validate network representations. The interaction among such relations as meronymy, hyponymy, and synonymy are only beginning to be understood. Correlatively, more work is needed to validate lexical structures in languages other than English.

Third, research is needed on how students acquire an integrated lexicon. Can browsing alone instill semantic links? Does browsing require interaction with real language uses, like reading and conversation, to ensure that words become tightly and multiply connected?

2.2 Semantic Representations in the Form of Pictures

Displaying visual images and scenes. In working with hypertext systems for second language instruction, we have come to see increasingly the need for pictorial forms of semantic representation: composite images, visual scenes, animation, and video.

A research rationale. The practical and pedagogical motivations for using pictures in second language teaching are discussed by Hamburger [23]. It is clear that pictures can create simulated immersion environments, reduce the need for first language explanation, and support a total physical response theory of teaching , [3]. The cognitive-theoretical motivations for pictures are equally strong. Research shows that semantic memory is integrated with a store of imagery, resulting in close ties between words and images of their referents. These ties are seen in the effects of imagibility on recall of words [44] and in the effects of words in priming pictures, described below.

Priming tasks in which people are asked to compare the meanings of pictures or of names suggest that these two forms have separate storage systems, and that the picture store is primary [31]. Specifically, categorization results show that when a category ("furniture") is named and thus semantically primed, yes/no decisions for items within the category are actually faster when the item is pictured than named -- that is, words semantically prime pictures even better than they prime words. In a related task, match/mismatch decisions for same/different categories are found to be faster for comparing pairs of pictures than for comparing pairs of words. Moreover, match/mismatch comparisons for mixed picture-word pairs produce decision times intermediate between picture-picture and word-word pairs [47]. Thus, studies exploring relationships between images and words point to a closer link between images and what we might call the semantic core of memory than exists between words and this semantic core.

The research further suggests that picture and word stores both access some kind of common semantic level in memory. For example, Kroll [30] gave students a "reality test" in which they had to discriminate words and pictures from non-words and non-pictures following related and unrelated sentences. Judgments were slightly faster for pictures than for words, even though pictures have many more ways of being non-pictures. Of greater consequence, the priming effect of related sentences was just as large for pictures as for words. Somehow, a sentence like "Because she was a religious person, she decided to become a ..." speeded up processing of both the word "nun" and a small picture of a nun. Pictures and words appear to make use of a common conceptual representation.

Similar kinds of evidence suggest that words in different languages also access a common conceptual level in memory. In research with bilinguals, Caramazza and Brones [9] examined the relationships between words in two languages. They found priming effects equally strong between languages as within a language. Just as in picture-word priming, interlingual priming implies the existence of a commonly accessible semantic store shared across languages. Additional evidence for a universal semantic store comes from Tulving and Colotla [56], who presented words in French, English, and Spanish to be recalled in multilingual lists. People had great difficulty remembering the language a word had been presented in and often recalled a word that was semantically correct but in the wrong language. Thus, words appear to access a universal semantic core and quickly lose their language-specific markings.

Note that the close contact between words and images in memory is confirmed by findings from psychophysiological studies. As recent observations of brain damaged individuals have shown [34] people can have semantic deficits for words that are removed by showing them pictures. For instance, a brain damaged individual can be asked what the word "elephant" means and respond with only "an animal," even after being prodded for more information. But when shown an iconic picture of an elephant, the same individual can give a verbal description of its habitat, characteristic sounds, actions, and a wealth of semantic information. The relationship between pictures and text, images and language, is manifested in brain physiology, which shows words and pictures functioning as an integrated unit.

The convergent findings from priming, recall, and psychophysiological research suggest that pictures and words access the same semantic core of patterned concepts, that pictures provide first access, and that this core has some interlingual universality. These findings imply that a sensible means of second language instruction is to meld words and pictures through immersion-like techniques that first build pictorial simulations, addressing the learner's existing semantic core, and then attach foreign language, connecting words with referents, utterances with actions.

Implementing pictures. The technology best suited for representing pictures with connections to language is found in hypertext, multimedia systems. The hotspots that appear on a hypertext screen, such as Figure 2, can be activated to bring up pictures, creating rich interlinkages of graphic and textual materials that are both flexible and controlled. Moreover, a rapid proliferation of commercial environments exploiting HyperCard© and visual imagery is beginning to let us manipulate images as easily as words. Apple© Computer has recently released an Educator's stack of basic ideas for HyperCard© that includes a visual immersion environment for moving objects around a room, shown in Figure 3. Wherever an object is placed, the stack pronounces a simple sentence that describes the location. The computer script for this stack could easily be adapted to different objects and locations. In fact, an encyclopedia of simple actions, objects, and environments could be built around this system, creating a large database of selectable images for second language instruction.

Figure 3. Example of a widely distributed HyperCard© stack that allows students to move objects (the hat, vase, book, or ball) around a room and receive correct descriptions (written and spoken) of the placement.

In most hypertext programs, pictures are added through painstaking hand drawings or through importing the small set of prefabricated icons that come with systems like HyperCard. But pictures can also be digitized from existing hardcopy, and we are pursuing the technology to digitize hardcopy imagery, or even video signals, as well as to store vast amounts of visual data on CD ROM.

Using pictures in vocabulary instruction. Picture technology can help build visual environments to which words are connected. Toward this end, pictures can be used (1) to define the referents of single words and phrases, (2) to depict the situations referred to by sentences, and (3) to set the scenes and frames that give language a communicative context. For example, in Yazdani's LINGER [58] pictures set scenes, while in Hamburger's FLUENT [23], pictures serve all 3 functions, creating a simulated immersion environment. To enhance immersion, FLUENT's visual scenes are not only dynamic but can be manipulated in response to second language directions, as in total physical response teaching [3].

We have found pictures especially important to clarify aspects of meaning not shown by network relations. Networks such as those in HyperLexicon are often insufficient to pinpoint the meaning of an unfamiliar word. Thus, it is not apparent just from the hierarchies in Figure 2 what part of the "body" a "head" is. We enhanced HyperLexicon by liberally invoking visual images to clarify meaning, sometimes developing running animations to explain a word. For example, a student buttoning first on "head" in the part-of hierarchies, and then on the camera icon, would get the set of referential pictures shown in Figure 4. By using what we hypothesized were universally understood images, we reduce the need for first language explanation in this system.

HyperLexicon presents pictures for unguided browsing, creating an exploratory environment for learning word-image connections. Alternatively, FLUENT sets up situations that call for students to manipulate and respond to pictures and scenes, thus motivating the ties between words and images and making them interactive.

Figure 4. Pictures in hypertext corresponding to "head" nodes in part-whole hierarchies from Figure 2.

Questions for research. A number of questions surround the use of picture technology (icons, images, graphs, animations, and videos) for second language instruction. First, our assumption that pictures will be universally understood raises the question of how speakers of different languages analyze visual information. Might there be differences in the order that pictorial information is parsed (e.g., scenes with several interrelated figures or objects), corresponding to syntactic demands of the viewer's native language? Are there cultural or linguistic differences in canonical imagery for common words and concepts?

Second, the possibility of constructing largescale visual databases thru hypertext raises the question of how to structure these databases. One possibility is to seek WordNet-like relationships among pictures (meronymy, hyponymy, synonymy, and antonymy), so as to organize them and capture pictorial abstractions.

Third, once we have constructed the necessary pictures -- or lexical networks, for that matter --

questions arise about how to sequence the course of instruction and what instructional techniques to employ. For example, how do exploratory learning environments like HyperLexicon compare in effectiveness to more directive environments like FLUENT? Our current pedagogical understanding yields no clear guidance on these issues [54].

Finally, practical questions remain about creating visual descriptions. There is no visual dictionary or thesaurus, no database of imagery, from which to select. If the choice is to digitize pictures fom existing hardcopy, then pictures to illustrate particular words are simply chosen as they are encountered in available sources. This is how we developed a program to teach military terms, drawing pictures from technical manuals and military magazines. Sometimes the pictures provided a good fit. More often, individual pictures were unrepresentative in ways that could be easily described in words but not easily changed in the pictures. For instance, to illustrate the meanings of "rifleman" and "sniper", we found images of soldiers abundantly available in source magazines. The problem was that both words call for an image of a soldier with a rifle. While it is possible to use the same picture to indicate roughly the meaning of each word, there are certainly characteristic ways in which the best picture of a rifleman and that of a sniper should differ. Perhaps one of these differences should include a sniper scope, while other differences should tap features of context. How to build representative images for "interlingua" purposes remains an open challenge.

One possibility we are employing to build representative images is a technique first suggested by Sir Francis Galton more than a century ago, that of averaging images to form a prototypical form. So far, we have built average images from individual photographs of faces, tanks, and airplane silhouettes. It might be argued that only such "basic level objects" can be averaged into useful, recognizable images; however, sophisticated averaging techniques are available with today's digital technology. It may be possible to use the averaging technique to produce prototype images of superordinate as well as basic level concepts.

A related question concerns how to access pictures in a hypertext visual database. Rather than verbally labeling pictures, the averaging technique could be used to create access paths in the form of icons and abstract visual imagery. Pictures in the database could be averaged to form an "abstract" icon, whose layers could be peeled off to find specific pictures. For instance, if an object of a certain size, color, and shape is needed, it could be found in the database simply by starting with a general shape and moving through a menu of alternative, more precise shapes until the correct, matching object is found. Words from a foreign language could be accessed not through native language translations but through relationships of complex imagery.

Testing these ideas and elaborating them into a real theory of visual concepts is a program of research that will last into the 21st century and perhaps beyond.

2.3 Semantic Representations in the Form of MultiMedia CyberSpaces

The ultimate form of representation for realistic semantic immersion is apparent 3-dimensional worlds that simulate multiple aspects of experience -- visual, tactile, and auditory. Such realistic environments are now possible through the technology of cyberspace [49].

Implementing cyberspace. Computational power and portability have made available cyberspace environments through devices like binocular goggles, power datagloves, and telecommunicating sensors. These devices can fundamentally change the nature of perception and meaning. Instead of just seeing and hearing a passive production, one can now interact dynamically with a virtual reality that may exist nowhere except in the creative imagination of an artist. Virtual realities allow one seemingly to walk through buildings or terrains, to see shifting perspectives, to touch and move objects -- all through computer interaction.

Using cyberspace in vocabulary instruction. How to take advantage of these virtual realities opens a brave new world of immersion for second language training. Cyberspace could be used to present to students an entire referring situation to which second language messages are tied. Instead of merely communicating with words, it should be possible to communicate with pictorial environments that appear to envelop the viewer. Moreover, a potential amplification of this powerful gadgetry could go far beyond the world of concrete imagery and into visual abstractions. If visual abstractions can be realized in a principled, theory-driven way, then instead of images and detailed video, generic prototypes of images could populate cyberspace.

Artificial realities are ways of exploiting hypertext and expert systems technology to improve second language training, making immersion more accessible and useful to a broad range of users. Cyberspace can demonstrate meaning in ways that should be clear to speakers across languages.

3. Integrating Forms of Representation

The forms of representation we have discussed are not independent or mutually exclusive. They correspond to forms of representation in memory that are themselves related. And they can be connected practically in a training system. We need criteria for how to make these connections, and for what are the most appropriate forms for displaying meaning under what conditions.

The intention behind the use of picture or cyberspace technology is to create immersion environments to which words can be connected. But visual environments cannot illustrate all concepts. Lexical networks that show links between words are sometimes a better way of representing meaning. Additional ways of representing meaning through words include a second-language continuation, or definition by linguistic context, as suggested by Hamburger [23]; a dictionary definition; and even a translation. Let us focus on how to relate the network and picture methods.

3.1 Integrating Word Networks and Pictures

In a sense, networks and pictures illuminate complementary aspects of meaning. Pictures are needed to define words with concrete referents, like "dog," which are generally at lower levels of a semantic hierarchy (basic level concepts). A picture shows which of several possible referents under "animal" is intended by "dog." Networks, alternatively, serve to illuminate where the word fits with respect to related words. Thus, in the case of concrete words, the picture supports what we might call first-time learning of word meaning, while the network supports what we might call lexical integration -- tying a newly learned word into the existing lexicon. A logical order of instruction would be first-time learning, with pictures, followed by integration, with networks.

For words superordinate in a semantic hierarchy, like "animal," networks serve a different and more defining purpose. A word like "animal" does not lend itself to pictorial depiction but is defined by its subsuming relationship to all kinds of animals. Not only will a single picture fail to clarify meaning, but pictures of the whole array of referents -- generically drawn cats, dogs, insects, etc. -- are impractical to show and possibly misleading. An obvious alternative is to define superordinate words through their links with other words. These links can be shown iconically, by positioning superordinates near the top of an "is-a" hierarchy. Thus, network hierarchies might be the best choice for first-time learning of superordinates, assuming that words lower in the hierarchy have already been acquired. Of course, another obvious way to convey meaning is a textual definition such as found in a dictionary ("an animal is a living thing with the ability to locomote..."). But pertinent research [20] suggests that definitions are ineffective ways to teach meaning.

Thus, networks and pictures provide complementary ways to describe meaning, depending on the nature of the words and the kind of learning desired. In fact, semantic networks can be seen as a bridge between definition by text and definition by image, between what Peirce [46] has called the purely symbolic system of language and the more realistic sign system of icons and images. Networks serve this bridge because they contain words, or symbols, but arrange them visually like an image.

In summary, visual descriptions are not well suited to higher levels of abstraction, which require conceptual descriptions in textual and hierarchical forms. Without a means of creating "abstract" visual representations, the abstractness of words constantly collides with the concreteness of imagery. So, it is only when textual and visual representations complement each other that we have adequately faithful models of semantic memory. To fully incorporate textual representations, however, we need to integrate networks and pictures with the text produced by parsers.

3.2 Integrating Parsers with Networks and Pictures

How can we link the semantic representations of hypertext to the more syntactic capabilities of parsing to create an intelligent foreign language tutor? The relationships between text and pictures that combine to make meaningful instructional materials are still only beginning to be explored [34]. Below, we summarize a few ideas.

In general, hypertext can create structural linkages and detailed, sometimes graphic explications of declarative knowledge; whereas parsers offer the environment for exercising and refining the skills that use that knowledge. Naturally, there is no way yet to have parsers analyze a picture or understand it, but pictures can sketch out a setting that constrains and illustrates meaning. For example, animated graphics can illustrate a conversational frame within which the parser generates dialogs with the student, as in the intelligent tutoring systems LINGER [58] and BRIDGE [14]. In addition, pictorial illustrations can furnish optional hypertext callouts when the student wants to know more about a word or phrase. This sort of structured lexical help is illustrated by the BRIDGE tutor. Beyond pictures, network descriptions are perhaps easier for a parser to deal with, since they can be encoded in computational form for symbolic analysis. Most simply, lexical networks can be presented as another mode of structured lexical help. But networks can also be read by a parser to estimate semantic appropriateness and discourse coherence of text passages. For example, a technical passage that contains words drawn from the same part-whole hierarchy could be rated as topically coherent with some degree of certainty.

Our first efforts to combine hypertext and parsers used Lexical Functional Grammar and Notecards on a Xerox Lisp Machine [48]. The enormous difficulty of integrating two very large software systems on the same machine has led us to examine the issues of parsers and hypertext separately. Still, it is our intent to integrate these two kinds of environments seamlessly into an efficient instrument for language training. In particular, we plan to create large semantic networks of words in different languages, according to the taxonomic structures natural to those languages. These structures can provide the basis for translating automatically from one language to another, and they can help second language instruction by pointing out places where knowledge of one language is likely to interfere with learning the semantic structure of another language.

4. Conclusion

As the powerful technologies of natural language parsing, hypertext, digital imaging, and cyberspace develop, they will support each other to create systems of unrivaled efficacy for language training. We are still a long way from recreating in these computational environments the full range of pictorial and symbolic representations that exist in the memory; but the analysis of language and the semantic supports that underlie it is beginning to pay off with representational systems that rival real intellectual functioning. It appears that intelligent tutoring systems are entering a new stage where the words are beginning to have real meaning.

References

1. Abeille, A.: A lexicalized tree adjoining grammar for French and it's relevance to language teaching (this volume)
2. Anderson, J. R.: A spreading activation theory of memory. Journal of Verbal Learning and Verbal Behavior, 22, 261-295 (1983)
3. Asher, J J.: The strategy of the total physical response: An application to learning Russian. International Review of Applied Linguistics, 3, 291-300 (1966)
4. Barlow, H., Blakemore, C., and Weston-Smith, M.: Images and understanding. Cambridge: Cambridge University Press 1990
5. Bower, G.H., Clark, M.C., Lesgold, A.M., & Winzenz, D.: Hierarchical retrieval schemes in recall of categorized word lists. Journal of Verbal Learning and Verbal Behavior, 8, 323-343 (1969)
6. Brown, G., and Yule, G.: Teaching the spoken language. Cambridge: Cambridge University Press 1983
7. Bui, K.: HyperLexicon, a hypermedia-based lexicon for vocabulary acquisition. MS project, Computer Science Department, George Mason University, 1988
8. Bush, V.: As we may think. The Atlantic Monthly, pp. 101-108, July 1945
9. Caramazza, A. and Brones, I.: Semantic classification by bilinguals. Canadian Journal of Psychology, 34, 77-81 (1980)
10. Clancey, W. J.: Qualitative student models. Annual review of computer science, 1, 381-450 (1986)
11. Collins, A. and Quillian, M. R.: Retrieval time from semantic memory. Journal of Verbal Learning and Verbal Behavior, 8, 240-247 (1969)
12. Columbo, L., and Williams, J.: Effects of word- and sentence-level contexts upon word recognition. Memory and Cognition, 18(2), 153-163 (1990)
13. Conklin, J.: Hypertext: An introduction and survey. IEEE computer, pp.1741, Sept 1987
14. Criswell, E., Byrnes, H., & Pfister, G.: Intelligent automated strategies for teaching foreign language in context (this volume)
15. Deese, J.: The structure of associations in language and thought. Baltimore, MD: Johns Hopkins University Press 1965
16. Feuerman, K., Marshall, C., Newman, D. and Rypa, M.: The CALLE project. CALICO Journal, pp. 25-34, March 1987
17. Forster, K.I.: Accessing the mental lexicon. In R.J. Wales & E. Walker (Eds.), New approaches to language mechanisms. Amsterdam: North-Holland 1976
18. Fredriksen, C.: Semantic discourse processing and tutoring systems for second language learning (this volume)
19. Fum, D., Giangrandi, P., Tasso, C.: The ET project: Artificial intelligence in second language teaching. Proceedings of the European Conference on Computers in Education, Lausanne, Switzerland 1988
20. Gildea, P. M., Miller, G. A., and Wurtenberg, C. L.: Contextual enrichment by videodisc: A first report. CognitiveScience Laboratory, Princeton University 1988
21. Halasz, F., Moran, T., and Trigg, R.: NoteCards release 1.2i reference manual. Palo Alto, California: Xerox Corporation 1985
22. Halliday, M.A.K., and Hansan, R.: Cohesion in English. London: Longman Press 1976
23. Hamburger, H.: Foreign language tutoring and learning environment (this volume)
24. Handke, J.: WIZDOM: A multi-purpose tutoring system based on AI techniques (this volume)
25. Johnson, K., and Porter, D.: Perspectives in communicative language teaching. London: Academic Press 1983
26. Kintsch, W.: The role of knowledge in discourse comprehension: A construction-intergration model. Psychological Review, 95, 163-182 (1988)
27. Kintsch, W., and Mross, E.: Context effects in word identification. Journal of Memory and Language, 24, 336-349 (1985)
28. Kostyla, S., and Holland, V.M.: Factors related to the acquisition, maintenance, and loss of second language skills. Paper presented at the American Educational Research Association, Boston MA, 1990
29. Krashen, S.: Principles and practice in second language acquisition. NY: Pergamon Press 1982
30. Kroll, J. F.: Recognizing words and pictures in sentence contexts: A test of lexical modularity. Journal of Experimental Psychology: Learning, Memory and Cognition, 16, 747-759 (1990)
31. Lupker, S. J.: Picture naming: an investigation of the nature of categorical priming. Journal of Experimental Psychology: Learning, Memory and Cognition, 14, 444-455 (1988)
32. Lytinen, S. and Moon, C.: Learning a second language. In Proceedings of the Seventh National

Conference on ArtiGcial Intclligence, St. Paul, MN, pp. 222-226, August 1988
33. MacWhinney, B.: The competition model and foreign language acquisition (this volume)
34. Mandl, H & Levin, J. R.: Knowledge acquisition from text and pictures. Amsterdam: North Holland 1989
35. Mandler, G.: Organization and memory. In K.W. Spence & J. T. Spence (Eds.), The psychology of learning and motivation. New York: Academic Press 1967
36. Marks, M. R., and Miller, G. A.: The role of semantic and syntactic constraints in the memorization of English sentences. Journal of Verbal Learning and Verbal Behavior, 3, 1-5 (1964)
37. Meyer, D. E. and Schvaneveldt, R. W.: Facilitation in recognizing pairs of words: Evidence of a dependence between retrieval operations. Journal of Experimental Psychology, 90, 227-234 (1971)
38. Miller, G. A.: Dictionaries of the mind. Proceedings, 23rd annual meeting of the Association for Computational Linguistics, Chicago, Illinois, pp.8-12 1985
39. Miller, G.A., Fellbaum C., Kegl J., and Miller, K.: WORDNET: An electronic lexical reference system based on theories of lexical memory, CSL Techical Report #11, Office of Naval Research, Arlington, VA., 1988
40. Miller, G. A., Heise, G. A., and Lichten, W.: The intelligibility of speech as a function of the context of the text materials. Journal of Experimental Psychology, 41, 329-335 (1985)
41. Miller, G. A., and Isard, S.: Some perceptual consequences of linguistic rules. Journal of Verbal Learning and Verbal Behavior, 2, 217-228 (1963)
42. Odlin, T.: Language Transfer. University of Cambridege Press, Cambridge 1989
43. Oxford, R. L.: Semantic mapping as a vocabulary learning toll for second or foreign language. Alexandria, Va: U. S. Army Research Institute, in preparation, 1988
44. Paivio, A.: Mental imagery in associative learning and memory. Psychological Review, 76, pp. 241-263,1969
45. Palermo, D. S., and Jenkins, J. J.: Word association norms: Grade school through college. Minneapolis: University of Minnesota Press, 1964
46. Peirce, C. S.: Collected Papers: Elements of logic. Cambridge, MA: Harvard University Press, Vol. 2 1965
47. Pellegrino, J. W., Rosinski, R. R., Chiesi, H. L., and Siegel, A.: Picture-word differences in decision latency: An analysis of single and dual memory models. Memory and Cognition, 5, 383-396 (1977)
48. Psotka, J., Holland, M., Swartz, M. L., and Hanfling, S.: Cognitive models of students' language structure: The view from intelligent computer assisted instruction. In C. S. Stansfield (Ed.), New directions in language aptitude testing 1988
49. Rheingold, H.: Travels in virtual reality. Whole Earth Review, pp. 80-87, Summer 1990
50. Rosch, E. and Mervis, C. B.: Family resemblances: Studies in the internal structure of categories. In E. Rosch and B. B. Lloyd (Eds.), Cognition and Categorization. Hillsdale, NJ: Lawrence Erlbaum Associates, Inc 1978
51. Rutherford, W.: Languagetypology and language transfer. In Gass, S., and Selinker, L. (Eds.), Language transfer in language learning. Newbury House, Rowley, MA 1983
52. Shneiderman, B. and Kearsley, G.: Hypertext: hands on! Reading, MA: Addison Wesley 1989
53. Smith, E. E., and Medin, D. L.: Categories and concepts. Cambridge: Harvard University Press 1981
54. Swartz, M. L. and Russell, D. M.: FL-IDE: Hypertext for structuring a conceptual design for computer-assisted language learning. Instructional Science, 18, 5-26 (1989)
55. Swinney, D. A.: Lexical access during sentence comprehension: (Re)consideration of context effects. Journal of Verbal Learning and Verbal Behavior, 18, 645-659 (1979)
56. Tulving, E., and Colotla, V. A.: Free recall of trilingual lists. Cognitive Psychology, 1, 86-98 (1970)
57. West, R., and Stanovich, K.: The neutral condition in sentence context experiments: Experimental studies. Bulletin of the Psychonomic Society, 26, 87-90 (1988)
58. Yazdani, M.: Steps toward an intelligent computer-assisted language learning systems (paper presented at the Workshop)

Subject Index

NATO ASI Series F

Including Special Programmes on Sensory Systems for Robotic Control (ROB) and on Advanced Educational Technology (AET)

Vol. 1: Issues in Acoustic Signal – Image Processing and Recognition. Edited by C. H. Chen. VIII, 333 pages. 1983.

Vol. 2: Image Sequence Processing and Dynamic Scene Analysis. Edited by T. S. Huang. IX, 749 pages. 1983.

Vol. 3: Electronic Systems Effectiveness and Life Cycle Costing. Edited by J. K. Skwirzynski. XVII, 732 pages. 1983.

Vol. 4: Pictorial Data Analysis. Edited by R. M. Haralick. VIII, 468 pages. 1983.

Vol. 5: International Calibration Study of Traffic Conflict Techniques. Edited by E. Asmussen. VII, 229 pages. 1984.

Vol. 6: Information Technology and the Computer Network. Edited by K. G. Beauchamp. VIII, 271 pages. 1984.

Vol. 7: High-Speed Computation. Edited by J. S. Kowalik. IX, 441 pages. 1984.

Vol. 8: Program Transformation and Programming Environments. Report on a Workshop directed by F. L. Bauer and H. Remus. Edited by P. Pepper. XIV, 378 pages. 1984.

Vol. 9: Computer Aided Analysis and Optimization of Mechanical System Dynamics. Edited by E. J. Haug. XXII, 700 pages. 1984.

Vol. 10: Simulation and Model-Based Methodologies: An Integrative View. Edited by T. I. Ören, B. P. Zeigler, M. S. Elzas. XIII, 651 pages. 1984.

Vol. 11: Robotics and Artificial Intelligence. Edited by M. Brady, L. A. Gerhardt, H. F. Davidson. XVII, 693 pages. 1984.

Vol. 12: Combinatorial Algorithms on Words. Edited by A. Apostolico, Z. Galil. VIII, 361 pages. 1985.

Vol. 13: Logics and Models of Concurrent Systems. Edited by K. R. Apt. VIII, 498 pages. 1985.

Vol. 14: Control Flow and Data Flow: Concepts of Distributed Programming. Edited by M. Broy. VIII, 525 pages. 1985.

Vol. 15: Computational Mathematical Programming. Edited by K. Schittkowski. VIII, 451 pages. 1985.

Vol. 16: New Systems and Architectures for Automatic Speech Recognition and Synthesis. Edited by R. De Mori, C.Y. Suen. XIII, 630 pages. 1985.

Vol. 17: Fundamental Algorithms for Computer Graphics. Edited by R.A. Earnshaw. XVI, 1042 pages. 1985.

Vol. 18: Computer Architectures for Spatially Distributed Data. Edited by H. Freeman and G.G. Pieroni. VIII, 391 pages. 1985.

Vol. 19: Pictorial Information Systems in Medicine. Edited by K. H. Höhne. XII, 525 pages. 1986.

Vol. 20: Disordered Systems and Biological Organization. Edited by E. Bienenstock, F. Fogelman Soulié, G. Weisbuch. XXI, 405 pages. 1986.

Vol. 21: Intelligent Decision Support in Process Environments. Edited by E. Hollnagel, G. Mancini, D.D. Woods. XV, 524 pages. 1986.

NATO ASI Series F

Vol. 22: Software System Design Methods. The Challenge of Advanced Computing Technology. Edited by J.K. Skwirzynski. XIII, 747 pages. 1986.

Vol. 23: Designing Computer-Based Learning Materials. Edited by H. Weinstock and A. Bork. IX, 285 pages. 1986.

Vol. 24: Database Machines. Modern Trends and Applications. Edited by A.K. Sood and A.H. Qureshi. VIII, 570 pages. 1986.

Vol. 25: Pyramidal Systems for Computer Vision. Edited by V. Cantoni and S. Levialdi. VIII, 392 pages. 1986. *(ROB)*

Vol. 26: Modelling and Analysis in Arms Control. Edited by R. Avenhaus, R.K. Huber and J.D. Kettelle. VIII, 488 pages. 1986.

Vol. 27: Computer Aided Optimal Design: Structural and Mechanical Systems. Edited by C.A. Mota Soares. XIII, 1029 pages. 1987.

Vol. 28: Distributed Operating Systems. Theory und Practice. Edited by Y. Paker, J.-P. Banatre and M. Bozyiğit. X, 379 pages. 1987.

Vol. 29: Languages for Sensor-Based Control in Robotics. Edited by U. Rembold and K. Hörmann. IX, 625 pages. 1987. *(ROB)*

Vol. 30: Pattern Recognition Theory and Applications. Edited by P.A. Devijver and J. Kittler. XI, 543 pages. 1987.

Vol. 31: Decision Support Systems: Theory and Application. Edited by C.W. Holsapple and A.B. Whinston. X, 500 pages. 1987.

Vol. 32: Information Systems: Failure Analysis. Edited by J.A. Wise and A. Debons. XV, 338 pages. 1987.

Vol. 33: Machine Intelligence and Knowledge Engineering for Robotic Applications. Edited by A.K.C. Wong and A. Pugh. XIV, 486 pages. 1987. *(ROB)*

Vol. 34: Modelling, Robustness and Sensitivity Reduction in Control Systems. Edited by R.F. Curtain. IX, 492 pages. 1987.

Vol. 35: Expert Judgment and Expert Systems. Edited by J.L. Mumpower, L.D. Phillips, O. Renn and V.R.R. Uppuluri. VIII, 361 pages. 1987.

Vol. 36: Logic of Programming and Calculi of Discrete Design. Edited by M. Broy. VII, 415 pages. 1987.

Vol. 37: Dynamics of Infinite Dimensional Systems. Edited by S.-N. Chow and J.K. Hale. IX, 514 pages. 1987.

Vol. 38: Flow Control of Congested Networks. Edited by A.R. Odoni, L. Bianco and G. Szegö. XII, 355 pages. 1987.

Vol. 39: Mathematics and Computer Science in Medical Imaging. Edited by M.A. Viergever and A. Todd-Pokropek. VIII, 546 pages. 1988.

Vol. 40: Theoretical Foundations of Computer Graphics and CAD. Edited by R.A. Earnshaw. XX, 1246 pages. 1988.

Vol. 41: Neural Computers. Edited by R. Eckmiller and Ch. v. d. Malsburg. XIII, 566 pages. 1988.

NATO ASI Series F

Vol. 42: Real-Time Object Measurement and Classification. Edited by A. K. Jain. VIII, 407 pages. 1988. *(ROB)*

Vol. 43: Sensors and Sensory Systems for Advanced Robots. Edited by P. Dario. XI, 597 pages. 1988. *(ROB)*

Vol. 44: Signal Processing and Pattern Recognition in Nondestructive Evaluation of Materials. Edited by C. H. Chen. VIII, 344 pages. 1988. *(ROB)*

Vol. 45: Syntactic and Structural Pattern Recognition. Edited by G. Ferraté, T. Pavlidis, A. Sanfeliu and H. Bunke. XVI, 467 pages. 1988. *(ROB)*

Vol. 46: Recent Advances in Speech Understanding and Dialog Systems. Edited by H. Niemann, M. Lang and G. Sagerer. X, 521 pages. 1988.

Vol. 47: Advanced Computing Concepts and Techniques in Control Engineering. Edited by M. J. Denham and A. J. Laub. XI, 518 pages. 1988.

Vol. 48: Mathematical Models for Decision Support. Edited by G. Mitra. IX, 762 pages. 1988.

Vol. 49: Computer Integrated Manufacturing. Edited by I. B. Turksen. VIII, 568 pages. 1988.

Vol. 50: CAD Based Programming for Sensory Robots. Edited by B. Ravani. IX, 565 pages. 1988. *(ROB)*

Vol. 51: Algorithms and Model Formulations in Mathematical Programming. Edited by S. W. Wallace. IX, 190 pages. 1989.

Vol. 52: Sensor Devices and Systems for Robotics. Edited by A. Casals. IX, 362 pages. 1989. *(ROB)*

Vol. 53: Advanced Information Technologies for Industrial Material Flow Systems. Edited by S. Y. Nof and C. L. Moodie. IX, 710 pages. 1989.

Vol. 54: A Reappraisal of the Efficiency of Financial Markets. Edited by R. M. C. Guimarães, B. G. Kingsman and S. J. Taylor. X, 804 pages. 1989.

Vol. 55: Constructive Methods in Computing Science. Edited by M. Broy. VII, 478 pages. 1989.

Vol. 56: Multiple Criteria Decision Making and Risk Analysis Using Microcomputers. Edited by B. Karpak and S. Zionts. VII, 399 pages. 1989.

Vol. 57: Kinematics and Dynamic Issues in Sensor Based Control. Edited by G. E. Taylor. XI, 456 pages. 1990. *(ROB)*

Vol. 58: Highly Redundant Sensing in Robotic Systems. Edited by J. T. Tou and J. G. Balchen. X, 322 pages. 1990. *(ROB)*

Vol. 59: Superconducting Electronics. Edited by H. Weinstock and M. Nisenoff. X, 441 pages. 1989.

Vol. 60: 3D Imaging in Medicine. Algorithms, Systems, Applications. Edited by K. H. Höhne, H. Fuchs and S. M. Pizer. IX, 460 pages. 1990.

Vol. 61: Knowledge, Data and Computer-Assisted Decisions. Edited by M. Schader and W. Gaul. VIII, 421 pages. 1990.

Vol. 62: Supercomputing. Edited by J. S. Kowalik. X, 425 pages. 1990.

Vol. 63: Traditional and Non-Traditional Robotic Sensors. Edited by T. C. Henderson. VIII, 468 pages. 1990. *(ROB)*

Vol. 64: Sensory Robotics for the Handling of Limp Materials. Edited by P. M. Taylor. IX, 343 pages. 1990. *(ROB)*

Vol. 65: Mapping and Spatial Modelling for Navigation. Edited by L. F. Pau. VIII, 357 pages. 1990. *(ROB)*

NATO ASI Series F

Vol. 66: Sensor-Based Robots: Algorithms and Architectures. Edited by C.S.G. Lee. X, 285 pages. 1991. *(ROB)*

Vol. 67: Designing Hypermedia for Learning. Edited by D.H. Jonassen and H. Mandl. XXV, 457 pages. 1990. *(AET)*

Vol. 68: Neurocomputing. Algorithms, Architectures and Applications. Edited by F. Fogelman Soulié and J. Hérault. XI, 455 pages. 1990.

Vol. 69: Real-Time Integration Methods for Mechanical System Simulation. Edited by E.J. Haug and R.C. Deyo. VIII, 352 pages. 1991.

Vol. 70: Numerical Linear Algebra, Digital Signal Processing and Parallel Algorithms. Edited by G.H. Golub and P. Van Dooren. XIII, 729 pages. 1991.

Vol. 71: Expert Systems and Robotics. Edited by T. Jordanides and B. Torby. XII, 744 pages. 1991.

Vol. 72: High-Capacity Local and Metropolitan Area Networks. Architecture and Performance Issues. Edited by G. Pujolle. X, 536 pages. 1991.

Vol. 73: Automation and Systems Issues in Air Traffic Control. Edited by J.A. Wise, V.D. Hopkin and M.L. Smith. XIX, 594 pages. 1991.

Vol. 74: Picture Archiving and Communication Systems (PACS) in Medicine. Edited by H.K. Huang, O. Ratib, A.R. Bakker and G. Witte. XI, 438 pages. 1991.

Vol. 75: Speech Recognition and Understanding. Recent Advances, Trends and Applications. Edited by P. Laface and Renato De Mori. XI, 559 pages. 1991.

Vol. 76: Multisensor Fusion for Computer Vision. Edited by J.K. Aggarwal. *(ROB)*

Vol. 77: Computer Algorithms for Solving Linear Algebraic Equations. The State of the Art. Edited by E. Spedicato. VIII, 352 pages. 1991.

Vol. 78: Integrating Advanced Technology into Technology Education. Edited by M. Hacker, A. Gordon, M. de Vries. VIII, 185 pages. 1991. *(AET)*

Vol. 79: Logic, Algebra, and Computation. Edited by F.L. Bauer. VII, 485 pages. 1991.

Vol. 80: Intelligent Tutoring Systems for Foreign Language Learning. The Bridge to International Communication. Edited by M.L. Swartz and M. Yazdani. IX, 347 pages. 1992. *(AET)*

MIX
Papier aus verantwortungsvollen Quellen
Paper from responsible sources
FSC® C105338

If you have any concerns about our products,
you can contact us on
ProductSafety@springernature.com

In case Publisher is established outside the EU,
the EU authorized representative is:
Springer Nature Customer Service Center GmbH
Europaplatz 3, 69115 Heidelberg, Germany

Printed by Libri Plureos GmbH
in Hamburg, Germany